FOLKLORE IN THE UNITED STATES AND CANADA

FOLKLORE IN THE UNITED STATES AND CANADA

An Institutional History

Edited by Patricia Sawin and
Rosemary Lévy Zumwalt

Indiana University Press

This book is a publication of

Indiana University Press
Office of Scholarly Publishing
Herman B Wells Library 350
1320 East 10th Street
Bloomington, Indiana 47405 USA

iupress.indiana.edu

Manufactured in the United States of America

First Printing 2020

Cataloging information is available from the Library of Congress.

ISBN 978-0-253-05287-2 (hardback)
ISBN 978-0-253-05289-6 (paperback)
ISBN 978-0-253-05288-9 (ebook)

Cover illustration, clockwise from upper left, then center:

Louis C. Jones, Fennimore House, New York State Historical Association, Cooperstown, NY, ca. 1967. *Photograph by Milo Stewart, by permission of Ruth Stewart.*

Christopher Lornell, Bruce Bastin, and Tom Davenport interview Arthur Jackson and Bill Jackson, 1975. *Photograph by Michael Higgins. From the Daniel W. Patterson and Beverly Bush Patterson Papers #20026, Southern Folklife Collection at Wilson Special Collections Library, University Libraries, University of North Carolina at Chapel Hill.*

Alan Dundes, KRON-TV, 1968. By permission of the Dundes family.

Austin and Alta Fife, Moab, UT, 1954. *Photograph by Austin Fife, by permission of Fife Folklore Archives, Utah State University.*

UNC Folklore MAs Victor Bouvéron, Zoe van Buren, Rach Garringer, Emily Ridder-Beardsley, Joshua Parshall, and Elijah Gaddis, 2017. *Photograph by Patricia Sawin.*

Parishioners of the Saint Elias church, Luzan-Toporiwtsi, Alberta, 2014. *Photograph by Natalie Kononenko.*

Anand Prahlad, University of Missouri. Photograph ca. 2010 courtesy of Anand Prahlad.

Marius Barbeau, 1942. *Photograph courtesy of Université d'Ottawa, Centre de recherche sur les Canadiens-français, Fonds Juliette Caron-Dupont, P97, Ph63-4.*

American Folklore Society Meeting, November 1972: Kenneth Goldstein, Frances Gillmor, Harry Middleton Hyatt, William Hugh Jansen, Américo Paredes, Daniel Crowley, Herbert Halpert, William Bascom, Warren Roberts, Roger Abrahams, Francis Lee Utley. *Photograph courtesy of Frances Terry.*

Contents

FOLKLORE IN THE UNITED STATES AND CANADA

Introduction

Patricia Sawin and Rosemary Lévy Zumwalt

ALMOST ALL FOLKLORISTS in the United States and Canada were educated in one or more of roughly two dozen graduate degree–granting programs in folklore. Notable exceptions—scholars who came to and even developed folkloristic approaches after earning degrees in related disciplines—are significant to the history of folklore study and include, perforce, some of the founders of academic programs in the early to mid-twentieth century. Most folklorists, however, proudly claim to be from the University of Pennsylvania, the University of Texas, Indiana University, the University of California, Berkeley, Laval University, Memorial University of Newfoundland, and so on, and they expect other folklorists to understand what that preparation and allegiance implies. Each folklore program has a distinctive ethos fostered by the personalities and theoretical commitments of the scholars who have taught there, the ways in which folklore could adapt to larger trajectories of a university's mission and development, the relative focus on regional as compared with national or international folklore, and perceptions of folklore by university administrators and regional publics.

Our goal in this book is to document the development of the academic folklore programs within which scholars have shaped the field, learned from one another, and passed on the discipline to their students. We have focused on graduate programs—with the exceptions of the early and influential program at Harvard and the recent Cape Breton program that hopes to develop a graduate certificate—because those who identify as folklorists usually studied folklore at the graduate level. Units that award folklore degrees have mostly been programs, curricula, or specializations in other departments rather than departments fully dedicated to folklore. We recognize that many academic folklorists succeed in introducing students to the subject matter and research methodologies of folklore while teaching in programs with other disciplinary labels, and we cannot claim to have established entirely consistent standards for what constitutes an academic unit that confers a graduate degree in folklore. We are likewise aware of lacunae even relative to our goal of including a chapter covering every program authorized to grant an MA, MS, or PhD in folklore in the United States and Canada. Notably, we were unsuccessful in soliciting a chapter on the University of Kansas, once characterized by Jan Harold Brunvand as "the famous stepping-off point for folklorists" (1986, 22). And we elected not to solicit a chapter on the Francophone program in folklore and ethnology at the University of Sudbury, Ontario, because it is solely an undergraduate program. The histories and challenges of folklore programs in Mexico seemed distinct enough (and, unfortunately, unfamiliar enough) that we did not attempt to cover them. With hope for the future of historical studies in folklore scholarship, we offer this collection as a beginning, as the one place where scholars can learn about and compare the development of twenty-six folklore programs in the United States and Canada, some long-lived, some sadly disbanded, some in a process of transformation, some just emerging.

This volume began with two sessions organized by Rosemary Lévy Zumwalt for the 2016 Western States Folklore Society (WSFS) meetings in Berkeley, California. Presenters included Charles Briggs, Lynne McNeill, Jill Terry Rudy, Patricia Sawin, Sharon Sherman, Michael Ann Williams, and Rosemary Lévy Zumwalt. The editors subsequently solicited the remaining chapters. Chapters 7 (UCLA) and 8 (the early decades at the University of Pennsylvania) are shortened versions of articles originally published in *The Folklore Historian*; we are grateful to American Folklore Society executive director Jessica Anderson Turner for permission to reprint them.

The chapters are organized according to when a university started conferring a graduate degree in folklore. Our chronology is inevitably a matter of interpretation. Scholars had often been teaching folklore at a university for decades before a formal degree-granting program was established. Students previously earned graduate degrees in other disciplines while being advised by professors who considered themselves folklorists. Tone and perspective vary among chapters. Some authors are retired faculty members looking back on the history of a program in which they played an influential role; others are current faculty members seeking both to uphold and to innovate beyond the tradition established by their predecessors; still others are graduate students or graduates who studied at the programs they describe.

The book is organized into three sections. The first covers programs established prior to the 1960s. These include the Harvard undergraduate program, the roots of which may be traced to Francis James Child; the program at the University of North Carolina, arguably not all that different from other state universities where folklorists expressed early interest in regional folklore, save for a dynamic leader who successfully proposed a folklore graduate degree to a sympathetic administrator; Laval University, which honored the Francophone history of French Canada; and the group of connected folklife programs—those that emphasized integrated study of the total folk culture of groups, especially their material culture—at Franklin and Marshall, Cooperstown, and Penn State and in the University of Pennsylvania Folklore and Folklife Program under the suasion of Don Yoder.

Zumwalt introduces the second section with a comparative analytical chapter on the efflorescence of folklore programs in the 1960s and 1970s—programs encouraged by, yet sometimes also shaped in reaction against the folk revival and the attention paid to traditional culture during the US Bicentennial. At many of these universities—Indiana, UCLA, Penn, UC Berkeley, Texas, Memorial, Western Kentucky, University of Oregon, University of Alberta, University of Louisiana, and Utah State University—faculty and students had studied folklore for many years. The expansion and generous funding of universities in the post-Sputnik era accompanied by the availability of federal funding—in the United States particularly through the National Defense Education Act of 1958, which supported both graduate study and the development of area studies at universities—and a renewed public interest in understanding the traditional sources of a rapidly changing culture paved the way for these schools to establish graduate folklore degrees. At Memorial, Herbert Halpert's efforts to build the folklore program were facilitated by "a series of university administrators [who] supported fully all individuals who showed genuine interest in studying any aspect of the Newfoundland environment, physical or human."[1] The program at the University of Alberta, a province with a substantial Ukrainian immigrant population, benefited from the energy and visionary fund-raising of a scholar who developed coursework in Ukrainian language and folklore.

The third section treats the programs that have arisen since the 1980s, again variable in origins. At George Washington University, the University of Wisconsin–Madison, Brigham Young University (Utah and Hawai'i campuses), George Mason University, the Ohio State University, and the University of Missouri, long histories of folklore study eventually came to fruition in the establishment of a folklore degree program as determined leaders seized opportunities to coordinate with university priorities (international relations at Ohio State; Upper Midwest studies at Wisconsin; at Brigham Young, the commitment of The Church of Jesus Christ of Latter-day Saints to the study of cultures; at George Mason, consistency with the university's guiding Mason Idea: innovative, diverse, entrepreneurial, and accessible). George Washington took advantage of its location in the US capital to involve employees of federal cultural agencies as faculty and to cultivate opportunities for students. The newest programs respond most evidently to contemporary cultural politics. Faculty at Goucher College have developed a unique MA in Cultural Sustainability to train students to identify and advocate for traditions and ways of life. At Cape Breton University, faculty capitalize on public perception of the traditionality of local Scots-derived culture while arguing for indigenous, French, and recent immigrant contributions. In the book's final chapter, the organizers of the Future of American Folkloristics conference report on the models and needs for innovative practice and teaching discussed by those who gathered in Bloomington in May 2017.

At the end of the WSFS presentations in 2016, Dan Ben-Amos asked that panelists pay attention to markers for success in folklore programs. What factors might we identify that have kept folklore programs alive? In the chapters that follow, authors highlight many markers that might be typified as a prescription for successful folklore programs. These include the importance of claiming an identity as a folklorist; the value of strong links to the local community; the significance of contacts across the institution; creativity in aligning folklore's contributions with broader institutional priorities; and the need for public and private funding. Folklore programs have also been subjected to challenges and conflicts over which the folklorists themselves have little to no control, crucially the interplay between economic factors and the academy (most fully explored by Mary Hufford in chapter 9 on Penn 1973–2013). The structure of interdisciplinary folklore programs poses additional challenges: the splitting of tenure-track positions between programs and the absence of a budget line for the folklore program nested in another disciplinary department.

McNeill remarked at the WSFS meeting that folklorists need "to take back the discipline of folklore," explaining, "When a good, cool thing comes out of folklore, it needs to be labeled as 'folklore.'" This idea melded with the "magical alchemy" that she saw emerging from the influence of charismatic leaders—she named Alan Dundes and Brunvand, although one might easily identify others—to form part of the "magical mixture." Sherman stressed the importance of recognizing folklore as a separate discipline—a creed she learned from Richard Dorson when she was an IU graduate student and still believes is crucial for sustaining folklore. Sherman emphasized that she always introduced herself as a folklorist. About Berkeley, Briggs writes, "Our program resolutely remains the Berkeley *Folklore* Program, and the 'f-word' is not hedged with any ands or buts." Rachel Kirby and Anthony Buccitelli's chapter explores Harvard folklorists' ability to present the discipline as "the very quintessence of humanities scholarship."

Memorial University's folklore program, McNeill explains, belongs to the community and exemplifies Diane Goldstein's argument that "Programs that are in places with a strong regional identity are the most secure." The folklore archive at Memorial, McNeill points out, is not regarded as "just a collection of information *about* the community, it truly belongs *to* the community." Marcia Gaudet and Barry Jean Ancelet likewise stress the close connection that folklore at the University of Louisiana has with the local community and the state. The University of North Carolina, Brigham Young, and Utah State have all emphasized both documenting local communities and devising outreach to share the results of folklore research. Ohio State arranges for materials from its field schools to be held both in the university archives and in the communities documented. The University of Oregon managed to bring the state folklorist position to campus to promote community connections. Natalie Kononenko emphasizes the importance of the University of Alberta's program serving the community through research, publications, and educational websites and by digitizing the archives to make them widely available. Claire Schmidt evokes the University of Missouri folklore program's connections to "ordinary citizens of genius." Both the state folklore societies and the Mizzou folklore program emphasize "collaboration among student, academic, public, and amateur folklorists, and the need to theorize new ways of knowing that challenge unequal power structures in order to build a better, more ethical field."

Randy Williams notes that Barre Toelken was a bridge builder. He saw no distinction between academic and public folklore. In "Building Bridges, Folklore in the Academy," William A. Wilson writes, "I began practicing what my wife calls 'hallology'—that is, I strolled the halls of the English department talking about folklore with any department members who would listen. But I did not just talk about my work. I asked these colleagues about their work and, when possible, tried to tie our interests together" (2006, 28). Briggs details the necessity of constantly tending to "strategies for building support. These efforts involve sustained diplomacy, tenacious insistence on administrative respect for policies and commitments, begging and cajoling, and lots of lunches."

Several authors comment on the crucial benefits of external funding. Richard Bauman reports that the National Endowment for the Humanities (NEH) provided funds for a grant, the application for which was titled "Expansion of the Archive of Folklore and the Training of Folklorists," that enabled the opening of the Center for Intercultural Studies in Folklore and Oral History at the University of Texas in fall 1967. In the late 1970s, as Kononenko notes, Bohdan Medwidsky secured private funds for the Huculak Chair of Ukrainian Culture and Ethnography at the University of Alberta. Christine Widmayer and Marcus Cederström stress the crucial support of the 1987 NEH grant for funding the UW–Madison folklore program. Randy Williams reflects on the funding from a 1993 National Historical Preservation and Records Commission grant that allowed the curating of Austin and Alta Fife's fieldwork tapes, and the 2016 funding from the Utah Department of Heritage and Arts that provided for digitizing the archives. Of course, there is also serendipity, as when a former student wrote a check to Dundes for $1 million to fund an endowed program in folklore at UC Berkeley.

At the WSFS meeting, presenters and audience members stressed the requisite link between university programs and public folklore. Lee Haring emphasized the obligation of folklore programs to train public folklorists, adding, "University programs who have not done that have failed." Margaret Magat, who works with cultural resource management, opined, "Folklorists need to infiltrate environmental and public folklore." Jeanne Harrah-Johnson comments on Bauman and others who followed him at IU as establishing "a concentration for MA and PhD students" in this area. Sawin describes UNC's range of outreach programs, including museum exhibits and K–12 curricula.

Was departmental status possible? How might it be achieved? Is it desirable? Accounts and opinions vary. Indiana's stability owes much to departmental standing in collaboration with ethnomusicology. The Memorial Folklore Department began, according to Herbert Halpert, because the English Department wanted to "get rid of us." The Penn English Department similarly determined to eject folklore, although the result was initially a folklore program rather than department. At North Carolina, Boggs "baptized [the program] with the name 'Curriculum' for fear the more logical term 'Department' might have given the Administration budgetary jitters," but seventy years later lack of departmental standing threatened the program in a time of austerity. Sherman, conversely, relates that both she and Toelken sought to make the folklore program visible but avoided departmental status, which they saw as "potentially treacherous. It was simply too easy to cut a department." The Ohio State program capitalizes on its status as an interdisciplinary center "to serve students across the humanities, arts, education, and social sciences." At George Mason, folklore thrives as a concentration within the English Department; at Louisiana, it is a major field in English or francophone studies.

Still, lacking departmental status often challenges a folklore program to function without control of its budget, resources, or faculty lines. At UCLA in 1970, Michael Owen Jones reports, D. K. Wilgus explained "to an administrator that, 'While the Folklore and Mythology [Program] is not a department, it functions as a department in many ways, particularly in relation to the instructional program' in that it possessed a large suite of disciplinary courses, administered the MA degree in Folklore (and the PhD in 1978), and had a core faculty who taught only Folklore-originated courses." This status as not-a-department but like-a-department was noted in a 1974 long-range planning document that remarked on the "lack of official status in the university, the difficulty of negotiating a budget, dependence on departments for full-time equivalent positions, lack of control over staffing and scheduling of folklore courses originating in departments, lack of status and compensation for the program chair, and the difficulty of maintaining interdepartmental relationships." Many other programs could report similar experiences.

While there is no single map for the success of folklore programs, some guideposts indicate a promising path. First, it helps to recognize that there are forces beyond any faculty member's or program's control: the economy buoyed universities up in the 1960s and brought them down with stagflation in the 1970s. The trajectory of the academy, dependent on national and state economies, continued downward. At state-supported universities—notably Indiana, Western Kentucky, Louisiana, Wisconsin, Missouri, and North Carolina—folklore suffers along with other humanities disciplines from conservative legislators' suspicion of "liberal agendas" behind cultural analysis. Furthermore, in any period when universities feel they need to portray themselves as forward-looking and as providing pathways to good jobs, folklore's association with the antiquarian and impractical, although undeserved, makes programs vulnerable. Many authors in this volume write about ways in which programs diversified the curriculum or the student body to maintain enrollments and about folklorists repurposing themselves and their programs to remain viable. At UC Berkeley, Briggs explains, "The Folklore Graduate Group thus proposed a designated emphasis in folklore, enabling PhD students recruited into other units to receive doctoral degrees in, say, French and folklore"; and students were allowed to pursue simultaneously an MA in folklore and a PhD in another discipline. At Goucher, Rory Turner recognized the potential of a program that would serve cultural activists and nontraditional students.

Friendly, collegial contact with administrators contributes significantly to the visibility and viability of often small folklore programs. Zumwalt, who served as dean of the college and vice president of academic affairs in a small liberal arts college for ten years of constant budgetary shortfall, often reminds colleagues that an administrator who cares wants to know what faculty members are doing in order to represent them well in meetings with higher administrators and the board of trustees. She advises getting to know one's dean, provost, and, if possible, president. Both Ben-Amos at WSFS and Harrah-Johnson in chapter 6 remark on Stith Thompson's connection with IU president Herman B Wells, including a fabled meeting in the barbershop (see Thompson 1996, 152) that helped persuade Wells that folklore "was one of the most important fields for a university to develop." Boggs recalled the "sympathetic ear" for folklore of UNC chancellor Bob House. Miller credits Dean Michael H. Jameson at Penn with a kinship toward folklore. Practical advice that Zumwalt recalls from a higher education conference—take a dean to lunch to maintain easy communication about academic matters—played out perfectly in a 1970s interaction recalled by North Carolina's Charles G. "Terry" Zug III:

> The faculty used to go over and eat lunch in the ground floor of Lenoir dining hall, right next to [the folklore offices in] Greenlaw Hall. You'd run into colleagues there, and the dean of arts and sciences ate there, so if you needed something that was a good chance to catch him—just walk over to his table and ask for what you needed. So, one time the folklorists wanted to bring in a guest speaker from out of town and we were going to need $500. So, I saw the dean in Lenoir and went over and explained. He just grabbed a paper napkin from the table and wrote on it, "Give Terry $500" and signed his name. And I walked up to South Building and the dean's secretary gave me the money.

Zug noted ruefully, "Things aren't like that now."[2]

Folklorists have made excellent administrators, both supporting folklore programs whose value they appreciate and drawing on folkloristic sensibilities to grasp the workings of the university. Randy Williams notes the benefit of having an administrator who is also a folklorist, like Jeannie Banks Thomas, who moved from the folklore program into the administration at Utah State. Debra Lattanzi Shutika reports on her ability as chair of English at George Mason to promote folklore within and beyond the department. At the 2017 Future of American Folkloristics conference, organizers Jesse Fivecoate, Kristina Downs, and Meredith McGriff recall that presenters recommended that folklorists capitalize on their disciplinary expertise to navigate relationships with administration, "pursuing an ethnography of universities in order to learn the cultures of deans, chairs, and other administrators, and to move effectively within those power structures."

Within the relatively small world of US and Canadian folklore, most programs are interconnected. Students and faculty have traversed the national border in both directions, although not without pushback from Canadians determined to defend their cultural distinctiveness. Laval's program, focused on French Canadian culture within a Francophone university, is perhaps not surprisingly the most self-contained. The authors of the chapters in this volume endeavor to convey the particular circumstances and character of each program, sketching historical context, sharing anecdotes and personalities, and analyzing their confluence. We encourage readers to pay particular attention to the trends and challenges outlined above as well as to patterns of influence as professors teach in several programs and graduates of one program become faculty in another. In the conclusion we will return to survey the landscape of losses and gains, especially over the past forty years, and the future prospects for graduate education in folklore in the United States and Canada.

Acknowledgments

The editors gratefully acknowledge Simon Bronner and Dan Ben-Amos for consultation on the history of American folklore studies, project manager Megan Odom Tice for organizational assistance, the anonymous reviewers for the press for careful reading and insightful comments that helped us strengthen the manuscript, and both Janice Frisch, the folklore acquisitions editor with whom we originally worked, and Allison Chaplin, who shepherded the project through its final stages.

Notes

1. Remarks quoted in the introduction without a citation are drawn from individual chapters in this volume. References supplied there.
2. Charles G. Zug III, personal communication to Patricia Sawin, June 15, 2018.

References

Brunvand, Jan Harold. 1986. Interview with Susan Domowitz. Indiana University Center for Documentary Research and Practice, IU Oral History Archive, 87-022.

Thompson, Stith. 1996. *A Folklorist's Progress, Reflections of a Scholar's Life*. Edited by John H. McDowell, Inta Gale Carpenter, Donald Braid, and Erika Peterson-Veatch. Special Publications of the Folklore Institute No. 5. Bloomington: Indiana University Press.

Wilson, William. 2006. "Building Bridges, Folklore in the Academy." In *The Marrow of Human Experience, Essays on Folklore*, edited by Jill Terry Rudy, 23–31. Logan: Utah State University Press.

PATRICIA SAWIN is Associate Professor and Coordinator of the Folklore Program in the Department of American Studies at the University of North Carolina, Chapel Hill. She is author of *Listening for a Life: A Dialogic Ethnography of Bessie Eldreth through Her Songs and Stories*.

ROSEMARY LÉVY ZUMWALT is Vice President Emerita and Professor Emerita of Anthropology at Agnes Scott College. She is author of *American Folklore Scholarship: A Dialogue of Dissent* and (with Isaac Jack Lévy) *Ritual Medical Lore of Sephardic Women: Sweetening the Spirits and Healing the Sick*.

Part I

Early Programs

1 The Quintessence of the Humanities

Folklore and Mythology at Harvard

Rachel C. Kirby and Anthony Bak Buccitelli

Established in 1967 under the guidance of Albert Bates Lord, the Committee on Degrees in Folklore and Mythology at Harvard University celebrated its fiftieth anniversary in 2017; however, the legacy of folklore research at Harvard is more than one hundred and fifty years old. In offering this undergraduate concentration, the committee formalized what was already a long-standing intellectual interest in folkloristics within the university (Committee on Degrees 2019b). Since 1851, Harvard has been an institutional home for many leading folklore researchers and a training ground for burgeoning public and academic folklorists.[1]

Tracing the development of folklore at Harvard from one professor's interest in ballads to the now fifty-year-old undergraduate curriculum illuminates the span of folkloristics as it developed in the United States. Graduates and faculty of Harvard were crucial in the early stages of professionalization in the field, with representatives falling on either side of the oft-noted divide between literary and anthropological folklore. Yet folklore research at Harvard preceded the establishment of distinct and formalized academic departments, and the current degree still depends on interdisciplinary work. In this way, the history of folklore at Harvard mirrors the development of the field as a whole in that it emerged out of work in distinct protodisciplines and is now maintained in the interstices between disciplinary departments.

Early Literary Folklore Studies at Harvard

In 1851, Frances James Child (1825–96) became Harvard's Boylston Professor of Rhetoric and Oratory. One of only fourteen faculty members in the 1850s, Child began the research that led to his canonical work, *The English and Scottish Popular Ballads*. The legacy of Child's scholarship and teaching is multifaceted, and his procedures for the ballad project are seen as a predecessor of the influential historic-geographic (Finnish) method. Documents and notes from his collecting efforts were eventually incorporated into Harvard's library, establishing the basis for Harvard's continuing importance in folktale research; and his work inspired the careers of generations of future folklorists in the United States (Lindahl 1988).

Perhaps the most notable of Child's early students was George Lyman Kittredge (1860–1941, Harvard class of 1882), who not only studied under Child but also succeeded him at Harvard in 1894, continuing Child's ballad research (Bynum 1974; Baker 1988; Lindahl 1988; Brown 2011). Together, Child and Kittredge defined folklore at Harvard and helped shape the field at large. The two are responsible for the Folklore Collection at the Harvard College Library, which Child established and Kittredge expanded by "more than 20,000 volumes" during his tenure (Bynum 1974, 12). The early instruction and collection of folklore at Harvard, led by two literary scholars, established Harvard as a locus for folklore research and teaching long before the school had any formal degree-granting program in folklore. Both scholars taught figures who ran the gamut of American intellectual and public life. Kittredge's notable students ranged from future US president Franklin Delano Roosevelt to the famed sociologist and public intellectual W. E. B. DuBois, who infamously ran afoul of Kittredge in an English composition course (Lewis 2009, 75), to Beat writer William S. Burroughs.

At the same time, the influence of Child and Kittredge could be felt more distinctly in an entire generation of literary folklorists. One student of both Child and Kittredge, Fred Norris Robinson, followed a path similar to Kittredge's and eventually became a fixture at Harvard as professor of English. Robinson is regarded as a foundational figure in what is now Harvard's Department of Celtic Languages and Literatures. The eminent American folklorist Stith Thompson would later describe Robinson as having "almost singlehandedly introduced Celtic Studies into America" (Shattuck 1966, 147; Department of Celtic Languages and Literatures 2018; Zumwalt 1988a, 61). Kittredge's folklorist students included John A. Lomax, Stith Thompson (see Harrah-Johnson, this volume), Sigurd Bernhard Hustvedt, Archer Taylor, Francis Lee Utley (see Mullen and Shuman, this volume), Samuel Preston Bayard, Duncan Emrich, and Lord (1912–91). Together the folklorists trained by Child and Kittredge made Harvard into the point of origin for a literary folkloristic genealogy that migrated westward across the United States (Baker 1988; Brown 1974). Taylor, for example, taught at the Pennsylvania State University, the University of Chicago, and then the University of California, Berkeley. Taylor's student, Wayland Hand, would later establish the folklore program at the University of California, Los Angeles. Similarly, Bayard helped establish folklore studies at Penn State, Utley at the Ohio State University, Lomax at the University of Texas, and Thompson at Indiana University.

American Folklore Society and Anthropological Folklore Studies at Harvard

Historiographies of American folkloristics have often outlined the divide between anthropological and literary folklore.[2] These histories have also noted the distance between the anthropologically oriented American Folklore Society (AFS) and the literary/philological folkloristics that was typically taught in early academic institutions (Bronner 1986; McNeil 1988; Zumwalt 1988a).[3] However, the involvement of Child, Kittredge, and other Harvard-affiliated folklorists in the AFS complicates this picture. While Child was the first president of the newly formed AFS in 1888, it was another Harvard affiliate, William Wells Newell (1839–1907, class of 1859), the first AFS secretary, who came to be regarded as the society's most important founding figure (Vance 1893, 595; Bell 1973, 10; Abrahams 1988, 66; Zumwalt 1988b). Though Newell was not a faculty member like Child or Kittredge, Harvard was, the site of his education under Child's tutelage, his primary academic affiliation, and Cambridge was his intellectual home (Bell 1973, 7–9; Abrahams 1988, 65, 69).

Michael J. Bell notes, "Newell was primarily responsible for the emergence of American folklore scholarship from random fact collection and speculative theory articulation to organized anthropological inquiry" (1973, 7).[4] Newell served as editor of the AFS's *Journal of American Folk-Lore* for its first twelve years, and he kept the journal so tightly focused on the empirical investigation of folklore that when the ownership of the *American Anthropologist* was transferred from the Anthropology Society of Washington to Franz Boas and W J McGee in 1899, there was discussion that the two periodicals should merge into a single scholarly publication (Abrahams 1988, 72–73; Zumwalt 1988a, 32–33).

In addition to being integral to the founding and early years of the AFS on the national level, Harvard intellectuals were among the Boston and Cambridge area members who, in 1889, almost immediately after the creation of the national society, founded a local Boston association—later called the Boston branch. Fourth-generation Harvard alumnus Frederick Ward Putnam (1839–1915, class of 1862) was a founding member of the group and served as its president from April 1890 until his death in 1915 (Peabody 1915).[5] Beginning his career as an assistant to the celebrated natural historian Louis Agassiz (1807–73), Putnam founded the university's anthropology department in 1890, was chief of the Department of Ethnology of the World's Columbian Exposition in 1893, and eventually served as Peabody Professor of American Archaeology and Ethnology (Radsken 2017). According to Charles Peabody's tribute to Putnam in the *Journal of American Folk-Lore*, Putnam's interest in tradition was mirrored in his family's legacy at Harvard, which extended back generations: "Perhaps it should not be so, but continuous tradition means much. Without it . . . folk-lore would not exist. With [Putnam] it culminated in a great loyalty and devotion to Harvard" (Peabody 1915, 303). Putnam's dedication to folklore, anthropology, and Harvard were equally significant in his life and works.

Fig. 1.1. Albert Bates Lord, late 1980s. Reproduced with the permission of the Curators of the Milman Parry Collection of Oral Literature, Harvard University.

Parry and Lord: The Next Generation of Folklore at Harvard

The next generation of folklorists at Harvard continued many of the traditions established by their predecessors, and they did so with an increasing integration of the anthropological and philological sides of the field. Two of the figures who most defined folklore at Harvard in the twentieth century are Milman Parry (1902–35) and his student, Lord.[6] Trained as a classicist in Paris, Parry studied Slavic oral tradition and Homeric tales but saw himself as a "literary anthropologist" (Bynum 1974, 28). Perhaps more aptly, he was a folklorist. His scholarship took him on multiple trips to Europe—especially to Yugoslavia—where he and Lord, who was invited to join Parry's expeditions after his graduation in 1934 and who played a key role in defining this research, studied the singers of oral epics (Mitchell and Nagy 2000, xi, xvi). These research travels left Parry with a massive collection of primary sources. On his death, his widow, Mrs. Marion Parry, donated the materials to Harvard (Mitchell and Nagy 2000, xvi n36). The core of his works established the Milman Parry Collection of Oral Literature housed in the Harvard College Library, further distinguishing Harvard as a national archive for the study of folklore.

Lord continued their research after Parry's death, bringing back more recordings from their former study sites in Yugoslavia as well as from subsequent trips to northern Albania (Mitchell and Nagy 2000, xv) and Bulgaria (Bynum 1974, 30). Based on the research that he had begun with his teacher, Lord published *The Singer of Tales* in 1960, a monumental work that established the oral-formulaic approach to studying folklore. This approach would influence the field's subsequent turn toward the study of folklore as performance in the late 1960s and early 1970s (Mitchell and Nagy 2000, xxi). Carl Lindahl explains Parry and Lord's research as combining "the best methods of folkloric and literary scholarship, conducting extensive fieldwork to collect oral performances which might help explain the oldest surviving works of western literature" (1988, 53).

The Committee on Degrees in Folklore and Mythology

On March 7, 1967—116 years after Child took his post as professor of English at Harvard—Lord formalized for the first time the procedure for granting degrees for the study of folklore. In the Faculty Room in University Hall—the very same room where the AFS was previously founded—the Faculty of Arts and Sciences voted to establish the Committee on Degrees in Folklore and Mythology. This choice of venue reinforced the close connection between the history of folkloristics in the United States and its history at Harvard University (Mitchell and Nagy 2000, xx; Committee on Degrees 2019b).

Seeking, as Child once did, a "freedom from departmental barriers" (Lindahl 1988, 52), Lord envisioned the curriculum as fundamentally cross-disciplinary, sustained through the cooperation of faculty from many departments. Stephen Mitchell observes that Lord's "vision of scholarship in the humanities" was that scholars "were most emphatically not to be segregated from their colleagues in the 'home departments,' but were expected to be scholars of both the 'high' and 'low' cultures of their language areas, students who could control the cultural history of the elite, as well as the oral literature of the peasantry" (1991, 13). True to folklore's history of interdisciplinary collaboration, students in Harvard's program have the ability to study a wide range of genres, periods, and geographic settings and to work with faculty in many different departments.

The breadth and scope of folkloristics at Harvard, as well as changes that have taken place in the field at large, are illustrated in the range of courses that have been taught and the faculty who have served on the committee since its inception. For example, in 1969–70—the third academic year after the formation of the committee—three courses were offered under the folklore and mythology designation: a junior tutorial taught by Gary Gossen on Mayan Folklore, a senior tutorial, and a class on African Folklore and its American Derivatives (see "Syllabi, Course Outlines and Reading Lists"). In addition, the course catalog lists classes in Scandinavian, comparative literature, and humanities that count toward folklore and mythology ("Courses of Instruction" 1969).[7] Around this time, the committee consisted of seventeen faculty members representing almost as many fields, including Far Eastern studies, English literature, Slavic and comparative literature, Celtic languages and literatures, Sanskrit, anthropology, music, and classical Greek literature. The affiliated classes also quickly expanded to include courses in Slavic, English, and music, suggesting that the program was establishing relationships that asserted its standing within the academic offerings at Harvard.[8]

Even with a wide range of geographic specializations and a steadily increasing number of affiliated courses in anthropology, ethnomusicology, and other humanistic social science disciplines, the folklore curriculum at Harvard has tended to emphasize rhetorical and literary inquiry, especially before Lord stepped down as chair of the program in 1979. Today the program holds true to these roots, maintaining course offerings that have a clear relationship to the literary pursuits of Harvard's founding folklorists but also expanding the topics of study to include music, performance, dance, and, most recently, folk art. The first designated folk art courses appeared in the 2008–9 course catalog, and since then, Felicity Lufkin has expanded these offerings to include classes on quilts and quilt making and a course titled Assertive Stitches: Domestic Arts and Public Conflict, which discusses tradition and craftsmanship through lenses of gender, ethnicity, class, and political resistance ("Courses of Instruction" 2008; Harvard University 2017–18).[9]

This expansion of boundaries is also reflected in the teaching and advising of Deborah Foster, who served for decades as senior lecturer and head tutor in the Folklore and Mythology Program. With a PhD in African languages and literature and a minor in dance performance and choreography from the University of Wisconsin–Madison, Foster previously taught at UW–Madison and in the Department of Folklore at the University of Khartoum, Sudan, before moving to Harvard (Deborah D. Foster 2018). Also serving as director of undergraduate studies for special concentrations, Foster was a leading supporter of interdisciplinary study by undergraduate students.

Fifty Years of the Degree, 160 Years of Folklore at Harvard

In his 1974 essay, "Child's Legacy Enlarged: Oral Literary Studies at Harvard Since 1856," David Bynum, an early member of the Committee on Degrees, lays out a genealogy of folkloristics at Harvard that begins with Child and progresses through Kittredge, Parry, and Lord. In the decades since Bynum's essay, a wide range of scholars has served on the committee. Current and past committee

Fig. 1.2. Conversation about the history of the program at the fiftieth anniversary symposium in 2017. *Left to right:* Maria Tatar, Stephen Mitchell, Hugh Flick (a former head tutor), Joseph Harris, Gregory Nagy, and Deborah Foster. Photograph courtesy of Lowell Brower.

members are too numerous to name, but recent significant contributions to the program have come from anthropologists Stanley Tambiah, Evon Vogt, Michael Herzfeld, and David Maybury-Lewis; medievalist Jan Ziolkowski; and classics scholars Kimberly Patton and David Elmer, the latter of whom currently serves as editor of the journal *Oral Tradition*. A recent important addition to the faculty is Joseph Nagy, Henry L. Shattuck Professor of Irish Studies (Harvard AB in folklore and mythology 1974; PhD 1978).

While both Maria Tatar and Joseph Harris have previously served as committee chairs, Gregory Nagy and Stephen Mitchell have served the longest terms since Lord's retirement. Gregory Nagy received his PhD from Harvard in 1966. In his long tenure on the faculty, he has directed or codirected more than fifty PhD dissertations and has continued to shape the next generation of scholars of oral tradition. Additionally, he has been actively involved with the Committee on Degrees in Folklore and Mythology, serving as committee chair from 1980 to 1987 (Gregory Nagy, PhD 2018; Gregory Nagy's Curriculum Vitae 2018). Most recently, he and a group of "Lord's students and successors" have created A Homer Commentary in Progress. This digital project was conceptualized as an open-source development of Lord and Parry's approach to studying Homer's works as a formulaic system (Stergios and Morse 2017). (For John Miles Foley's continuing Lord's legacy at University of Missouri, see Schmidt, this volume.)

Mitchell has maintained the program's legacy connections to Lord and the study of oral literature. In fact, in 2000, Mitchell and Nagy co-edited the fortieth-anniversary edition of Lord's classic *The Singer of Tales*. Additionally, both have served as curators of the Milman Parry Collection of Oral Literature. Mitchell, like Parry, did not train at Harvard, though his educational trajectory embodies the blending of anthropology and literature within folklore that was characteristic of the Parry/Lord approach. Mitchell has taught in and directed a Viking studies program in Scandinavia; developed a class called HarvardLore, which focuses on historic and contemporary folklore on the college campus; and researched and taught in diverse areas, including Scandinavian ballads, Nordic culture, witchcraft and magic, memory studies, and popular culture ("Courses of Instruction" 1998, 334).

Since 2003, Harvard Folklore and Mythology has hosted an annual symposium designed to bring together current faculty and students with the program's alumni as well as other scholars from around the world. The themes of these symposia indicate the breadth of approaches to folklore at Harvard. The first, "All Eyez on Me": Tupac Shakur and the Search for the Modern Folk Hero, was followed by themes such as Feminist Folklore & Masculine Myths, Folklore & Nationalism, Netlore: Globalizing Folklore in a Digital World, Kinetic Folklore, and, to mark the program's fiftieth anniversary in 2017, Folklore and Mythology in and Beyond Harvard: F&M at 50. These yearly gatherings reflect the interdisciplinary nature of folklore at Harvard and speak to the latest efforts to strengthen the program's relationship to the broader discourses of folklore in the United States (Committee on Degrees 2019c).

Reflecting on Lord's dedication to folklore at Harvard, Mitchell once observed that, "in its broadest sense, folklore was for Albert not a 'rude' area of intellectual enquiry, but rather the very quintessence of humanities scholarship" (1991, 14). This view is reflected in Harvard's Folklore Program as it has taken shape. While serving as a major base of undergraduate teaching that has produced many of the most important folklore scholars since 1967, the Harvard program has steadfastly held to its founder's vision. It is not just a disciplinary home for folklore training but "a liberal education in itself" (Committee on Degrees 2019a).

Notes

1. At Harvard University, undergraduate students are awarded AB degrees with concentrations rather than the more typical designation of a major. Degrees from the Concentration in Folklore and Mythology are administered by the Committee on Degrees, established in 1967, and are not a designation within any other course of study.

2. The term *literary* with regard to folklore studies can be applied in two slightly different ways. At times, it has referred to the belletristic study of folklore, such as the approach promoted by Fletcher S. Bassett (1847–93), organizer of the Chicago Folklore Society and its journal, *The Folk-Lorist* (Bell 1973, 17–18). While his career was clearly shaped by and around the study of literature (see, for example, Chamberlain 1907), Newell was decidedly not in that mold. Instead, influenced both by the philological tradition of his teacher Child and by the anthropological thinking of his close friend Boas, Newell took the view that folklore was shaped by its development within a cultural and historical context (Bell 1973, 17–18; Abrahams 1988, 72–73).

3. The society was originally founded as the American Folk-Lore Society, but the hyphen was eventually dropped from the name.

4. See similar comments by Vance (1893, 595), Robinson (1907, 59), and Abrahams (1988, 66). Franz Boas, for example, pointed out that Newell, "without assuming to become an anthropologist . . . exerted a lasting influence upon many investigators" (1907, 209). Bell has also argued that there was a strong theoretical continuity between Child and Newell (1988, 306–7; see also Bendix 1997, 89).

5. Other founding members of the Boston branch who were still involved at the time of Putnam's death included Kittredge, Clarence J. Blake, Charles P. Bowditch, Albert Matthews, and Crawford Howell Toy.

6. Lord recounts that on returning from Yugoslavia with Parry in 1935, he began a PhD in comparative literature under the direction of Kittredge (1991, 5). He had completed his AB at Harvard in classics in 1934.

7. Additionally, an introductory folklore course and courses on folktale, Scandinavian mythology and folklore, and oral epics were listed with other course prefixes.

8. As an indication of the range of committee members, it is notable that, in addition to Lord, the affiliated faculty that year included David E. Bynum, assistant professor of Slavic languages and literatures; Cedric H. Whitman, professor of classical Greek literature; Daniel H. H. Ingells, professor of Sanskrit; David Mitten, James Loeb professor of classical art and archeology; John M. Ward, professor of music; David H. P. Maybury-Lewis, professor of anthropology; and Evon Z. Vogt, professor of social anthropology ("Courses of Instruction" 1969). In 1972, Joseph C. Harris offered a course in the program on English folklore, though he was not listed as a committee member ("Courses of Instruction" 1971).

9. Historian Laurel Thatcher Ulrich was an early proponent of the expansion of material culture courses at Harvard as well.

Archival Sources

"Courses of Instruction 1969–1970." 1969. Harvard and Radcliffe Faculty of Arts and Sciences, Cambridge, MA. Courtesy of the Harvard University Archives, 8500.16.

"Courses of Instruction 1971–1972." 1971. Harvard and Radcliffe Faculty of Arts and Sciences, Cambridge, MA. Courtesy of the Harvard University Archives, 8500.16.

"Courses of Instruction, 1998–1999." 1998. Harvard College, Radcliffe College, and the Graduate School of Arts and Sciences, Cambridge, MA. Courtesy of the Harvard University Archives, 8500.16.

"Courses of Instruction 2008–2009." 2008. Harvard College and the Graduate School of Arts and Sciences, Cambridge, MA. Courtesy of the Harvard University Archives, 8500.16.

Mitchell, Stephen. 1991. "Address." In "In Memoriam: Albert Bates Lord." (The Memorial Church, Harvard University, September 27, 1991), 11–14. Courtesy of the Harvard University Archives, Accession 2018.170.

"Syllabi, Course Outlines and Reading Lists in Folklore and Mythology, 1967–1980." Courtesy of the Harvard University Archives 8529.4.1.

References

Abrahams, Roger D. 1988. "Rough Sincerities: William Wells Newell and the Discovery of Folklore in Late-19th Century America." In *Folk Roots, New Roots: Folklore in American Life*, edited by Jane S. Becker and Barbara Franco, 61–75. Lexington, MA: Museum of Our National Heritage.

Baker, Ronald L. 1988. "The Folklorist in the Academy." In *100 Years of American Folklore Studies: A Conceptual History*, edited by William M. Clements, David Stanley, and Marta Weigle, 65–69. Cambridge, MA: American Folklore Society.

Bell, Michael J. 1973. "William Wells Newell and the Foundation of American Folklore Scholarship." In "American Folklore Historiography." Special issue, *Journal of the Folklore Institute* 10, no. 1/2: 7–21.

Bendix, Regina. 1997. *In Search of Authenticity: The Formation of Folklore Studies*. Madison: University of Wisconsin Press.

Boas, Franz. 1907. "In Memoriam: William Wells Newell." *Folklore* 18, no. 2: 209–11.

Bronner, Simon J. 1986. *American Folklore Studies: An Intellectual History*. Lawrence: University Press of Kansas.

Brown, Mary Ellen. 2011. *Child's Unfinished Masterpiece: The English and Scottish Popular Ballads*. Champaign: University of Illinois Press.

Bynum, David E. 1974. "Child's Legacy Enlarged: Oral Literature Studies at Harvard since 1856." *Publications of the Milman Parry Collection*, 1–37. Preprinted from *Harvard Library Bulletin* 22, no. 3.

Chamberlain, Alexander F. 1907. "William Wells Newell—1839–1907." *American Anthropologist* 9, no. 2: 366–76.

Committee on Degrees in Folklore and Mythology, Harvard University. 2019a. "About: An Introduction to the Committee on Degrees in Folklore and Mythology." Last modified August 21, 2019. https://folkmyth.fas.harvard.edu/about.

Committee on Degrees in Folklore and Mythology, Harvard University. 2019b. "A Brief History of Folklore and Mythology at Harvard." Last modified August 21, 2019. https://folkmyth.fas.harvard.edu/brief-history-folklore-and-mythology-harvard.

Committee on Degrees in Folklore and Mythology, Harvard University. 2019c. "Symposiums and Conferences." Last modified August 21, 2019. https://folkmyth.fas.harvard.edu/symposiums-conferences.

Deborah D. Foster. 2018. Accessed June 1, 2018. https://tdm.fas.harvard.edu/people/deborah-d-foster.

Department of Celtic Languages and Literatures, Harvard University. 2018. The History of Celtic Studies at Harvard. Accessed June 1, 2018. https://sites.fas.harvard.edu/~celtic/history.shtml.

Gregory Nagy, PhD. 2018. Harvard Extension School. Accessed April 29, 2018. https://www.extension.harvard.edu/faculty-directory/gregory-nagy.

Gregory Nagy's Curriculum Vitae. 2018. Center for Hellenic studies. Accessed April 29, 2018. https://chs.harvard.edu/CHS/article/display/1503.

Harvard University. 2017–18. Faculty of Arts and Sciences Course Catalog Preview. Harvard Faculty of Arts and Sciences Registrar's Office. Last modified on January 24, 2019. https://registrar.fas.harvard.edu/files/fas-registrar/files/2017-2018.pdf.

Lewis, David Levering. 2009. *W.E.B. Du Bois: A Biography.* New York: Henry Holt.

Lindahl, Carl. 1988. "The Folklorist and Literature: Child and Others." In *100 Years of American Folklore Studies: A Conceptual History*, edited by William M. Clements, David Stanley, and Marta Weigle, 52–54. Cambridge, MA: American Folklore Society.

Lord, Albert Bates. 1991. *Epic Singers and Oral Tradition.* Ithaca, NY: Cornell University Press.

McNeil, W. K. 1988. "The Folklorist and Anthropology: The Boasian Influence." In *100 Years of American Folklore Studies: A Conceptual History*, edited by William M. Clements, David Stanley, and Marta Weigle, 55–57. Cambridge, MA: American Folklore Society.

Mitchell, Stephen. 2018. Bio. Accessed April 29, 2018. https://scholar.harvard.edu/smitchell/biocv.

Mitchell, Stephen, and Gregory Nagy. 2000. "Introduction to the Second Edition." In *The Singer of Tales*, edited by Stephen Mitchell and Gregory Nagy, vii–xxix. Cambridge, MA: Harvard University Press.

Peabody, Charles. 1915. "Frederick Ward Putnam." *Journal of American Folklore* 28, no. 109: 302–6.

Radsken, Jill. 2017. "The World in an Exhibit." *Harvard Gazette* (May 5). https://news.harvard.edu/gazette/story/2017/05/harvards-peabody-museum-fetes-150-years-with-unusual-exhibit/.

Robinson, F. N. 1907. "William Wells Newell." *Journal of American Folklore* 20, no. 76: 59–60.

Shattuck, Henry L. 1966. "Fred Norris Robinson." *Proceedings of the Massachusetts Historical Society* 78: 147.

Stergios, Gosia, and Christopher Morse. 2017. "Homer and the Web." *A Homer Commentary in Progress.* http://darthcrimson.org/portfolio/homer-commentary-progress/.

Vance, Lee J. 1893. "Folk-Lore Study in America." *Popular Science Monthly* 43: 586–98.

Zumwalt, Rosemary Lévy. 1988a. *American Folklore Scholarship: A Dialogue of Dissent.* Bloomington: Indiana University Press.

———. 1988b. "On the Founding of the American Folklore Society and the *Journal of American Folklore.*" In *100 Years of American Folklore Studies: A Conceptual History*, edited by William M. Clements, David Stanley, and Marta Weigle, 8–10. Cambridge, MA: American Folklore Society.

RACHEL C. KIRBY is a doctoral candidate in the American & New England Studies Program at Boston University.

ANTHONY BAK BUCCITELLI is Associate Professor of American Studies and Communications at Penn State Harrisburg. He is author of *City of Neighborhoods: Memory, Folklore, and Ethnic Place in Boston* and editor of *Race and Ethnicity in Digital Culture: Our Changing Traditions, Impressions, and Expressions in a Mediated World.*

2 Bringing Ethnographic Research to the Public Conversation

Folklore at the University of North Carolina

Patricia Sawin

Faculty and students have studied folklore at the University of North Carolina at Chapel Hill (UNC) for roughly a century. Whether one traces the program's origins to the arrival of drama professor Frederick Koch in 1918, sociologist Howard Odum in 1920, or Ralph Steele Boggs—the first professor formally trained in folklore—in 1930, the distinctive features of Carolina folklore are consistent: dedication to documenting the regional culture of the American South and "to doing ethnography and bringing it to the public conversation" through popular and creative as well as scholarly media.[1]

Folklore at UNC contributed to early twentieth-century efforts to transform a small college that prepared North Carolina's white sons to become lawyers and ministers into a research university by hiring the first professors with PhDs, expanding the curriculum to include emerging disciplines, and establishing the University of North Carolina Press (The Carolina Story 2016). In 1940 UNC became the first US university to offer a graduate degree in folklore. The fortunes of the UNC folklore program have depended on societal appreciation of folklore, dynamic leadership, and sympathetic reception by administration. While folklore is now part of the Department of American Studies, the influence of its origins as a multidisciplinary coalition persists. Four overlapping generations of folklore faculty have promulgated UNC's distinctive contributions—elaborating ethnographic methodology, helping to define the South's traditional culture, and preparing students to apply folklore training in public-facing endeavors.

1910s to 1920s

UNC's English Department recruited Koch to teach playwriting "after H. L. Mencken observed that the South lacked a theater that could present a decent play" and "to expand the university's public service mission to the arts" via the Carolina Playmakers student theater troupe (The Carolina Story 2016). "Prof" Koch, as he was affectionately called, assigned drama students to write "folk plays." Boggs was suspicious until he gathered that Koch "wanted them to compose original plays [featuring] folk elements of the environment in which they grew up" and that, "to help them recognize and evaluate these elements, he was happy to have them study Folklore" (1981, 2). Koch's early students included novelist Thomas Wolfe and dramatist Paul Green (Zug 1968).

Sociologist Howard Odum, invited to UNC to form a department of sociology and direct the Institute of Social Welfare, devoted his career to seeking "new standards for the [South] in race relations, . . . public welfare, higher education, regional planning, and penal reform" (Sills 1968, 271). Odum and Guy Johnson quickly collaborated to publish *The Negro and His Songs* (1925), *Negro Workaday Songs* (1926), and Johnson's *John Henry* (1929), recorded from the "gangs of pick-and-shovel men" who constructed the expanding university (Guy Johnson and Guion Johnson 1980, 133), presenting African American folklore as a contribution to human civilization, an expression of community values, and a key to the group's "inner life" (Odum and Johnson 1925, 8). They hoped the books would "spark widespread public interest in and awareness of the [institute]'s work," "generat[e] financial support from well-heeled foundations," and make their more subversive research palatable to conservative legislators (Matthews 2018, 4; Patterson 2015).

Among the Black laborers Odum met was singer and storyteller John Wesley Gordon, on whom Odum based a trilogy of "folk novels" about a peripatetic "Black Ulysses" (Odum 1928). Odum narrated Gordon's life in the Jim Crow South and as a World War I soldier, punctuating the story with poetry and song and emphasizing the indignities Gordon/Ulysses experienced. Odum "found Gordon impressive as a human being, and . . . wanted readers to admire the man as he did" (Sanders 2003, 55). The books were widely popular, serving to counter contemporary racist depictions of Black men as violent and lazy.[2]

Odum's prominence partly reflects the "institutional racism . . . that minimized and marginalized the work of [pioneering] Black scholars like [W. E. B.] Du Bois" (Matthews 2018, 5). Yet he established a charter to which the UNC Department of American Studies (2018) continues to subscribe when it asserts: "The study of Folklore focuses on creativity in everyday life, looking to the worlds of creative action . . . that communities fill with meaning."

1930s to 1950s

Two of Archer Taylor's students from the University of Chicago—Ralph Steele Boggs and Arthur Palmer Hudson—anchored UNC's second generation of folklorists. Hired to a linguistics professorship in Spanish, Boggs "had a not-so-secret love: folklore" and was permitted to offer a "general introduction to the science of folklore course in the Comparative Literature department" (Boggs 1981, 1). Hudson completed his MA at Chicago with Taylor and Louise Pound, taught at the University of Mississippi, and began doctoral studies in English at UNC, with Boggs on his dissertation committee. In 1930, in a feud with the University of Mississippi trustees, Mississippi governor Theodore Bilbo dismissed the head of the Department of English, David Horace Bishop, with whom Odum had studied.[3] Offered the position, Hudson could not accept "without making myself a party to the forces that had devastated [Mississippi's] higher institutions of learning" (Krause 1999, 18; Patterson 2012a, 1). Boggs encouraged UNC's English Department to hire Hudson and have him offer a "course on Anglo-American balladry" that was "already an established practice" elsewhere (Boggs 1981, 1). Hudson's *Folksongs of Mississippi and Their Background* (1936a) and *Humor of the Old Deep South* (1936b) are classics of Southern folklore.

"A contributing factor in the rise of folklore studies in the university was that in 'the decade from 1931 to 1940 . . . America suddenly became aware . . . that it had a folk tradition'" because of various "'New Deal forces'" (Bronner 1986, 97, quoting Louis D. Jones). In precisely this period, actors and opportunities converged to create UNC's Curriculum in Folklore. Boggs "discovered an amazing variety of interests in . . . folklore around the campus" (1981, 2): Odum and Johnson in Sociology; Koch in English; and Harvard-trained medievalist Urban Tignor Holmes Jr. in French (Patterson 2012a, 2); and in the Music Department Jan Schinhan, who was "well trained in Vienna, where *Volksleid* was a highly respected term," and who both agreed "to give a course on folk music" (Boggs 1981, 2) and "directed probably the first and the third theses on American fiddle tunes" (Patterson 2012a, 2).

In 1937, Boggs "induce[d] the administration to replace" the departing chair of the German Department with Richard Jente, who had known Archer Taylor at Washington University in Saint Louis (Zumwalt 1988, 53), and "who added . . . a fine course on the proverb" (Boggs 1981, 2). On October 3, 1939, Boggs "sent to Dean Pierson of the Graduate School a memo with the general statement and list of courses of the just-born Curriculum in Folklore." Boggs "baptized [the program] 'Curriculum' for fear the more logical term 'Department' might [give] the Administration budgetary jitters." The folklore MA was "first published in the Graduate School catalogue, April 5, 1940," although for thirty years, most graduate students interested in folklore earned their degrees in other departments. "Above all of these diverse elements out of which the Curriculum in Folklore grew," Boggs avers, "there was a sympathetic ear in UNC Chancellor Bob House, who was always ready . . . to fish his harmonica out of his pocket and blow a folksy tune that could . . . make any group feel the common bonds of folk tradition" (Boggs 1981, 2).

When Duke English professor Frank C. Brown, "perennial secretary . . . of the North Carolina Folklore Society," died in 1943, Boggs joined Brown's Duke colleague Newman Ivey White in "organizing [Brown's "attic full" of folklore] for publication" (Boggs 1981, 1). White asked Boggs "to recommend editors for the different categories." Boggs identified "Hudson for the ballads and songs, Schinhan for their music, my old friend Wayland Hand of UCLA for beliefs, Archer Taylor for proverbs and riddles, Stith Thompson for legends and tales, and Paul Brewster for games." The seven-volume *Frank C. Brown Collection of North Carolina Folklore* was aimed not only at folklore scholars but also at the North Carolina public, with copies sent to local libraries all over the state.[4] In the late 1940s, Boggs founded the *North Carolina Folklore Journal.* By 1948, the UNC Folklore Council—including Boggs, Hudson, and Schinhan and part of the Extension Division—arranged with Bascom Lamar Lunsford to direct the Carolina Folk Festival in the university's football stadium, "with more than 600 entertainers from the coast to the mountains" (Records of the Carolina Folk Festival 1948–53).

In 1950, Boggs left for the University of Miami, "a more advantageous base from which to develop contacts with Latin American folklorists" (Patterson 1990). Hudson headed the Curriculum until his retirement in 1968 and then briefly passed leadership to John Keller, who "taught medieval Spanish language and literature and wrote about legends" (Patterson 2012a, 2).

1960s to 1990s

As a graduate student at UNC in 1953, Daniel Patterson took Hudson's long-standing English and Scottish Ballad course. Hired to teach Southern literature, Patterson modestly reports that when Hudson retired, "There was nobody else but me, . . . the eccentric one around who was interested enough, and . . . they offered [the course] to me" (2015). Hudson had studied with Taylor, who had studied with George Lyman Kittredge, who had taken over Harvard's ballad course after James Francis Child's death in 1896 (Zumwalt 1988, 49, 52). Fifth in this lineage, Patterson initiated significant change.

Descended from generations of North Carolinians, Patterson loved haunting modal hymn tunes and started collecting rare old songs from elderly relatives after his parents gave him a tape recorder for his 1949 Duke University graduation (2015). In all of his scholarship—on folk songs, the Shakers (1979), the Frankie Silver legend (2000) (for which book he won the 2001 Chicago Folklore Prize), a Presbyterian North Carolinian style of tombstone carving (2012b)—Patterson connects minutely observed aesthetic expression with specific (mostly) Southern histories and characters. Folklore for Patterson connects past and present and brings skill and motivation to life. Patterson's story of transforming Hudson's course into his own British and American Folksong reflects a shift from the text-based folklore of the Hudson years toward a style that echoes Johnson's love for song tune and Odum's admiration for the individual performer.

> I taught it his way for the first year or two. . . . Hudson had used the Kittredge one-volume edition of Child. That was his textbook. And he played recordings in class that were 78 rpm disks, . . . by the end, he may have had one or two LPs, too. . . . Some of the pieces were John Jacob Niles or Richard Dyer-Bennet performing a ballad like "The Golden Willow Tree." Dyer-Bennet . . . *throws* himself into the song . . . and dramatizes it. And then, [Hudson]'d put on another record that would be Horton Barker from southwestern Virginia, blind ballad singer, so restrained and . . . objective way of performing it, and the real way, and without this strumming guitar. . . . And it just astonished me that Hudson couldn't hear there was any difference. . . . He would smile as beatifically for the one as for the other. And I was just writhing when he played the Richard Dyer-Bennet. Even without having read Lomax, . . . it was obvious that there was a difference, . . . and the style was violated in this, and not violated there. (2015)

Patterson taught his folksong course for thirty years, amassing a collection of sound recordings and films to illustrate authentic traditional singing and, legendarily, whistling all the ballad tunes to teach students that "what they're hearing on the recording of a traditional singer is not bad singing; it's singing in a different system" (2015). He recalls humorously the challenge of lining up examples for a class with various analog media and then clearing the classroom before the next professor got annoyed. His teaching collection became the basis for the Southern Folklife Collection, UNC Libraries, a premier research source of professional and field recordings for Southern music. Patterson was also instrumental in gathering the field recordings of Johnson, Schinhan, and later D. K. and Eleanor Long Wilgus and Archie Green, and in negotiating with UCLA to purchase the John Edwards Memorial Collection, created by the Australian collector of early country music (Patterson 1991). Patterson assumed leadership of the folklore program after "some issue exploded in the Department of Romance Languages" and "Keller left for the University of Kentucky," taking with him "all the faculty and graduate students in the Spanish wing of the department" (Patterson 2012a, 2). In 2009, Patterson received the American Folklore Society's Kenneth Goldstein Award for Lifetime Academic Leadership in recognition of his work in strengthening the folklore program.

In 1968, just as Keller was departing, Charles G. "Terry" Zug III "sent a letter of inquiry at the completion of his graduate studies at Pennsylvania" (Patterson 2012a, 2), and Patterson arranged for Zug to be hired immediately into the English Department. Zug, who had studied with Tristram Potter Coffin and Kenneth Goldstein and wrote his dissertation on Sir Walter Scott, taught Folk Narrative and Introduction to Folklore. Exposed to material culture studies through his classmate Henry Glassie and Professor Don Yoder, Zug became fascinated with North Carolina pottery (Zug 1986, 2018); did fieldwork with potters, rag rug weavers, and boat builders; and introduced material culture to the curriculum. Thus, in the late 1960s, folklore "began to rebuild at a moment when many of the earlier generation were retiring and dying" (Patterson 2012a, 2). Patterson and Zug assembled another interdisciplinary team: "James Peacock in Anthropology, Wilton Mason in Music, John Florin in Geography, and Leon Fink and the stirrings of Oral History in History" (Patterson 2015).

Patterson and Zug alternated leadership of the Curriculum in Folklore for thirty years and are remembered for faculty-student collaboration on public-facing projects. Only one student had actually earned the folklore MA (in 1962) since the degree became possible in 1940. From 1971 on, however, a steady stream of graduate students—as many as six per year—has completed the MA. The resurgence of folklore study in the 1970s was inspired by the political and cultural tenor of the time (Patterson 2015). Many students played string band music and did research with traditional North Carolina musicians. By the 1980s, Trudier Harris and David Whisnant had joined the English Department, contributing expertise in the role of folklore in African American and women's literature (Harris 1996, 2001) and in film and the critical history of the discovery of "folklore" in Appalachia (Whisnant 1983). Archie Green became an ardent supporter of the program, establishing an endowment to fund student research and spearheading a conference on labor folklore (Zug 2018).

In 1981, Zug organized an exhibit of North Carolina pottery, accompanied by graduate students Laurel Horton and Joyce Joines Newman's pioneering exhibit of North Carolina quilts, and it became the first wildly popular show at the university's then somnolent Ackland Art Museum. Patterson began collaborating with filmmaker Tom Davenport on documentaries—including *Born for Hard Luck* (about one of the last medicine show performers) (Davenport, Patterson, and Tullos 1976), and *A Singing Stream* (about an African American family bonded by their shared landholdings and singing of gospel music) (Davenport, Patterson, and Tullos 1986)—and students were involved in those documentation and public presentation projects. In 1976, Patterson also obtained a grant from the National Endowment for the Arts that supported graduate students in producing five hour-long radio broadcasts about North Carolina folklore for the university's WUNC radio station. The students drew on material already in the folklore archive and also did their own fieldwork to produce programs on Primitive Baptist songs, Durham blues, Piedmont blues, fiddler Tommy Jarrell, and ballad singer Cas Wallin (North Carolina Folklore Broadcast Collection, 1976). Patterson and Zug's edited collection *Arts in Earnest* (1990) comprises essays by students on the aspects of North Carolina folklore they had researched, and faculty encouraged students to publish their research in the *North Carolina Folklore Journal* to make their work available to scholars and those with informal interests in local folklore (Zug 2018). Zug was central in establishing the North Carolina Pottery Center in Seagrove, designed as "a place where people of all backgrounds, ages,

Fig. 2.1. Graduate students Christopher Lornell (*with microphone*) and Bruce Bastin (*seated*) assist filmmaker Tom Davenport (*with camera*) in interviewing Arthur "Peg Leg Sam" Jackson (*far left*) and his brother Bill Jackson for the film *Born for Hard Luck*, 1975. Photograph by Michael Higgins. From the Daniel W. Patterson and Beverly Bush Patterson Papers #20026, Southern Folklife Collection at Wilson Special Collections Library, University Libraries, University of North Carolina at Chapel Hill.

and interests discover the beauty and the stories behind North Carolina's world-class clay culture" (North Carolina Pottery Center 2019). He served not only as a longtime board member but also, upon retirement from UNC, as interim director (Zug 2018).

1990s to 2010s

Transition from the third to fourth generation began in the 1990s with the retirements of Patterson and Zug and the hiring of Glenn Hinson and myself, who have since shared leadership. In 2005, the Curriculum in Folklore merged with the Curriculum in American Studies to form the Department of American Studies, which, since 2008, has offered a PhD in American studies within which students may select folklore as their specialization. The department also forged a productive connection with Duke University's Center for Documentary Studies, long led by folklore MA Thomas Rankin, facilitating students' developing skills in photo-documentation and creative nonfiction. The folklore core faculty continue a tradition in which scholarship and collaboration with students

Fig. 2.2. Students in Glenn Hinson's Descendants Project class gather in 2018 in Oak Level Cemetery, Warren County, NC, burial place of 1921 lynching victim Plummer Bullock. Students in the class trace victims' lineages, interview their descendants, and assist local communities to publicly memorialize those murdered by lynching. Hinson (*center*); Cosmos George, head of the Warren County NAACP (*right*). Photograph by Megan May.

feed accessible public-facing presentations and prepare students for public and creative careers.

Glenn Hinson (PhD folklore, University of Pennsylvania) was hired particularly to teach a course on public folklore (Zug 2018). Hinson's Art of Ethnography course puts graduate students through the paces of fieldwork while they grapple with ethical dilemmas. His collaboration with colleagues in UNC's School of Education—the Curriculum, Music, and Community project—developed fourth-grade curricula focusing on local traditional music and empowering students as ethnographic researchers (Hinson et al. 2004). Hinson won the Chicago Folklore Prize for his book evoking African American worshippers experiencing the Holy Spirit (Hinson 2000) and continues research on identity-affirming legacies of Black oral poetry, misrepresentations of Voodoo in New Orleans tourism, and, with American studies colleague Seth Kotch, documenting stories of resilience among descendants of North Carolina lynching victims.

Patricia Sawin (MA University of Texas; PhD folklore, Indiana University) was hired to develop the graduate course on folklore theory and to teach courses on narrative, discourse, and gender (Sawin 2004). I served as the first director of graduate studies for the merged department, shepherding the fledgling PhD program. I currently study experiences of families formed through transnational adoption through the lenses of narrative and festival theory (Sawin 2017).

William R. Ferris (PhD folklore, University of Pennsylvania) came to UNC as Joel R. Williamson Eminent Professor of History after an illustrious career teaching Afro-American studies at Yale, establishing Southern Studies at the University of Mississippi, and heading the National Endowment for the Humanities under President Clinton. Until his retirement in 2018, he served as senior associate director of UNC's Center for the Study of the American South, where he catalyzed public-university collaborations, including a project with an association of Black towns across the South, and sought out archival materials for the Southern Folklife and Southern Historical Collections. In collaboration with the University of North Carolina Press, he is transforming his lifetime of research into books on Southern culture valuable to both scholarly and popular audiences (W. Ferris 2013, 2016). Ferris won a Grammy Award for the box set of his field-recorded music, interviews, and documentary films (W. Ferris 2018).

Marcie Cohen Ferris (PhD American studies, American University) taught courses on the Jewish Southern experience and foodways until her retirement in 2018. She has been instrumental in making UNC a vibrant center of Southern food studies, collaborating across the campus with scholars of nutrition, food supply, and local agriculture (M. Ferris 2010, 2014). Students in her Carolina Cooks, Carolina Eats (2015) course contributed photos and oral histories to a website documenting North Carolina foodways by region, an adjunct to upcoming publications on North Carolina food.

Jocelyn Neal (PhD music theory, Eastman School of Music) in the Department of Music, brings a musicologist's perspective to the study of country music and dance (Neal 2009, 2013).

Katherine Roberts (PhD folklore, Indiana University) joined the Department of American Studies as an assistant professor and introduced courses on The American Home and Images of the American Landscape (Roberts 2013). Roberts decided not to continue on the tenure-track path.

Bernard L. Herman (PhD folklore, University of Pennsylvania) joined the faculty as George B. Tindall Professor of Southern Studies after many years at the University of Delaware and served as chair of American studies from 2011 to 2017. Herman promulgates an expansive view of visual and material culture, interpreting quilts, self-taught art, foodways, historical archaeology, and vernacular photography, and articulating theoretical approaches to the study and interpretation of objects (recent publications include Herman 2016a, 2016b, 2019). His courses involve students in research leading to public engagement, including *Thornton Dial: Thoughts on Paper*, a book and exhibition with the Ackland Art Museum (2011).

Gabrielle Berlinger (PhD folklore, Indiana University) joined the American studies faculty in 2015 as Babette S. and Bernard J. Tanenbaum Fellow in Jewish History and Culture. She expands the Jewish folklore offerings and contributes new perspectives on ritual and festival and on vernacular architecture as a process of homemaking, exemplified in her book on Sukkot booths in Tel Aviv immigrant neighborhoods (Berlinger 2017) and her work with the Lower East Side Tenement Museum in New York City (2018). With additional retirements anticipated within five years, Berlinger will likely lead UNC Folklore into its second century. The folklore faculty hope to hire colleagues that expand the study of African American and Latinx culture in the South.

The merger of Folklore and American Studies initially provoked concern that folklore's disciplinary identity would be submerged. Being part of a larger department, however, has made the program less vulnerable to budget cuts. Previously Curriculum in Folklore faculty members were hired into other departments and allowed to teach only half folklore courses; now folklorists are hired with appointments in American Studies, make the annual case for position requests among department priorities, and have capitalized on endowments to support professorships in Southern material culture and Jewish culture. Undergraduates can now major in American studies with a concentration in folklore instead of crafting an individual major.

UNC's offering only the master's degree in folklore proper has influenced the program's role and profile within the discipline. Under time-to-degree pressures and limits on student funding, the curriculum has been streamlined so most students complete the MA, including an article-length thesis, in two academic years. A few folklore MA students go on to pursue professional degrees or PhDs. Many are making their mark in institutions dedicated to arts administration, production, and documentation from the local to the regional and national levels and in related endeavors where their folklorist's perspective informs their work as librarians, record producers, musicians, authors of poetry and novels, photographers, videographers, journalists, and creators of web content.

Across nine decades and substantial change in US society and the university, UNC folklorists adhere to three unifying commitments: recognizing the American South's connection to larger areas and movements (the British Isles, the African and Jewish diaspora, and Latin America); conducting empathetic, detailed, historical documentation of a range of Southern lives and experiences that subtly probe sectional issues of race, hierarchy, and justice; and a dedication to the broad sharing of research results—via not only books and journal articles but also dramatic works, museum exhibits, conferences, films, recordings, performances, K–12 curricula, current collaborations in digital humanities and web design, and more—in order to make their work accessible to the public and to inform debate and understanding. UNC folklorists endeavor to make students and publics aware of the ways that communities express their struggles and values through vernacular creativity and of how supporting and understanding these forms of expression are crucial to cultural survival, to cultural and political inclusion, and to developing an honest, productive, and forward-looking understanding of this troublesome and beloved region.

Acknowledgments

Thanks to Glenn Hinson for insightful reflection; Jacquelyn Solis, Director of Research and Instructional Services, UNC Libraries, for substantiating the date of UNC's first folklore MA; Chris Fowler for sharing his independent study essay on Odum and Johnson; and Aaron Smithers of UNC Libraries for guiding my search for images and calling my attention to the 1976 student radio show.

Notes

1. Glenn Hinson, personal communication with author, February 2, 2018.
2. Ibid.
3. William R. Ferris, personal communication with author, February 26, 2018.
4. Hinson, 2018.

References

Berlinger, Gabrielle Anna. 2017. *Framing Sukkot: Tradition and Transformation in Jewish Vernacular Architecture*. Bloomington: Indiana University Press.

———. 2018. "Balancing Memory and Material at the Lower East Side Tenement Museum." *Museum Anthropology Review* 12, no. 1: 14–29.

Boggs, Ralph Steele. 1981. "Reminiscences on the Prenatal Care and Birth of the Curriculum by Its Father, Ralph Steele Boggs." *Newsletter of the Curriculum in Folklore*, 1–2. University of North Carolina at Chapel Hill.

Bronner, Simon J. 1986. *American Folklore Studies: An Intellectual History*. University of Kansas Press.

Carolina Cooks, Carolina Eats: Documenting the Voices of North Carolina Foodways. 2015. http://carolinacooks.web.unc.edu/.

The Carolina Story: A Virtual Museum of University History. 2016. Accessed April 6, 2016. https://museum.unc.edu/exhibits.

Davenport, Tom, with Daniel Patterson and Alan Tullos. 1976. *Born for Hard Luck: Peg Leg Sam Jackson*. Delaplane, VA: Davenport Films. http://www.folkstreams.net/film,1.

———. 1986. *A Singing Stream: A Black Family Chronicle*. Delaplane, VA: Davenport Films http://www.folkstreams.net/film,2.

Ferris, Marcie Cohen. 2010. *Matzo Ball Gumbo: Culinary Tales of the Jewish South*. Chapel Hill: University of North Carolina Press.

———. 2014. *The Edible South: The Power of Food and the Making of an American Region*. Chapel Hill: University of North Carolina Press.

Ferris, William R. 2013. *The Storied South: Voices of Writers and Artists*. Chapel Hill: University of North Carolina Press.

———. 2016. *The South in Color: A Visual Journal*. Chapel Hill: University of North Carolina Press.

———. 2018. *Voices of Mississippi: Artists and Musicians Documented by William Ferris*. Box set of field recordings and film. Atlanta: Dust-to-Digital.

Harris, Trudier. 1996. *The Power of the Porch: The Storyteller's Craft in Zora Neale Hurston, Gloria Naylor, and Randall Kenan*. Athens: University of Georgia Press.

———. 2001. *Saints, Sinners, Saviors: Strong Black Women in African American Literature*. New York: Palgrave.

Herman, Bernard L. 2011. *Thornton Dial: Thoughts on Paper*. Chapel Hill: University of North Carolina Press in association with the Ackland Art Museum.

———. 2016a. *Building the British Atlantic World: Spaces, Places, and Material Culture, 1600–1850*. Chapel Hill: University of North Carolina Press.

———. 2016b. *Fever Within: The Art of Ronald Lockett*. Chapel Hill: University of North Carolina Press.

———. 2019. *A South You Never Ate: Savoring Flavors and Stories from the Eastern Shore of Virginia*. Chapel Hill: University of North Carolina Press.

Hinson, Glenn. 2000. *Fire in My Bones: Transcendence and the Holy Spirit in African American Gospel*. Philadelphia: University of Pennsylvania Press.

Hinson, Glenn, Dwight Rogers, Sydney Brown, and Amy Bauman. 2004. "Music Matters: Asking Questions, Fostering Agency, and Building Community in Arts-Based Educational Programming." *Journal of Thought* 39, no. 4: 15–34.

Hudson, Arthur Palmer. 1936a. *Folksongs of Mississippi and Their Background*. Chapel Hill: University of North Carolina Press.

———. 1936b. *Humor of the Old Deep South*. New York: Macmillan.

Johnson, Guy B. 1929. *John Henry: Tracking Down a Negro Legend*. Chapel Hill: University of North Carolina Press.

Johnson, Guy B., and Guion Johnson. 1980. *Research in Service to Society: The First Fifty Years of the Institute for Research in Social Science at the University of North Carolina*. Chapel Hill: University of North Carolina Press.

Krause, Bonnie J. 1999. "Arthur Palmer Hudson: Mississippi Folklorist." *Mississippi Folklife* 32, no. 1: 16–21.

Matthews, Scott L. 2018. *Capturing the South: Imagining America's Most Documented Region*. Chapel Hill: University of North Carolina Press.

Neal, Jocelyn. 2009. *The Songs of Jimmie Rodgers: A Legacy in Country Music*. Bloomington: Indiana University Press.

———. 2013. *Country Music: A Cultural and Stylistic History*. New York: Oxford University Press.

North Carolina Folklore Broadcast Collection. 1976. Collection 20105. Wilson Special Collections Library. University of North Carolina at Chapel Hill.

North Carolina Pottery Center. 2019. Overview. Accessed June 19, 2019. http://ncpotterycenter.org/overview/.

Odum, Howard. 1928. *Rainbow Round My Shoulder: The Blue Trail of Black Ulysses*. Indianapolis: Bobbs-Merrill.

Odum, Howard, and Guy Johnson. 1925. *The Negro and His Songs: A Study of Typical Negro Songs in the South*. Chapel Hill: University of North Carolina Press.

———. 1926. *Negro Workaday Songs*. Chapel Hill: University of North Carolina Press.

Patterson, Daniel W. 1979. *The Shaker Spiritual*. Princeton, NJ: Princeton University Press.

———. 1990. "Boggs Donates Recordings and Papers." *Newsletter of the Curriculum in Folklore*. University of North Carolina at Chapel Hill.

———. 1991. "The History of the Southern Folklife Collection. I. The Era of Surprise." In *Sounds of the South: A Report and Selected Papers from a Conference on the Collecting and Collections of Southern Traditional Music Held in Chapel Hill, April 6–8, 1989, to Celebrate the Opening of the Southern Folklife Collection with the John Edwards Memorial Collection in the Manuscripts Department of the Academic Affairs Library, University of North Carolina*, edited by Daniel W. Patterson, 127–39. Chapel Hill: Southern Folklife Collection, Manuscripts Department, Wilson Library, University of North Carolina.

———. 2000. *A Tree Accurst: Bobby McMillon and Stories of Frankie Silver*. Chapel Hill: University of North Carolina Press.

———. 2012a. Email to Marcie Cohen Ferris, "Re: Chronology/history of founding of UNC Folklore Program," January 13. UNC Folklore Program Records. Collection 40362. Wilson Special Collections Library. University of North Carolina at Chapel Hill.

———. 2012b. *The True Image: Gravestone Art and the Culture of Scotch Irish Settlers in the Pennsylvania and Carolina Backcountry*. Chapel Hill: University of North Carolina Press.

———. 2015. Interview with Elijah Gaddis and Patricia Sawin, November 4. UNC Folklore Program Records. Collection 40362. Wilson Special Collections Library. University of North Carolina at Chapel Hill.

Patterson, Daniel W., and Charles G. Zug III. 1990. *Arts in Earnest: North Carolina Folklife*. Durham, NC: Duke University Press.

Records of the Carolina Folk Festival 1948–53. Collection 40175, Box 1. Wilson Special Collections Library. University of North Carolina at Chapel Hill.

Roberts, Katherine. 2013. "The Art of Staying Put: Managing Land and Minerals in Rural America." *Journal of American Folklore* 126, no. 502: 407–33.

Sanders, Lynn Moss. 2003. *Odum's Folklore Odyssey: Transformation to Tolerance through African American Folk Studies*. Athens: University of Georgia Press.

Sawin, Patricia. 2004. *Listening for a Life: A Dialogic Ethnography of Bessie Eldreth through Her Songs and Stories*. Logan: Utah State University Press.

———. 2017. "'Every Kid Is Where They're Supposed to Be, and It's a Miracle': Family Formation Stories Among Adoptive Families." *Journal of American Folklore* 130, no. 518: 394–418.

Sills, David L., ed. 1968. "Odum, Howard W." In *International Encyclopedia of the Social Sciences* Vol. 11, 270–72. Gale Virtual Reference Library.

UNC Department of American Studies. 2018. Folklore. Accessed June 12, 2018. https://americanstudies.unc.edu/areas-in-american-studies/folklore/.

Whisnant, David E. 1983. *All That Is Native and Fine: The Politics of Culture in an American Region*. Chapel Hill: University of North Carolina Press.

Zug, Charles G. III. 1968. "Folklore and the Drama: The Carolina Playmakers and Their 'Folk Plays.'" *Southern Folklore Quarterly* 32, no. 4: 279–94.

———.1986. *Turners and Burners: The Folk Potters of North Carolina*. Chapel Hill: University of North Carolina Press.

———. 2018. Interview with Patricia Sawin and Trista Reis Porter, February 2. UNC Folklore Program Records. Collection 40362. Wilson Special Collections Library. University of North Carolina at Chapel Hill.

Zumwalt, Rosemary Lévy. 1988. *American Folklore Scholarship: A Dialogue of Dissent*. Bloomington: Indiana University Press.

PATRICIA SAWIN is Associate Professor and Coordinator of the Folklore Program in the Department of American Studies at the University of North Carolina at Chapel Hill. She is author of *Listening for a Life: A Dialogic Ethnography of Bessie Eldreth through Her Songs and Stories*.

3 Teaching and Research at Laval University (Québec, Canada)

From Folklore to Ethnology

Laurier Turgeon

The hundredth anniversary of the first inquiries by Marius Barbeau—one of the founding fathers of folklore and ethnology in Canada—into the oral traditions of Québec's and Canada's French-speaking populations provides an ideal opportunity to discuss the evolution of the discipline at Laval University, the first and still main home base for folklore and ethnology in French Canada. This critical review describes the development of programs, research topics, and student enrollment. I examine four pivotal periods: foundations and expansion (1940–71), changes and growth (1971–92), fragmentation and decline (1992–2006), and refounding and difficult new beginnings (2006–18).

Foundations and Expansion (1940–71)

The founding in Canada of the discipline initially called folklore but now known as ethnology goes back to 1940, when Luc Lacourcière undertook the teaching of folklore and ethnology at Laval University with a course on French Canadian folklore and popular song. This young graduate in classical and French studies had already taught one year at Collège Saint-Charles de Porrentruy in Switzerland (1936–37). Lacourcière met Marius Barbeau in Ottawa in 1938 and, through him, discovered ethnology, which was then still called folklore. Lacourcière quickly developed a passion for this field. Barbeau helped him obtain his first scholarship from the Royal Society of Canada in 1939–40, and then a second from the Guggenheim Foundation in 1943–44, to conduct research on the French origins of Canadian popular songs in the libraries of Boston, New York, Philadelphia, Charlottesville, and Washington, DC (Pichette 2004, 13, 22–23).

In 1942, Lacourcière began teaching summer courses and carrying out fieldwork at Clermont in the Charlevoix region near Québec City (Du Berger 1997, 7). Thanks to the success of the summer courses as well as prestigious scholarships and Barbeau's support, Lacourcière was named to the newly established chair of folklore at Laval University in 1944 at age thirty-four (Pichette 2004, 23).

The chair was generously endowed with a budget, a documentation center, and a teaching program. From the start of the folklore program, there were about forty students from the arts and social sciences faculties along with noncredit students (Pichette 2004, 25; Du Berger 1997, 8). Lacourcière prepared a second basic thematic course on French and Canadian storytelling; and for the methodology and theory course, he called on his master, Marius Barbeau, who, at age sixty-two, already had some thirty years of field experience across Canada.

Barbeau's course, In Search of Anthropological Knowledge in North America, consisted of forty-five lessons (including six public conferences) to be given in three units in spring 1945, fall 1945, and spring 1946. The first unit featured the "geographic and ethnic environments" of Canada and an overview of Barbeau's research findings on the Amerindians and French Canadian folklore. The second unit dealt with methodology—more precisely, field methods based on his personal experiences. It was a veritable field guide and remains surprisingly relevant today (Thériault 2011). The third unit is more theoretical in scope with its depiction of the great masters of the French, English, and American schools of anthropology. Barbeau was already associating folklore and ethnology by using together the expressions "folklore research" and "ethnographic research." He was also using the word *ethnology* to designate the combined fields of the discipline—namely, oral traditions (associated with folklore) and customs, artistic trades, and crafts (a field designated as folklife in the United States). Barbeau was influenced by the French school of thought that had abandoned the word *folklore* after World War II. French-speaking scholars judged the term negatively because of its widespread use and misuse by the Pétain government that collaborated with the German Nazi regime. Thus, in naming the discipline, they turned to the more politically correct and academic term *ethnology*.

The chair's research component was focused on the documentation center, called the Folklore Archives, whose goal—like that of many archives associated with folklore programs at universities in the United States and in other parts of Canada—was to house oral materials. Lacourcière envisioned "preparing a vast program of research projects in all the French parts of Canada" (Lacourcière 1945, 3). He introduced numerous graduate students to fieldwork case studies dedicated to traditional practices with the intention, through multiple monographs, of forming a vision of folklore over the whole territory. His research program expanded rapidly to all of French America. In his essay addressed to the Massey Commission in 1950, Lacourcière emphasized that his sound collection already comprised 1,500 recordings (Du Berger 1997, 12–13). Within six years, the influence of the Folklore Archives was being felt in North America's major centers of French-speaking populations.

The program developed steadily through the 1950s and 1960s. In 1952, it gained specific recognition with the creation of a degree in classics with the

Fig. 3.1. Marius Barbeau, 1942. Photograph courtesy of Université d'Ottawa, Centre de recherche sur les Canadiens-français, Fonds Juliette Caron-Dupont, P97, Ph63-4.

mention of "French Canadian civilization" (Du Berger 1997, 14). One could henceforth specialize in Canadian studies. This trend toward specialization increased a few years later, when the certificate was reworked and became a certificate in traditional ethnography—a designation that would be retained until the 1970s. At the same time, the field of ethnology expanded to include the study of traditional technology and material culture. The sharp increase in enrollment in the undergraduate as well as the graduate programs demanded more teaching staff. In the 1960s, the number of professors increased from two to six. Madeleine Doyon became professor in the field of costume and textiles in 1954 after the retirement of Marius Barbeau; Roger Matton was hired in 1963 to teach traditional music; Jean Du Berger in 1964 to teach tall tales and legends; Conrade Laforte in 1965 to work on traditional songs; and Jean-Claude Dupont in 1968 to teach material culture. Luc Lacourcière oversaw, on average, the defense of one doctoral thesis a year during that period, several of which were published. He was awarded a prestigious Killam Research Fellowship by the Canada Council for the Arts in 1971, enabling him to establish a team to focus on folklore research, compile bibliographies, and catalog and publish the holdings of the Folklore Archives.

Fig. 3.2. Laurier Turgeon and Helgi Paccinin recording Marc Cormier (*left*) and his brother Jack Cormier, two Franco-Newfoundland musicians, at Cape Saint George, on the Port au Port Peninsula in Newfoundland, August 2017. Photograph by Laurier Turgeon.

Changes and Growth (1971–92)

At the close of the 1960s, the discipline continued to develop and mature. The reform of the study program in 1970 brought into being an honors degree involving a major and a minor; folklore studies would henceforth be carried out in terms of a minor in traditional ethnography. However, no sooner had the restructuring been completed than the Department of Canadian Civilization was dismantled. The ethnography professors and the program would become part of the History Department in the Faculty of Arts. The program acquired the status of a major and was renamed Ethnology of French America. While the professors of the program embraced the new title, the anthropologists in the Social Science Faculty contested the use of the word *ethnology*, which they claimed was a subdiscipline of anthropology. After two years of discussion and debate, the program was renamed Popular Arts and Traditions—reflecting the name of the new French ethnology museum, the Musée des arts et traditions populaires, which was then enjoying great success (see Segalen 2005). As Jean Simard—then professor of Folklore—conveyed to me,[1] the teaching staff then restructured the program by defining four main sectors of the discipline: language and oral literature, customs and beliefs, song-music-dance, and arts and technologies. The program was relaunched with these new foundations and quickly bore fruit. Professor of folklore Jean-Claude Dupont informed me that the number of undergraduate students grew rapidly to between fifty and sixty new enrollments per year at the end of the 1970s.[2]

The research structures also underwent some significant changes. In 1974, Lacourcière asked "to be relieved of his responsibilities as administrative director of the Folklore Archives," which he had directed for thirty years (Du Berger 1997, 22, quoting Lacoucière). The oral and written archives were gradually integrated into the university library holdings, and the management of the archives was entrusted to Laval University's Department of Administrative Archives. To replace the Folklore Archives, judged by some to be too focused on collection and not enough on research, the Arts Faculty established in 1975 the Centre d'études sur la langue, les arts et les traditions populaires des francophones en Amérique du Nord (Center for the Study of Language, Popular Arts and Traditions of French-Speaking North America, or CÉLAT). It was the first research center for the humanities and social sciences founded at Laval University and was intended to focus on scientific research in ethnology from an interdisciplinary perspective. CÉLAT brought together a new generation of researchers and became a center for research in ethnology. However, the ethnologists became gradually marginalized. They no longer controlled the Folklore Archives, which were now part of the university archives, and had limited influence at CÉLAT, an interdisciplinary research center headed by a historian.

In response to the increase in enrollment, the teaching staff continued to grow and to expand its areas of expertise. Three new professors were hired during the 1970s and four in the 1980s to teach in the following areas: popular art, religious heritage, theory of storytelling, textiles and domestic life, historical archeology, material culture, language practices and discourse analysis, ethnohistory, foodways, museology, and festivals and rituals. At the close of the 1980s, the discipline counted ten professors, some fifty graduate students, and a hundred undergraduate students—making Laval University among the most important institutions teaching ethnology in Canada, and even in North America.

Fragmentation and Decline (1992–2006)

The beginning of the 1990s marked another important turn for the discipline. Hope was high for a bright future. The designation Popular Arts and Traditions had fallen out of use and was abandoned in 1992 to be replaced by that coveted since the 1970s, Ethnology of French Speakers in North America. Enthusiastically embraced, this new moniker corresponded to what was being practiced, and this time the anthropologists consented. An international symposium was organized in 1994 to mark the fiftieth anniversary of the founding of the Folklore Archives and to provide an overview of the development of the discipline in

Québec, in Canada, and abroad. The most prominent ethnologists in Canada, the United States, and France came to share views about the development of the discipline. The collection of essays published from the symposium, *Ethnologies francophones de l'Amérique et d'ailleurs*, became a point of reference for researchers and a course manual for the introductory course in the discipline at Laval University (Desdouits and Turgeon 1997). The work served as a resource for the course titled Étude de sa culture taught by Anne-Marie Desdouits and for Introduction à la culture matérielle taught by Laurier Turgeon after the retirement of Dupont in 1999.

The only journal of the discipline in Canada, *Ethnologies*, was published under the auspices of the Folklore Studies Association of Canada and was connected with Laval University in 1990. In 1992, the journal received a grant from the program for learned journals of Canada's Social Sciences and Humanities Research Council; the following year, it received a grant from the program for journals of the transfer of Fonds québécois de recherché—société et culture. *Ethnologies* has been regularly financed by these two organizations and has remained linked to Laval.

Despite these successes, fragmentation led to a certain breakdown in the discipline. Historical archeology evolved into its own discipline, forming undergraduate programs and a minor in 1987 and a major in 1996 (Dupont 1997, 37). Museology, too, became independent; it created its own program with a graduate diploma and gradually pulled away from ethnology. A growing gap between the specialists in oral traditions and literature and those in material culture created tensions between the two groups. Pressures imposed by granting agencies required CÉLAT to redefine itself since it had become an interdisciplinary and interuniversity center, thus recruiting more and more researchers in other disciplines (history, geography, architecture, archeology, linguistics, and literature) and from other universities (McGill, Université du Québec à Montréal, Université du Québec à Chicoutimi). In the mid-1990s, only three ethnologists remained at CÉLAT.

The discipline declined at the end of the 1990s. The enrollments in undergraduate studies fell to seven or eight new students per year. Graduate and postgraduate study enrollments fell as well due to the lack of professors and projects being supported financially by research grants. Three professors took their retirement in 1999–2000 and a fourth in 2004. This left only three professors of ethnology for the undergraduate and the graduate programs (MA, PhD). The ethnology program was threatened with closure for lack of professors and students.

Refounding and Difficult New Beginnings (2006–20)

A wind of renewal blew through the folklore and ethnology programs beginning in 2003. Following a national competition, an endowed Canada Research Chair in Ethnological Heritage Research was awarded to Laurier Turgeon in July 2003 for a fourteen-year period.[3] Along with the granting of two new academic positions, the chair managed an annual budget to finance research activities, two annual scholarships for MA and PhD students, and a postdoctoral scholarship. Moreover, in 2004, the chair received a major grant from the Canada Foundation for Innovation to form a laboratory for ethnological and multimedia research equipped with the latest digital technologies for the collection, treatment, study, and dissemination of ethnological data. The chair acquired equipment to fill twelve work positions for researchers to respond first to its own needs and then to the teaching needs of the BA, MA, and PhD in ethnology. The chair and his laboratory initiated several major national research projects, both in the fields of fundamental and applied research and in tangible and intangible heritage, drawing in an average of $1 million per year in research money from 2006 to the present.

More importantly, the department was able to recruit two young professors to help renew its teaching staff: the first, Martine Roberge in 2005, in the fields of festivals, rituals, and heritage; and the second, Habib Saïdi in 2006, in the areas of material culture, museology, and cultural tourism. These hires made possible an investment in promising new fields of the discipline. In 2007, to take advantage of the developing field of heritage studies, many new courses—such as Intangible Cultural Heritage, Heritage and Sustainable Development, Religious Heritage, Museums and Cities, and Cultural Tourism—were added to the undergraduate and graduate programs. The programs were renamed Ethnology and Heritage. The staff increased from three to five professors, and all managed to secure research grants from the Social Sciences and Humanities Research Council and Fonds québécois de recherché—société et culture. The addition of the word *heritage* to the programs and grant-financed research projects enabled ethnology professors to recruit even more graduate and postgraduate students from Québec and from overseas. Enrollment in the program—and especially in the PhD program—became increasingly international, with more students from central Europe (Romania, Bulgaria, and Moldavia), the Maghreb (Tunisia and Morocco), French-speaking Africa (Senegal, Cameroon, and Benin), and the Caribbean (Haiti and Guadeloupe). As a whole, the discipline gained a feeling of renewed momentum.

To revitalize teaching methods and increase enrollment at the undergraduate level, the chair fostered the development of summer schools, as Lacourcière and Barbeau had done in the early days. These courses were organized in collaboration with museums, cultural centers, municipalities, and heritage associations—all to provide students with an opportunity to conduct fieldwork and collaborative research in the public sector. The summer schools—intensive ten-day training programs—have been immensely successful, attracting between twenty and thirty-five students each year. Since 2014, two summer school programs have been held each year, one in Québec and the other internationally (Haiti, Spain, and France) to give students an opportunity to do fieldwork abroad.

In contrast, the experience with online courses was a catastrophe. With support from Laval University, professors in the program were encouraged to offer online courses and, in 2009, to establish a thirty-credit certificate in ethnology, based on the study of traditional and contemporary Québec culture, entirely online. The goal of the certificate program was to promote ethnology and to recruit students outside the Québec City area who did not have the means to attend classes in person. The option of completing a certificate program on a part-time basis on an adaptable timetable offered flexibility that enabled professionals to progress at their own rate (see Laval University 2018). At its inception, the certificate program attracted on average six or seven new enrollments per year, but enrollment quickly decreased to three or four. The certificate had been developed without much consultation and forethought. There was a mistaken assumption that online courses would attract outside students who would flock to the virtual classes. But instead of complementing and strengthening the new bachelor's degree, the certificate program became a competitor in two ways. First, it duplicated the bachelor's degree in ethnology and heritage because it proposed exactly the same courses, soliciting an already reduced clientele. Second, the new certificate in ethnology required offering at least four compulsory courses online and six optional courses from the bachelor's program. Often the new BA students were forced to take three or four of the five obligatory courses online in their first trimester. They were thus in front of their computer screens at home. Those involved in this project learned that virtual presentation is not a format well suited to ethnology, which is based, first and foremost, on practice, observation, and analysis of human relationships. About half the new bachelor's students left the program for this reason and, at the same time, dissuaded new students from enrolling. Unfortunately, the certificate program structure created a threat to the bachelor's degree program, the driving force behind the undergraduate programs, in favor of an online certificate.

The general decline in enrollments in the humanities and the Québec government's budget cuts for universities beginning in 2013–14 intensified the programs' problems. The situation in the Faculty of Arts of Laval University was especially precarious, with a soaring deficit due to poor management. In fall 2014, at the request of the university administration, the dean developed a draconian plan for recovery by eliminating support personnel positions, calling for a moratorium on the hiring of new professors, and suspending enrollment in certain small programs. The ethnology programs were targeted. At the outset of May 2015, the dean suspended enrollments in the bachelor's program in ethnology but maintained the online certificate and kept the master's degree and doctorate in ethnology and heritage. The dean was seeking reelection at this time and hoped to find support among the university administration who wanted to do away with the smaller programs while keeping the online programs deemed, at least in their view, generally more feasible. In the end, the plan did not work, the deficit increased dramatically, and the dean lost the election.

The following year, the new dean revived the interdisciplinary heritage studies undergraduate program offering a minor (thirty credits) in ethnology. Students of ethnology are able to earn a bachelor's degree in heritage studies with ten core courses in heritage (thirty credits) while taking a minor in ethnology (thirty credits) and other courses in historical sciences (thirty credits in history, art history, archaeology, archival studies, and museum studies). This interdisciplinary heritage approach to the discipline appears promising. Enrollment is up again from seven new students in 2016, to thirteen in 2017, nineteen in 2018, and twenty-eight in 2019. The MA and PhD programs are drawing local as well as an increasing number of international students. Approximately twenty-five students are currently enrolled in the graduate programs compared to seventeen in 2016. And the staff is hopeful again that there is a future for the discipline at Laval University.

Conclusion

Although the oldest and still the largest in French Canada, the ethnology program at Laval University has faced some serious challenges over the last thirty years. It has had to deal with the rise of competing disciplines such as anthropology, archaeology, museum studies, archival studies, and heritage studies. It has had to adapt to sharp budgetary restrictions and an ever-changing job market that tends to favor managers and professionals of heritage rather than scholars of popular culture. At Laval University, the ethnology undergraduate and graduate programs were restructured and renamed Ethnology and Heritage in order to broaden the scope of ethnology studies and embrace the new and developing field of heritage studies. Although these changes have enabled the programs to survive, it will be necessary in the coming years for administrators to be very creative and to think of new venues for the discipline. It will be requisite to train students in the use of digital technologies to put the folklore archives online and to use digital technologies in the field as well as in the interpretation and transmission of tangible and intangible heritage. Given the current importance and proliferation of communication via online video content, ethnologists trained in the production of ethnographic films could be in a good position to take advantage of this social trend. The exponential development of cultural tourism worldwide also offers ethnologists a wealth of opportunities in the interpretation of tangible and intangible heritage, in the organization of festivals, and in the creation of guided tours.

Acknowledgments

I thank the late Jean-Claude Dupont and Jean Simard for the interviews and information that they provided on the teaching of ethnology at Laval University before the 1980s. My thanks go to Jean-Pierre Pichette and to Simard for their comments and corrections on this chapter.

Notes

1. Jean Simard, personal communication to the author, October 25, 2019.
2. Jean-Claude Dupont, personal communication to the author, October 5, 2014.
3. The chair was obtained following an international competition organized by the Faculty of Arts of Laval University, which had announced the creation of a chair in heritage without specifying a particular field. Candidates were asked to justify the area of heritage proposed. Once selected by Laval University, the submission underwent a national review by a committee of peers at the secretariat of Canada Research Chairs.

References

Desdouits, Anne-Marie, and Laurier Turgeon, eds. 1997. *Ethnologies francophones de l'Amérique et d'ailleurs*. Québec: Presses de l'Université Laval.

Du Berger, Jean. 1997. "Folklore et ethnologie à l'Université Laval." In *Ethnologies francophones de l'Amérique et d'ailleurs*, edited by Anne-Marie Desdouits and Laurier Turgeon, 3–24. Québec: Presses de l'Université Laval.

Dupont, Jean-Claude. 1997. "L'Étude de la culture matérielle à l'Université Laval." In *Ethnologies francophones de l'Amérique et d'ailleurs*, edited by Anne-Marie Desdouits and Laurier Turgeon, 25–37. Québec: Presses de l'Université Laval.

Lacourcière, Luc. 1945. "Les Études de folklore français au Canada." *Culture* 6: 3–9.

Laval University. 2018. Certificate in Ethnology. Accessed April 2, 2018. www2.ulaval.ca/les-etudes/programmes/repertoire/details/certificat-en-ethnologie.html.

Pichette, Jean-Pierre. 2004. "Luc Lacourcière et l'institution des Archives de folklore à l'Université Laval (1936–1944). Autopsie d'une convergence." *Rabaska* 2: 11–29.

Segalen, Martine. 2005. *Vie d'un musée*. Paris: Stock.

Thériault, Benoît. 2011. "Marius Barbeau, en quête de connaissances depuis 1911." *Rabaska* 9: 171–81.

LAURIER TURGEON holds the Canada Research Chair in Intangible Cultural Heritage and is Professor of History and Ethnology at Laval University. He is author of *Patrimoines métissés: Contextes Coloniaux et Postcoloniaux*.

4 The Folklife Connection

Ethnological Organization at Franklin and Marshall, Cooperstown, and Penn State Harrisburg

Simon J. Bronner

Planting Academic Folklife Education and Public Engagement at Franklin and Marshall College

Working on his dissertation about the folk culture of the Amish, Alfred Shoemaker in the late 1930s consulted ethnological scholars working in European folklife institutes more than literary and anthropological folklorists who were prevalent in America (Bronner 1998, 266–312). He realized that these institutes devoted to the study of community life in their regions were engaged in scholarship that differed sharply from what was available in North America. After his military service during World War II, Shoemaker grasped an opportunity to introduce ethnological perspectives into the American academy when he became the founding chair of the Department of Folklore at Franklin and Marshall College (F&M). Organizing the program along ethnological lines, he quickly set into motion publications, an outreach center, and archives.

The college had a long legacy of connection to the surrounding Pennsylvania German culture, including being home to the Pennsylvania German Folklore Society since the 1930s, and Shoemaker convinced administrators that adding folklore studies defined ethnologically would anchor the college in the regional culture and also provide academic legitimacy. The move made news as the nation's first independent department of folklore. Religion expert Don Yoder and Germanicist J. William Frey joined Shoemaker on the folklore faculty. All of them had Pennsylvania German backgrounds and set about to counter anti-German feeling lingering from the war with a celebration of the folk culture of central Pennsylvania.

Shoemaker bucked the trend in graduate programs at the University of North Carolina and Indiana University, where fledgling programs emphasized the literary and oral aspects of folklore. Essential to Shoemaker's vision was the centrality of material culture and social life to the study of diverse religious-ethnic communities in America. Indeed, Shoemaker openly challenged his American colleagues at the Midcentury International Folk Conference in 1950 by proclaiming, "I have never seen why we should limit ourselves exclusively to the oral tradition. To my mind that is only a very small segment of folklore and in the life of the people may not get as much attention as folk art, games, gambling, and so forth" (Thompson 1953, 246).

Lodged in a small undergraduate liberal arts institution, Shoemaker had a choice to make. He could fall into line with the other programs and integrate those ethnological concerns together with literary and oral interests under the broad umbrella of comparative folklore; he could rename the department to publicize its ethnological offerings (the department had six courses listed); or he could leave academe and concentrate on independently building folk museums, festivals, and archives at the heart of a regional folklife or folk cultural approach. With the smashing success of the Pennsylvania Dutch Folklore Festival he launched in Lancaster and the rising sales of the *Pennsylvania Dutchman* magazine tapping into a growing tourist market, he chose the latter. Frey stayed in the German Department but did not have the commitment to folklife studies that Shoemaker had. Further ending F&M's central ethnological role, in 1956 Yoder moved on to the Department of Religious Thought at the University of Pennsylvania.

A pioneer of public folklife programming, Shoemaker formed the Pennsylvania Folklife Society and changed the name of the *Pennsylvania Dutchman* to *Pennsylvania Folklife*. For Shoemaker, the goals he set as a scholar were regionally oriented to document and revitalize Pennsylvania German culture. This attitude was evident while he was teaching at F&M, where, in addition to an introduction to folklife that sent students to conduct ethnographic field research of Pennsylvania German communities, his other courses were locally oriented with titles including Pennsylvania Dutch Folklore, Pennsylvania Dutch Folk Art, and Folklore of Southeast Pennsylvania. Plagued by health issues, Shoemaker made a premature exit from scholarship in the early 1960s, and his colleague Don Yoder stepped up to take the reins of *Pennsylvania Folklife* and the folk festival.

Six years after Don Yoder arrived at the University of Pennsylvania, literary scholar MacEdward Leach from the English Department formed a Group Committee on Folklore Studies (see Miller 2004 and this volume). But Yoder was not part of it. When Penn's president in 1966 was unsuccessful in getting an external candidate to replace Leach as chair of the committee, he turned in-house to Yoder to take over. As chair from 1966 to 1969, Yoder's most significant move was to rename the program, and later the department, Folklore and Folklife. As they were at the University of Pennsylvania, courses at

Indiana mostly addressed music and narrative, and the main gateway courses at the departments on theories and methods were not ethnologically centered. Although Yoder boasted as editor of *Pennsylvania Folklife* that it had the largest circulation among folkloristic periodicals, at the academic organizational level, the American Folklore Society was dominated by narrative and music studies. Nonetheless, Yoder declared that a "folklife studies movement" had taken hold in the United States, and he sought to expand it academically (Yoder 1963). By the time of the department's twentieth anniversary, almost half of the dissertations addressed folklife concerns (Samuelson 1983, 7).

Sprouting a Fieldwork and Museum-Centered Collaborative Folk Culture Program at Cooperstown

The breakthrough for a stand-alone ethnological folklife program came out of a museum rather than a large university setting. It occurred in 1964 when Louis C. Jones, director of the New York State Historical Association (NYSHA), worked with the State University of New York at Oneonta to create separate graduate programs in American Folk Culture and History Museum Studies at the association's location in Cooperstown (Rath 1975, 5–6). Jones had been teaching literary studies in English since 1934 at what was then the New York State College for Teachers at Albany (now the University at Albany). Anthropologist George Herzog at Columbia mentored Jones in his doctoral work, but it was his older colleague at Albany, Harold Thompson, founder of the New York Folklore Society, who influenced Jones's move to the study of local and regional folklore (Hand 1975, 7–8). A native of Albany, Jones moved from the historical-literary study of local murder cases to documenting the ghost legends associated with them (McDade 1975). With Thompson's departure for Cornell in 1940 and Jones's expanded research on supernatural beliefs and legends in community context, Jones took over the folklore class at Albany and compiled an archive, for which he consulted European ethnological models.

The trustees of NYSHA tapped Jones for the directorship because of his combination of folkloristic and historical interests that were relevant to the Farmers' Museum, defined as a "folk museum" of upstate New York village life in the early nineteenth century, in addition to Fenimore House, an art and historical museum focusing on New York State (Rath 1975, 1–2). With his background as an educator, Jones, beginning in 1948, supervised the Seminars on American Culture held at the museum complex during the summers. Recognizing the Farmers' Museum as comparable to Scandinavian open-air museums, he introduced seminars led by European as well as American ethnologists on traditional practices such as blacksmithing, cookery, farming, and weaving. Set against the backdrop of the museums, the seminars were among the first in the country to offer college credit in material culture and folklife topics. Jones also developed

Fig. 4.1. Louis C. Jones in the folk art gallery of the Fenimore House (now Fenimore Art Museum), New York State Historical Association, Cooperstown, NY, ca. 1967. Photograph by Milo Stewart.

the folk art collections of the Fenimore House and brought in folklorists to work together with art historians on the new genre. He had been a participant in Indiana University's summer Folklore Institutes during the late 1940s with an emphasis on oral tradition, and he realized that his Cooperstown seminars could be distinguished by their ethnological and museological bent.

Emboldened by the numbers of young students at the seminars, Jones sought to expand the Cooperstown educational offerings into a year-round degree-granting program. In pursuing this plan, he had several advantages over Shoemaker's experience at F&M. Cooperstown had an existing folk museum with professional staff, but, more importantly, Jones was an administrator who could allocate resources toward the project. Unlike other museum directors, Jones was a NYSHA trustee and served with Frank Moore, chair of the State University of New York board. Moore helped broker a deal with the Oneonta campus to extend degrees to Cooperstown. Jones's plan got a boost with a $30,000 lead grant from the Scriven Foundation to fund fellowships and equipment; additional funding came from the Rockefeller Brothers Fund and the American Association for State and Local History (Jones 1965, 105). Keeping the attention to regional-ethnic communities in a national context that Shoemaker championed, Jones labeled the MA program American Folk Culture to distinguish it from existing academic folklore programs and connect it to the emphasis at Cooperstown's Seminars on American Culture.

The first class attracted twenty-seven students, including Henry Glassie, who would go on to teach folklife and material culture in folklore departments at Penn and Indiana. The enrollees arrived from fifteen states and Turkey. Coupled with another MA program, History Museum Studies, Cooperstown would have more of an applied framework than the existing folklore programs and would encourage students to pursue careers in museums, archives, media, and historical-cultural agencies (Jones 1965, 103–4). The first full-time professor in folk culture was Bruce Buckley, who had received his PhD in folklore from Indiana University in 1962. Although Buckley had studied folk ballads and oral tradition at Indiana, Jones was impressed that he had produced educational films on American folklife. Complementing him in museum studies was Frank Spinney, who had been president of Old Sturbridge Village, another outdoor museum. Per Guldbeck, who had previously been employed at the Museum of International Folk Art in Santa Fe, New Mexico, taught a hands-on course on Folk Technology—the first of its kind—that included preindustrial practices of log-building construction, gathering edible wild plants, and farming (Jones 1965, 106). Jones participated in the program as instructor of folk art courses.

Whereas Don Yoder in "The Folklife Studies Movement" (1963) had described folklife museums and universities as separate locations for ethnological research, Jones conceived the Cooperstown programs as integrating them. Whether students were majoring in American folk culture or history museum studies, they were required to take two gateway courses: Folklife Research and History Research. The pedagogy thus included learning through ethnographic fieldwork with contemporary communities and archival research with historical documents (see Jones 1982). The former meant training in documentary technology of photography, audiovisual recording, and field notes, while the latter emphasized interpreting artifacts, reading various types of primary documents such as broadsides and merchant ledgers, and working with photographs and paintings as social historical evidence. The outcomes were not only written papers but also exhibitions, multimedia presentations, and ethnographic films. Students submitted their documentary projects to the newly created Archive of New York State Folklife (which was based on a European model), and future students would consult these files to build a comprehensive cultural profile of the region (Donaldson 2009). As a program, the pedagogy underscored teamwork and hands-on experiences, with the museums treated as laboratories for enacting traditional practices. In his director's report for 1964, Jones gave, as an example, students in the folk technology course who "built a forest shelter and furnished it, using only the equipment available to a frontiersman in 1800; the class worked on this project as a group and out of it has come a joint report which not only is interesting reading but also reflects an unusual kind of educational experience" (1965, 106).

Buckley reflected years later that the "pedagogy represented by the Programs was not a formula approach, not necessarily a particular methodology, and not even a theoretical school, but rather more of an attitude, a sensitive and inquisitive attitude toward people as individuals and as members of groups, and a respect for their traditions and the meanings they give to them" (1984, 29). Yet the main contribution that the programs wanted to achieve, unlike what Buckley called the "separatist, ivory-tower" outlook of the other folklore programs, was a "synthesis of folklife and museology" geared especially to the North American cultural context (28).

With Jones gone from leadership and NYSHA refocusing on its state historical mission during the late 1970s, the folk culture program received less support from administrators than it had in the 1960s. The number of students did not appear to be the problem. Buckley counted 461 graduates of the programs through spring 1979, with folk culture claiming 159, or over 34 percent of the total. The folk culture program also touted high-profile folklorists as alumni. In addition to Henry Glassie were Roderick Moore at Ferrum College, W. K. McNeil at the Ozark Folk Center, Thomas Adler at the University of Kentucky, and Gerald Parsons at the American Folklife Center. Regardless, the State University of New York dropped the Folk Culture Program at Cooperstown in fall 1979.

Flowering of Ethnological Education at Penn State

I received my degree from Cooperstown in 1977 and then went to Indiana to obtain the PhD. Two years after the Cooperstown program closed, I began teaching at the Pennsylvania State University branch in Middletown, known then as the Capitol Campus. A Cooperstown connection was the establishment by Henry Glassie of coursework on folklife and material culture at the Capitol Campus within the American Studies graduate program. In the region including Harrisburg and Lancaster, where Alfred Shoemaker had been based, a number of growing institutions called for student participation, including the State Archives and State Farm Museum (now the Landis Valley Village and Farm Museum, a Pennsylvania German Heritage Site) and America's largest regional folk festival at Kutztown.

Glassie recalls that the courses at the newly established campus (1966) in Middletown were broad, umbrella courses with names such as Regional America and Seminar in American Culture, and he was given great leeway to design course content that emphasized material culture. Glassie left a year later to go to Indiana University, and the college dean, who came out of American Studies, continued the faculty line as a folklorist with specialization in folklife, material culture, and museology. Folklorist Jay Anderson, who had studied historic material culture and museology with Don Yoder at the University of Pennsylvania, was hired, and when he left, another material culture specialist, Yvonne Milspaw, holding a PhD from Indiana University, continued in the position.

During the 1980s, a number of folklore degree programs—including at the University of Texas, Indiana University, University of Pennsylvania, Memorial University of Newfoundland, and University of California, Los Angeles—offered courses with the terms *folklife* and *material culture* in their titles. John Michael Vlach in the American Studies Doctoral Program at George Washington University led a concentration in folklife. The loss of the Cooperstown Folk Cultural Program created a void of locations taking ethnological approaches in the United States, and there was only a small likelihood that the George Washington University program would expand the folklife option into a stand-alone program. In response, I added courses on Material Culture and Folklife to the Penn State curriculum, coordinated a vibrant folklife internship program, and created the Center for Pennsylvania Culture Studies (renamed in 2017 the Pennsylvania Center for Folklore) with multiple folklife archives (including the papers of folklife researchers Mac E. Barrick and Sue Samuelson and the Pennsylvania Folklife Archives from the Pennsylvania Council on the Arts) as an anchor for outreach programs in regional folklife. Students who wanted to continue their studies past the ethnologically oriented MA could apply to the Department of Folklore and Folklife at the University of Pennsylvania or transfer to the American Studies Program at George Washington University with its folklife concentration if they wanted to stay in the region. But when Penn suspended admissions in Folklore and Folklife and George Washington dropped its Folklife Concentration after John Vlach's retirement, I felt the need to work on a doctoral program that would keep students at home and be attractive to a global pool transferring from other MA programs.

With concerns about competition from the history and English departments at Penn State, the proposal for a doctoral program as it went through the complex bureaucracy of one of America's largest universities evolved to emphasize distinctive features among the ethnological offerings of a concentration in community studies, folk culture, and a connection to public heritage, which included government, media, and community work in addition to museums and archives (Bronner 2012a). While professing a global scope, the proposal also highlighted Penn State's land-grant mission to serve regional interests and public outreach. My teaching focused on folklife, material culture, heritage studies, folklore (around the theme of culture and aging with special attention to youth cultures), and Jewish studies. Tenure-track professors Michael Barton, John Haddad, and Anthony Buccitelli, respectively, led seminars on ethnography and community studies, taught courses on Chinese culture and on popular culture and folklife, and designed courses on digital culture and media, religious cultures, and race

Fig. 4.2. Graduate students in the Material Culture and Folklife course at the Pennsylvania State University, Harrisburg, documenting folk architecture, Middletown, PA, 2014. Photograph by Simon J. Bronner.

and ethnicity. Skill-oriented courses were available in oral history, archives and records management, historic preservation, and museum studies.

In 2009, Penn State Harrisburg (the new name for the Capitol Campus) admitted the first class of doctoral students in American Studies that included a number of students specializing in folk culture, including Trevor Blank, Amy Milligan, Jennifer Dutch, Zachary Langley, and Spencer Green. The program grew quickly and leapfrogged adult education as the largest doctoral program in the college. With admissions to the program stabilizing between eight and ten students annually, complementary graduate certificate programs were launched in Folklore and Ethnography and Heritage and Museum Studies. These programs proved to be popular, especially among the MA students (at the doctoral level, students could declare folklife as a field of study). An added feature was support for various national publications and reference works that involved faculty and students, such as editing the *Encyclopedia of American Folklife*, *Youth Cultures in America*, *Cultural Analysis*, and *Western Folklore*. The endowed Center for Holocaust and Jewish Studies (founded in 2008) also regularly featured programming in Jewish folklife studies. The doctoral program attracted a national pool of students, and interest and visiting scholars from abroad (e.g., Turkey, Andorra, Trinidad, Tajikistan, Russia, and China).

The program has given opportunities to professionals working in heritage institutions to extend their expertise and make Penn State Harrisburg a hub of folklife activity. Participating in the program, for example, were Charles Camp with foodways, Lisa Rathje in public folklife, Patricia Levin in folk medicine, Sue Samuelson on festivals, and Troy Boyer with Pennsylvania German folklife. To be sure, although Penn State's doctoral program shares with the Cooperstown precedent an American cultural purview, an ethnological methodological and pedagogical core, and a significant applied component, it differs from Jones's model set against the backdrop of the Farmers' Museum in a remote locale. Penn State's folklife programming is centered on a college campus but reaches out to a greater variety of heritage institutions and ethnic-religious communities—urban, rural, and suburban—in an area that is crowded with museums, cultural and community organizations, and international traffic (Bronner 2012a). Folklife courses are embedded within American Studies and are more concerned than those at Cooperstown with the interrelations of popular and folk cultures of ethnicity, race, religion, and gender. The influence of the cultural landscape known as Amish and Dutch country, the neighboring ethnic-industrial community of Steelton and its many folk music and dance groups, and publicity for the Susquehanna Folk Music Society and Kutztown Folk Festival all make *folklife* and *folk art* recognizable terms in the area. Penn State Harrisburg also takes advantage of its location near state and national capitals to feature governmental partnerships and to work with public and community affairs organizations.

These advantages for expanding a program for ethnological studies in the American folkloristic landscape are balanced by organizational challenges. The doctoral program is housed in a school of humanities that is not ideal for the social science foundation of ethnology and folklife. In addition, other areas of concentration such as humanities, English, and history that faced enrollment declines have viewed the folklorists with intellectual suspicion and believed they lured students away from them. In 2016, the School of Humanities' strategic plan with the "signature" programming of American studies and folklife in mind, called for rebranding humanities as a culture and communication unit, and I boldly suggested a possible shift of the programming to the School of Public Affairs. This labeling issue is important for proposals such as the one I put forward for technological laboratories for material culture analysis and exhibition. Labs and studios are less likely to be approved for humanities than for other units.

The Changing Landscape of Folklife and Ethnology in American Academe

The rise of Penn State's program signals the story of ethnological education in America coming full circle from its seeds in central Pennsylvania and showing strength for the future of folkloristics. Another interpretation is of an often-faltering arc for folklife and ethnology as research and pedagogical approaches as compared with those in Europe, where the field appears more dominant and widespread. Looking to the past, I might explain the academic difficulty of folklife study in the United States resulting from its precarious position as an outlier to English and anthropology. With many American universities in the post–World War II period not viewing their missions in terms of their regional location, the community-centric orientation of folklife and ethnology also faced the hurdle of identifying ethnological study in the dispersed, individualistic society of the United States relative to more rooted, group-oriented institutions in Europe and Asia (see Jackson 1984 on American folkloristic pedagogy, which omits ethnological approaches, and Bendix 1998 for ethnological criticisms of folklore terminology from a European perspective). Indeed, the roots of European ethnology were based on studies of a regionalized peasant class, which was largely absent, or perceived to be absent, in North America. The term *ethnology* has been applied in the United States mostly in research of Native Americans, as exemplified by the Smithsonian Institution's Bureau of American Ethnology (1879–1965).

The folklife studies movement claimed roots in European ethnology but used the term *folklife* to distinguish its community work from American ethnology. Central Pennsylvania became fertile ground for the movement's development because of thriving tradition-centered communities such as the Amish, agricultural and hunting enclaves, and ethnic-industrial neighborhoods (Bronner 1989). Not far from Penn State, the 1967 Festival of American Folklife (later the Smithsonian Folklife Festival) and the American Folklife Center (incorporating the Archive of Folk Culture) in the Library of Congress in 1976 attracted attention to ethnological perspectives. As a result, many state and regional organizations incorporated the word *folklife* in their names, but academe still lagged behind.

In the twenty-first century, amid concerns about the meaning of digital culture, physical mobility, and globalization for traditions that provide senses of place and social belonging, there is more cause to embrace a broadened view of folklife in American academe, particularly as universities increasingly understand the urgency to reach out to surrounding communities for social as well as economic support (see Bronner 2016). When folklorist William Ferris was chair of the National Endowment for the Humanities (1997–2001) as an appointee of President Bill Clinton, he envisioned funding a network of regional centers connected to universities that would build on ethnological principles. However, in the politics of a country without a cultural policy, the funding initiative disappeared with a new administration (National Endowment for the Humanities 1999). Still, the best hope for expanding degree-granting programs such as Penn State's is in collaboration with outreach centers, museums, and archives that are often linked to local governments.

Some trends in American folkloristics proved to be a problem for the expansion of ethnologically oriented programs in the United States. Although material culture was generally acknowledged after the 1960s to be part of what folklorists study, the ascendancy of performance theory in line with a narrowing concern for verbal art gave rise to more, rather than less, exclusive emphasis on narrative in the discipline, often within the context of humanities departments (see Bronner 2019, 278–80). The situation was different in Europe, where ethnological institutions grew by developing a niche, often within social sciences, with the broadening work of practice theory and community-centric work (see Bronner 2012b; Bronner 2019, 282–86). An opening exists, however, for ethnologically oriented programs that respond comprehensively to digital culture, or image culture, in the twenty-first century as well as the phenomena of rituals and festivals, organizational and corporate culture, bodylore and sexuality, adult play and video games, and new age beliefs and religion as folklife topics (indeed, a trajectory of folklorist Jeffrey Tolbert, hired in 2018 by Penn State Harrisburg). In addition, many of the communities thought to be doomed, such as the Amish and Hasidim, have in fact proliferated, suggesting the value of comparative studies for other groups drawing ethnological attention such as South Asians, Mormons, Cajuns, Chicano/a, French Canadians, Afro-Caribbeans, LGBTQ people, urban dwellers, athletes, youth gangs, fan cultures, maritime groups, and refugees. The increasing number of folklorists in public heritage positions also suggests a need for more ethnological education and the kinds of applied work that is conducted in folklife programs. These aspects of folklife might pragmatically be embedded in existing folklore programs and interdisciplinary units (Bronner 2012a; Wilson 2006, 23–31), but conceptually a need remains for stand-alone, community-centric centers educating for life with a spectrum of traditions and groups as their purview.

References

Bendix, Regina. 1998. "Of Names, Professional Identities, and Disciplinary Futures." *Journal of American Folklore* 111, no. 441: 235–46.

Bronner, Simon J. 1989. "Folklife Starts Here: The Background of Material Culture Scholarship in Pennsylvania." In *The Old Traditional Way of Life*, edited by Robert E. Walls and George H. Schoemaker with Jennifer Livesay, 230–43. Bloomington, IN: Trickster Press.

———. 1998. *Following Tradition: Folklore in the Discourse of American Culture*. Logan: Utah State University Press.

———. 2012a. "Folklore Studies within American Studies: The Penn State Harrisburg Model." *AFS Review* (February 13). https://www.afsnet.org/news/news.asp?id=83354.

———. 2012b. "Practice Theory in Folklore and Folklife Studies." *Folklore* 123, no. 1: 23–47.

———. 2016. "Toward a Definition of Folklore in Practice." *Cultural Analysis* 15: 6–27.

———. 2019. *The Practice of Folklore: Essays toward a Theory of Tradition*. Jackson: University Press of Mississippi.

Buckley, Bruce R. 1984. "New Beginnings and Old Ends: Museums, Folklife, and the Cooperstown Experiment." *Folklore Historian* 1: 24–31.

Donaldson, Ryan A. 2009. "Dynamic Yet Fragile: Reconsidering the Archive of New York State Folklife." *Voices: The Journal of New York Folklore* 35: 4–11.

Hand, Wayland D. 1975. "Louis C. Jones and the Study of Folk Belief, Witchcraft, and Popular Medicine in America." *New York Folklore* 1: 7–13.

Jackson, Bruce, ed. 1984. *Teaching Folklore*. Buffalo, NY: Documentary Research.

Jones, Louis C. 1965. "The Director's Report for 1964." *New York History* 46: 103–44.

———. 1982. *Three Eyes on the Past: Exploring New York Folk Life*. Syracuse, NY: Syracuse University Press.

McDade, Thomas M. 1975. "After the Fact or the Murderous Career of Louis Clark Jones." *New York Folklore* 1: 15–20.

Miller, Rosina S. 2004. "Of Politics, Disciplines, and Scholars: MacEdward Leach and the Founding of the Folklore Program at the University of Pennsylvania." *Folklore Historian* 21: 17–34.

National Endowment for the Humanities. 1999. "NEH Launches Initiative to Develop 10 Regional Humanities Centers Throughout the Nation." Press release (May 10). https://www.neh.gov/news/press-release/1999-05-10.

Rath, Fred. 1975. "The Great Adventure: Louis C. Jones and the New York State Historical Association." *New York Folklore* 1: 1–6.

Samuelson, Sue, ed. 1983. *Twenty Years of the Department of Folklore and Folklife at the University of Pennsylvania: A Dissertation Profile*. Philadelphia: Department of Folklore and Folklife, University of Pennsylvania.

Thompson, Stith, ed. 1953. *Four Symposia on Folklore*. Bloomington: Indiana University Press.

Wilson, William A. 2006. *The Marrow of Human Experience: Essays on Folklore*. Edited by Jill Terry Rudy. Logan: Utah State University Press.

Yoder, Don. 1963. "The Folklife Studies Movement." *Pennsylvania Folklife* 13, no. 3: 43–56.

SIMON J. BRONNER is Dean of the College of General Studies and Distinguished Professor of Social Sciences at the University of Wisconsin–Milwaukee and Distinguished Professor Emeritus of American Studies and Folklore at the Pennsylvania State University, Harrisburg. He is author of *Folklore: The Basics* and *The Practice of Folklore: Essays Toward a Theory of Tradition*.

Part II

1960s–70s Efflorescence

5 "The Great Team" of American Folklorists

Characters Large in Life and Grand in Plans

Rosemary Lévy Zumwalt

The Great Team

In an interview on the history of the Indiana University (IU) Folklore Institute conducted in 1986, Jeanne Harrah-Conforth (now Harrah-Johnson) asked Alan Dundes what question he would pose to Richard Dorson if Dorson were still alive. Dundes replied, "I'd say to him, 'Why didn't you ever write a history of American folklorists and folklore scholarship, the way you did for England?'" (Dundes 1985, 28).[1] Dorson had a response; and when I was a student in the Folklore Program at University of California, Berkeley (UCB) in the early 1970s, I heard Dundes give the answer: "Dorson always said that there was never the great team of folklorists in America as there had been in Britain." However, as Roger Abrahams recalled, "the great team" was used to refer to three American folklorists. Abrahams recounted that he, Dorson, and Dundes had a wonderful time in the 1960s: "We went to Yugoslavia . . . [and] Argentina together, and we always would hook up for a meal at the AFS [American Folklore Society] the first night. And we kiddingly called ourselves 'The Great Team.'" Thus, if only in jest, "the great team" was used as an emic term for, and here another playful self-reference, "the triumvirate" (Abrahams 1986, 12).

The Spirit of the 1960s

The great team of American folklorists and the development of specific graduate folklore programs emerged in the United States in the 1960s at a time of organizational efflorescence in academia. In 1963, the IU Folklore Institute became an independent department of folklore; the University of Pennsylvania (Penn) created a graduate group on folklore studies also in 1963; the University of California, Los Angeles (UCLA) established the Interdepartmental MA Program in Folklore

Fig. 5.1. International Congress of Americanists, Buenos Aires, September 1966. *Left to right*: William Hurt, Robert Jerome Smith, Roger Abrahams, Alan Dundes, Gloria Dorson, and Richard Dorson. Photograph courtesy of Roger Abrahams; permission courtesy of Rod Abrahams.

and Mythology with students entering in 1965; UCB created the MA Folklore Program in 1965; and the University of Texas established the Center for Intercultural Studies in Folklore and Oral History in 1967.[2]

Roger Abrahams gives a personal account of the political and cultural forces that played out in his life as an undergraduate at Swarthmore College (1951–55):

> And there I was a "folkie." We didn't call them "folkies" quite yet, . . . and I was a singer [and played] a four-string guitar and banjo. And I was politically involved . . . , and that meant that I kind of fell into folk singing groups. . . . There was a Swarthmore folk festival in those days. And actually I could date to the exact moment when I fell in love with folklore, when I said, "That's what I'm going to do." I was sitting next to Ralph Rinzler at a Pete Seeger concert in 1952, at the Swarthmore Folk Festival. And we went out and bought our banjoes the next day. (1986, 12)

With the pull of the practical, Abrahams entered law school at Penn in 1956: "And I looked in the catalog, and there in the English Department was a course called, 'Selected Topics in English and American Folklore,' with MacEdward Leach. I thought, 'My God! People *study* that?' And I . . . met MacEdward, and we became very close friends. And I took a course with him" (Abrahams 1986, 1–2, emphasis in original; see also Muthukumaraswamy 2002, 11–12).

Leach would later say that "his 'greatest seduction'" was luring Abrahams away from law school (Abrahams 1968, 99).

Indiana University

Dundes made the crucial link to visionary IU president Herman B Wells, "a greatly beloved administrator . . . [who] was sympathetic to Folklore." It took not only Stith Thompson, Dundes said, who was "not your most charismatic person, . . . [but also] an enlightened administration to see the possibilities." The administration at IU at that time was willing to take "intellectual chances . . . with . . . disciplines like folklore" and to take chances with "maverick-type professors" (Dundes 1985, 11–12). Richard Bauman observed that "the general strategy of Indiana University [was] to cultivate in some way or another . . . these things that the deans call the jewels in the crown." Resources were channeled to build up a program, so that in the case of folklore, "everywhere in the world, when somebody thinks about folklore . . . they think about Indiana University" (1987, 21, 22). Jan Brunvand commented on the strengths of IU, which built on the "tradition that Thompson established." Brunvand continued, "He was known internationally. 'Bloomington' was all you had to say to Europeans, ironically, more than Americans, and they knew what you meant" (1986, 49).

William Wilson reflected on his time at Indiana University from 1961 to 1965 as "the golden era at IU, it was the golden era of my life, too." When Harrah-Conforth asked him why he thought that folklore grew at Indiana, Wilson replied with a description of the people and the place: "Stith Thompson was this gentleman scholar, this old school grand gentleman who worked his tail off, frankly, you look at his knowledge of languages, his work that went into the type and motif indexes, his reputation not just in this country but in Europe, and particularly among the followers of the Finnish school." Thompson had moved "into a place where a proper setting was there, where the spirit was." Wilson continued, "And so I think that Thompson working first, and then Dorson moving into that with a kind of . . . brutalness, almost, of slaying dragons on all sides to get what he wanted, but working in a place where what he wanted was already accepted. I'm not sure that could have happened any place else." Referring to Dorson's earlier place of employment, Wilson said, "I don't think Dorson at Michigan State would have become Dorson, and I don't think the folklore program without Dorson would have become what it became." Continuing with the metaphor of the golden era, Wilson said, "You almost have an origin myth with people who were with Dorson in the beginning" (1986, 85, 77–78, 71).

Harrah-Conforth asked Bauman about his time at IU when he had come midyear in January 1961. He recalled this early period by listing the people, beginning with Hasan El Shamy, Neil Rosenberg, Barbro Klein, and Dan Ben-Amos. He continued, "Jerry Mintz was a year or 2 out. Elli Köngäs came back that summer to defend her dissertation. Jan Brunvand finished . . . the end of that spring. Sandy Ives was here that year. . . . Alan Dundes finished the year after that. But the program was small enough and there was just a sense of excitement and esprit de corps about it that was very stimulating. And Bob Georges was here." Harrah-Conforth posited, "These are names that most people know now" and then queried, "But at the time, did you have any sense of the strength of these people?" Bauman replied in the affirmative and emphasized that there was "a sort of effervescence about the place" (1987, 7–8).

When Harrah-Conforth asked Robert Georges to "put yourself back," he very quickly described the location where all the graduate students came together: "The main gathering place was the Folklore Library on the 3rd floor of the old library. . . . And the library was a good place to meet people. We had one of our classes, and they'd just close the library down and they had a seminar. My first class was in that room" (1985, 4). Bauman said, "The old folklore library was a great place" and was available at night for studying. He continued, "I have very vivid memories of discussions of this, that, or the other theoretical issue going on there. Dundes stomping up and down and saying, 'You don't have to do your master's thesis or your dissertation on yet another god-damned historic geographic thing—you can do other things besides'" (1987, 8).

Michael Owen Jones articulated what was special about Indiana University when he came in 1964 from the University of Kansas: "It was IU, it was us." He continued, "So many of us had been through . . . a period of searching for ourselves, for our topic, for our direction. And then we finally 'found'—and that's usually the way it's put—finally found folklore studies." They also benefited from the results, as Jones said, of what Dorson "was able to accomplish at IU, bringing these visiting faculty members. We had faculty members coming in right and left! Thinking back on it, it's astonishing" (1986, 22).

When asked about Dorson's impact on the field of folklore, those interviewed by Harrah-Conforth referred repeatedly to his missionary zeal for spreading folklore studies. Dundes remarked on his "endless enthusiasm for the subject matter" and his desire "to convert people to . . . folklore, and to straighten out people who were amateurs or misguided." Dorson undertook, Dundes said, "a one-person campaign for folklore as an academic discipline." Dundes continued, "He had this enthusiasm and willingness to travel and, really, to put folklore before everything else, even before his own family" (1985, 27). Bauman remarked, "Thompson laid the foundations and opened the doors, but it was [Dorson's] energies and his efforts that made it a . . . real program. Thompson never did that. He was in the English department." Dorson was, Bauman continued, "a sort of ideologue and an energetic and forceful person who was able to persuade partly through his own achievements, which were considerable, and his place in academe generally, and his total commitment to the importance of folklore and its place in the academy" (1987, 29). Georges described Dorson as "the nerve center of the program. He was the energy" (1985, 8). Wayland Hand opined, "No one could have done what Dorson could have done. Certainly I couldn't, I have a different approach to things and wouldn't drive the way he drove" (1986, 23).

University of Pennsylvania

At the University of Pennsylvania, MacEdward Leach lacked the administrative support that was available for folklore at IU. "By hook and crook," and by persistence of effort, Leach managed to situate folklore in the English Department (Glassie 1968, 107, quoting Leach). In 1959, Leach recruited his former student Tristram P. Coffin, who had been at Denison College from 1949 to 1958, to teach in the English Department. As Abrahams commented, the program at Penn "essentially started with just" Leach and Coffin and remained that way from 1962 to 1965 (1986, 29; see Miller 2004, 21, 29).

As Rosina Miller details in chapter 8, Abrahams was the last folklore student in the English Department at Penn. In 1961, the faculty in the English Department, Abrahams recounted, were "outraged" by his dissertation, "Negro Folklore from South Philadelphia" (Abrahams 1961). They decided that there would be "no more folklore dissertations," and that resulted in the creation of the Folklore Program. Abrahams said he learned about this only after MacEdward Leach had died. "That was a secret because he didn't want my career affected in any way" (1986, 28, 29).

Rivalry among Programs

The established folklore program at IU and the nascent folklore programs—at Penn, UCLA, UCB, and Texas—were linked through recruitment of faculty and separated often by fierce rivalry. During this period, the rivalry between IU and Penn erupted at the 1961 American Folklore Society meeting in Austin. Acknowledging that he had not attended this "seminal conference," Hand recounted what he had heard from others: "The Pennsylvania people openly assailed the Indiana people, that all they'd done out there is index and they had not analyzed. . . . It was simply sterile codification and taxonomy" (1986, 20). This was the first time Georges had attended a meeting of the society, and he recalled that Kenny Goldstein had spoken "about how barren the field was." There were no new directions, Goldstein emphasized, because everyone was "doing the same thing" (Georges 1985, 14–15). In a letter fragment with no indication as to whom it was addressed, Dundes wrote of what he had heard of the AFS meeting: "Dorson tells me that there was quite a fight at the meetings in Austin. Pennsylvania and Indiana telling each other that one was good and the other bad. Leach and Coffin and Goldstein etc. versus Dorson, Jansen, Baughman, etc. Sorry to have missed it."[3]

Dorson twisted the affectionate term used for Leach's students, "Mac's Pennsy Gang" (Coffin 1968, v), to the "Pennsy crumb-bums." He planted his worst insult on Penn: it was "a popularizing place," where "they weren't serious about scholarship."[4] As Wilson remarked, "He used to say some fairly unkind things about their not being serious. And then he didn't like folk music. He had a wooden ear and he didn't like it, and [Penn] had MacEdward Leach [with] a strong emphasis on ballad scholarship" (1986, 64–65). Harrah-Conforth asked Abrahams how Penn viewed IU and Dorson and how they were viewed "from within AFS." Abrahams replied succinctly, "Well, they were viewed as hegemonic bullshit." And then he expanded, "That is, having a dominant elitist methodology, which they were going to impose on the entire world. They had gotten the word in Finland and they had brought it to the United States, and they were going to . . . impose this yoke upon folklore studies in the United States" (1986, 15–16). The schism still reverberated in 1967, when Goldstein wrote to Dundes, "I am still in the process of mending fences between Indiana and Penn and have invited Dick to come down here to discuss AFS matters and, while he is at it, to talk to our students."[5]

"Things Were Stirring in the West"—UCLA and UCB

As Hand recounted, he carried news to those attending the 1946 IU Folklore Institute, when he was codirector with Stith Thompson, of the organizational beginnings of folklore in California: "And so, like the minstrels of old, I brought tidings from the West, and things were stirring." Having built up folklore studies over a period of years, Hand felt on the verge of securing an institutional hold for folklore at UCLA. In 1954, while Hand was at IU for the summer Folklore Institute, dean of the Graduate School John Ashton extended an offer to him to lead the folklore program on Stith Thompson's retirement the following year: "They had me back to look me over and make final arrangements. So I turned them down with a heavy heart, because things [at UCLA] were looking very . . . good." Hand traveled back home by car with his family. "I knew I was not going to accept the job." So did his family: "One or other member of the family cried all the way to the Wabash River. They wanted so badly to go there, you know. All the swimming, all of the parties" (1986, 10, 12, 15). Linguistic anthropologist Thomas Sebeok recounted the ultimate and significant result: "Ashton went ahead and telephoned Japan," where Dorson was on a Fulbright, "and offered it to Dorson" (1988, 18, 20).

Almost simultaneously, faculty at UCLA and at UCB had begun planning for graduate degree-granting programs in folklore. In November 1964, Dundes, who had been at UCB in the Department of Anthropology since his move from the University of Kansas in 1963, wrote D. K. Wilgus, "The news that your MA had been approved was hailed up here. Congratulations. I read your program with interest. It seems to be just great. There are quite a few courses which I don't think are offered anywhere else in the country. . . . I think there'll be some students here who might be interested in the MA in folklore and mythology. We've heard nothing yet on our program. I suspect that *if* it is approved that it is a couple of years away."[6] Dundes was wrong: the UCB Folklore Program was approved in April 1965.

William Bascom, the impetus behind the Berkeley Folklore Program, wrote Dundes that he had thought of establishing the program since his arrival at UCB in 1957, but he had so many other commitments that he was not able to devote the time to it. Dundes replied that a committee on folklore at Berkeley was "a natural." Thinking strategically about developing a program that would not duplicate the offerings of other institutions, Dundes wrote of his idea "to build a center for the study of primitive folklore." He continued, "At the moment, there is no place in the country where one can find this emphasis. Pennsylvania's new graduate department of folklore is purely ballad; UCLA's is European (Germanic) and folk song; Indiana's is the most comprehensive, but is still weak in primitive coverage. Since it will be the anthropologists who will bring the folklore committee into existence at Berkeley (if it does come into existence), I think it is only appropriate that this emphasis be given." Dundes added, "It also has the advantage of not antagonizing UCLA since there will be no conflict of interest."[7]

Dundes wrote Hand about the plans that he and Bascom were crafting for a folklore program. Hand responded, "I am interested in your plans for establishing some sort of a center for the study of Primitive Folklore at Berkeley. This seems to me a logical corollary of the work going on in Los Angeles, and would not throw our respective institutions into conflict for the small amount of money available." Hand offered to support the effort.[8] The Graduate Council of the Berkeley Division of the Academic Senate approved the program in March 1965.

University of Texas

Of his move from Pennsylvania to Texas, Abrahams wrote, "In 1959, I had only been in school for a semester and a half but Leach asked if I wanted to teach at the University of Texas" (2002, 13). Abrahams had no desire to stay on in Philadelphia. "I wanted to teach and this job at Texas came along, and MacEdward recommended me for it. . . . I snapped at it, and went to Texas and wrote my dissertation there the first year I was down there [1960–61] . . . while I was preparing seven new courses" (1986, 3). Abrahams delighted in Austin, "where I found a number of colleagues with whom I was very comfortable." He continued, "More specifically, Mody Boatright, who was a working class guy who had come from the oilfields, who was then head of the English department at the University of

Texas. Then there was my buddy, . . . Américo Paredes. Then Dick Bauman who was the first person we hired down there . . . and Barbara Kirshenblatt-Gimblett was the second. So we had a great group . . . in Texas" (2002, 13).

Abrahams reflected on his initial years with Paredes and Boatright: "And I started to agitate for . . . having an organization for the discipline in the English Department." Abrahams notes that Richard N. Adams, who was the new chair of the Anthropology Department, arranged to split the positions for Paredes and Abrahams between English and Anthropology and to advocate for a new anthropology position "that would be set aside for a folklorist" (1986, 5). Paredes recalled, "In 1966, when I already was a full professor, the Anthropology department took over half my salary, and I began at last to have graduate students and to teach graduate courses in Hispanic folklore" (Abernethy and Satterwhite 1994, 231).[9]

Dorson had plans for Texas. In October 1964, he confided to Abrahams, "I just wrote . . . a strong letter for Américo's promotion. With you and Américo and Mody Boatright and the Dobie tradition all at Austin, it seems that Texas should really blaze forth now, and be one of the major folklore centers." Through his position on the AFS executive board (1962–69), Dorson intended "to move through AFS toward strengthening academic folklore programs around the country." He continued, "For instance, I think that Texas is ripe for a big forward push, and one of the AFS offices should go there, perhaps the publications; I nominated you for Secretary-Treasurer if Tris resigns."[10]

Three years later, in 1967, the University of Texas had, indeed, blazed forth as Dorson had anticipated. "As Américo might have told you," Dundes wrote Bascom, "Texas has put in a MA AND PhD in folklore program. This plus Harvard's new undergraduate major in folklore are good signs."[11] In April 1965, in his capacity as chair of the Department of Anthropology at Texas, Adams had written Dundes of "the very strong intent of the Administration and the Department to support a program in folklore which will allow the person so involved the widest range for development." He concluded, "May I add that the entire staff was very positively impressed by your visit and are very anxious that you consider the offer favorably."[12] The letter from Adams came on the cusp of the approval of the MA program in folklore at UCB. Two weeks later, Dundes wrote Adams to decline, with his decision "largely influenced by the offer of tenure here coupled with the fact that the MA in folklore program is already in existence." Dundes continued, "However, nothing here can compare with the teaching load, salary, and program potential at Texas."[13]

The search at Texas continued. In gathering suggestions for possible candidates, Abrahams recalled, "We asked around who's the hottest young folklorist that would fit into an anthropology department, and we kept hearing the same thing, 'Get Bauman.' . . . So at the next AFS meeting, I met Dick, and I said,

Fig. 5.2. American Folklore Society Meeting, November 16–19, 1972. *Left to right*: Kenneth Goldstein, Frances Gilllmor, Harry Middleton Hyatt, William Hugh Jansen, Américo Paredes, Daniel Crowley, Herbert Halpert, William Bascom, Warren Roberts, Roger Abrahams, and Francis Lee Utley. Photograph courtesy of Frances Terry.

'You know, we have this job that's going to come open. You really should come.' And . . . eventually a year and a half later, here he came. . . . And that's how the connection with anthropology was forged" (1986, 5). In 1967–68, the Center for Intercultural Studies in Folklore and Oral History was officially established; and in 1970, the center was granted advanced-degree status with Bauman serving as director from 1970 to 1986 (see Abernethy and Satterwhite 1994, 228).

Recruiting from Outside for Penn

Just as Dorson wanted to see the Texas folklore program strengthened, so he worked to achieve the same results for Penn. Ben-Amos recounted, "You know that our program would not have existed without Dorson" (1985, 32). The administration had invited Dorson for consultation on the folklore program at Penn, particularly with the pending retirement of Leach at the end of the 1965–66 academic year, and with Coffin having moved from the English Department into administration as vice provost (Miller 2004, 30). Ben-Amos continued, "Dorson came, and evaluated the program and said that . . . they had to hire people from different institutions," since the only faculty at Penn were "Tris Coffin and Ken Goldstein and Don [Yoder]" (1985, 32).

Dell Hymes, Dundes's close friend and colleague in the Anthropology Department at Penn, was the central figure in recruiting Dundes. In his letter to Francis Lee Utley, Dundes remarked, "The move to get an anthropological folklorist from outside was made by Dell Hymes not Kenny [Goldstein], although Kenny has been enthusiastic."[14] Dean of the College of Arts and Sciences Otto Springer issued the invitation to Dundes to visit the campus. Into this perfect storm Alan Dundes stepped with his indefatigable optimism. Ben-Amos recalled that "Tris hated Alan Dundes." Resentful that Dundes was invited by the anthropologists on the committee, Dell Hymes and Anthony Wallace, MacEdward Leach refused to attend the lunch because Coffin would not attend. Ben-Amos continued, Goldstein, "who was a good friend of Alan, would not come to the lunch because MacEdward Leach did not come and Tris Coffin did not come. So Alan said to himself, 'If my friends would behave that way, why should I come?' So, Alan turned them down" (1985, 33).

Penn persisted in the recruitment for the position in folklore. Ben-Amos wrote Dundes in November 1966, from his position in the UCLA Department of Anthropology, "I knew about Penn consideration. I know that last year they made you an offer, and if they come up with anything for me, I would really like to hear your opinion about the situation there."[15] In January 1967, Goldstein wrote Dundes, "Dan called me on Saturday to inform me that he is accepting the offer at Penn. You are right—it's great for Penn—but don't feel that it is a bad loss for UCLA as they will probably get an excellent replacement for him."[16] Miller notes that the hire of Ben-Amos was "an attempt to alleviate the Penn-Indiana competition and ameliorate Penn's deficiency in prose narrative." At the same time, in 1967, Yoder was appointed chair, and the program changed its name to Folklore and Folklife (Miller 2004, 31).

Interconnection of Folklore Programs

The great team of American folklorists in the 1960s did not develop from one center outward but was an interconnected flow of people and ideas among centers of folklore. There were continual attempts to hire senior people to strengthen programs. In 1965, Dundes wrote Utley, who was professor of English at the Ohio State University, "I was somewhat sorry to learn that you decided against moving to Indiana. Your great knowledge would have boosted the folklore institute quite a bit."[17] Reflecting on the one that got away, Sebeok told Harrah-Conforth, "And that was one of the real mistakes . . . to let him go in the first place, because when Dundes left for . . . Kansas, I remember saying to Dorson, 'This guy will never come back.' 'Oh,' Dorson [said], 'Let him season there, he will come back.' I said, 'He'll never come back.'" Harrah-Conforth asked, "Why didn't you think he'd come back?" Sebeok replied, "Because he's too good. . . . I mean, I think Alan is crazy in some ways, but he's marvelous. He's so stimulating, so witty, so charming." Sebeok returned to the refrain of regret, "But I wanted Dundes, I wanted Bauman, I wanted Ben-Amos, I wanted Barbara Kirshenblatt-Gimblett" (1988, 44–45, 77).

Wilson remarked that Dorson "may have seen Roger Abrahams as one of the first great stars coming out of" Penn. Dorson had respect for Abrahams, and "he may have started changing his view about Penn" (1986, 65). Along with trying to recruit Dundes, Dorson had tried to hire Abrahams. "Well, he couldn't get Dundes and me to come," Abrahams said. "He made offers . . . year after year to Dundes and myself and Dick Bauman and Dan Ben-Amos." He regarded them along with Bob Georges as "the young Turks and people that were going to lead the field." When asked why Abrahams would not leave Texas for Indiana, he responded, "What can I say? Texas was taking off. We had a really good thing going. I *loved* Austin" (1986, 20, emphasis in original).

The development of folklore programs in the United States in the 1960s was dependent on key figures, characters large in life and grand in plans, with vision and energy. Drawn by the free spirit of the 1960s and the government funding of the Sputnik era, students gravitated to the graduate programs that these key figures created to pursue the study of folklore; and the students, in turn, became the leaders who spread across the country to develop and teach in other folklore graduate programs. This was a story of commitment, passion, and conflict, of strategizing for leadership and battling for academic territory.

Acknowledgments

I am grateful to the following people for permission to quote from archival material: Rod Abrahams, Dan Ben-Amos, Roland Dorson, David Dundes, Diane Goldstein, and Barbara Truesdell of Indiana University's Center for Documentary Research and Practice. I am also grateful to Rod Abrahams and Frances Terry for permission to use the photographs.

Notes

1. Harrah-Conforth conducted the interviews on file at the Center for Documentary Research and Practice, which was supported by the Skaggs Foundation of Oakland, California. Dundes was referring to Dorson (1968).
2. In this volume, see chapter 6 for IU, chapter 7 for UCLA, chapters 8 and 9 for Penn, chapter 10 for UCB, and chapter 11 for Texas. See also Miller 2004, Jones 2011, Harrah-Conforth 1989, and Zumwalt 2017.
3. Dundes Papers, Bancroft Library, Carton 2, fragment of an undated letter, p. 2, signed, Alan and Carolyn. From internal evidence, it clearly followed the December 28–30, 1961, AFS meeting in Austin.
4. Dundes Papers, Bancroft Library, 39:17, Dorson to Dundes, December 10, 1962.
5. Dundes Papers, Bancroft Library, 3:11, Goldstein to Dundes, February 15, 1967.

6. Dundes Papers, Bancroft Library, 7:34, Dundes to Wilgus, November 23, 1964, emphasis in original.

7. Bascom Papers, Bancroft Library, Carton 2, Dundes to Bascom, February 2, 1963; and see Carton 2, Bascom to Dundes, January 14, 1963. Dundes later used "anthropological folklore," and eschewed the term "primitive." See Zumwalt 2017, 26 n37.

8. Dundes Papers, Bancroft Library, 3:28, Hand to Dundes, February 5, 1963.

9. Abernethy and Satterwhite are quoting from Paredes's letter of July 30, 1991, in which he explained why he had to give up the direction of the Texas Folklore Archive.

10. Letter from Dorson to Abrahams, October 28, 1964; appended to interview with Abrahams 1986. J. Frank Dobie was known for his "'creative' and literary treatment of folklore" (Limón 2012, 77). Although Dorson in this singular instance saw Dobie's influence as a positive one for the development of academic folklore at UT, in general he was skeptical about Dobie's scholarship and influence on the discipline, even referring to him facetiously elsewhere in the same letter to Abrahams as "the voice of the coyote," alluding to Dobie's book of that title (1949). Paredes, Abrahams, and Bauman held a view more congruent with that negative assessment (see Bauman, this volume).

11. Bascom Papers, Bancroft Library, Carton 2, Dundes to Bascom, May 26, 1967, emphasis in original.

12. Dundes Papers, Bancroft Library, 40:21, Adams to Dundes, April 21, 1965.

13. Dundes Papers, Bancroft Library, 40:21, Dundes to Adams, May 4, 1965.

14. Dundes Papers, Bancroft Library, 7:31, Dundes to Utley, February 27, 1966. See also Dundes Papers, 3:55, Hymes to Dundes, December 7, 1965. For more detail on Hymes's role, see Zumwalt 2017, 17 and 30n64.

15. Dundes Papers, Bancroft Library, Ben-Amos to Dundes, November 5, 1966.

16. Dundes Papers, Bancroft Library, 3:11, Goldstein to Dundes, January 18, 1967.

17. Dundes Papers, Bancroft Library, 7:31, Dundes to Utley, October 19, 1965. For Utley, see Mullen and Shuman, this volume.

Archives and Collections

Bancroft Library, University of California Berkeley
Alan Dundes Papers
William R. Bascom Papers
Center for Documentary Research and Practice (CDRP), Indiana University Bloomington

References

Abernethy, Francis Edward, and Carolyn Fiedler Satterwhite. 1994. *The Texas Folklore Society, 1943–1971*, Vol. 2. Denton: University of North Texas Press.

Abrahams, Roger. 1961. "Negro Folklore from South Philadelphia: A Collection and Analysis." PhD diss., University of Pennsylvania.

———. 1968. Comments in "MacEdward Leach, 1892–1967," in MacEdward Leach Memorial Issue, edited by John Greenway, *Journal of American Folklore* 81, no. 320: 99.

———. 1986. Interview with Harrah-Conforth, April 30. CDRP, 87-018.

———. 2002. "The People Are Not There When You Isolate Text from Everything Else." In *Voicing Folklore: Careers, Concerns and Issues, A Collection of Interviews*, interview and edited by M. D. Muthukumaraswamy, 10–19. Chennai, India: National Folklore Support Centre.

Bauman, Richard. 1987. Interview with Jeanne Harrah-Conforth, February 25. CDRP, 87-030.

Ben-Amos, Dan. 1985. Interview with Jeanne Harrah-Conforth, September 28. CDRP, 87-005.

Brunvand, Jan Harold. 1986. Interview with Jeanne Harrah-Conforth, September 19. CDRP, 87-022.

Coffin, Tristram. 1968. *Our Living Traditions*. New York: Basic Books.

Dobie, J. Frank. 1949. *The Voice of the Coyote*. Lincoln: University of Nebraska Press.

Dorson, Richard. 1968. *The British Folklorists, A History*. Chicago: University of Chicago Press.

Dundes, Alan. 1985. Interview with Jeanne Harrah-Conforth, September 26. CDRP, 87-3-1, 2.

Georges, Robert. 1985. Interview with Jeanne Harrah-Conforth, September 25. CDRP, 87-002.

Glassie, Henry. 1968. Comments in "MacEdward Leach, 1892–1967," in MacEdward Leach Memorial Issue, edited by John Greenway, *Journal of American Folklore* 81, no. 320: 107–8.

Hand, Wayland. 1986. Interview with Jeanne Harrah-Conforth, March 12. CDRP, 87-014.

Harrah-Conforth, Jeanne. 1989. "Dorson and the Indiana University Folklore Program: Oral Histories." *Western Folklore* 48, no. 4: 339–48.

Jones, Michael Owen. 1986. Interview with Jeanne Harrah-Conforth, March 12. CDRP, 87-016.

———. 2011. "UCLA's Folklore and Mythology Program and Center: A History." *Folklore Historian* 28: 37–69.

Limón, José E. 2012. *Américo Paredes: Culture & Critique*. Austin: University of Texas Press.

Miller, Rosina S. 2004. "Of Politics, Disciplines, and Scholars: MacEdward Leach and the Founding of the Folklore Program at the University of Pennsylvania." *Folklore Historian* 21: 17–34.

Muthukumaraswamy, M. D. 2002. *Voicing Folklore: Careers, Concerns and Issues, A Collection of Interviews*. Chennai, India: National Folklore Support Centre.

Sebeok, Thomas. 1988. Interview with Jeanne Harrah-Conforth, January 25. CDRP, 87-041.

Wilson, William. 1986. Interview with Jeanne Harrah-Conforth, September 18. CDRP, 87-021.

Zumwalt, Rosemary Lévy. 2017. "'Here Is Our Man': Dundes Discovered, the Development of the Folklore Program at the University of California, Berkeley." *Journal of American Folklore* 130, no. 515: 3–33.

ROSEMARY LÉVY ZUMWALT is Vice President Emerita and Professor Emerita of Anthropology at Agnes Scott College. She is author of *American Folklore Scholarship: A Dialogue of Dissent* and (with Isaac Jack Lévy) *Ritual Medical Lore of Sephardic Women: Sweetening the Spirits and Healing the Sick.*

6 The Jewel in the Crown

Hallmarks of Success in Indiana University's Folklore Program

Jeanne Harrah-Johnson

I LOOK TO the development and achievements of Indiana University's Department of Folklore and Ethnomusicology (IUFE) and attempt to answer Dan Ben-Amos's question, "What makes a folklore program successful?" (see introduction to this volume). I identify the sources of IUFE's success from archival and secondary sources and from two phases of oral history interviews that I conducted with IUFE faculty, alumni, administrators, students, and emeriti. I conducted forty-three interviews in the mid-1980s and fifteen during 2016–17. Every paragraph draws from information and the ideas of the people I interviewed. I focus on folklore, not ethnomusicology.[1]

A successful folklore department requires a combination of ambitious departmental leadership, supportive department and higher administration relationships, and chairpersons and faculty members driven by their vision and advocacy for the field realized through teaching, publications, public programs, research, and related projects. External funding, participation at conferences, ties to related departments, visits from national and international scholars, and cohesive, involved groups of graduate students generate new ideas and strengthen the profile and name recognition of the program (Baughman 1987; Boggs 1940; Bronner 2011, 2017; Clarke 1986; Clements 1988, 65–70; Dolby 2018; Griff-Sleven 2018; Halpert 1985; Marsh 2017; Wolford 2018).

Administration

As of 2019, there have been thirteen chairs, co-chairs, or associate chairs at the IUFE.[2] Three people—Stith Thompson, Richard Dorson, and Richard Bauman—are prominent for their roles in defining the structure and substance of the department. Understanding their influence is central to identifying a formula for success. The impact and recognition of their leadership reaches well beyond the individual chairperson (Bauman 1987; Dundes 1985; McDowell 2018; Zumwalt 1988, 132–42).

Stith Thompson (1885–1976) earned a PhD in English at Harvard University (1914). He studied under George Lyman Kittredge, who was a protégé of Francis J. Child. Thompson was hired at Indiana University (IU) as director of freshman English in 1921. He began teaching folklore courses in Bloomington and Indianapolis in 1923. In 1939, IU president Herman B Wells offered Thompson the first professorship of English and folklore in the United States, along with research and conference support; funding to purchase folklore books, which he had already begun collecting for the IU Library; and support to establish a special series of folklore publications (Martin 1976; Roberts 1976; Wells 1985).[3]

Thompson was also dean of the IU Graduate School from 1947 to 1950. He established the doctoral program in folklore. Thompson's student, Warren Roberts, was the first to receive a PhD (1953) in folklore (Roberts 1986). Thompson's publications, *The Motif-Index of Folk Literature* (1955–58) and the Aarne-Thompson *Types of the Folklore* (1961) were groundbreaking folklore publications and continue today as references for folklorists (Dundes 1997).

In the early part of the twentieth century, one of Wells's foremost objectives was to launch the university on a path to "become a cosmopolitan center of learning with an international reputation" (Capshew 2012, 13; Wells 1980). Stith Thompson brought clout to IU with his network of international colleagues. During his travels to meetings and conferences, "he met a number of prominent European folklorists, thereby beginning a lifelong . . . exchange of ideas and facts with major scholars of his field. Stith Thompson's reputation as a folklorist was international, bringing fame to the man and to Indiana University" (Martin 1976, 8). Thompson's travels reached beyond contact with folklore scholars. He cultivated friendships while traveling and reciprocated by inviting scholars and philanthropists to his home in Bloomington (Clements 1988; Letsinger 1985; Wells 1985, 3; Wells, personal communication, December 18, 1985).[4]

For Wells, the IU Folklore Program was exemplary. "I had a feeling that this was one of the most important fields for a university to develop. . . . I think any intelligent person, if they understand the field, would realize that it was an important and emerging field that had been more or less overlooked in this country, compared to what was happening abroad. And, now, I guess, under Stith's leadership, with Dorson, Sebeok, and others that have come along since, America's ahead of the world, isn't it?" (Wells 1985, 3). Wells was a strong believer in and supporter of intellectual freedom and civil rights. These were the underpinnings for many of his business decisions, hiring practices, and goals for the university (Wells 1980). In a 1985 interview, Alan Dundes says, "Indiana was in a period of exploration and growth and they liked the interdisciplinary things. They brought people here who were a little off-beat. And they took chances with disciplines like folklore" (1985, 12).

Fig. 6.1. Richard Dorson (*left*) and Dan Ben-Amos (*right*), December 10, 1962. Photograph courtesy of Indiana University Archives.

With funding and administrative support from the offices of the university president, Thompson organized the first Summer Folklore Institute in 1942 on the IU campus. These were held every four years for two decades. IU folklore faculty, graduate students, and invited scholars from across the United States taught and participated in the Summer Folklore Institutes. In 1950, Thompson expanded the summer institute into the Midcentury Folklore Congress, an international seminar that attracted folklorists from across America and folklorists and their students from Europe. Its aim was to show that folklore could be an established academic discipline in the United States as well as in Europe (Bronner 1986; Rudy 2000; Sebeok 1988; Thompson 1956).

The summer institutes were established during the time that IU was cultivating smaller, distinctive departments. Wells and the deans called these "the jewels in the crown," which they typified as world-class programs not commonly offered at other universities. In turn, the university became a draw for students and other scholars. While Thompson was thorough and methodical in his approaches to his scholarly research and in organizing the folklore program in order to sustain it as one of the jewels, his role was overshadowed quickly by the level of enthusiasm and commitment to folklore that followed once he retired: that of Richard M. Dorson (Bauman 1987; Dorson 1977; Hand 1986; Wells 1985).[5]

Dorson (1916–81) received his PhD (1942) in the history of American civilization at Harvard. After teaching at Harvard for a year and at Michigan State University from 1944 to 1957, Dorson was hired by Indiana University in 1957 to chair "the committee on folklore." In 1963, Dorson founded the Folklore Institute, and in 1978, he became the first director and chairman of the Indiana University Folklore Department. He died September 11, 1981, as Distinguished Professor of History and Folklore and Director of the Folklore Institute at IU. His publications are both foundational and controversial. Dorson coined the term "fakelore," one of the concepts for which he is best known. He repeatedly sought to distinguish between what he considered genuine folklore versus fakelore, which he defined as "the presentations of spurious and synthetic writings under the claim that they are genuine folklore" (Dorson 1976). (See Briggs, this volume, for a different viewpoint on fakelore and Dorson.) He maintained that there is authentic folklore worthy of scholarly study, and there are imitators who cultivate stories, songs, and other items for entertainment, money, or for political reasons. This position put him at odds with Benjamin Botkin and others. Sometimes Dorson's distinctions between folklore and fakelore were convincing, and in other important ways they failed.[6]

While Stith Thompson had been dedicated to working with IU to enhance its international status via folklore, Dorson was devoted to establishing folklore as an autonomous department and elevating it to the ranks of other disciplines. He managed the program so that its international associations continued to grow while the study of American folklore gained importance. His goal was to make folklore a recognizable field throughout academe. The organizational structure of IU already provided financial, administrative, and research support along with a core folklore faculty. (See Jones, this volume, for a contrasting structure in a folklore program.) The department was solidly positioned so that Dorson's professional and personal vision could thrive (Bronner 2011; Hand 1986; Montenyohl 1989; Rudy 2000).

With energy to spare, Dorson developed the curricula, syllabi, and reading lists for the three required graduate courses: Survey of Folklore, Folklore Theory and Techniques, and History of Folklore. He established the undergraduate folklore major and the *Journal of Folklore Research*, sponsored and participated in dozens of conferences, secured research funding through grants, and coordinated graduate student assistantships. He continued to build IU's Folklore Library, developed the IU Folklore Archives, authored MA and PhD comprehensive exams, facilitated dissertation clinics, taught classes, and chaired eighty-six PhD dissertations (his goal was one hundred). He did not do this alone. Many people assisted him, but it was, to paraphrase several people, the imprint of Dick Dorson that people carried away from IU, and that had formative effects (Bauman 1987; Janelli 1986; McDowell 2018; Wolford 2018).[7]

Students

Key to Dorson's undertaking was the expansion of the folklore program and strict definitions of the field. He expected faculty members to be equally dedicated to the field and to adhere to his high standards, and he expected the same from his students. Graduate student enrollments climbed, and, "to a great extent, the students made the reputation of Dorson" (Bronner 2017). To Dorson's dismay, the majority of students who sought degrees in folklore at Indiana came because of their involvement in the folk song revival movement. Throughout the 1960s and early 1970s, a steady flow of students was accepted into the program and landed under Dorson's guidance. Urging them on was a brew of social movements, dissatisfaction with the status quo, and mutual encouragement. Dorson agreed with the conviction that societal inequities needed to be addressed, but performing folk music and other genres, he felt, threatened his views on folklore as a scholarly field. It signaled to him a devolution into the realm of fakelore (Abrahams 1986; de Caro 1986; Georges 1985; Jones 1986; Reuss 1985; see Miller, this volume, for the importance of the folk song revival on the growth of folklore departments.)

The folklore graduate students of the late 1960s initiated the Folklore Students' Association, the student-run publication *Folklore Forum* (1968), and the Folklore Publications Group. They instigated an uprising and demanded more rigorous folklore courses and opportunities to share their research and their concerns about the field and to study theory. (David Bidney, IU professor of anthropology and Spinoza scholar, taught theory to folklore students.) The Folklore Students' Association, *Folklore Forum*, and folklore publications were part of the solution to their frustrations. The association and publications continue to be outlets for students' participation in the department. And though the lack of a theoretical orientation at IU was a source of continual disenchantment for students, the department's syllabi—without a specific theoretical bent—could be deemed an advantage. IUFE graduates disseminate wide-ranging ideas and interpretations and are not identified with a specific paradigm. They do, however, speak their minds (Abrahams 1986; Dundes 1985; Hickerson 1986; Ives 1985; McDowell 2018; Reuss 1985).

For decades, Nick's English Hut (a bar) served as the meeting place for folklore graduate students. In addition to official departmental gatherings, parties, and meetings of the Folklore Students' Association, there were annual daylong pig roasts, "the 516 club" (named after the number for one of the core courses), student-run dissertation clinics (originally held by Dorson), and study groups for the MA and PhD exams that were based on standardized exam reading lists and previous exam questions. The regularity of these gatherings strengthened the bonds among students (Griff-Sleven 2018; Marsh 2017; Warren 2018; Wolford 2018).

Faculty

As the 1970s progressed, Dorson championed his folklore ideology, and the students and graduates of the program developed a folklore identity. The majority of Dorson's departmental colleagues did not challenge his centrality in the folklore program but pursued their own research specialties and support of students. For example, Warren Roberts was the material culture and field study leader. Students became his "converts" and developed a new way of seeing landscapes and buildings. Linda Dégh, a rival to Dorson, had "disciples" who were not dissuaded by her rigorous European model of teaching and expectations. In fact, every faculty member is recognized in the oral histories for contributions to the Folklore Department and for dedication to specific students and their academic interests. Students had the added advantage in that they could choose to complete the requirements for a double PhD in American studies, a minor in a related field (such as anthropology or history), or expand their education in one of the many IU area studies programs (such as Uralic-Altaic) and gain dissertation committee members from those specialties (Bronner 2017; Evans 2018; Marsh 2017; Wolford 2018).

Richard Dorson "constituted a frame of reference for people." He is credited with advancing a folklore ethos that permeated the department, securing departmental autonomy for the IUFE, and, to a great extent, procuring the disciplinary autonomy of folklore in general (see Zumwalt, this volume; Miller, this volume). His students and IUFE's program seeded every folklore program throughout the country. The program taught folklorists from every continent in the world, who then directed students and colleagues back to Indiana University. This history and cycle are part of the reason that the program continues to thrive (Ben-Amos 1985; Brunvand 1986; Harrah-Conforth 1989; Oinas 1988).

Richard Bauman joined the faculty of the IUFE in 1986. He received an MA in folklore at Indiana University (1962) and an MS in anthropology and PhD in American civilization from the University of Pennsylvania (1968). He was chair of the IUFE from 1986 to 1991 and again from 2003 to 2007; he directed IU's Research Center

Fig. 6.2. Stith Thompson in his office, May 24, 1955. Photograph courtesy of Indiana University Archives.

for Language and Semiotic Studies from 1992 to 1998 and was a founding member of IU's Department of Communication and Culture. He is best known in the folklore world for bringing together the literary and anthropological approaches using folkloristics, anthropology, and linguistics and analyzing folklore as a performance event and in situational contexts. His model frames the object of study as an artistic event and emphasizes how folklore is used, understood, and works within communities (Bauman 1987; McDowell 2018; Zumwalt 1988; also see Bauman, this volume).

Bauman's interdisciplinary education and perspective unveiled a new agenda for the IUFE. Without Dorson's presence, and with predictable faculty retirements, Bauman inherited the stability of the department allocations and a structure that allowed him freedom to explore the boundaries of the program. Self-described as someone who "does not believe in the disciplinary autonomy of folklore," Bauman was diverging from the past and had the potential to change the Folklore Department and decades of its systemized structures (Bauman 1987). There were concerns about the possible shifts in the department's direction, particularly with regard to being maintained as an autonomous entity and nurturing IU's folklore identity (Bronner 2017; Griff-Sleven 2018; Marsh 2017; McDowell 2008, 2018).

Yet many students and colleagues found that Bauman's chairmanship offered transparency in the decision-making processes and open-mindedness about theory, topics for study, qualifying exams, and curricula. His appointment as chair was perceived as changing the trajectory of the program, which in part resulted in the reinvigorated department that it is in 2019 (Lloyd 2018; Marsh 2017; McDowell 2008, 2018).

During the years of Bauman's leadership and since his retirement, Henry Glassie (retired) and other, new faculty members joined the department. Positions such as professor of practice have been established, and public folklore is a concentration for MA and PhD students. Public folklore courses and the public practice concentration were late additions to the IUFE program, as compared to the offerings in other folklore programs (see M. A. Williams, this volume, for a description of an early public folklore program). Unlike other universities, IU's public folklore footprint is institutionalized through Traditional Arts Indiana, initiated in 1998, and the Mathers Museum of World Cultures (Evans 2018; McDowell 2018).[8]

The offices of the American Folklore Society (AFS) moved from the Ohio State University to the Indiana University campus in 2015. The move was preceded by the development, over several years, of a partnership between AFS and the IU Library based in large part on the accessibility of folklore publications. The IU College of Arts and Sciences provides space on the IU campus, salary, and other support to AFS, while the society maintains its institutional independence. The support from the College of Arts and Sciences is a major affirmation of the continued importance of folklore at Indiana. With AFS on campus, students have more opportunities to get involved in the field, and new initiatives and collaborations—such as the Indiana University and the Ohio State University student conference—are emerging (Lloyd 2018; Marsh 2017; McDowell 2018).

While the oral history interviews uncovered elements critical to building a successful folklore department, a single theme is woven through all the descriptions of achievements and motivations necessary to secure a lasting folklore program: folklore studies lead to a deeper understanding of ourselves and society. Folklorists recognize that folkloristics and its definitions of traditions encompass a wide range of peoples and cultures, particularly marginalized communities. We are motivated by our awareness of the social processes and expressive culture that communicate, heighten, and sometimes encumber social justice (Dolby 2018; McDowell 2018; Warren 2018).

Folklorists have a passion for the substance of folklore and for what it explains about humans. Financial support, brilliant teachers, and theory are insufficient without a central conviction that the field has a purpose. What is important is understanding our field and proclaiming to colleagues, other academics, and the public how folklore plays a pivotal role in deciphering human interactions and in compassion. This is a driving force in the discipline (Abrahams 1986; Bronner 1991; Dorson 1976; Glassie 1986).

For the Folklore Department at Indiana University, Stith Thompson and Herman B Wells deserve credit for forward and strategic thinking. Had Dorson arrived without their accomplishments paving the way, it is likely that his goals would not have been realized. Dorson was the dynamism behind the growth of the field and the establishment of an autonomous department. Richard Bauman opened the program's definition and boundaries and, along with the faculty and the chairpersons who followed, transformed components of the perception and fundamentals of the department (Dorson 1977; Hays 1985; Richmond 1967).

Folklore, as an academic jewel in the crown, is vulnerable. Without a strong identity and purpose, the ties between the department and administration and between the department and the larger academic and nonacademic communities are tenuous. To strengthen folklore's place in the academy and beyond requires folklorists to communicate the unique position and responsibility of folklore study in revealing who we are. Folklore is not an appendage, it is lifeblood.

Notes

1. Audio and transcribed oral history interviews may be accessed at the Indiana University Center for Documentary Research and Practice in the IU Oral History Archives. This collection was formerly held at the Indiana University Center for the Study of History and Memory, originally named the Indiana University Oral History Research Center, and the Indiana University Bicentennial Oral History Program. Interviews consulted for this chapter are included in the references. Jeanne Harrah-Johnson, the author of this chapter and identified as interviewer in 2017–18, was known as Jeanne Harrah-Conforth when she conducted the interviews in 1985–87.
2. Christopher Roush, email to author, March 5, 2018.
3. Stith Thompson donated his books to the Indiana University Libraries' Folklore and Ethnomusicology collection. This initiated the largest, most comprehensive library collection on the subject in the world. The collection contains 50,500 distinct titles, including 1,100 journals and periodicals, 125 current journal subscriptions, 2,570 sound recordings, and more than 1,000 musical scores.
4. During my interview with Herman B Wells and in conversation after the interview, he told me that Axel and Marguerite Wenner-Gren held Stith Thompson in high regard and visited him in Bloomington. The Wenner-Gren Foundation (formerly the Viking Fund) focuses on funding anthropology research. Axel Wenner-Gren was one of the richest men in the world at the time he began supporting projects at Indiana University.
5. Wayland Hand was offered the position prior to it being offered to Richard Dorson. Hand decided to remain at UCLA to develop the folklore program (see Zumwalt this volume).

6. In the late 1950s, Richard Dorson, then president of the American Folklore Society, wrote a letter to the National Defense Education Act (NDEA) committee requesting folklore graduate students be eligible for NDEA funding. He used his fakelore argument to emphasize the importance of academic study of real folklore, as opposed to "longhaired folksingers" and how real folklore study met the objectives of the NDEA. The committee disagreed (Ivey 2018, 81–83). Folklore students who might have benefited from the funding and who may have chosen to pursue folklore graduate studies based on this support were cut short. In 1964, the NDEA was amended to include funding for additional academic fields, including area studies. Depending on topic and career goal, some folklore students became eligible for NDEA support.

7. Inta Carpenter, assistant research scholar emerita, was instrumental in the success of the Special Projects at IUFE. Dorson donated his Michigan State Folklore Archives collection to build the IU Folklore Archives when he joined the IU faculty in 1957. The Folklore Archives contain two major collections: accessioned student field collections and professional papers of folklorists tied to Indiana University.

8. Traditional Arts Indiana was developed with collaboration between Indiana University's Folklore Institute (the department's title in 1998) and the Indiana Arts Commission. Traditional Arts Indiana director and professor of practice is Jon Kay, whose office is at the Mathers Museum of World Cultures. Jason Baird Jackson, professor of folklore and anthropology, is director of the Mathers Museum.

References

Aarne, Antti, and Stith Thompson. 1961. *The Types of the Folktale: A Classification and Bibliography*. Helsinki: Finnish Academy of Science and Letters.

Abrahams, Roger. 1986. Interview with Jeanne Harrah-Conforth. The History of the Indiana University Folklore Institute 87-018. Indiana University Center for Documentary Research and Practice; IU Oral History Archive (hereafter CDRP).

Baughman, Earnest. 1987. Interview with Jeanne Harrah-Conforth. CDRP, 87-031.

Bauman, Richard. 1987. Interview with Jeanne Harrah-Conforth. CDRP, 87-030.

Ben-Amos, Dan. 1985. Interview with Jeanne Harrah-Conforth. CDRP, 87-005.

Boggs, Ralph Steele. 1940. "Folklore in University Curriculum in the United States." *Southern Folklore Quarterly* 4: 93–109.

Bronner Simon J. 1986. *American Folklore Studies, and Intellectual History*. Lawrence: University Press of Kansas.

———. 1991. "A Prophetic Vision of Public and Academic Folklore, Alfred Shoemaker and America's First Department of Folklore." *Folklore Historian* 8: 38–55.

———. 2011. "American Folklorists' Voices in Print: A Critical Survey." *Folklore Historian* 28: 3–16.

———. 2017. Interview with Jeanne Harrah-Johnson. Bicentennial Oral History Project. Indiana University (hereafter BOHP).

Brunvand, Jan. 1986. Interview with Susan Domowitz. CDRP, 87-022.

Capshew, James H. 2012. *Herman B Wells: The Promise of the American University*. Bloomington: Indiana University Press.

Clarke, Kenneth. 1986. Interview with Jeanne Harrah-Conforth. CDRP, 87-015.

Clements, William, ed. 1988. *100 Years of American Folklore Studies: A Conceptual History.* Washington, DC: American Folklore Society.
De Caro, Frank. 1986. Interview with Jeanne Harrah-Conforth. CDRP, 87-025.
Dolby, Sandra. 2018. Interview with Jeanne Harrah-Johnson. BOHP.
Dorson, Richard M. 1976. *Folklore and Fakelore: Essays toward a Discipline of Folk Studies.* Boston: Harvard University Press.
———. 1977. "Stith Thompson (1885–1976)." *Journal of American Folklore* 90, no. 355: 3–8.
Dundes, Alan. 1985. Interview with Jeanne Harrah-Conforth. CDRP, 87-003.
———. 1997. "The Motif-Index and the Tale Type Index: A Critique." *Journal of Folklore Research* 34, no. 3: 195–202.
Evans, Timothy. 2018. Interview with Jeanne Harrah-Johnson. BOHP.
Georges, Robert. 1985. Interview with Jeanne Harrah-Conforth. CDRP, 87-002.
Glassie, Henry. 1986. Interview with Jeanne Harrah-Conforth. CDRP, 87-023.
Griff-Sleven, Hanna. 2018. Interview with Jeanne Harrah-Johnson. BOHP.
Halpert, Herbert. 1985. Interview with Jeanne Harrah-Conforth. CDRP, 87-006.
Hand, Wayland. 1986. Interview with Jeanne Harrah-Conforth. CDRP, 87-014.
Harrah-Conforth, Jeanne. 1989. "Dorson and the Indiana University Folklore Program: Oral Histories." *Western Folklore* 48, no. 4: 339–48.
Hays, Margarite Thompson. 1985. Interview with Harrah-Conforth. CDRP, 87-004.
Hickerson, Joe. 1986. Interview with Jeanne Harrah-Conforth. CDRP, 87-024.
Ives, Edward. 1985. Interview with Jeanne Harrah-Conforth. CDRP, 87-008.
Ivey, Bill. 2018. *Rebuilding an Enlightened World: Folklorizing America.* Bloomington: Indiana University Press.
Janelli, Roger. 1986. Interview with Jeanne Harrah-Conforth. CDRP, 87-017.
Jones, Michael Owen. 1986. Interview with Jeanne Harrah-Conforth. CDRP, 87-016.
Letsinger, Dorothy. 1985. Interview with Jeanne Harrah-Conforth. CDRP, 87-004.
Lloyd, Timothy. 2018. Interview with Jeanne Harrah-Johnson. BOHP.
Marsh, Moira Smith. 2017. Interview with Jeanne Harrah-Johnson. BOHP.
Martin, Peggy. 1976. *Stith Thompson: His Life and His Role in Folklore Scholarship, with a Bibliography.* Folklore Monograph Series, Vol. 2. Bloomington, IN: Folklore Publications Group.
McDowell, John H. 2018. Interview with Jeanne Harrah-Johnson. BOHP.
Montenyohl, Eric. 1989. "Richard M. Dorson and the Internationalization of American Folkloristics." *Western Folklore* 48, no. 4: 349–57.
Oinas, Felix. 1988. Interview with Jeanne Harrah-Conforth. CDRP, 87-042.
Reuss, Richard. 1985. Interview with Jeanne Harrah-Conforth. CDRP, 87-007.
Richmond, Edson, ed. 1967. "Short Biographical Sketch." *Studies in Folklore. In Honor of Distinguished Service Professor Stith Thompson.* Folklore Series, 9, Bloomington: Indiana University Press.
Roberts, Warren. 1976. "Stith Thompson." *Indiana Folklore* 9: 138–46.
———. 1986. Interview with Eric Montenyohl. CDRP, 87-019.
Rudy, Jill Terry. 2000. "The Lazy Susan and Beyond: Studying Four Symposia and Stith Thompson at Midcentury for the Twenty-First Century." *Folklore Historian* 17: 11–22.
Sebeok, Thomas. 1988. Interview with Jeanne Harrah-Conforth. CDRP, 87-041.
Thompson, Stith. 1956. *A Folklorist's Progress: Reflections of a Scholar's Life.* Bloomington: Indiana University Press.

———. 1955–1958. *Motif-Index of Folk-Literature: A Classification of Narrative Elements in Folktales, Ballads, Myths, Fables, Mediaeval Romances, Exempla, Fabliaux, Jest-Books, and Local Legends*, Vols. 1–5. Bloomington: Indiana University Press.

Warren, Greer Trotter. 2018. Interview with Jeanne Harrah-Johnson. BOHP.

Wells, Herman B. 1980. *Being Lucky: Reminiscences and Reflections*. Bloomington: Indiana University Press.

———. 1985. Interview with Jeanne Harrah-Conforth. CDRP, 87-010.

Wolford, John B. 2018. Interview with Jeanne Harrah-Johnson. BOHP.

Zumwalt, Rosemary Lévy. 1988. *American Folklore: A Dialogue of Dissent*. Bloomington: Indiana University Press.

JEANNE HARRAH-JOHNSON is an independent scholar in Reno, Nevada.

7 Folklore and Mythology Studies at UCLA

Michael Owen Jones

Wayland D. Hand, The Group, and the Center

The study of folklore at the University of California, Los Angeles, dates from 1933, when noted ballad scholar Sigurd B. Hustvedt began teaching the first folklore course on the popular ballad (Hand 1964a). In 1937, Germanic Languages hired Wayland Debs Hand to develop folklore courses; he offered an introductory class in 1940 (Cattermole-Tally 1989; Newall 1987). Hand, who died in 1986, was born in 1907 in Auckland, New Zealand, of Mormon parents who later moved to Utah. He conducted his missionary work in Germany for three years. At the University of Utah, he earned the BA (1933) and MA (1934) in German. His 1936 dissertation at the University of Chicago, directed by Archer Taylor, concerned *Die Schnaderhüpfel*, an Alpine folk lyric (Cattermole-Tally 1989), although he was noted later for work on folk medicine. Hand edited the *Journal of American Folklore* (1947–51) and *Western Folklore* (1954–66) as well as presided over the American Folklore Society (1957–58) and the California Folklore Society.

In his youth, the red-haired Wayland played minor league baseball. Teammates called him "Red" Hand, he told me. He stood about six feet tall. Later in life, he had white hair neatly parted on the left and a trim mustache; with his well-defined features and courtly manners, many found him charming. He is best known for editing and organizing data in the two volumes of the *Frank C. Brown Collection* on popular beliefs (Hand 1961, 1964b), which garnered him the Giuseppe Pitrè Prize for International Folklore (Coffin 1968; Cattermole-Tally 1989), as well as for the edited volume *American Folk Medicine* (1976), and his still-relevant *Magical Medicine* (1980).

Hand came to UCLA at the invitation of Gustave O. Arlt, chair of Germanic Languages and later dean of the Graduate Division, who, like Hand, had been a student of Taylor's at the University of Chicago (Taylor and Hand 1966). By the mid-1940s, a loosely knit association supporting folklore had formed at UCLA, consisting of, among others, Hand and Arlt in Germanic Languages, Ralph Beals in Anthropology, Charles Speroni in Italian, and Stanley Robe in Spanish. In 1954, Dean Paul A. Dodd officially recognized this affiliation of faculty as the Folklore Group, which supervised courses and conducted research; seventeen faculty members were associated with the Group, seven folklore courses were offered, and seventeen related courses were listed in the catalog (Hand 1964a). Its regular courses, listed under "Folklore" in the college catalog, consisted of undergraduate offerings in introductory folklore, American folklore, and folklore theory as well as a graduate course on the folktale.

With funding from the Ford Foundation, the Institute of International and Foreign Studies was founded in 1958 and included under its auspices the Center of Latin-American Studies, Near-Eastern Studies, and African Studies. On May 6, 1960, Hand submitted a proposal to establish a fourth research unit, the Center for the Study of Comparative Folklore and Mythology.[1] Hand referred to himself in the proposal as a "comparative folklorist," William Lessa in Anthropology represented cross-cultural studies of tribal societies and "primitive mythology," and Jaan Puhvel in Classics assumed the title of "comparative mythologist."

From its founding in 1961 until 1968, the Center launched major fieldwork projects in Mexico, Colombia, and the Philippines as well as the California Ethnic Folklore Project. The last, undertaken from 1962 through 1965, resulted in extensive documentation of Serbo-Croatian, Russian, African American, and Mexican folklore in Los Angeles, contributing substantial data to the Center's archive as well as supporting dissertations. As Hand wrote in a report in 1961, "Ever since the founding of the Folklore Group in 1954, and even before that, the folklore of ethnic groups has been of primary concern to people connected with the development of Folklore studies on the UCLA campus." By 1961, twenty-seven faculty members were associated with forty course offerings in folklore and mythology (Hand 1964a).

D. K. Wilgus and the Folklore and Mythology Program

When the Center for the Study of Comparative Folklore and Mythology was established, Hand changed the name of the Folklore Group to the Folklore and Mythology Group, consistent with the Center's title. A division of labor ensued as the Center oversaw research, and the Group took charge of the curriculum, although there was still no degree in folklore. That soon changed.

Since the mid-1950s, Hand had attempted to hire an American folk song and ballad specialist. Because the Folklore Group could not hire faculty on its own, Hand prevailed on the English and Music Departments. UCLA's English Department finally agreed to hire D. K. Wilgus as associate professor of English and Anglo-American folk song to teach courses on fieldwork, American folklore, and British and American folk song and ballad (Hand 1964a). Some of Wilgus's courses were to bear only the folklore prefix; others were to be cross-listed with English or music.

Under the guidance of Francis Lee Utley, Wilgus completed his dissertation on Anglo-American folklore scholarship at the Ohio State University in 1954 and subsequently published the work as a book (Wilgus 1959). In contrast to Hand, a teetotaler who sometimes rewarded informants by "setting them up at the bar" while abstaining himself (Cattermole-Tally 1989), Wilgus would quaff a few rounds; more than once he showed me a bottle of Wild Turkey he kept in his desk drawer. Rather short, he sported a goatee, combed his thick, wavy hair forward and over his ears, smoked unfiltered cigarettes, and occasionally wore cowboy boots. He often used proverbial expressions, sometimes told jokes, and knew a great many traditional ballads that he sang a cappella.

Born Donald Knight Wilgus in West Mansfield, Ohio, December 1, 1918, he died on Christmas Day 1989 of complications following emergency cardiovascular surgery (Montell 1991). He earned his BA (1941), MA (1947), and PhD (1954) at Ohio State. From early 1942 to December 1945, he served in the US Army. Wilgus taught at Western Kentucky State College, now Western Kentucky University, from 1950 to 1961 (see M. A. Williams, this volume). He founded and edited *Kentucky Folklore Record* (1955–61), edited *Western Folklore* (1970–75), served as record review editor of the *Journal of American Folklore* (1959–73), and presided over the California Folklore Society and later the American Folklore Society (1971–72).

Prior to Wilgus's being hired at UCLA in 1963, Hand asked what facilities he needed. With special funding from the dean's office, Hand created the Folk Song Laboratory, a recording and dubbing studio also equipped with portable tape recorders for fieldwork. Wilgus transferred from Western Kentucky University copies of the E. C. Perrow and Josiah Combs folk song collections, his own regional collection of about a thousand audiotapes of field-recorded songs and narratives, and an extensive paper collection of wide-ranging folklore materials that he added to the archival holdings of Center for the Study of Comparative Folklore and Mythology. Over the next two decades, Wilgus created another archive in the center that housed thousands of commercial recordings of folk song and music.

Hired to oversee the Folklore and Mythology Group's curriculum, Wilgus soon proposed the creation of a program that would grant the MA degree. By 1963, Wilgus wrote Hand (1964a, 36), the Group's "course offerings now number fifty-nine, including twenty-one graduate courses" taught by "thirty-three instructors drawn from twelve academic departments." In a 1974 budget planning document, Wilgus described the degree program as having been "designed to provide the student, who is required to have had introductory courses in general folklore and American folklore, with basic training in Folkloristics, including theory, and both library and field research, knowledge of the basic genres, to specialize in a genre or culture area." Students were permitted to enter in the fall of 1965. It was christened the Interdepartmental Program to Administer the MA Degree in Folklore and Mythology, or IDP (the PhD was added in 1978). Calling this interdepartmental program both folklore and mythology coincided with the name of the Center. The IDP had its own core identity and courses while also drawing faculty and courses from both ethnological disciplines (anthropology, ethnomusicology, dance ethnology) and literary and historical fields (classics, Indo-European studies, and language and literature departments). As the program's curriculum developed, however, myth and mythology, especially European myth and mythology, played a diminished role compared with the field documentation and analysis of contemporary behaviors.

Budget and Archives

Even after the establishment of the MA in 1965, the Program "was without a budget, as all normal support funds remained in the home departments of the faculty" of the Program, wrote Wilgus in a 1966 memo. A draft of the 1972 PhD proposal states that funds were to be budgeted through the English, Germanic Languages, Slavic, and Music Departments. Funding involved "difficult bookkeeping," contended Wilgus, because support funds in humanities were transferred to a special subaccount in English slated for folklore while fine arts funds were dispersed through the Music Department. If and when the funds reached folklore, they were often insufficient. There was no provision to purchase audiovisual equipment needed by students and faculty to do fieldwork, replace office furniture, or purchase typewriters and computers.

Despite ongoing budget problems, the Program and the Center managed to develop (often with extramural funding) a library with 7,000 books and serial publications and five major archives: one on folk medicine with 750,000 cards (which included cross-references); another on popular beliefs with half a million cards; a third on folk music with about 8,000 commercial recordings; a fourth on California and Western folklore with extensive audiotape and paper collections of ethnic folklore; and a fifth on visual media, including 30,000 slides and 350 field and commercial videotapes on folklore.

Over the years, the Center and Program sponsored important conferences, curricula, and festivals focusing on ethnographic research and performances of the folk arts. In 1963, Wilgus directed the UCLA Folk Music Festival; the first of five, it boasted forty-two performers and 12,000 paid admissions (Hand 1964a). The year 1963 also saw the first UCLA Summer Institute on Latin American Folklore directed by Hand and Robe. The second such institute occurred in 1967, when the Folklore Center cosponsored with the Museum of Ethnic Arts and Technologies (later the Fowler Museum of Cultural History) a twelve-week lecture series on folk arts around the world. In 1968, the Center sponsored a Finnish folk festival directed by Inkeri Rank. In 1971, the Center held a conference on American folk legend. The Folk Musicians, a UCLA Extension course directed by Wilgus in 1972, featured performances and presentations by noted folksingers and instrumentalists.

Robert A. Georges, Core Faculty, and Expanded Curriculum

In 1965, there were only two full-time folklorists, Hand and Wilgus. They taught the few core folklore courses in the program: Introduction to Folklore, American Folklore, Folklore Theory, Fieldwork, The Folktale, Folk Song, and Folk Belief and Custom. The first folklore hire following Wilgus was Robert A. Georges in 1966. All faculty members who taught in this IDP had to be housed in departments; Georges was placed in English. Hand wrote in a memo that "the Center has gained a specialist in the folklore of immigrant groups in America. The Center plans to take advantage of this fact, and launch an ongoing program in the collecting of ethnic folklore in Los Angeles." Indeed, in 1975–76, Georges was the principal investigator of the Traditional Arts and Oral History of Chicanos of Greater Los Angeles, an ethnic heritage studies grant funded by the Department of Health, Education, and Welfare. Trained at Indiana University as a folklorist, Georges taught only folklore courses at UCLA for the next twenty-eight years, until retiring in 1994.

Born in Sewickley, Pennsylvania, Georges earned his BS degree (English and French majors) from Indiana State Teachers College (now Indiana University of Pennsylvania) in 1954 and then taught high school English classes in Bound Brook, New Jersey, from 1954 to 1956; did a two-year stint in the army; and taught English in Manahawkin, New Jersey, from 1958 to 1960. He then went to the University of Pennsylvania, where he earned an MA in English and American literature in 1961. From there he went to Indiana University, where he studied folklore, linguistics, and English Romantic literature (Wehmeyer 1997), filing his dissertation in 1964, a year after having been hired by the English Department at the University of Kansas. Ballad scholar MacEdward Leach at Penn triggered Georges's interest in folklore. Georges also was intrigued by the approach of behaviorist B. F. Skinner, from whom he took a course and some of whose ideas he later realized were implicit in folklore studies (Georges 1990).

Georges's background in linguistics led him initially to a structural approach to the study of riddles, play activities, and folktales; his Greek American heritage stimulated extensive research on ethnic folklore. Incisive and decisive, Georges focused many of his publications on fundamental concepts in folkloristics, such as his landmark essay within a behavioral perspective concerning narrating as communicative event, legend, motif and tale type, the historic-geographic method, the folklorist as comparatist, and repertoire (see Georges 1997 for a list of his publications). He taught courses on folklore theories and methods, ethnic folklore, folk speech, narrative, and other topics. Above all, Georges brought to the Folklore and Mythology Program an intellectual rigor that established the field as a discipline, not simply an interest area appealing in varying degrees to faculty members scattered throughout the university unschooled in the concepts and methods of folkloristics (Georges 1991).

In 1968, the Folklore and Mythology Program obtained two institutional full-time equivalent positions—one from humanities on loan to the social sciences and the other split between fine arts and the humanities. I was hired for the first position and was placed in History. James Porter, who had an MA from the School of Scottish Studies, was offered the second, and he was housed in Music. Porter taught introductory folklore and folk music courses as well as specialized courses on the popular ballad and on folk music transcription and analysis. He returned to Scotland in 1998.

Having completed BA requirements at the University of Kansas for a triple major in history, art, and international relations, I enrolled in the fall of 1963 in Introduction to Folklore taught by Robert Georges, who had just been hired by English. I knew before the first class period ended that I wanted to devote my life to the study of folklore. After taking a graduate course on the folktale taught by Georges at the University of Kansas in the spring of 1964, I headed for the Folklore Department at Indiana University, where I earned the MA in folklore and the PhD in folklore and American studies. During my forty-year career at UCLA, I taught courses on folk art, American folklore, fieldwork, film and folklore, folk medicine, foodways, and other subjects.

Additional faculty constituted the core of the UCLA program for a few years each: Shirley Arora (Spanish and Portuguese), Inkeri Rank (Scandinavian), Beverly Robinson (Theater Arts), Peter Tokofsky (Germanic Languages), and Patrick K. Ford (English). Many visiting folklorists taught in the IDP in the 1980s and 1990s, among them Sharon R. Sherman, Elliott Oring, Hugh Shields, Betty Belanus, and Sabina Magliocco.

Five other faculty members were active longer in the central functioning of the program. Hired by Germanic Languages in 1965, Donald Ward (PhD, UCLA) occasionally taught courses on German folklore and increasingly one on folklore theories. In 1978, Joseph Nagy, with a PhD from Harvard in Celtic languages and literatures, was hired by English to fill an appointment advertised by that department specifically for a "literary folklorist." In 1982, Donald Cosentino (PhD, University of Wisconsin, African languages and literature) began teaching a variety of African folklore and mythology courses for the program on a temporary basis. He was appointed to a permanent position in 1988. Stephen Stern was hired

Fig. 7.1. *Left to right:* Robert A. Georges, D. K. Wilgus, Wayland D. Hand, and Michael Owen Jones at a conference celebrating the twentieth anniversary of the teaching program and the twenty-fifth anniversary of the Research Center in Folklore at UCLA, May 1986. Photograph by Jane Jones. Courtesy of Michael Owen Jones.

in 1982 but ultimately did not obtain tenure in the School of Library Science. In 1992, Timothy Tangherlini was hired on a split appointment between East Asian and the Scandinavian section in Germanic Languages; he has taught courses on shamanism, ritual, folk narrative, and other subjects.

Challenges and Changes

In addition to detailing ongoing budgeting issues, many documents attest to the anomalous nature of the Folklore and Mythology Program as an IDP with a separate research center. In 1970, Wilgus explained to an administrator that "while the Folklore and Mythology [Program] is not a department, it functions as a department in many ways, particularly in relation to the instructional program" in that it possessed a large suite of disciplinary courses, administered the MA degree in folklore (and the PhD in 1978), and had a core faculty who taught only folklore-originated courses.

A long-range planning document of 1974, however, listed many problems and disadvantages of the teaching program's remaining an IDP: lack of official status in the university, the difficulty of negotiating a budget, dependence on departments for full-time equivalent positions, lack of control over staffing and scheduling of folklore courses originating in departments, lack of status and compensation for the program chair, and the difficulty of maintaining interdepartmental relationships. In addition, later hires in the Program had to teach at least half time in their home department and satisfy expectations of research and publishing in that field; as a result, many core members of the Program suffered, being denied merit increases and even tenure.

In 1974, the administration threatened to close the Folklore and Mythology Center, invoking the "sunset clause" in Center agreements. University administrators finally disestablished the Center in 1994, precipitated partly by the university's financial problems. The Center's collections were dispersed to the Ethnomusicology Archive, the English Department's reading room, and other sites. In June 1997, the Graduate Council suspended student admission to the Program. Ultimately, the teaching program merged with the Department of World Arts and Cultures to form one of the concentrations in a new graduate curriculum. This department had been established in 1972 as the undergraduate, interdepartmental Ethnic Arts Program in which folklore studies was one of seven possible concentrations.

Summary and Concluding Remarks

Organizationally, folklore studies at UCLA was at first simply a number of faculty members in the arts, humanities, and social sciences interested in one or another aspect of folklore forms and specializing in a particular place or period. Some were texturally and historically oriented, others more concerned with analyzing contemporary behaviors. Hand located and brought them together in what became officially recognized in 1954 as the Folklore Group. He spearheaded the establishment of an interdepartmental research entity in 1961. Wilgus succeeded in establishing a teaching unit to grant the MA in 1965 (and with Georges's participation, a PhD in 1978). In large measure owing to Georges, the Program's core curriculum grew to epitomize folklore studies as an academic discipline. By the end of the 1990s, after the Center's dissolution and then the Program's disestablishment owing to financial problems, diminished faculty, and lack of administrative support, folklore studies became a graduate concentration within a department where it survived, even thrived, for a decade. Folklore has come full circle at UCLA: it exists now as a topic of interest, even a specialization, among several faculty in the arts, humanities, and social sciences.

As a discipline, folklore studies had the potential to become a department with a stable budget and dedicated faculty. That never happened. The diversity of folklore's subject matter appealed to a wide range of academic specializations and attracted a large number of courses around its core that gave the field a multidisciplinary character—and with it, both complementary and competing interests. In addition, because departments do not have research centers, many students and faculty over the years feared the loss of the Center's archives of field data as well as its sound laboratory and field equipment along with the three research assistantships that constituted much of students' financial support. Few departments have their own libraries or archives; continuing the teaching program as an IDP therefore seemed preferable to departmentalization. There were personal and professional reasons as well: some faculty enjoyed their joint status in the Program and in a department; others feared that a small department might not survive during a budget crisis; and yet others did not regard folklore studies as a discipline with its own methods, questions, and hypotheses.

Many of those who studied in the Folklore and Mythology Program's MA or PhD curricula became noted in the entertainment industry, such as folk singer John Fahey, choreographers Anthony Shay and Roberta Evanchuck, radio personality Barret Hansen (Dr. Demento), and Academy Award–winning scriptwriter Eric Roth. Others developed folklore and folk arts programming with city or state agencies, including museums, historical societies, and arts councils in California, Oregon, Washington, Kansas, Pennsylvania, Connecticut, New York, and Florida. They contributed significantly to (and in some instances chaired) folklore departments, programs, or concentrations at Indiana University, the University of Oregon, Utah State University, Western Kentucky University, Otis College of Art and Design, University of Texas, University of Missouri, University of Wisconsin, University of Glamorgan in Wales, Sophia and Beppu Universities in Japan, and the University of Botswana, among others. Alumni and core faculty members brought to the fore the importance of folkloristics in understanding immigrant cultures and ethnic enclaves, narrating and aesthetic expression in daily interactions, alternative medicine, traditions at work in contemporary organizations, vernacular religion and alternative spirituality, ritual arts and healing practices in the African and Latin American diaspora, and digital culture and communication, to name a few areas of influential studies. Overall, these seem noteworthy accomplishments for a small, often beleaguered folklore and mythology program.

Acknowledgments

A longer version of this chapter was originally published in 2011 as "UCLA's Folklore and Mythology Program and Center: A History," *Folklore Historian* 28: 37–69.

Note

1. This and subsequent unattributed quotations concerning the administration of the Center and teaching program are derived from documents in the author's possession.

References

Cattermole-Tally, Frances. 1989. "Wayland Debs Hand (1907–1986)." *Journal of American Folklore* 102, no. 404: 183–85.

Coffin, Tristram III, ed. 1968. *American Folklore: Voice of America Forum Lectures.* Washington, DC: United States Information Service.

Georges, Robert A. 1990. "Skinnerian Behaviorism and Folklore Studies." *Western Folklore* 49, no. 4: 400–405.

———. 1991. "Earning, Appropriating, Concealing, and Denying the Identity of Folklorist." *Western Folklore* 50, no. 1: 3–12.

———. 1997. "Publications of Robert A. Georges." *Western Folklore* 56, no. 3/4: 195–97.

Hand, Wayland D., ed. 1961. *Popular Beliefs and Superstitions from North Carolina.* Vol. 6, *The Frank C. Brown Collection of North Carolina Folklore.* Durham, NC: Duke University Press.

———. 1964a. "Folklore and Mythology at UCLA: Folklore, Mythology, Folk Music, and Ethnomusicology." *Western Folklore* 23, no. 1: 35–37.

———, ed. 1964b. *Popular Beliefs and Superstitions from North Carolina.* Vol. 7, *The Frank C. Brown Collection of North Carolina Folklore.* Durham, NC: Duke University Press.

———, ed. 1976. *American Folk Medicine: A Symposium.* Berkeley: University of California Press.

———. 1980. *Magical Medicine: The Folkloric Component of Medicine in the Folk Belief, Custom, and Ritual of the Peoples of Europe and America.* Berkeley: University of California Press.

Montell, William Lynwood. 1991. "D. K. Wilgus (1918–1989)." *Journal of American Folklore* 104, no. 411: 72–73.

Newall, Venetia. 1987. "Professor Emeritus Wayland D. Hand (1907–86)." *Folklore* 98, no. 1: 105.

Taylor, Archer, and Wayland D. Hand. 1966. "Twenty-Five Years of Folklore Study in the West." *Western Folklore* 25, no. 4: 229–45.

Wehmeyer, Stephen C. 1997. "Introduction [to Festschrift for Robert A. Georges]." *Western Folklore* 56, no. 3/4: 189–93.

Wilgus, D. K. 1959. *Anglo-American Folk Song Scholarship since 1898.* New Brunswick, NJ: Rutgers University Press.

MICHAEL OWEN JONES is Professor Emeritus of World Arts and Culture at UCLA. He is author of *Corn: A Global History* and editor (with Lucy M. Long) of *Comfort Food: Meanings and Memories.*

8 Of Politics, Disciplines, and Scholars

MacEdward Leach and the Founding of the Folklore Program at the University of Pennsylvania

Rosina S. Miller

On November 4, 1962, newspapers across the country shared a press release from the University of Pennsylvania News Bureau: "The first graduate department of folklore in the United States has been established at the University of Pennsylvania." The announcement boasted, "Only two other American universities, Indiana University and the University of California at Los Angeles, have programs in folklore, but not departments."[1] While the news item conferred prestige on folklore at Penn, it was actually a misstatement. It would take many years for folklore to become a department at the university. A graduate group in folklore, authorized to grant PhDs, was approved in May 1962, but it was not an independent department. This miscommunication established not just the folklore program at Penn but a legacy of contested status that endured throughout the program's existence.

Equally important was the legacy of interdisciplinary scholarship, avid collecting, and enthusiastic teaching bequeathed to the folklore program by its founder, Professor MacEdward Leach. The relationship between folklore and the university was established when the first meeting of the American Folklore Society (AFS) was held at Penn in 1889, called to order by anthropologist Daniel G. Brinton; and it was maintained with anthropologists Frank Speck and Alfred Irving Hallowell at Penn well into the twentieth century. The graduate folklore program, however, traces its lineage through the English Department and Leach, who entered the department as a doctoral student and instructor of English in 1920. Trained as a philologist and medievalist, he earned his PhD in English in 1930 and was hired in 1931 as an assistant professor of English. He climbed the ranks to full professor and devoted his entire career to teaching and working at Penn. He retired in 1966, a year before his death. Leach's intellectual pursuits led him to the discipline of folklore and to leadership roles in the AFS.

Fig. 8.1. The Program in Folklore and Folklife at Penn occupied the fourth floor of Logan Hall until 2006. The building's name had been changed to Claudia Cohen Hall by the time this photograph was taken in 2013. Photograph by Bohao Zhao, (https://commons.wikimedia.org/wiki/File:Claudia_Cohen_Hall_-_panoramio.jpg), converted to black and white [CC BY 3_0 (https://creativecommons.org/licenses/by/3_0)].

Leach's interest in folklore developed from his study of medieval literature, which led him to the ballad. John Greenway counts among Leach's influences the anthropologist Speck and the English professor Cornelius Weygandt: "The one let him put his feet in the earth of life; the other showed him how to speak about the experience" (Greenway et al. 1968, 98). Leach's interests next turned to the folk song, especially the Child ballad and the cante fable. He pursued fieldwork in Cape Breton, Labrador, Newfoundland, Jamaica, Virginia, Pennsylvania Dutch country, Maine, Rhode Island, and the New Jersey Pine Barrens.

Trained in English yet interested in fieldwork, Leach brings together the two intellectual histories from which folklore emerges—the literary and anthropological approaches—differentiated by an emphasis on literary works and the unwritten tradition from which they derived on the one hand, and on oral cultures and fieldwork on the other (Zumwalt 1988, 10). As Ben-Amos notes, literary and anthropological folklorists were marked by their different institutional affiliations, with the anthropological approach dominant in the AFS for many years and the literary approach dominant in the universities (1973). It was the English Department that, at the time of Leach's tenure, offered courses in folklore and even granted a PhD in English with a concentration in folklore. Despite the long-standing place of folklore in English, in the spring of 1962, folklore at Penn split to become a freestanding program with Leach as chair. Though an interdisciplinary committee was listed, the graduate program in folklore was essentially Leach's one-man show, with Tristram P. Coffin, his colleague in English, former student, and beloved friend, helping to teach the core courses.

Speaking to the press about the motivation for separating the folklore program from the English Department, Leach emphasized the freedom to accept students majoring in subjects other than English (*Daily Pennsylvanian*, November 13, 1962). The student newspaper reported that graduates in folklore trained in museum practice were increasingly in demand to staff the folklore museums springing up throughout the country. "We have never been able to fill all the demands," declared Leach. Another early article about the graduate program (*Philadelphia Inquirer*, January 13, 1963) pictures students listening to a professional folk singer. Leach stressed that studies involve more than singing: "Of course, we want the students to experience the vitality of the songs and stories. But there are other aims: to explain much of literature and other arts, to gain understanding of the process and power of tradition, to explode a lot of misbeliefs in history and to achieve insight of the attitudes and thinking processes of people in many lands."

Despite these explanations, one still might ask why it was important to Leach and others to separate folklore from English at this time, only four years before he retired. Leach had taught folklore in the English Department for decades; his leadership role in the AFS conferred prestige and significant power within the university. A partial explanation lies in the academic expansion of the 1960s, with the federal government and foundations pouring money into academia. As this was the era of the sexual revolution, civil rights, and language expansion, folklore's independence from the English Department also took strength from the liberating politics of the times and the expanding bounds of proper academic study. Notably, the *Journal of American Folklore* published its "obscenities" issue (volume 75, 1962) at this time, announcing folklore as the academic location for the study of such subject matter. One interpretation of folklore's break from English highlights the material being studied by folklore graduate students.

Coffin explained the circumstances that brought the program into existence:

> The way it actually started was a little bit oblique. Roger [Abrahams] wrote a thesis with MacEdward, which was called *Deep Down in the Jungle*, he later made it into a book, and it was full of obscenities of all kinds. The English department at that time was very, very conservative and a little bit on the Victorian side, perhaps. And they couldn't stomach that thesis, and Mac had been

> trying for a long time to get a folklore program started and that thesis sort of broke the back of the English department and they said, "Get out of here! We don't want anything more to do with you. Start your graduate program." And it started as a graduate program.[2]

Abrahams, a student of Leach's, had begun collecting folklore in the African American neighborhood where he lived during graduate school. "I want to be clear on this," Abrahams explained: "I did not set out to work in a radically different community. My interest first was picked up when I was living in Black Philadelphia because they were playing singing games outside my door and ball bouncing and hand-clapping and I thought, that's my stuff, I'm going to write some articles here. This is just great stuff."[3]

Later Abrahams discovered that he had observed the traditional oral genres of "playing the dozens" and "toasts." What began as play for Abrahams and his neighbors fit well within folklore's field of inquiry, if not within the English Department's conservative canon. Thus, Abrahams was the last student of Leach's to earn a folklore degree through the English Department. The next dissertation completed—and the first in the independent folklore program—was Kenneth Goldstein's in 1963, whose *A Guide for Fieldworkers in Folklore* was published under the same title.

Leach's establishment of a separate folklore program thus enacted a shift away from an overdependence on a literary repertoire regarded as "appropriate." Instigated by the explicit language in Abrahams's dissertation, the folklore program's steps to independence mirrored larger issues addressed by the discipline at that time, recreating folklore as an independent discipline, not a subspecialty of English or anthropology. Notably, the performance-centered approach had already begun to ferment, ultimately providing folklore with the conceptual framework needed to bring together the field's previously disparate strands (Dwyer-Shick 1979, 339).

Scholars at Indiana University were simultaneously trying to establish folklore as a serious scholarly discipline, first under Stith Thompson and later, Richard Dorson (see Harrah-Johnson, this volume; and Zumwalt, this volume). As the two major graduate programs in folklore at the time, Penn and Indiana were bound to develop a rivalry with Dorson and Leach leading the opposing teams. Coffin believes the rivalry was based less on intellectual differences than on personality, specifically Dorson's jealousy of Leach's rapport with students, what Dorson called—according to Coffin—"Mac's 'Pennsy gang.'"[4] Abrahams agrees that Dorson was competitive but characterizes the competition as between insiders and outsiders. Dorson was anxious to make a name for himself. He entered the Europeanist History Department of Indiana University as an Americanist and immediately set out to become a world scholar. Abrahams argued that Dorson succeeded, but "did it in the face of what looking back was a cabal. Between MacEdward and Tris [Coffin] and Wayland [Hand] and Archie [Green] and his ex-students and Louis Jones, the New York bunch."[5] Dorson was an outsider to a whole generation of Leach's students and friends.

Not everyone agrees with this interpretation of the Penn-Indiana rivalry, however. Another aspect lies in the two departments' responses to the folk song revival. In the 1960s, the discipline seemed ambivalent toward the popularization of folklore. The folk song revival helped establish the Penn folklore program; folk songs and the interests they inspired, consequently, were accepted as appropriate topics for scholarly study at Penn. However, this revival was also responsible for colloquial uses of the term *folk*, which some felt undermined the discipline's scholarly reputation.

In this same period, Dorson wrote: "What does the Folk-song Revival have to do with the study of folklore? As matters stand, quite a good deal. The collecting and scrutiny of folk-songs have obsessed numbers of American scholars since the days of Francis James Child and Cecil Sharp; a ballad specialist will be found on college faculties where there is otherwise little or no interest in folklore" (1963, 437). Dorson's dismissal of ballad scholarship and the study of folk song is obvious from his 1968 monumental study of British folklore, in which he makes no mention of the Scottish and English ballad scholars. The conflict between Dorson and Leach over the popularization of the term *folk* spilled into debates about the expansion of the AFS. Simon Bronner reports that Dorson "unleashed a firestorm by discouraging figures he called 'popularizers' and 'amateurs' from the leadership" of the AFS. In Dorson's view, "the popularizers undermined the serious study of folklore, destroyed the integrity of authentic traditions, misrepresented folklore's meaning, and endangered the academic growth of a folkloristic discipline." Leach, on the other hand, was secretary-treasurer of the AFS for all those years and "thought that popularizers did a service by keeping folklore interests before the public hungry for colorful regional literature" (Bronner 1998, 334).

Dan Ben-Amos, however, preferred to characterize the Penn-Indiana rivalry as a debate about intellectual practice.[6] Dorson, he argues, was committed as part of the Indiana tradition to developing folklore into a scientific discipline. Thompson's legacy was the motif and type indexes, scientific tools for the scholarly study of folklore. Developing folklore in consonance with scientific principles of rigorous scholarship was central to the project that Dorson inherited and carried out as leader of folklore at Indiana University. Yet Dorson was also an avid fieldworker.

Leach, according to Ben-Amos, emphasized the *human* element of folklore rather than the scientific.[7] Despite motif analysis's application to ballad scholarship, Leach was uninterested in Thompson's scientific approach to tradition. Under the influence of the folk song revival, scholars of the ballad moved toward field collecting and interaction with people, as opposed to motif and type analysis, which kept the scholarly project at the level of the text. Leach's dedication to fieldwork and his interest in interacting with all kinds of people are obvious in his scholarship, research trips, and governance of the graduate program. The literary-anthropological split in folklore thus became another feature of the Penn-Indiana rivalry (see Zumwalt, this volume).

The controversy over the folklore program at Penn did not remain within disciplinary politics or theoretical debates. Disciplines must exist within university structures, and the folklore program's relationship to the administration also began with contestation. On March 4, 1963, Chester Tucker, vice president for development and public relations, wrote to Provost David R. Goddard that he "detected an overtone of criticism" from Goddard regarding a press release his office had written about the new folklore program. Goddard wrote back to Tucker the same day:

> I have the news release of Sunday, November 4 concerning the graduate program in Folklore at the University. First, I might say that we consider Folklore a completely legitimate field of academic study, particularly at the graduate level at the University. I might point out that for many years my father was editor of the American Journal of Folklore [*sic*], published by the organization of which Dr. MacEdward Leach is now president. We have not organized a department of Folklore; what we have organized is a graduate group permitted to direct students for a doctor's degree, but this is not a University department, nor does it have a chairman, nor does it have a budget. The University of Pennsylvania has a fair number of graduate groups without departments and this is what was organized here. I do not know who furnished the information to your office concerning the alleged department, and I am sorry that our communications in the University break down occasionally. I am sure that the members of your staff cannot be expected to recognize the intricacies of academic organization in all cases. I feel that no real harm has been done; my criticism was directed at the assumption that we had organized a department when no such department exists. Certainly, any effort to correct the matter with the daily press would create far more harm, and I think the matter should be forgotten. P.S. Dr. MacEdward Leach is chairman of the graduate group in Folklore.[8]

Leach himself referred to the folklore program as a department in the press and other official communications; Goldstein as chair followed suit. It is unclear whether this terminological misrepresentation was the source of friction between Goddard and Leach or a symptom of larger problems. As late as August 31, 1966 (after Leach had retired!), Goddard continued to try to set Leach straight about folklore's status. Coffin explains it as a matter of personalities and style: "Mac [Leach] was unorthodox. He didn't follow the normal lines of academia. And, he'd ruffle feathers as he went along. But you couldn't dislike the guy, nobody disliked him. But they just felt he was taking advantage of things."[9]

There seemed to be universal agreement that Leach's greatest abilities lay in teaching. In memoriam, Wayland Hand wrote, "Great as was his work as a field collector and scholar in folklore, MacEdward Leach will be remembered as one of the most successful teachers of folklore in the country" (1968, 43–44). Thirty-five years later, Coffin echoed Hand's praise: "Mac [Leach] had an amazing ability of capturing students," he explained. "He was a real pied piper. . . . He just got guys, you know, and everybody hung around his office, and that's the way it operated."[10] Among his students count many scholars who have made serious contributions to the field, including Coffin, Abrahams, Goldstein, Green, G. Malcolm Laws, Edith Krappe, Horace Beck, William Simeone, John Greenway, David Fowler, Ellen Stekert, David Elder, Mary Washington Clarke, and Lionel Wyld.

For the first three years, Leach and Coffin were considered the faculty of the folklore program, with their appointments in the English Department. In 1965, Goldstein was hired as a nondepartmentally affiliated temporary appointment in the Graduate School, and Leach announced his plans to retire from Penn, forcing the administration to decide the future of folklore. According to a Memorandum on the Folklore Program dated November 15, 1965, a committee was appointed to make recommendations and identified three problems that demanded the administration's attention: Leach's pending retirement, the anomalous administrative structure of the program (under the budget of the English Department but administered by an independent committee), and the inadequate size of the faculty for the number of students and courses offered. The committee recommended six courses of action, including establishing a separate department with, potentially, an undergraduate major; recruiting a new chair from outside the university; appointing a new graduate group committee; and increasing the number of faculty. The committee's primary concern was securing a "distinguished professor" as chair who "should be prepared to develop folklore vigorously and with concern for hardminded research."[11]

Needless to say, these recommendations were not all heeded. Records of the administration's actions in the 1965–66 academic year reveal only the end result of their drive to hire a "distinguished professor" to lead the folklore program. The administration appears to have had a single-minded ambition to hire Alan Dundes to replace Leach as chair. According to Coffin, Dean Otto Springer was determined to hire Dundes, and, according to Ben-Amos, the Anthropology Department supported this plan.[12] Coffin reports, however, that Leach was just as determined that Springer not hire Dundes.[13] Abrahams explains what happened next. Dundes was invited to Penn for a luncheon and to give a lecture. Leach, Coffin, and Goldstein closed ranks against Springer by ignoring Dundes's visit. Abrahams described the effect on Dundes: "He said it was just the strangest experience of his life because he was brought in by the dean to interview and the dean was pulling a flanker's move. He was not called in by MacEdward. Well, this is perfectly legitimate. You're not supposed to pick your own successor, you see. But, as a result, Alan gave his speech, and none of the folklorists came."[14]

Dundes's candidacy was likely complicated by his perceived criticism of the Penn program; he had written a scathing review of Coffin's anthology of tales published by the AFS: "The editor is a folklorist trained in the history of literature and seems to use this as an excuse for ignoring the anthropological aspects of the tales" (Dundes 1963, 69). Whether or not this review motivated Leach, Coffin, and Goldstein's actions, Dundes picked up on their sentiment and declined the offer of chair to stay at the University of California, Berkeley, and build the folklore program there (see Briggs, this volume; see also Zumwalt, this volume).

By the end of spring 1966, Leach was still without a replacement as chair of the folklore program. Goldstein had just been appointed to the faculty—his temporary appointment having been made permanent retroactively—and Coffin was now vice provost, unable to serve as chair. On May 18, 1966, President Gaylord P. Harnwell wrote a letter to Don Yoder of the Department of Religious Thought. With nearly identical wording to the one written by Harnwell to Leach four years earlier, the president asked Yoder to assume the chair of the Group Committee in Folklore.[15] Yoder was a logical choice to draft into the folklore program. He came to Penn from Franklin and Marshall College, which established the first department of folklore in the United States (see Bronner, this volume), and taught the first folk religion class at Penn in 1957. However, interestingly, Yoder and Leach's paths rarely crossed, despite the fact that Yoder succeeded one of Leach's teachers, Professor Weygandt.[16] Penn had a distinguished history of scholarship of the Pennsylvania German community, to which Yoder devoted much of his own work. Once chair, Yoder quickly broadened the field of folklore to include folklife studies and helped to get the term registered in the Library of Congress. Shortly thereafter, the program changed its name to the Program in Folklore and Folklife.

On October 31, 1966, Dean Michael H. Jameson wrote a confidential letter to Provost Goddard about the folklore program. Jameson proved a strong advocate for folklore and made careful recommendations in the best interests of the program. He supported continuing the program and recognized its various strengths. He alluded to "last year's fight" over the Dundes hire and made more modest suggestions to improve the program. He discussed anthropological-versus-literary approaches to folklore and argued that this division was no longer valid. "Goldstein and Yoder are interested in an independent Folklore, concentrating on collecting, field work, musical and visual records, area studies, and the like," he wrote. "They are glad to take advantage of Sapir's, Hymes' and Wallace's work in Anthropology. They need an appointment in the folktale (who could be of use to English as well)." Later in the letter, he stated, "I would not want to

Fig. 8.2. MacEdward Leach, ca. 1965. Courtesy of the Folklore Archives, Penn Museum Archives.

see the Folklore program collapse but would like to give it a chance to develop greater strength. Very likely a single, vigorous appointment on the assistant professor level is all they need at the moment. One candidate they have suggested is an Israeli teaching at UCLA who could handle the folktale and has had African fieldwork."[17]

Thus, in 1967, Ben-Amos, who earned his PhD at Indiana University, joined the folklore faculty as assistant professor. His hire was an attempt to alleviate the Penn-Indiana competition while ameliorating Penn's deficiency in prose narrative. Although folklore seemed on its way to establishing itself within the university, its status remained tenuous in the eyes of the faculty. On May 17, 1971, Goldstein wrote to Provost Curtis Reitz asking for a decision "concerning the status of the Folklore Department" and of the promotions of Ben-Amos, Yoder, and himself. He was on his way to the AFS's annual meeting and wanted to "squash once and for all the rumors concerning the demise and destruction of the Graduate Folklore and Folklife Program here at Penn."[18]

There is more history between Ben-Amos's hire in 1967 and Goldstein's 1971 letter to Reitz, of course. Clearly, however, in this era while folklore was on its way to establishing itself as a vital and independent discipline within the academy, faculty and students still had to fight for status and recognition within the university. The model for the program at Penn, shaped by the inimitable Leach and expanded by Yoder and Goldstein, established folklore at this institution and in the academy as an independent discipline, autonomous of English and anthropology, and, as the next decade would reveal, capable of forging new connections to education, linguistics, and related fields (see Hufford, this volume).

Acknowledgments

A longer version of this chapter was originally published in 2004 as "Of Politics, Disciplines, and Scholars: MacEdward Leach and the Founding of the Folklore Program at the University of Pennsylvania," *Folklore Historian* 21: 17–34.

Notes

1. University of Pennsylvania Archives, a. University Relations News and Public Affairs Records, Subject Files [UPF 8.5], Box 101, Folder 4.
2. Tristram P. Coffin, telephone interview with the author, 2003.
3. Roger D. Abrahams, interview with the author, 2003, Penn Folklore Archives.
4. Coffin 2003.
5. Abrahams 2003.
6. Dan Ben-Amos, conversation with the author, 2003.
7. Ibid.
8. University of Pennsylvania Archives, Office of the Provost, General Files [UPA 6.4], Box 48, Folder 5.
9. Coffin 2003.
10. Ibid.
11. University of Pennsylvania Archives, Tony Garvan's Papers [UPT50 G244], Box 22, Folder 41.
12. Ben-Amos 2003.
13. Coffin 2003.
14. Abrahams 2003.
15. University of Pennsylvania, Office of the Provost, Box 48, Folder 5.
16. Don Yoder, telephone interview with the author, 2003.
17. Office of the Provost, Box 48, Folder 5.
18. Ibid.

References

Ben-Amos, Dan. 1973. "A History of Folklore Studies: Why Do We Need It?" *Journal of the Folklore Institute* 10, no. 1/2: 113–24.

Bronner, Simon J. 1998. *Following Tradition: Folklore in the Discourse of American Culture.* Logan: Utah State University Press.

Dorson, Richard M. 1963. "The American Folklore Scene, 1963." *Folklore* 74, no. 3: 433–49.
Dundes, Alan. 1963. Review of *Indian Tales of North America*, by Tristram P. Coffin. *Journal of American Folklore* 76, no. 299: 69–71.
Dwyer-Shick, Susan A. 1979. "The American Folklore Society and Folklore Research in America, 1888–1940." PhD diss., University of Pennsylvania.
Greenway, John, Roger D. Abrahams, Russell K. Alspach, Horace P. Beck, Katharine M. Briggs, Ray B. Browne, Tristram P. Coffin, et al. 1968. "MacEdward Leach, 1892–1967." *Journal of American Folklore* 81, no. 320: 95–120.
Hand, Wayland. 1968. "MacEdward Leach (1896–1967)." *Western Folklore* 27: 43–44.
Zumwalt, Rosemary L. 1988. *American Folklore Scholarship: A Dialogue of Dissent.* Bloomington: Indiana University Press.

ROSINA S. MILLER is Founding Director of Stanford in New York at Stanford University.

9 Groundtruthing the Humanities

Penn Folklore and Folklife, 1973–2013

Mary Hufford

Introduction

The story of the University of Pennsylvania's Department of Folklore and Folklife—never formally constituted yet undoable only by fiat of the university's trustees—suggests a kind of wonder tale. I begin with the 1970s golden age, when the faculty built an innovative curriculum that would persist until 2013, when the last PhD candidate in folklore graduated. I then consider the unraveling context for folklore and folklife at Penn as institutional supports collapsed and academic straitening shut down an internationally recognized flagship graduate program.

"Groundtruthing," the cartographic practice of checking maps against the territories they represent, supplies an apt metaphor for folklore's paradigmatic shift in the 1960s and 1970s. The Penn program's foundation narrative (Miller, this volume) dramatizes folklore's move from text-centered to field-based research. Scandalized by Roger Abrahams's dissertation (1961) on profane African American speech play, an elite, conservative English department proposed that MacEdward Leach start his own graduate program.

Abrahams's dissertation, and more than three hundred to follow, engaged the field-based study of folklore in lively conversation with the humanities, social sciences, sciences, and professions at Penn and beyond. As forms of social communication with literary merit, recoverable through fieldwork, folklore was, in the words of Tristram Potter Coffin (1962–85),[1] the "bastard child that anthropology begat upon English" (Coffin 1968, v).

From the beginning, the study of folklore and folklife at Penn was distinguished by reliance on ethnographic fieldwork to recover folklore's disciplinary object. In an interview with Rosemary Lévy Zumwalt, Dan Ben-Amos credited Kenneth Goldstein and Leach for "a scholarly approach that put the fieldwork . . . as the priority rather than some classificatory system that was possibly . . . scientific. If you ask why it was a great department at that time and for twenty years, I think it was because it was a department that was ready to look at folklore in the field."[2]

The field-based approach to folklore fostered both multisectoralism and interdisciplinarity. Because folklore is metaculture (Noyes 2004), fieldwork can stimulate collaborative reflection by scholars and community members on conditions subtending social life. Folklore at Penn in the 1960s anticipated the rise, through the 1970s and 1980s, of public folklore as a means of "amplifying voices in a democratic polity" (Gross Bressler 1995). Democratic values, hardwired into the methods of folklore research, would come to be deeply at odds with university policies that in the 1990s supplanted traditional faculty governance with market-driven structures of decision making.

Between the 1960s and 2000s, Penn, like most US universities, abandoned what political scientist David Schultz terms the "Deweyan business model of higher education," based on public investment in the education of a democratic citizenry, for a corporate, market-driven business model (2015). Given that many folklore programs withstood corporatization, I ask how Penn's transition to a market-driven institution altered folklore's context so profoundly that it could not survive.

The 1970s and 1980s

Penn's Department of Folklore and Folklife, in the 1970s, broke from the Enlightenment project of assembling and classifying texts. "New Perspectives" were regrounding and revitalizing the field. Celebrating linguistic creativity in the ordinary lives of his Camingerly neighbors, Abrahams had elevated the poetics of artfully performed social routines like playing the dozens to the status of canonical texts of literary and classical studies. The department's 1992 Five Year Plan explicitly articulated this groundtruthing function of folklore studies: "The verbal art [folklorists] study possesses many of the qualities literary scholars and philosophers have recently discovered in written texts" (Department of Folklore and Folklife 1992). Thus, John Dewey's lifelong project—"restoring the continuity of aesthetic experience with normal processes of living" (Dewey 1934, 10)—consistently informed the work of Penn folklorists.

When I began graduate studies at Penn in 1975, this paradigm shift suffused the department's curriculum. Goldstein, the first Penn folklore PhD and author of *A Guide for Fieldworkers in Folklore*, taught courses in fieldwork and folklore of the British Isles and Ireland (1965–92). Dell Hymes, author of "The Contribution of Folklore to Sociolinguistic Research" (1971), taught Ethnography of Speaking (1965–87). Don Yoder, who brought the term *folklife* to the department's name, introduced the study of vernacular custom and material culture (1966–96) (see Bronner, this volume). Ben-Amos taught Folktale, Minor Genres, and History of the Discipline (1967 to present). John Szwed taught Jazz and Blues and Folklore and Culture. Barbara Kirshenblatt-Gimblett taught Folklore and

Fig. 9.1. Kenneth Goldstein at Elliot Ephraim's Book Barn in Northford, CT, 1976. Courtesy of Diane Goldstein. Photograph by William R. Ferris. In the William R. Ferris Collection (KGP 1-76-5 #742), Southern Folklife Collection at Wilson Special Collections Library, University Libraries, University of North Carolina at Chapel Hill.

History, Foodways, and Folklore of Immigrant Groups (1973–81). Henry Glassie taught Vernacular Architecture and other courses in material culture (1976–88).

In the 1970s, Penn magnificently supported folklore's interdisciplinarity. As Rosemary Stevens (dean of the School of Arts and Sciences, 1991–96) later recalled to Ben-Amos: "Folklore was an exciting, important interdisciplinary program, drawing faculty from the Museum, English Department, African-American Studies and others."[3] Making sense of folklore as socially constitutive, metacultural processes, folklore graduate students studied with Erving Goffman, Anthony Wallace, Arjun Appadurai, Ray Birdwhistell, William Labov, Barbara Herrnstein Smith, and other transdisciplinary luminaries. Such free-range grazing across disciplines resisted the departmentalized university's legacy of siloed professions where "illumination achieved in one area is apt to get sealed off from others" (Wilshire 1990, 99).

Kirshenblatt-Gimblett and Szwed departed in the early 1980s. Margaret Mills (1983–98), Abrahams (1985–2002), and John Roberts (1982–96) ensured Penn folklore's continuing leadership in both academic and public spheres. Through the 1980s, Goldstein secured large student cohorts, partly by subdividing fellowships. Occupying most of the fourth floor of Logan Hall, the Folklore and Folklife Department included a graduate student lounge and archive that, with a folklore reading room in Van Pelt Library, incubated an enduring esprit de corps among students. Contributing to a growing field, students instituted a colloquium series, edited *Keystone Folklore Quarterly*, and launched a foodways journal titled *The Digest*. Penn folklore faculty and alumni would join the ranks of MacArthur fellows, Guggenheim fellows, Botkin fellows, state folklorists, Academy Award–winning filmmakers, National Heritage fellows, and chairs of national endowments.

The Rise of Public-Sector Folklore

From the 1960s on, Penn folklore faculty, students, and alumni actively cultivated folklore's place in the public sphere. Such efforts were controversial. Academic folklorists, including Ben-Amos, cited historical lessons on dangers of government-sanctioned cultural intervention. Many, however, embraced emerging opportunities to engage and support culturally pluralist values distinctive to the American democratic project (Muthukumaraswamy 2002). Penn folklorists joined colleagues across North America to influence the creation and administration of the National Endowments for the Arts and Humanities, the inauguration of the Smithsonian Folklife Festival, and the passage of the American Folklife Preservation Act (AFPA), establishing the American Folklife Center at the Library of Congress. In 1974 Hymes, then president of the American Folklore Society, exhorted Congress to enact the AFPA, for which Penn folklore alumnus Archie Green had spent a decade lobbying. Hymes's testimony in support of the AFPA became a manifesto for public folklorists: "Folklorists believe that capacity for aesthetic experience, for shaping of deeply felt values into meaningful apposite form, is present in all communities. . . . Our work is rooted in recognition that beauty, form, and meaningful expression arise whenever people have a chance, even half a chance, to share what they enjoy or must endure" (1975, 346).

The Penn Folklore Archive

Archives logically go hand in hand with folklore programs. Inaugurated concurrently with the program in the 1960s, Penn's folklore archive had by the 1970s become a means of training students in the building and archiving of field-based knowledge (Ben-Amos 1970; Department of Folklore and Folklife 1982). With financial support from the Philadelphia Folksong Society, folklore graduate students served as archivists for several decades. Faculty emphasized folklorists' obligation to shield from harm those entrusting us with their words and images on tape and film. Consistent with Dewey's theory of the critical role of shared inquiry in democratic self-governance, Penn's Archive of Folklore and Folklife came to embody a compact between university-based researchers and a public formed through the research activity itself.

Through the 1980s, Penn folklore rode the crest of a transdisciplinary shift toward community-based research models. Glenn Hinson, then a graduate student, recalled Penn folklore's participation in democratizing the research process: "With the performance paradigm now taken for granted, students were pushing on the ethnographic front . . . increasingly experimenting with ideas of ethnographic collaboration. The term 'informant' gradually gave way to 'consultant' in student conversations, while students pressed faculty for more discussions about public engagement and ethical practice."[4] Still, by the 1990s, questions regarding the raison d'être for PhD folklore training were troubling folklore's identity and standing at Penn.

The 1990s: The Fate of Folklore in the University of Excellence

The 1973 publication of *One University: Report of the University Development Commission* was a harbinger of Penn's corporatization: "Our academic development calls for the strengthening of graduate programs, but our resources and our energies do not permit across-the-board strengthening, nor is it wise to contemplate such an idea. Instead, the concept of *selective excellence* in graduate education has been put forward" (University Development Commission 1973, 13). Over the next twenty years, the board of trustees grew Penn's endowment (from $164 million in 1976 to more than $3 billion in 1998) and trimmed the annual operating budget through downsizing, outsourcing, and, crucially, reducing the proportion of endowment funds that could be used to run the schools to 2.5 percent (Ruben 2000).

By the time of Judith Rodin's presidency (1994–2004), Glassie (who accepted a university professorship at Indiana University), was replaced by Robert Blair St. George (1989–99). Hymes left for an endowed chair at the University of Virginia and was not replaced in folklore (his faculty line reverted to the School of Education).[5] Both Yoder and Goldstein retired after more than thirty years on the folklore faculty. Thus, when Regina Bendix joined the department in 1993, the faculty was still down by two, although David Hufford, a Penn folklore alumnus on the faculty of the Hershey Medical School, taught folk belief and folk medicine, and Janet Theophano, a folklore alumna and a dean in the College of General Studies, taught courses in foodways and folklore and aging at no cost to the department.

Decisions about downsizing were increasingly market-based. The university ignored differences between the fund-raising capacities of departments in the School of Arts and Sciences and those in schools with wealthy alumni—such as Wharton, medicine, and law—in a struggle that favored the strong.[6] Cross-disciplinary conversations on which folklore had flourished withered as each department strategized to increase undergraduate enrollments and to appear unique and indispensable. The departures of Hymes, Glassie, and Goldstein were, in Mills's words, "natural events," but it was clear that the university had no intention of replacing them. "Regina [Bendix] was the last hire, a brilliant hire," but the department was "below a critical mass in numbers. . . . The situation was lethal."[7]

Given the phenomenal growth of the endowment by 1998, why had the fortunes of the Folklore and Folklife Department not improved with those of the university? Matthew Ruben argues that the function of the endowment had changed: "For the trustees, capital growth, facilities expansion, and the cutting of labor costs are not merely a means to an end. They are *social values in and of themselves*—values that signal to the financial world, the media, and the public that Penn is sufficiently possessed of that elusive quality, 'excellence,' to compete with the nation's most elite universities" (2000, 202, emphasis in original). Folklore felt the university's corporatizing policies as an existential threat. In 1997, Bendix invited faculty and alumni to read Bill Readings's *The University in Ruins* (1997), which resoundingly critiques "excellence," before a meeting to "help us find ways to maintain and perhaps reorient the graduate program." Bendix recalls: "Of course we felt the business model. It was after all our small undergrad major numbers that added to the reasons why we should not be a department. We were a field that fueled into other enterprises, our grad students often made a little money teaching freshmen writing seminars, or when they were farther along, Theophano gave them opportunities to teach for [the College of General Studies]. (Meanwhile CGS, too, was pressured into developing money generating degrees, such as the Masters in Liberal Arts that Janet built there)."[8] President Rodin assured the university community that departments could succeed by changing with the times (Ruben 2000). For many, "changing with the times" would be code for "disappearing."

The university eliminated nearly four thousand positions during the 1990s (Ruben 2000). Struggling to do much more with much less, units found themselves in fierce competition for favors from the administration. During the 1990s, the administration also stopped the folklore department's practice of dividing fellowships among graduate students.[9] Such a practice did not, in the administration's view, support a reputation for selectivity rivaling Harvard's.

After Goldstein and Yoder retired, the Folklore and Folklife Department had six standing faculty while maintaining a chair, graduate chair, and undergraduate chair. In 1996 and 1998, respectively, Roberts and Mills left Penn for Ohio State's program in folklore (see Mullen and Shuman, this volume). With no prospect of replacements, in 1998, three of the remaining faculty negotiated with deans in the School of Arts and Sciences to close the department, creating in its stead a graduate program and a research center. Only Ben-Amos opposed the dissolution. In 1999, the board of trustees dissolved the department and established the Graduate Program in Folklore and Folklife and the Center for Folklore and Ethnography, the latter directed by Abrahams, the Hum Rosen Professor of Folklore and Folklife. Program faculty were relocated to English (Abrahams), History (St. George), Anthropology (Bendix), and Near Eastern Languages and Civilizations (Ben-Amos).

The 2000s: The Graduate Program in Folklore and Folklife and the Center for Folklore and Ethnography

In 2001, the School of Arts and Sciences authorized two new folklore positions. Jay Dautcher (2001–4) was hired as assistant professor in anthropology with teaching responsibilities in folklore. I was hired to direct the Center for Folklore and Ethnography, with an appointment to the Folklore Graduate Group. Bendix resigned in 2001, accepting a position at the University of Göttingen, Germany. Abrahams went into semiretirement in 2002. From the Department of Near Eastern Languages and Civilizations Ben-Amos continued to chair the graduate program, which admitted two to three graduate students annually with full funding.

As director of the Center for Folklore and Ethnography, I developed externally funded field practica for graduate students, taught core courses in folklore, co-organized conferences and speaker series with graduate students, and inaugurated, with alumna Meltem Turkoz, a community-based academic service learning course: Exploring Memory and Tradition in Philadelphia Communities (Hill 2007).[10] As a repository for the associated manuscripts and documentation, the folklore archive continued to comprise, in the words of a reporter for *The Daily Pennsylvanian*, "a very active hub for student research and work in the discipline" (Rockar 2005).

When Dautcher resigned, Dean of the School of Arts and Sciences Sam Preston suspended admissions to the folklore graduate program. Associate Dean Jack Nagel, in an interview with the *Daily Pennsylvanian*, rejected folklore's status as "an interdisciplinary study incorporating anthropology, sociology, English and history," calling it "a mere 'topic' for these disciplines" (Rockar 2005). A contradiction was not lost on the student reporter, who concluded: "As Penn increases its efforts to compete with both the selectivity and endowment of the Harvard Corporation, we should keep in mind what we risk losing along the way. Penn's aggrandizement could come at the cost of the very things President Gutmann claims to want to embrace" (Rockar 2005). Despite concerted efforts by faculty, alumni, and colleagues around the world, the university never reinstated

Fig. 9.2. Members of Penn's Graduate Faculty in Folklore and Folklife during a gathering in the Moose Room of Fiji House in the fall of 2008. *Left to right:* Roger D. Abrahams, Mary Hufford, David Azzolina, and Dan Ben-Amos. Photograph by Leah Lowthorp, who in 2013 would become the last person to graduate with a PhD in folklore and folklife from Penn.

admissions. In 2006, the folklore offices and archives were moved from Logan Hall to Fiji House (a Scots Gothic structure nicknamed for its once and future occupants, the Phi Gamma Delta fraternity). It was there that the program and center lived out their last days. Only the archive would survive.

Postlude: The Folklore Archive

Compressed into the form of the archive are icons and indices of fifty years of the life of folklore and folklife at Penn. Course syllabi and bibliographies register the evolution of the program and the field, along with hundreds of student papers, recordings of guest presentations from colloquia, and complete runs of student publications, including *The Digest* and *The Archivist.*

The archive, which in 2006 challenged the weight-bearing capacity of Fiji House floorboards and so overflowed into the basement, included gifts given over the years by faculty, alumni, and visiting scholars: gongs and agricultural implements from Korea given by Roger Janelli, a whimsical Ferris wheel made by the subject of Skye Morrison's dissertation, and a collection of Haitian paintings given by Roger Abrahams to the Center for Folklore and Ethnography. Shelves were lined with dozens of autographed books and offprints, and hanging on a coatrack were costumes created and worn by graduate students during Christmas mummings performed annually from the late 1970s until the mid-1990s.

Working to migrate the archive to digital format, my students and I wondered, "What fairy tale are we in?" Initially it seemed we might share the predicament of the miller's daughter in Rumpelstiltskin, spinning a dwindling supply of straw into gold. Perhaps our tale was among the oldest in the world, the Dragon Slayer (Thompson 1977, 32). What could appease the guardians of the endowment's gleaming hoard? Clearly, we needed a princely sum to endow a chair and rescue the program. Would such a benefactor find us if we dangled a colossal yellow braid through the parapets outside the archive window?

Or had we already ventured into Barbe Bleue's forbidden chamber?

The final act of dismemberment had been planned for the archive. Deans in the School of Arts and Sciences had directed the dispersal of the folklore archive by format into separate divisions of the university's library system. In preparing materials for distribution within what seemed an impossibly short time, we faced the daunting curatorial challenge of preserving linkages among the archive's multiple formats. Then, lo! A technicality of the humblest sort came to the rescue. The folklore archive contained materials deposited over the decades by multiple stakeholders for research and safekeeping. Library officials pointed out that accepting materials not donated outright as gifts would violate university policy. We might say that through its own public, democratic nature, the archive saved itself. And so it came to pass that, in 2009, the archive migrated across campus, linkages intact, to join the archive of the University of Pennsylvania Museum of Archaeology and Anthropology. No longer active, even as it slumbers, the archive indexes every aspect of five decades of folklore and folklife at the University of Pennsylvania.

Notes

1. Dates indicate when a faculty member taught in folklore at Penn.
2. Dan Ben-Amos, interview with Rosemary Lévy Zumwalt, June 2018.
3. Rosemary Stevens, letter to Dan Ben-Amos, 2017.
4. Glenn Hinson, personal communication to Patricia Sawin, June 27, 2018.
5. Janet Theophano, personal communication to the author, March 22, 2019.
6. Regina Bendix, personal communication to the author, May 10, 2019.
7. Margaret Mills, personal communication to Rosemary Lévy Zumwalt, June 2017.
8. Bendix 2019.
9. Ibid.
10. See the center's website at https://www.sas.upenn.edu/folklore/center/index.html (accessed May 17, 2019).

References

Abrahams, Roger. 1961. "Negro Folklore from South Philadelphia: A Collection and Analysis." PhD diss., University of Pennsylvania.

Ben-Amos, Dan. 1970. "The University of Pennsylvania Folklore Archives: A Progress Report." *Keystone Folklore Quarterly* 15, no. 3: 148–57.

Coffin, Tristram Potter. 1968. *Our Living Traditions: An Introduction to American Folklore.* New York: Basic Books.

Department of Folklore and Folklife. 1982. Self-Study. University of Pennsylvania Archives. Office of the President, Hackney Records [UPA 4], Box 652, Folder 1.

———. 1992. Five Year Plan. University of Pennsylvania Archives. Office of the President, Hackney Records [UPA 4], Box 652, Folder 1.

Dewey, John. 1934. *Art as Experience.* New York: Minton, Balch.

Gross Bressler, Sandra Jill. 1995. "Culture and Politics: A Legislative Chronicle of the American Folklife Preservation Act." Dissertations available from ProQuest. AAI9532184. https://repository.upenn.edu/dissertations/AAI9532184.

Hill, Judy. 2007. "South Philly's Indonesian Community as a Focus for Service Learning." *Penn Current*, March 1.

Hymes, Dell. 1971. "The Contribution of Folklore to Sociolinguistic Research." *Journal of American Folklore* 84, no. 331: 42–50.

———. 1975. "Folklore's Nature and the Sun's Myth." *Journal of American Folklore* 88, no. 350: 345–69.

Muthukumaraswamy, M. D., ed. 2002. *Voicing Folklore: Careers, Concerns and Issues: A Collection of Interviews.* Chennai, India: National Folklore Support Center.

Noyes, Dorothy. 2004. "Folklore." In *The Social Science Encyclopedia*, 3rd ed., edited by Adam Kuper and Jessica Kuper, 375–78. New York: Routledge.

Readings, Bill. 1997. *The University in Ruins.* Cambridge, MA: Harvard University Press.

Rockar, Amara. 2005. "A Dying Myth: Once Well Renowned, Penn's Folklore Program Is Fading Away." *Daily Pennsylvanian*, March 25. https://www.thedp.com/article/2005/03/a_dying_myth.

Ruben, Matthew. 2000. "Penn and Inc.: Incorporating the University of Pennsylvania." In *Campus, Inc.: Corporate Power in the Ivory Tower*, edited by Geoffrey D. White with Flannery C. Hauck, 194–217. Amherst, NY: Prometheus Books.

Schultz, David. 2015. "The Rise and Coming Demise of the Corporate University." *Academe* 101, no. 5. https://www.aaup.org/article/rise-and-coming-demise-corporate-university.

Thompson, Stith. 1977. *The Folktale.* Berkeley: University of California Press.

University Development Commission. 1973. "Pennsylvania, One University." *Almanac* 19, no. 20, Special Supplement, January 29. Penn University Archives and Records Center.

Wilshire, Bruce. 1990. *The Moral Collapse of the University.* Albany: State University of New York Press.

MARY HUFFORD is Associate Director of the Livelihoods Knowledge Exchange Network. She is author of *Chaseworld: Foxhunting and Storytelling in New Jersey's Pine Barrens* and editor of *Conserving Culture: A New Discourse on Heritage.*

10 Toward a Multigenealogical Folkloristics

The Berkeley Experiment

Charles L. Briggs

Here I present a disciplinary history of the future. My focus is on the Folklore Graduate Program at the University of California, Berkeley. Outlining two periods, 1963–2005 and 2005–18, it would seem that my concern is actually with the past. Taking a cue from contemporary work in the philosophy of history (see Koselleck 2004), however, my concern is with ways that charting tactics for navigating the present involve imagining pasts and futures. Sketching the first four decades of the history of the Berkeley Folklore Program, I stress Alan Dundes's emphasis on building a program with strong theoretical, interdisciplinary, and international dimensions. Turning to the program's recent history, I offer critiques of how theory building in folkloristics has subordinated and often erased contributions by Latinx and African American folklorists. This discussion suggests the importance of a multigenealogical folkloristics that explores different sites and experiences in multiplying ways of defining folklore and configuring folkloristics. Returning to the Berkeley case, I examine how challenging Eurocentric genealogies structures the program's emphasis on theoretical, interdisciplinary, and international dimensions in different ways as a small graduate program attempts to build a vibrant future in the face of shifting institutional agendas and uncertain financial resources. In presenting one perspective on one folklore program, my broader goal is to contribute to debates about the pasts, presents, and futures of folkloristics.

Alan Dundes, Forms of Folklore, and the Berkeley Folklore Program

Rosemary Lévy Zumwalt (2017) drew on the papers of Alan Dundes and William Bascom in Berkeley's Bancroft Library to detail the program's inauguration and Dundes's role in shaping it. I thus only outline this history here. William Bascom joined Berkeley's Department of Anthropology and the (then) Lowie Museum of Anthropology in 1957. An African specialist with deep interest in art, Bascom

Fig. 10.1. Alan Dundes giving a lecture on folk narrative for the KRON Television series on folklore, 1968. Permission courtesy of the Dundes family.

worked with Franz Boas's student Melville Herskovits at Northwestern University, meaning that folklore was part of his training. Bascom served as president of the American Folklore Society in 1953–54. Dell Hymes joined the Berkeley faculty in 1960. Trained at Indiana University in anthropology, folklore, and linguistics, Hymes became the only person to serve as president of the scholarly societies of all three fields—the American Anthropological Association, the American Folklore Society, and the Linguistic Society of America. Along with John Gumperz, Hymes was forging the "ethnography of speaking" perspective he used in reshaping theoretical premises. Hymes grasped the quality of Dundes's intellect and imagined how he could help establish a folklore program.

After coming to Berkeley in 1963, Dundes created his signature undergraduate course, The Forms of Folklore. Dundes's perhaps unparalleled knowledge of folklore and folklore scholarship around the world along with his charisma, enthusiasm, sense of humor, and deep love of folkloristics made the course an instant success. Enrollments reached five hundred or more students, making Dundes one of Berkeley's most celebrated teachers. The course shaped the Folklore Graduate Program in several ways. First, the course included, as it still does, a collection component, transforming undergraduates into contributors to folklore scholarship. After the Berkeley Folklore Archive outgrew a collection of filing cabinets in Dundes's office, the archive became a social space in Kroeber Hall where graduate students could build a sense of community. Second, legions of undergraduates volunteered to file the mountains of contributions that flooded the archive each time the course was offered, enabling them to interact with folklore graduate students and Dundes himself. Third, the course's scale garnered important financial support for graduate students, providing readerships that paid fees and stipends. Finally, the course enabled Dundes to entice outstanding students into pursuing folklore graduate study. It is still a common occurrence for undergraduates to discover submissions by folklorists of the stature of Regina Bendix and Barbara Kirshenblatt-Gimblett—realizing that they began their careers in that introductory class.

Although the Department of Anthropology provides administrative support, folklore is a separate graduate program. For decades Berkeley only offered the MA in folklore; students could obtain PhDs through departmental doctoral programs or in the Ad Hoc Interdisciplinary Doctoral Program. The graduate program thrived, in part, because its launch in 1965 benefited from the post–World War II boom in US support for higher education. Second, as Zumwalt (this volume) details, Dundes declined numerous offers of employment elsewhere, remaining a formidable figure on campus for forty-two years and offering a strong sense of continuity.

This stability was tragically disrupted on March 30, 2005, with Dundes's sudden death. Joining the faculty just a few months later, I faced not the smooth transition that we had planned but the need to forge quickly an intellectual vision for the future and to secure the program's financial and institutional base, knowing that it would soon be buffeted by changing institutional priorities and fluctuations in resources. Fortunately, the Folklore Faculty Graduate Group, drawn from departments across the humanities and social sciences, then consisting of Ronelle Alexander, Ben Brinner, John Lindow, Dan Melia, Candace Slater, and Bonnie Wade, provided guidance, support, and deep knowledge of the Berkeley campus. Sustaining a small academic MA program in a university whose major orientation is toward PhD programs and professional degrees is a much more difficult task in the new millennium than it was in the 1960s. The expansionist visions and abundant funding of past decades had often given way to contractionist administrative agendas and the cycles of boom and bust that have affected California's public universities since the 1980s. Moreover, in 1965, California resident graduate students paid no fees. In 2018–19, resident graduate students were charged over $19,000 for fees and nonresidents an additional $15,000 per academic year—costs that the program seeks to avoid passing along to its students.

Deepening connections to PhD-granting departments and expanding the presence of folklore in graduate education was crucial, given the vulnerability of freestanding, academic master's programs. The Folklore Graduate Group thus proposed a designated emphasis in folklore, enabling PhD students to receive doctoral degrees in, say, French and folklore. Several preceding steps increased the likelihood of success. We built broader support by recruiting colleagues with folkloristic expertise to the Folklore Faculty Group from as many humanities and social science departments as possible; faculty members with decades of experience at Berkeley became "informants" on administrative intricacies. We worked closely with Associate Dean of the Graduate Division Joseph Duggan (a folklorist!). We kept requirements minimal—an introductory folklore course, a yearlong graduate core seminar, a graduate methodology course (generally taken in the PhD home department), substantial folklore content on qualifying examinations and dissertations, and a graduate group member on qualifying examination and dissertation committees. Our pitch was that the designated emphasis would enhance PhD programs' efforts to recruit graduate students and faculty members and to place their graduates, who could offer folklore classes in addition to their disciplinary specialty.

Happily, our projections proved accurate on all three scores. In addition to students who elected a designated emphasis in folklore, others opted to pursue an MA in folklore and a PhD simultaneously. These moves boosted applications to the Folklore MA Program and helped PhD-granting departments recruit top candidates, thereby increasing support across campus and benefiting folklore MA students, who join a larger folklore graduate student community.

Two initiatives served simultaneously to honor Dundes's contributions and to secure Berkeley folklore's future. First, funds from the Alan Dundes Distinguished Professorship in Folklore permit an annual Alan Dundes Lecture, drawing campus-wide attention to the work of leading figures in the field and emerging research agendas and perspectives. Second, the Dundes family, along with Dundes's friends, colleagues, and former students, contributed to an endowment whose income enables the program to name an Alan Dundes Graduate Fellow each year and provide a modest stipend.

Securing Folkloristics' Place amid Shifting Social and Academic Landscapes: Toward a Multigenealogical Folkloristics

The preceding remarks tell only one part of the story—the institutional component—of changes emerging since 2005. My sense is that it is possible to move from ideas to administrative structures but that it is harder go in the reverse direction. A main focus has thus been on critically rethinking the underpinnings of folkloristics, examining its relationship to shifting academic and social/political landscapes, and imagining vibrant disciplinary futures.

In his American Folklore Society presidential address, John Roberts reflected on how important shifts in the academy "threatened the viability of folklore

Fig. 10.2. Visiting professor John McDowell performing a corrido during a podcast interview with (*left to right*) Charles Briggs and graduate students Cameron Johnson and Leah Simon, 2019. Photograph by Elena Klonsky.

as an independent discipline" (1999, 134). He suggested that folkloristics lost relevance in shifting cultural and political landscapes due to "our origins in romantic nationalism" and "refusal to expel the phantoms, to engage the politics of romantic nationalism by challenging those discourses and practices that we have embraced in our efforts to make our work conform to its silent dictates." Folkloristics thus largely failed to join African American studies, ethnic studies, women's studies, performance studies, and queer studies in challenging caricatures and stereotypes; work by folklorists accordingly became "invisible" (123). Clinging to romantic nationalism in claiming autonomy in the context of shifting "politics of disciplinarity" exacerbated long-standing doubts regarding folkloristics' disciplinary status (136–37).

Gerald Davis called attention to how folklorists' own ethno-racial positionalities affect the research they do. In particular, the experience of folklorists from racialized, underrepresented populations can engender scholarship and public-sector work that challenge dominant conceptions and practices (1992, 110). A report card of sorts emerged from a recent essay by Rachel González-Martin, who reflects on how graduate training can still "unsettle" minority scholars' place in "a discipline that remains uncertain of who we are and what we do" (2017, 21). Her experience suggests that deeper engagement with folkloristics can ironically produce a diminished sense of belonging in the discipline and a debilitating sense that minority scholars are "never capable of directing its future" (30). What role can graduate programs play in addressing these issues? These concerns certainly resonate with Fivecoate, Downs, and McGriff's (this volume) report on concerns expressed by today's graduate students.

The Berkeley Folklore Program stresses forging contexts in which teaching and scholarship critically reexamine genealogies and theoretical underpinnings, generating new alternatives. Again, creating new futures requires creating new pasts. Folkloristics began long before romantic nationalism; multiple and competing logics have been at play for three centuries (Bauman and Briggs 2003). Richard Dorson (1968) promulgated a genealogy for folkloristics that seemingly required the sort of American folkloristics he consolidated at Indiana. Projecting a single future for folkloristics—shielded carefully from fakelore (thus from nearly everything we study today) and encroachment by other disciplines—required a single genealogy that led unilinearly from William Camden and John Aubrey to Dorson, a single file of white Euro-American elites. This genealogy intersected with race and colonialism only when folkloristics traveled with the British Empire. As Roberts suggests, building a monolithic, bounded genealogy to rationalize folkloristics' claim to disciplinary status can ironically engender intellectual narrowness and institutional weakness. Rather than trying to enshrine a single vision of folkloristics' pasts and futures, Berkeley's program fostered a multigenealogical folkloristics.[1]

First, Dorson's genealogy performed disciplinary boundary work (see Briggs 2008), designed to isolate folkloristics from contemporaneous scholarly endeavors. Aubrey worked in a late seventeenth-century milieu and an institution—the Royal Society—that simultaneously produced the domains of nature, language, and politics and the autonomous provinces of knowledge required to understand them: science, semiotics (linguistics), and the social sciences. Folkloristics' precursor, antiquities, enshrined the three epistemologies as central to modern knowledge by projecting them as opposites of premodern beliefs and subjects. Exploring how research on folklore helped make dominant disciplines thus demonstrates that folkloristics is relevant not just to purportedly déclassé and disappearing objects but to scrutinizing other disciplines.

Second, Américo Paredes's work (1958) forms a central focus of the core seminar, sparking reflections on how he constructed folklore as revolving not around a single, homogeneous, national shared culture but around difference, race, power, borders, and conflict (see Bauman, this volume). Each year we debate in the core graduate seminar how genealogies get inflected by racial inequalities—from Paredes's time through the present—and where folkloristics might be today if Paredes's epistemological and political challenge to dominant genealogies had been placed center stage in 1958. South Asian and Latin American scholarship similarly provides alternative genealogies. In short, rather than placing folklore from around the world in Eurocentric frameworks, we explore globally dispersed analytic traditions of folkloristics.

Third, building alternative genealogies involves more than rejecting the canon; it requires developing new ways of reading canonical texts. For example, Dorson positioned Aubrey as a key folkloristic father figure through his discovery of Englishness in rural people who differed not in race but in class and space. Rereading Aubrey critically through the lens of colonialism suggested how his texts formed heteroglossic, multilingual compendia of fragments in which English peasants' folklore was constantly in dialogue with that of peoples of Asia, the Americas, North Africa, and colonized Ireland. Accordingly, Aubrey's work was shaped by British imperialism, the expansion of English capital, missionization, and dialogues Aubrey shared with John Locke, Isaac Newton, and other Royal Society members. Using the literature in science-technology studies and in postcolonial and decolonial, feminist, queer theory, and disability studies to rethink folkloristics advances not a simple charge that folkloristics is complicit with colonialism—which is hardly news—but awareness of how multiple, complex forms of difference have been woven into the fabric of folkloristics from its beginning through the present, as González-Martin's stark assessment of contemporary graduate training suggests.

Fourth, a persistent feature of Berkeley's program has been its international reach, recruiting folklorists from outside the United States as visiting faculty members. Visitors during the past ten years have included Pertti Anttonen, Rahile Dawut, Valdimar Hafstein, Galit Hasan-Rokem, Sadhana Naithani, Diarmuid Ó Giolláin, and Kwesi Yankah. Each taught a semester of the core graduate course. Scholars from China, Finland, Iceland, India, Ireland, Israel, and Ghana have thus helped shape critiques of Eurocentric genealogies and proposed alternatives. For example, Sadhana Naithani (2006) extended critiques of folklore collecting by British colonial officials and missionaries by exploring the complex agency of Indian "translators" or "assistants," whose linguistic and cultural capital enabled them to collect, translate, and edit these texts. Many international visiting students, postdocs, and scholars have similarly augmented the global reach of the conversations. US-based visitors—including JoAnn Conrad, Steven Feld, Ruth Goldstein, Lee Haring, Mary Hufford, Jeana Jorgensen, Amanda Martinez-Morrison, John McDowell, Jay Mechling, Amy Shuman, Timothy Tangherlini, and Katharine Young—have similarly deepened and broadened multigenealogical dialogues.

Finally, our students make crucial contributions to the multigenealogical ethos of Berkeley's Folklore Graduate Program. Indeed, the program's central goal is to provide an environment in which students are not consumers but producers of diverse genealogies. We recruit students who have specific forms of training or life experience that position them to read the canon against the grain in particular ways and construct alternatives. Here are just a few examples: Having directed a dance troupe, Naomi Bragin (2010) used popping, a subgeneric style of hip-hop, as a basis for rethinking folk dance. Trained as an ethnobotanist, Ruth Goldstein (2009) drew on her experience in coordinating a community garden in Costa Rica to reposition folkloristics at the center of the posthumanist turn, rethinking folk medicine through new cartographies of human-plant relations. Carl Schottmiller (2009) reconfigured Dundes's work on latrinalia from queer theory perspectives, questioning the women's/men's bathroom binary years before it became a political flash point. Héctor Beltrán (2012), trained at the Massachusetts Institute of Technology in computer science, drew on insider understandings of hardware and software in documenting narratives and social media among Central American migrants in Oakland. My goal is not to single out these alumni—I wish I could provide many more examples. Rather, I point out that the heart of the Berkeley Program lies in how students rethink folkloristics in their own ways. We seek to train new generations of folklorists who will help sustain the discipline into the future.

Conclusion: Which Pasts? Which Futures?

Berkeley's Folklore Program is lucky to have been shaped by one of the most visible figures in the field and to have received the million-dollar check that endowed the Alan Dundes Distinguished Professorship in Folklore. Neither of these advantages renders it immune, however, to the forms of precarity—including fluctuating fiscal resources and shifts in disciplinary fashions and administrative agendas—that often threaten folklore programs. Like other programs, its continuing vitality rests on continually devising strategies for building support, which involve performing diplomacy, tenacious insistence on administrative respect for policies and commitments, begging and cajoling, and lots of lunches.

I have emphasized the importance of critical, creative intellectual work to sustaining the field. Our program resolutely remains the Berkeley *Folklore* Program, and the "f-word" is not hedged with any ands or buts. This disciplinary commitment does not signal, however, acceptance of the sort of boundary work that fosters intellectual isolation or limits efforts to challenge the discipline's geopolitical and historical underpinnings, its silences and contradictions. I spent a day in 2005 with the late Anna-Leena Siikala. At one point, she suggested that we should not have to choose between just doing things the way we did them in the nineteenth century or morphing into cultural studies. Folklore training programs can play a crucial role in crafting a broader range of futures for the discipline by involving graduate students, faculty, and other interlocutors in countering received forms of exclusion by critically revising and multiplying folkloristics' pasts.

It could be argued that we are now comfortably postgenealogical, that we should bury pasts and focus on disciplinary futures. I reject this position for three reasons. First, the pasts of folkloristics are less history lessons you learn in graduate school than commonsense understandings that continue to shape presents and futures. If our students are to make new futures for the discipline, they need to construct their own histories. Second, such erasure would reproduce racialized hierarchies. In the face of demands to recognize women's contributions and those of scholars from US racialized minorities and from countries beyond the Europe–North America orbit, declaring "game over—no more genealogies, please!" would leave those exclusions in place, impoverishing the range of ideas that count as folkloristics' stock-in-trade. Third, Dipesh Chakrabarty (2000) transformed subaltern studies by suggesting that Indian history is less valuable as a separate, bounded intellectual box than as a space that affords unique tactics for "reprovincializing Europe," for dismantling such prominent and supposedly universal boxes as philosophy, political economy, art, and so forth. To paraphrase Shakespeare, so let it be with folkloristics. By viewing the discipline relationally rather than in isolation, folklorists can explore how they have shaped other disciplines by drawing boundaries between what are projected as folk versus elite, popular, or, formerly, "primitive" spheres. This approach can similarly reveal how other intellectual traditions have defined themselves by drawing on and often subordinating folkloristics.

In sum, the more we are open to critically and creatively exploring folkloristics' pasts and presents, the more we can fashion vibrant futures.

Note

1. Sadhana Naithani played a crucial role in developing this approach; see Briggs and Naithani (2012).

References

Bauman, Richard, and Charles L. Briggs. 2003. *Voices of Modernity: Language Ideologies and the Politics of Inequality*. Cambridge: Cambridge University Press.

Beltrán, Héctor. 2012. "Echándole Ganas across Borders: Narratives of la Frontera Sur from the Everyday into the Mainstream." Master's thesis, University of California, Berkeley.

Bragin, Naomi. 2010. "Popping and Other Dis/Appearing Acts." Master's thesis, University of California, Berkeley.

Briggs, Charles L. 2008. "Disciplining Folkloristics." *Journal of Folklore Research* 45, no. 1: 91–105.

Briggs, Charles L., and Sadhana Naithani. 2012. "The Coloniality of Folklore: Towards a Multi-Genealogical Practice of Folkloristics." *Studies in History* 28, no. 2: 231–70.

Chakrabarty, Dipesh. 2000. *Provincializing Europe: Postcolonial Thought and Historical Difference.* Princeton, NJ: Princeton University Press.

Davis, Gerald L. 1992. "'So Correct for the Photograph': 'Fixing' the Ineffable, Ineluctable African American." In *Public Folklore,* edited by Robert Baron and Nicholas R. Spitzer, 105–18. Washington DC: Smithsonian Institution Press.

Dorson, Richard M. 1968. *The British Folklorists.* Chicago: University of Chicago Press.

Goldstein, Ruth Elizabeth. 2009. "An Ecology of the Self and Other Wild Thoughts." Master's thesis, University of California, Berkeley.

González-Martin, Rachel V. 2017. "A Latinx Folklorist's Love Letter to American Folkloristics: Academic Disenchantment and Ambivalent Disciplinary Futures." *Chiricú* 2, no. 1: 19–39.

Koselleck, Reinhart. 2004. *Futures Past: On the Semantics of Historical Time.* Translated by Keith Tribe. New York: Columbia University Press.

Naithani, Sadhana. 2006. *In Quest of Indian Folktales: Ram Gharib Chaube and William Crooke.* Bloomington: Indiana University Press.

Paredes, Américo. 1958. *"With His Pistol in His Hand": A Border Ballad and Its Hero.* Austin: University of Texas Press.

Roberts, John W. 1999. "'. . . Hidden Right Out in the Open': The Field of Folklore and the Problem of Invisibility." *Journal of American Folklore* 112, no. 444: 119–39.

Schottmiller, Carl. 2009. "If These Stalls Could Talk: Gendered Identity and Performativity through Latrinalia." Master's thesis, University of California, Berkeley.

Zumwalt, Rosemary Lévy. 2017. "'Here Is Our Man': Dundes Discovered, The Development of the Folklore Program at the University of California, Berkeley." *Journal of American Folklore* 130, no. 515: 3–33.

CHARLES L. BRIGGS is the Alan Dundes Distinguished Professor of Folklore in the Department of Anthropology of the University of California, Berkeley. He is author (with Richard Bauman) of *Voices of Modernity* and (with Clara Mantini-Briggs) *Tell Me Why My Children Died.*

11 The Texas School

Richard Bauman

Antecedents

Folklore first gained an institutional foothold at the University of Texas (UT) in the early years of the twentieth century, with the founding of the Texas Folklore Society (TFS) in 1909.[1] Leonidas Payne, a UT professor of English, was the society's first president, succeeded by Stith Thompson, also a member of the English Department (1914–18) and the founding editor of the society's serial publications. Neither Payne nor Thompson, however, left a discernible mark on the intellectual life of UT. Nor, I would suggest, did J. Frank Dobie, perhaps the most widely known figurehead of the TFS in the following decades. Notwithstanding his on-again-off-again stints as a UT faculty member, Dobie was far more dedicated to writing literary adaptations of folklore for popular audiences than to scholarship, which he held in conspicuously low regard. Dobie's opinion that "a great deal of folklore is inane, banal, stupid, dull, and tedious. Nobody should feel under compulsion to 'preserve it for posterity'" would not, in any event, serve very productively as a charter for an academic program (quoted in Abernethy 1994, 72).

In charting the foundations of the UT folklore program, the pivotal figure was Mody C. Boatright, who began his distinguished career at UT in 1926 while working on his PhD and went on to serve the English Department for more than four decades until his retirement in 1968 (Speck 2010). Boatright credited Dobie for launching his career as a folklorist, and in 1937 he joined Dobie in editing the society's annual publication. Six years later, he succeeded Dobie as secretary and editor, serving in that position until 1964.

In marked contrast to Dobie, however, Boatright was a true scholar, dedicated to advancing the field beyond mere collection and literary adaptation to the practice of critical, analytical scholarship. While Texas and the Southwest continued to serve as the point of departure for his work, Boatright approached the region as a cultural historian, within the context of broader cultural and historical currents, including the relationship between traditional culture and the mass media, the formation of cultural ideologies, the shaping influence of cultural pluralism, the advent of modernity, and industrial capitalism (Boatright 1973).

In his dual capacity as head of the TFS and chair of the English Department, Boatright set in motion an extended process that led to the eventual founding of the UT graduate program in folklore. The first step in the process was his establishment, in 1958, of the UT Folklore Archive to house the growing collection of field recordings deposited at the TFS office by various collectors (Paredes 1959). The founding of the archive, in turn, provided the basis for bringing Boatright's former student Américo Paredes back to Austin from Texas Western College in El Paso to serve as director of the archive and assistant professor of English. Two years later, Boatright was able to hire Roger Abrahams as well, fresh from his graduate studies at the University of Pennsylvania (Muthukumaraswamy 2002, 13).

Laying the Groundwork

By the mid-1960s, the viability of the Folklore Archive increasingly came into question as Paredes's professional responsibilities multiplied and the English Department's financial support proved less adequate to sustain it.[2] In December 1964, in response to Paredes's efforts to set the archive on a solid footing, the dean of the College of Arts and Sciences appointed a committee on folklore "to advise appropriate officials on the folklore collection."[3] Boatright was chair of the committee. Other members were Paredes; Richard Adams, chair of the Department of Anthropology; and William Goetzmann, director of the nascent program in American Studies. Chester Kielman, director of the University Archives, served ex officio. This committee laid the foundations of what was to become the UT Folklore Program.

The committee's initial effort was to recruit a folklorist who would divide his efforts between directing the archive and teaching courses in folklore. Adams, as chair of anthropology, was in a position to take the lead in this effort. In the work of the advisory committee, he saw an opportunity to build the anthropology faculty by making a place in the department for the prospective folklore hire. Knowing of the existence at Penn of a distinguished folklore program and a highly ranked anthropology department, Adams contacted Anthony Wallace, then chair of anthropology at Penn, to see if he could recommend a candidate for the position. Wallace recommended me, and Adams wrote to me to ascertain my possible interest in the position. At that point, in the spring of 1965, I had barely begun my dissertation research and was not ready to take a job. Adams also approached Alan Dundes, who found the prospect attractive but ultimately decided to remain at Berkeley (Zumwalt 2017, 15; see also Zumwalt, this volume). The committee suspended its recruitment efforts at that point, though Adams was able to bolster his folklore faculty by other means. As a Latin Americanist, he developed a collegial relationship with Paredes through their mutual engagement in Latin American studies. In 1966, he arranged for half of Paredes's line to be transferred to anthropology, and the following year, once Abrahams got tenure, Adams brought in half of Abrahams's line as well. Thus, as of 1967, there was a significant folklore presence in anthropology.

What really got things rolling, though, was the October 1966 submission of an application to the National Endowment for the Humanities titled "Expansion of the Archive of Folklore and the Training of Folklorists." The application abstract sets out the following goals: "We propose: to establish an interdisciplinary group for the purpose of studying cross cultural influences in the oral traditions of the various ethnic and occupational groups in Texas and other parts of the Southwest; to expand and make more widely available existing facilities in the Archive of Folklore and Oral History at the University of Texas; and to implement an interdisciplinary program . . . to train young scholars in folklore and related fields, with a special emphasis on the folklore and popular cultures of Southwestern United States and Latin America."[4]

The third of the goals set forth in the proposal, the establishment of a training program, marks an especially significant point in the development of folklore at UT. Only two years earlier, in answer to a query from Tristram Coffin concerning the status of folklore studies at UT, Boatright had responded, "I do not at this time advocate any change in our program, even though I am aware that meeting degree requirements in the departments leaves the student too little time for the mastery of folklore I could wish."[5] By October 1966, however, he was ready to endorse the establishment of a formal program.

The grant application was initially unsuccessful, but the endowment came back to Boatright with a greatly reduced offer of $12,000, and the Center for Intercultural Studies in Folklore and Oral History (generally referred to as the Folklore Center) was established in fall 1967 with Paredes as director.[6] Frances Terry, who was a mainstay of the center throughout its existence, was hired as secretary in January 1968.

With an eye toward the establishment of a training program, the committee turned its attention once again to recruitment. In those halcyon days of institution building, UT established a program of internally funded postdocs as a means of attracting potential faculty members. Among them, the members of the committee had a fair degree of institutional clout, and they banded together to secure one of those postdocs for me, with the prospect of a tenure-track appointment in anthropology the following year.[7] By this point, I was ready. I arrived in Austin in fall 1967, just as the Center for Intercultural Studies in Folklore and Oral History was getting under way. A couple of months later, in December 1967, Boatright made a formal request to the dean of arts and sciences on behalf of the committee that an assistant professorship be created for me in anthropology, and so I became a member of the anthropology faculty in fall 1968.[8] One of my most vivid memories of that moment in my professional life was walking into a reception room at the 1967 American Folklore Society meetings in Toronto with Boatright, Paredes, and Abrahams, just a couple of months after I arrived at UT, and hearing Bob Byington exclaim, "Here come the Texans!" It took me a couple of seconds to realize that "the Texans" included me. For a newly minted, wet-behind-the-ears folklorist to be included in that company was a powerful feeling indeed. Boatright's request amounted to his last contribution to the development of a folklore program at UT; he retired at the end of that academic year. Paredes, Abrahams, and I used to joke among ourselves that Boatright, scion of a West Texas ranching family and for many years the mainstay of the TFS and the custodian of folklore at UT, left the future of folklore at the university in the hands of two eastern Jews and a Mexican.

The establishment of the Folklore Center gave folklore a new footing at UT, independent for the first time from the TFS. The society maintained a presence at the university for a few more years, with English professor Wilson Hudson, who succeeded Boatright, serving as secretary-editor from 1964 to 1971. Hudson played no role in the establishment of the Folklore Center, however, and when he was succeeded by Francis Abernethy of Stephen F. Austin State University, the society moved its headquarters to Nacogdoches, thus ending the sixty-two-year bond between the TFS and the University of Texas. The separation was far more, though, than a mechanical matter of the society following a new secretary-editor to his home institution. The roots of the rupture went back years—even decades—in fact.

As a young scholar at UT, Paredes maintained a dutiful involvement in TFS, even serving a term as president in 1961. Indeed, the society distributed his book, *With His Pistol in His Hand* (1958), as its extra publication in 1958, well before it attained the status it came to enjoy as a foundational contribution to the Chicano movement with its pioneering documentation of a tradition of Mexican American resistance to Anglo domination. Still, Paredes never considered the society a venue for serious scholarship. He viewed Dobie, lionized as the greatest expert on Mexican culture, "as something of a fraud" for his inability to speak Spanish and his perpetuation of shallow stereotypes (Saldívar 2006, 117). Moreover, he viewed the society's annual meetings essentially as "literary entertainments" and a holding area for anti-Mexican stereotypes on the part of the WASP-dominated old guard (López Morín 2006, 63).

Abrahams's engagement with the Texas Folklore Society was a mismatch from the start. In his first year at UT, he offered a paper at the annual meeting of the society that drew on his dissertation research on African American expressive culture in South Philadelphia. His paper charted new directions in conceptions of the African American hero, but it was far too analytical and revisionist for the older members of the group. As Paredes later recalled, "He was received with open sarcasm by some of the audience. This wasn't folklore as they knew it" (quoted in McNutt 1982, 325).

Having no experience with or investment in the TFS, I did not attend its 1968 spring meeting in Alpine. Paredes and Abrahams did attend, though, and they came home fed up and ready to be done with the society, which they described to me as a venue for racists and anti-intellectual good old boys. This period, then, marked a serious, conscious shift in direction for folklore at the University of Texas.

Founding Principles

If we positioned ourselves as the not-TFS group of Texas folklorists, what was the positive intellectual ground on which we came together as we sought to define a new direction for our nascent project? One way that readers might understand what was emerging from our conversations as we began to work together would be to read our respective contributions to *Toward New Perspectives in Folklore* (Paredes and Bauman 1972), a compilation that we considered from the beginning as the charter document of our intellectual and institutional project. In his foreword to the collection, Paredes made clear that the core concern was a theoretically informed folkloristics (1972). To be sure, simply to say that we were committed to theory was sufficient to set us apart from the anti-intellectualism of TFS. But Paredes went on to establish other guiding principles: to be part of a global dialogue, especially with colleagues in Latin America, a key mission of UT at that time and still today; and a self-conscious, explicit, and critical engagement with theory without a priori commitment to received and routinized concepts, definitions, methods, and conceptions of disciplinary boundaries and canons.

In brief, our common ground rested on five principles. First, we were committed to a reorientation from folklore as item—bounded, durable cultural objects passed down through time by successions of "tradition bearers"—to folklore in use, as a resource for the situated accomplishment of social life. *Performance* and *situational contexts of use* were the keywords that seemed best suited to identifying what we were trying to understand. Second, we were committed to ethnography as an empirical principle. We understood folklore forms, practices, and contexts of use to be cross-culturally variable and to be discovered by ethnographic fieldwork, not assumed a priori. How were expressive forms and practices understood, and how did they work in the communities in which they served as a social resource?

Third, and closely related to our shared commitment to ethnography, we were committed to the principle that languages matter. This principle was not simply a nod to the basic notion that one should learn the "native language" of the community in which one worked; rather, it was based on a more complex understanding of language and community. The conception of language with which we operated went beyond lexicon and grammar to comprehend ways of speaking, genres, routines, registers, and language ideologies that gave shape to expression within those communities. I use the plural form, *languages*, because we understood speech communities as heterogeneous, with complex repertoires of communicative means—a strong departure from the "one culture, one language" understanding of the language-culture nexus in the Herderian tradition. A concomitant feature of this orientation to language was that our graduate program maintained close ties with the linguistic anthropology faculty and program within the Anthropology Department.

Fourth, we were engaged in exploring ways of reconceptualizing and recalibrating the dynamic tension between the ready-made, traditional aspects of folklore and the emergent aspects of folk expression. In particular, we converged in our thinking toward developing critical correctives to conceptions of the social base of folklore that posited shared identity, collective repertoire, and group solidarity within the homogeneous folk community as essential qualities of folk expression. Paredes came at the problem from a career-long engagement with the Texas-Mexico border region and the recognition that this conflict zone might serve as a generative seedbed of emergent folklore forms, such as the *corrido* of border conflict or forms of intercultural joking (1993). Abrahams, newly embarked on his research in the West Indies, was concerned to elucidate the agonistic dimension of African American expression and the ways in which folklore might serve as a resource for the assertion of personal power in interaction (1983). For my part, energized by Wallace's (1970) powerful understanding of society as an organization of diversity as against a replication of uniformity, I was interested in exploring how folklore in use might serve as an expression of differential identity, as against a mechanism of sharedness and group solidarity; how identity might be emergent in interaction; and how complementarity, rather than uniformity, was the necessary basis for communicative interaction.

Finally, we were strongly committed to engaged scholarship, the ideological principle that scholarly work should be responsible to and be carried out in collaboration with the communities in which we worked and lived for the mutual benefit of all parties to the intellectual dialogue. In the early years of our collegial project, our engagement was focused largely on research and advocacy for educational programs that would overturn the legacy of prejudice and neglect to which Mexican American and African American children in Texas had been subjected by deeply rooted institutional policy. This was the heyday of deprivationist ideologies in education, founded on racist notions of cultural impoverishment, and we were all immersed in organized efforts to bring to the attention of educators our folklorists' recognition of the expressive richness of what children in the Mexican American and African American communities knew and could do with language.

Launching the Graduate Program

With the core faculty on board, and the Center for Intercultural Studies in Folklore and Oral History as an institutional base, conditions were finally ripe for the organization of a graduate program in folklore. The problem we faced was how to situate our program vis-à-vis already established departments and within the shifting environment of the university. This was a period of rapid growth and institutional experimentation in graduate education at UT as the university worked to position itself as a research institution of the first rank.

In spring 1969, Paredes prepared a document titled "Institutional Request for PhD and MA Degrees in Folklore."[9] The request proposed an interdisciplinary but administratively independent program with degree-granting status:

> Proposed is an Interdepartmental Graduate Degree Program in Folklore. The Folklore Program is projected as an interdisciplinary and intercultural study of the expressive aspects of culture, combining the methods of both the humanities and the social sciences.
>
> The granting of PhD and MA degrees is contemplated, with two types of degrees to be offered: (1) a PhD or MA in Folklore, for which the candidate would meet requirements set up by the Folklore Program and do supporting work in a department, or in combination with other interdisciplinary programs such as American Studies and Latin American Studies; (2) a degree in Folklore and another major subject (Anthropology, English, German, History, Linguistics, Spanish, etc.), for which the candidate would meet the usual requirements of the participating department, take a certain number of hours in Folklore, and write his thesis or dissertation on a folklore subject.

Proposals for new graduate degrees were first reviewed by the Committee on Graduate Program Policy of the Graduate Assembly, which then made a recommendation to the full assembly. If approved by the assembly, the proposal went to the dean of the graduate school and then on up the administrative chain. The most important gatekeeper in this bureaucratic process, however, was the Committee on Graduate Program Policy. If its recommendation was favorable, the proposal had a good chance of receiving favorable action from the administration.

In mid-fall, in informal consultation with the committee chair, we learned that some members of the committee had raised questions about the value of a graduate program in folklore, including reservations about the legitimacy of the field itself and the potential for employment for degree recipients in folklore. In light of these stumbling blocks, the chair advised us to submit a supplemental document detailing the rationale for a graduate program in folklore. Accordingly, Paredes, Abrahams, and I composed a supporting document and submitted it to the committee in mid-December 1969. Our argument centered on four basic points.[10]

The first was that, for a number of years, we had attempted to meet the needs of graduate students with an interest in folklore by crafting ad hoc joint degrees that combined folklore with another discipline. Although we had achieved some measure of success with this approach, interest in the field was increasing and it had become cumbersome to have to petition for each individual student. Accordingly, we felt the need to regularize our procedures and standardize our requirements. Second—and clearly designed to feed the competitive impulses of the university among research universities—we were in competition with other institutions for the best graduate students in folklore, such as Indiana University, the University of Pennsylvania, and the University of California, Los Angeles. Moreover, potential applicants who were already accomplished scholars and were attracted by the resources of UT would welcome the opportunity to obtain a PhD in folklore if it were possible. Third, in regard to the employability of people with folklore degrees, we cited a range of opportunities open to folklorists, with the demand exceeding the supply: at colleges and universities, state and local historical societies, state folklore commissions, libraries, archives, teacher-training programs, and so on. Finally, and with a discernible touch of grumpiness, we addressed the perennial problem of disciplinary validity:

> We regret the necessity of having to emphasize yet again the position of our discipline as a whole within the scholarly community. . . . Allow us then to point out that we conceptualize Folklore not simply as an antiquarian discipline, but as a field which is part of the study of human thought and behavior. Our own work, as indicated in the accompanying documents [our CVs], deals with intercultural relations, expressive patterns, expressive forms, sociolinguistics, and culture history, and these are the subjects on which our programs are to be founded. The rigor of our proposed degree programs will be apparent to anyone who assesses them fairly; we are confident that they will not suffer by comparison with any other interdisciplinary programs presently available at the University.

In the end, we were only partially successful. The dean of the graduate school was reluctant to move the proposal forward. The situation lingered until mid-fall 1970, by which time I had become director of the Folklore Center, as Paredes had become director of the new program in Mexican American Studies for which he had lobbied long and hard. Abrahams, who would have been next in line, became director of the equally new program in Afro-American and African Studies. That left me, the new kid, to take over folklore. The dean asked to meet with me in early November to offer a new solution. To the best of my recollection, he had reached a point where he wanted to slow down the proliferation of new degree-granting programs and had turned to the graduate assembly for alternative procedures. What they had come up with, and what he proposed for folklore, was a mechanism for the constitution of ongoing graduate studies committees in interdisciplinary and interdepartmental fields. The committees would not have independent degree-granting authority but could establish and monitor standard program requirements and procedures, receive applications from prospective graduate students, and administer qualifying exams for the PhD. Crucially, however, the committee would have to work out accommodations with established, degree-granting departments, articulating its admissions procedures and degree programs with theirs. The resultant degrees would be anthropology or English, or whatever, with a specialization in folklore.

Not having a viable alternative, we assented to the dean's proposal. Accordingly, he constituted the first Graduate Studies Committee in Folklore in November 1970.[11] I was chair of the committee, and the other members were Paredes, Abrahams, and Barbara Kirshenblatt-Gimblett, who held a visiting appointment in English that year. Kirshenblatt-Gimblett was only with us for two years (her second year's appointment was in Anthropology)—not enough time to play a shaping role in the development of the program, but she was such a charismatic teacher that she played a big role in attracting members of our first cohort of graduate students from within UT, including Beverly Stoeltje and Robbie Davis.

The final task, then, to get the program fully launched, was to negotiate arrangements with established departments in which to place our students. We focused our efforts on English and anthropology, the disciplines that had the strongest ties to folklore.[12] Although we did work out a graduate folklore track in English, it never suited the needs of our students because of the insistence of the English faculty that students in folklore also satisfy all the graduate degree requirements in English. Anthropology was far more accommodating. The standard division of disciplinary labor in anthropology was built on a four-subfield conception of the field: sociocultural anthropology, archaeology, physical anthropology, and linguistic anthropology. The UT graduate curriculum in anthropology rested on a foundation of core courses in each of the four subfields. MA students were required to take two core courses; PhD students, four. The department agreed to institute a fifth core course in folklore, which gave graduate students an additional option. Beyond the core courses, graduate students had to pursue further coursework in one major subfield and one minor subfield within the department. Almost all the students doubled up in linguistic anthropology, with which I was closely identified (Bauman 2018), or sociocultural anthropology. The arrangement worked out well for graduate students in folklore, with the result that virtually all of them, with only a couple of exceptions, graduated with degrees in anthropology with a specialization in folklore. In addition to the major department requirements, the Graduate School required that PhD students complete an outside minor in another department or interdisciplinary program.

Fig. 11.1. Members of the founding Graduate Studies Committee in Folklore, University of Texas, waiting to testify at the congressional hearings considering the establishment of an American Folklife Center in the Library of Congress, May 10, 1974. *Second row, seated, right to left*: Américo Paredes, Richard Bauman, Barbara Kirshenblatt-Gimblett. *Standing, second from right*, is Archie Green, who led the effort to establish the center and subsequently taught at the University of Texas from 1975 to 1982. Photograph by and courtesy of Carl Fleischhauer.

For folklore graduate students, the most popular outside minors were American studies, English, and Latin American studies—all programs with which Paredes, Abrahams, or I had formal connections.

Epilogue

There you have it: the antecedents, foundations, and processes that brought about the establishment of the UT Graduate Program in Folklore in the late 1960s and early 1970s. The program was very much a product of its times, the era in which the American research university assumed its current shape. The heyday of the program extended from the early 1970s to the mid-1980s. At its height, about twenty-five to thirty students were in residence and engaged in coursework, with another dozen or so taking exams, doing fieldwork, or writing their dissertations. The courses, especially those with a performance orientation, also drew graduate students from adjacent departments, mainly Speech Communication, Radio-TV-Film, Ethnomusicology, and various foreign language and literature departments. During those years, in common with all academic departments and programs, folklore underwent a range of adjustments and transformations as conditions changed and new opportunities presented themselves.

One major change occurred in 1974, when the Center for Intercultural Studies in Folklore and Oral History became the Center for Intercultural Studies in Folklore and Ethnomusicology in response to the addition to the anthropology faculty of Marcia Herndon and the development of a program in ethnomusicology in the School of Music, under the direction of Gerard Béhague. Ethnomusicology became a strong partner of the Folklore Program in the years that followed (Bauman 2014).

During the 1970s, the folklore faculty grew beyond the three founders. After Kirshenblatt-Gimblett left for Penn, Roger Renwick—a specialist in ballad, folk song, and folk poetry—was the first addition to the group, with a position in English. Then, in succession, we hired John Vlach, later succeeded by Jane Young, to teach material culture; Archie Green, who introduced folklore in the public sector to the curriculum; Barbara Babcock, who attracted a number of folklore students to pursue minors in comparative literature; José Limón, who bolstered the curriculum in Chicano folklore; and Beverly Stoeltje, who added ritual and festival to the program. Vlach, Young, and Limón had primary appointments in Anthropology; Green and Babcock in English. Stoeltje began in English and later shifted to Anthropology. The founding group began to exit the scene in 1979 with Abrahams's departure for Scripps College. Paredes retired in 1984, though he continued to teach on an occasional basis for a few years thereafter. Then Stoeltje and I left for Indiana University in 1986.

After that, the folklore component of the program waned, supplanted by a growing emphasis on cultural studies, which accorded better with the interests of newer faculty members in Anthropology. Echoes of the former program exist under the auspices of the Américo Paredes Center for Cultural Studies. "Our starting point," according to the online statement of the center's charter, "is ethnographic approaches to performance, representation, visual culture, aesthetics, affect, space, and publics. Our principal attention is geared towards how people perform, produce, and project cultural forms through verbal, visual, musical, kinesthetic, material, and dramatic means."[13] I can live with that, and so, I believe, could most of the faculty and students who passed through our Folklore Program.

Acknowledgments

I would like to thank Olivia Solis, John Wheat, and especially Beverly Stoeltje for help in the research and writing of this article; Guha Shankar for locating the photograph of Américo Paredes, Barbara Kirshenblatt-Gimblett, and me in the

American Folklife Center collection; and Carl Fleischhauer for granting permission to include the photograph in this article, nailing down the precise date, and providing a high-resolution copy for publication.

Notes

1. On the early history of the Texas Folklore Society, see Abernethy (1992).
2. Américo Paredes to Clarence Cline, April 19, 1963. Américo Paredes Papers, Nettie Lee Benson Library, University of Texas, Austin (hereafter cited as Paredes Papers).
3. Memorandum from J. A. Burdine to Mody C. Boatright, Richard N. Adams, William H. Goetzmann, Américo Paredes, Chester V. Kielman, December 4, 1964. Paredes Papers.
4. Cover page, National Endowment for the Humanities application, October 6, 1966. Mody Coggin Boatright Papers, Briscoe Center for American History, University of Texas, Austin (hereafter cited as Boatright Papers).
5. Mody Boatright to Tristram P. Coffin, April 13, 1964. Boatright Papers.
6. Saunders Redding to Mody C. Boatright, January 3, 1967. Boatright Papers.
7. James E. Boggs to Roger D. Abrahams, April 24, 1967. Boatright Papers.
8. Américo Paredes to John Silber, December 20, 1967. Paredes Papers.
9. Institutional Request for PhD and MA Degrees in Folklore: A New Program at the University of Texas at Austin, Paredes Papers.
10. Roger D. Abrahams, Richard Bauman, Américo Paredes to Committee on Graduate Program Policy, December 19, 1969. Paredes Papers.
11. W. Gordon Whaley to Richard Bauman, November 11, 1970. Paredes Papers.
12. For more detail, see Sawin (1985).
13. University of Texas at Austin, Américo Paredes Center for Cultural Studies, https://liberalarts.utexas.edu/culturalstudies. Accessed December 28, 2017.

References

Abernethy, Francis Edward. 1992. *The Texas Folklore Society, 1909–1943*. Publications of the Texas Folklore Society 51. Denton: University of North Texas Press.

———. 1994. *The Texas Folklore Society, 1943–1971*. Publications of the Texas Folklore Society 54. Denton: University of North Texas Press.

Abrahams, Roger D. 1983. *The Man-of-Words in the West Indies: Performance and the Emergence of Creole Culture*. Baltimore: Johns Hopkins University Press.

Bauman, Richard. 2014. "Foreword." In *Soundscapes from the Americas: Ethnomusicological Essays on the Power, Poetics, and Ontology of Performance*, edited by Donna A. Buchanan, xiii–xiv. Farnham, UK: Ashgate.

———. 2018. "Others' Words, Others' Voices: The Making of a Linguistic Anthropologist." *Annual Review of Anthropology* 47: 1–16.

Boatright, Mody C. 1973. *Mody Boatright, Folklorist*. Edited by Ernest B. Speck. Austin: University of Texas Press.

López Morín, José R. 2006. *The Legacy of Américo Paredes*. College Station: Texas A&M University Press.

McNutt, James. 1982. "Beyond Regionalism: Texas Folklorists and the Emergence of a Post-regional Consciousness." PhD diss., University of Texas, Austin.
Muthukumaraswamy, M. D. 2002. *Voicing Folklore: Careers, Concerns and Issues*. Chennai, India: National Folklore Support Center.
Paredes, Américo. 1958. *"With His Pistol in His Hand": A Border Ballad and Its Hero*. Austin: University of Texas Press.
———. 1959. "The University of Texas Folklore Archive." *Folklore and Folk Music Archivist* 2, no. 3: 1, 4.
———. 1972. "Foreword." In *Toward New Perspectives in Folklore*, edited by Américo Paredes and Richard Bauman, iii–iv. Austin: University of Texas Press.
———. 1993. *Folklore and Culture on the Texas-Mexican Border*. Edited and with an introduction by Richard Bauman. Austin: University of Texas Press for the Center for Mexican American Studies.
Paredes, Américo, and Richard Bauman, eds. 1972. *Toward New Perspectives in Folklore*. Austin: University of Texas Press.
Saldívar, Ramón. 2006. *The Borderlands of Culture: Américo Paredes and the Transnational Imaginary*. Durham, NC: Duke University Press.
Sawin, Patricia. 1985. "MA and PhD Programs in Folklore at the University of Texas at Austin." *Folklore Forum* 18, no. 1: 69–76.
Speck, Ernest B. 2010. "Boatright, Mody Coggin." *Handbook of Texas Online*. Texas State Historical Association. http://www.tshaonline.org/handbook/online/articles/fbo01.
Wallace, Anthony F. C. 1970. *Culture and Personality*. 2nd ed. New York: Random House.
Zumwalt, Rosemary Lévy. 2017. "'Here Is Our Man': Dundes Discovered, the Development of the Folklore Program at the University of California, Berkeley." *Journal of American Folklore* 130, no. 515: 3–33.

RICHARD BAUMAN is Distinguished Professor Emeritus of Folklore and Anthropology at Indiana University, Bloomington. He is author of *Verbal Art as Performance* and *A World of Other's Words: Cross-Cultural Perspectives on Intertextuality*.

12 Memorial University's Folklore Program

Outsiders and Insiders

Lynne S. McNeill

> I ended up becoming the Head of the Folklore Department, full professor, with a staff of zero. I did have a part-time secretary to type up questionnaires on proverbs and so on, and that's how the Folklore Department started, primarily for the English Department to get rid of us.
>
> —Herbert Halpert

I BEGIN THIS history of the folklore program at Memorial University of Newfoundland (MUN) by expressing my indebtedness to Jeff A. Webb, professor of history at MUN, who has done much of my work for me. When I set out to write about the formation of the folklore program, I discovered that someone else had already done it, and quite recently, too. In his substantial book *Observing the Outports* (2016), Webb gives a comprehensive description of the history and development of Memorial's folklore program and the Folklore and Language Archives, from their inception through the 1980s. Given that the work of description and documentation has largely been handled by another, my goal here is not only to share that history but to expand beyond it, to describe something of its texture by drawing out several larger themes from the story of one of the most successful folklore programs in North America. As this essay will illustrate, the strength of MUN's folklore program rests on several foundations, many of which have grown from the unique—and sometimes challenging—tension between insiders and outsiders (or, to put it colloquially, between Newfoundlanders and come-from-aways).

Newfoundland, a small island on the east coast of Canada, was the first part of North America discovered by Europeans. It joined Canada, along with its continental counterpart Labrador, in 1949, having previously existed as a self-governing British colony. The university in St. John's, on the east coast of the

Avalon Peninsula, opened in 1925 as a teachers' college and began offering arts and science degrees in 1949.

While the university as a whole had been interested in Newfoundland culture from the start, one of the first people to push for a folklore program was the first university librarian, Sadie Organ. In the late 1950s, Organ corresponded with Seamus Delargy of the Irish Folklore Commission, hoping to encourage him or one of his assistants to visit the province to "engage in the work of rescuing our folklore from oblivion" (Webb 2016, 146). Her efforts fell through, but in 1962, Edgar Ronald Seary and George Story of the English Department (and, for Story, of eventual *Dictionary of Newfoundland English* fame [Story, Kirwin, and Widdowson 1982]), invited US folklorist Herbert Halpert, who they had heard was looking for a position, to come to MUN and add his folkloristic expertise to their ongoing linguistic and dialectical research.

Halpert turned the job down. He had visited Newfoundland once before, as a member of the US Armed Forces, in winter. Newfoundland in winter, especially on the military bases in Stephenville and Gander, seemed remote and unappealing, despite Halpert's burgeoning folkloristic inquiry into the local culture and stories, which led the Newfoundlanders on the base to conclude that Halpert was "obviously unlike the usual Yankee."[1] After some persuading (specifically, an offer to fund the move of his 10,000-volume personal library), Halpert and his wife, Violetta, or "Letty," accepted the offer, though their journey to the farthest eastern point of North America is one that Halpert described with humorous dismay: "All right, so our books got packed and got into . . . a fine sturdy car, and oh Lord it was wonderful that it was sturdy. We drove to Sydney, found about getting on the ferry and crossed, a miserable crossing, night, and then early in the morning, Port-aux-Basques looming up before, and it was a grey day, and my wife is a very brave person, but she said, 'let's go back.'"[2] Indeed, a hearty soul, Letty was one of the first women to enlist in the US Navy during the war, and she made the rank of lieutenant before being honorably discharged in 1951. She was also a folklorist, trained by Stith Thompson, and it was she who designed the format of the MUN Folklore and Language Archives.

Halpert's eventual decision to relocate was surely motivated by the difficulty he had had in securing work as a folklorist in the United States. He spent time in Kentucky at Murray State College, where he began his lifelong emphasis on turning students into collectors. He went from Kentucky to Blackburn College in Illinois, where he served as dean of English—a job that he said left him feeling "deaned to death by deanish piddlings" (Webb 2016, 153). He then took a visiting position at the University of Arkansas, at which point Letty began writing letters—more than a hundred of them—to find him a permanent job. Her efforts resulted in a one-year appointment as a visiting professor in New Paltz, New York. In his own descriptions of his struggle to find a position as a folklorist, Halpert actively and proudly displays his disdain for most administrators. He describes one university president as "a tall, handsome idiot," and later noted in general that "I have a long history of disliking [university] presidents."[3] This is noteworthy, given his glowing praise, described below, of MUN's upper administration.

When he finally accepted the job offer at MUN, it was because the English Department had expressed an interest in creating a new folklore program. As Halpert explained, "Memorial University was both new and small, but it was *flexible*. It was run by men who had no hesitation about doing things for the first time in English-speaking Canada. Introducing Folklore as a university subject is one example. . . . Besides daring to try new ventures, a series of university administrators supported fully all individuals who showed genuine interest in studying any aspect of the Newfoundland environment, physical or human" (Webb 2016, 158). The regional focus of the new program and of the university as a whole was significant to the successful establishment of the folklore program. University administrators, most of whom were native Newfoundlanders, saw immediate value in the documentation and preservation of their local culture, and Halpert, driven by his early work with questionnaires and survey cards used by his students, set to work. Halpert's early collaborations with George Story and John Widdowson led to fruitful work and publications such as *Christmas Mumming in Newfoundland* (1969). While Halpert was initially limited to the creation of eight folklore classes (because he was the only folklorist available to teach them), two additional folklore instructors were brought in in 1967: A. E. Green and Richard Buehler (editor of *Abstracts of Folklore Studies*) to teach Folk Song and American Folklore, respectively.

The Department of Folklore was officially created in 1968 and began with four MA students and two PhD students. Being a graduate student in the folklore program meant both collecting Newfoundland folklore and cataloging the information that Halpert and Widdowson had gathered. Students were regularly called on to fill out survey cards both with their own folklore and folklore they collected from others. Halpert was a strong proponent of survey cards as a way to encourage not only student fieldwork but also successful interactions with informants. He believed that full sheets of paper were too demanding—informants would feel as though they needed to write formally. In his own words, "I found that cards were particularly effective in Newfoundland because a lot of Newfoundlanders when they're faced with a blank sheet of paper remember what their English teacher told them. . . . I've told people, write the way you heard it and don't worry about the English. Just in your own language."[4]

In 1968, Halpert hired Neil V. Rosenberg, a scholar of folk music and a musician himself, who formally established the MUN Folklore and Language Archives, better known as MUNFLA. MUNFLA soon became a well-recognized

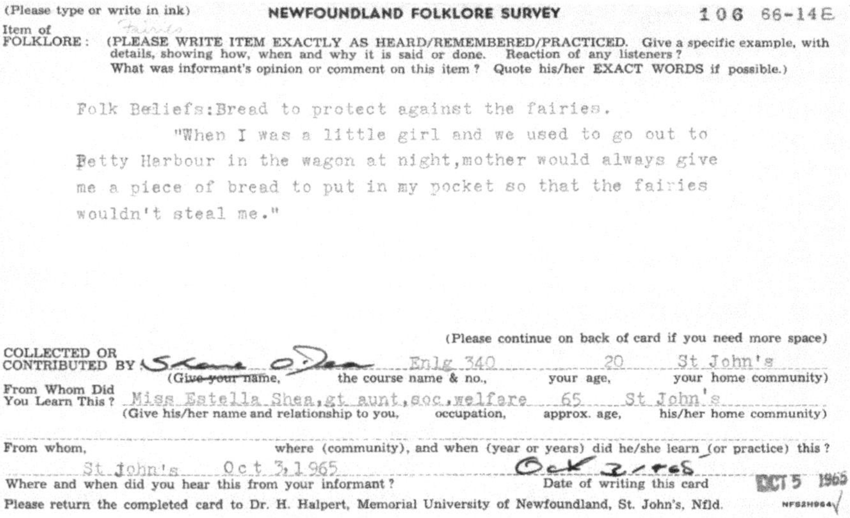

(Please type or write in ink) **NEWFOUNDLAND FOLKLORE SURVEY** 106 66-14E

Item of
FOLKLORE: Fairies (PLEASE WRITE ITEM EXACTLY AS HEARD/REMEMBERED/PRACTICED. Give a specific example, with details, showing how, when and why it is said or done. Reaction of any listeners? What was informant's opinion or comment on this item? Quote his/her EXACT WORDS if possible.)

Folk Beliefs:Bread to protect against the fairies.
"When I was a little girl and we used to go out to Petty Harbour in the wagon at night,mother would always give me a piece of bread to put in my pocket so that the fairies wouldn't steal me."

(Please continue on back of card if you need more space)

COLLECTED OR CONTRIBUTED BY Shane O'Dea Enlg 340 20 St John's
(Give your name, the course name & no., your age, your home community)

From Whom Did You Learn This? Miss Estella Shea,gt aunt,soc.welfare 65 St John's
(Give his/her name and relationship to you, occupation, approx. age, his/her home community)

From whom, where (community), and when (year or years) did he/she learn (or practice) this?

St John's Oct 3,1965 Oct 3/1965
Where and when did you hear this from your informant? Date of writing this card OCT 5 1965

Please return the completed card to Dr. H. Halpert, Memorial University of Newfoundland, St. John's, Nfld. NFS2H964

Fig. 12.1. A survey card from the MUN Folklore and Language Archives, collected in 1965 by Shane O'Dea, now professor emeritus, Department of English, Memorial University of Newfoundland. MUNFLA FSC 66-014E 106. Courtesy of MUNFLA and Shane O'Dea.

folklore archive, being chosen as the repository for MacEdward Leach's collection of Atlantic Canadian folk music and Carole Carpenter's collection of interviews with Canadian folklorists.

Halpert was fifty-seven years old when the Department of Folklore and MUNFLA were formed. He brought in a number of additional faculty members: David Hufford, Richard Tallman, Larry Small, and Wilfred Wareham. The latter two were rural Newfoundlanders, trained as folklorists at MUN. When Hufford left in 1974, the department hired Peter Narváez, another folk musician and another student of Richard Dorson's. Later hires included Philip Hiscock, Kenneth Goldstein, Gerald Pocius, Martin Lovelace, Gerald Thomas, David Buchan, and Paul Smith. Diane Goldstein, hired in 1986, was the first woman faculty member in the Folklore Department, and it would be nine years before another woman, Diane Tye, was hired. Many of the second generation of folklorists at MUN have retired or are now retiring, but according to one faculty member's estimation, there were at one time thirteen folklorists working together at MUN.

Today, MUN's folklore program is thriving, with nine faculty members on the St. John's campus. Current faculty include Holly Everett, Diane Tye, Cory Thorne, Harris Berger, Jillian Gould, Mariya Lesiv, Sarah Gordon, Daniel Peretti, and Kelley Totten. Cognate faculty, at the Grenfell campus across the island in Corner Brooke, include John Bodner and Doreen Klassen. Since 1993, the Folklore

Department, through Pocius's efforts, has offered an English Cultural Landscape Program at its Harlow-based sister campus in England. The program has been offered fifteen times and has provided students with hands-on experience with vernacular architecture and cultural landscape studies. This focus on practical experience is also found in the department's field school, developed in 2012 in part to reestablish the early connections between the folklore program and local communities and to counteract the developing trend of current students not being comfortable talking to people they do not already know. This renewed focus on interacting with the folk is something Halpert himself initially emphasized. He described himself as anti-theory, unless "the theory comes from the material itself": "The trouble is if you start with a theory then you're going to chop off anything that doesn't fit the theory and push it aside, put it under the rug, and it'll be the kind of material that probably has the most value."[5]

The department accepts about a dozen graduate students each year and, at any given time, has about forty to fifty active students in varying stages of their degree programs, not counting undergraduates. It is, overall, hard to identify a bad time to have been or to be a folklorist at Memorial University of Newfoundland.

I can attest to this experience myself, having attended the program from 2002 to 2005. When I was finishing my MA at Utah State University and applying to PhD programs, I arranged to meet with students from various folklore departments at that year's American Folklore Society meeting. I met with a young Canadian man who was several years into a PhD at Memorial, and we had a pleasant conversation about the program. At the end of our talk, however, he said—mysteriously, it seemed to me—"You know, they won't think you're special because you're American." It had not, I can say honestly, occurred to me that they would think I was special because I was American, and I was mildly offended at the suggestion. The fact that Memorial University of Newfoundland was in another country, making me an international student were I to choose to attend, had not crossed my mind. This, of course, was the problem.

As Laurel Doucette, in a scathing critique of folklore studies in Canada in general and at Memorial in particular, has noted, "Because they have come into a country where the majority of citizens are the same colour as themselves and speak the same language, foreign academics frequently do not realize that we [Canadians] perceive ourselves as different and may resent their intrusion into our culture and their appropriation of its study" (1993, 127). Over the following four years that I spent at MUN, I would slowly become aware of an undercurrent of mild tension over the issue of insiders and outsiders: Canadians and Americans, Canadians and British, and Canadians and Newfoundlanders themselves, who often do not strongly identify as Canadian and refer to anyone from off the island as "come-from-aways." The question of insiders and outsiders is central to both the department's struggles and its successes.

MUN's folklore program was, of course, founded by an American and rapidly populated by other US and British faculty members. This was probably because there were few trained anglophone Canadian folklorists at the time, but it created a strain within a program so clearly focused on regional Newfoundland studies, especially as the graduate student pipelines from the US programs that MUN's faculty had attended were established. Memorial became perceived as something of an outpost or embassy of either the British or the American Folklore Societies. As Doucette elaborates, "The continual separation of the people studied from the people doing the studying, creating an alienation of the discipline from the local reality, is particularly visible in Newfoundland, the site of the country's only English language degree program in Folklore Studies" (1993, 127).

Halpert's nationality was not the only factor in determining whose perspectives were being promoted or overlooked in MUN's folklore program; until Diane Goldstein's arrival in 1986, the faculty was a veritable boys' club, and several faculty members noted in interviews that Halpert sometimes alienated women. Doucette describes the sentiments of a group of women scholars who convened to support one another's work: "Among Canadian born participants in particular, the process has revealed a shared sense of oppression in relation to the discipline of folklore itself, a feeling that goes beyond the particular frustrations and affronts experienced within institutions of work or study" (1993, 121). She notes further, "When any department is made up chiefly of scholars with personal and professional ties elsewhere, who perceive the centers of intellectual activity to be elsewhere, and who utilize theoretical paradigms developed elsewhere, there can be little hope of the development of intellectual approaches which will reflect the realities of life as it is lived by local people" (127).

Not everyone agreed with Doucette's description of the situation at Memorial, and two demonstrable points contradict her assessment. First, there have always been native Newfoundlanders at Memorial University on the faculty and especially among students (and it was these local students doing much of the collecting from their own communities). Second, Doucette's approach denies the valid research conducted by many students and faculty members—all over North America, not just in Newfoundland—whose interests lie outside their own home culture. Halpert may have been American, and Widdowson may have been British, but, as Goldstein puts it: "Those two scholars probably did more fieldwork than any other two human beings in Newfoundland."[6]

Halpert's identity as an American in Newfoundland is an interesting one. In his own writing and lecturing, he moves easily between identifying himself as an insider and an outsider. In a 1969 lecture about the Department of Folklore, he opens with a nice piece of metafolklore, making a joke about Newfie jokes, and takes an insider stance against those who might tell them: "We only collect Newfie jokes from Newfoundlanders. What's black and blue and black

Fig. 12.2. Herbert Halpert recording a folktale from James L. Conklin, New York, 1946. Photograph by Violetta M. Halpert.

and blue and floating in the harbor? The first Torontonian that tells a Newfie joke in St. John's."[7] At other times, however, he plays up the fact that he came to Newfoundland from away, observing, for example, that locals who would clam up in his presence would often open up to other faculty members. Of course, by the end of his career, Halpert had been living and working in Newfoundland for longer than some of his students had been alive; whether that qualifies him to adopt an emic perspective on the culture is a determination best left to Newfoundlanders themselves.

But the question of transregional or nonregional interest in folkloristics is an important one, and the issue is at the heart of the shifting contemporary identities of many current folklore programs. Halpert may have been regionally focused and anti-theory, but Hiscock explains that embedded local research is not what scholars are expected to produce these days. "Our department has become less a department of Newfoundland studies, and there's push and pull on that. The pull is that the university is judging tenure on professors' abilities to work with other professors in other countries, to give papers at international conferences, and to be published in all the big journals, and the big journals have moved from being documentary or descriptive, over 40 years or so, to being much more interested in theory or abstraction. So any regional and celebratory folklore work becomes demeaned in the profession as a whole."[8]

Hiscock points out that in programs such as MUN's, where the undergraduate student body is almost entirely local, the move away from celebratory regional studies can alienate students, making the work less relevant to their lives. Many students now expect to learn about exotic, unfamiliar cultures in their folklore classes rather than their own recognizable cultural milieu, despite the discipline having more roots in emic studies than in etic studies. Possibly the biggest change in MUN's departmental culture in the last several decades has been this slow shift away from regional studies of Newfoundland culture. Plenty of that still takes place, to be sure, especially through the field schools, but as Hiscock explains, it is likely unsustainable. He used the example of replacing Martin Lovelace, a British scholar who had conducted extensive narrative and ballad research in Newfoundland and who was retiring that year: "When he retires, and we go to the dean to replace him, the dean will say 'okay, what kind of person do you want,' and the department won't say 'we want someone who has a specialty in Newfoundland,' we'll ask for a ballad scholar or a folktale scholar. Someone whose experiences were shaped elsewhere will get that job. And why should they start doing Newfoundland work when they've just showed up in Newfoundland?"[9]

Why indeed? Halpert did, because that was both his own interest and the driving interest of the administration that hired him. But today, especially with the advent of the internet and the more globalized study of new communications media, regional hires make less sense. Folklore is such a broad field of study that most faculty positions are genre-based rather than culture-based, and yet all the MUN faculty members with whom I have spoken cited the Folklore Department's connection to the local community as a source of its resilience. "MUN survived and thrived," Hiscock says, "because it really was linked to a sense of *celebration* in the overall community." He continues, describing how local folk performers valued the folklore program's work: "They were a backstop to everything we did. And the University had an ideology right at the top in that period of developing Newfoundland studies, and we were seen as the frontrunners in that. We were the avant-garde."[10] Goldstein sums it up succinctly: "Programs that are in places with a strong regional identity are the most secure." Her comments mirror Hiscock's with regard to the community's use of the archive's holdings: "People can see themselves in a local folklore program."[11] She described how community members would regularly call, trying to remember the words to their grandfather's favorite song or to get advice with supernatural issues. MUNFLA is not just a collection of information about the community; it truly belongs to the community.

Paul Smith brought up the same idea in an anecdote about his time as department head:

> I went to a heads of folklore programs meeting at the American Folklife Center, and I thought, there's something wrong here, because all I was doing was listening to people complain about the treatment of them and their programs, however large or small they were within the university context. It took me until about Thursday afternoon to work out what the difference was: it was the way people in Newfoundland think about us. In the university as well. You can walk around here and there'll be a sign in a bar window saying "folk Music, Thursday night." People don't snigger, it's there. . . . So you don't always have to explain what the hell folklore is.[12]

As Smith put it, "The university saw us as something that was very unique. If you wanted to say, what's special about Memorial, you'd say, the Marine Institute and the Folklore Program. University Presidents used to trot that out all the time."[13]

The idea of people not "sniggering," or "sneering," as Halpert put it in one interview, is important. As Halpert often noted, the university administration, typically made up of native Newfoundlanders, highly valued the program. He explained, "They backed us all the way when other . . . department budgets were being cut. By some accident we would get ours increased. They supported our activities when we had some graduate students who had papers that were accepted for the American Folklore Society. They were given travel [funds]. I had spent my life not getting travel when I was at any number of different institutions, or half the fare if you go by bus or something like that. Here students, for a whole glorious period, could get to the meetings."[14]

Will a slow reorientation away from regional studies affect the folklore program at Memorial University of Newfoundland? That remains to be seen. When I called this trend a hazard during my interview with Goldstein, she reframed it as a challenge. A notable strength of the department, touched on by all the faculty members I spoke with, is its commitment to a comprehensive approach to folklore studies, and that has not changed. Classes are offered on almost every major genre of the field, and the diverse faculty does not hold to a single theoretical approach. Students come away with a sense of the field at large, not simply an in-depth understanding of their own thesis topics. This commitment to the field of folklore studies in all its expansive manifestations surely bodes well for the future.

Notes

1. Herbert Halpert, "The Early Years of the Folklore Department," November 10, 1982, St. Johns, Newfoundland, transcript of talk recorded by Janet McNaughton. MUNFLA F6073/C5999/Accession Number 82-286.

2. Ibid.

3. Ibid.
4. Ibid.
5. Ibid.
6. Diane Goldstein, interview with the author, May 22, 2016.
7. Herbert Halpert, talk given at Memorial University of Newfoundland, St. John's, June 1969. Audio recording by Neil V. Rosenberg. MUNFLA F11923/C2012/CD-F2400-Copy/Accession Number 74-233_F1932.
8. Philip Hiscock, interview with the author, February 2016.
9. Ibid.
10. Ibid.
11. Goldstein 2016.
12. Paul Smith, interview with the author, May 2016.
13. Smith 2016.
14. Halpert 1982.

References

Doucette, Laurel. 1993. "Voices Not Our Own." *Canadian Folklore Canadien* 15, no. 2: 119–37.

Halpert, Herbert, and G. M. Story, eds. 1969. *Christmas Mumming in Newfoundland: Essays in Anthropology, Folklore, and History.* Toronto: University of Toronto Press.

Story, G. M., W. J. Kirwin, and J. D. A. Widdowson, eds. 1982. *Dictionary of Newfoundland English*. Toronto: University of Toronto Press.

Webb, Jeff A. 2016. *Observing the Outports: Describing Newfoundland Culture, 1950–1980.* Toronto: University of Toronto Press.

LYNNE S. McNEILL is Associate Professor of Folklore and Chair of the Folklore Program in the English Department at Utah State University. She is author of *Folklore Rules* and editor (with Trevor J. Blank) of *Slender Man Is Coming.*

13 A Century of Folklore Research and Teaching at Western Kentucky

Michael Ann Williams

In 1917 Gordon Wilson, a teacher at Western Kentucky State Normal School, announced in his diary his intent to pursue the study of folklore. "Ever since I first began to teach Vergil, January, 1912, I have been interested in local folk-lore," Wilson noted. While his interest may have been piqued by the teaching of the classics, his research was firmly rooted in collecting lore from his own community. With work on his "Purchase Stories" well under way, Wilson wrote, "I already have in the book over 175 'cuss-words' and over 100 well-known superstitions in my home neighborhood. When I go to Calloway County next week I hope to get a great deal of help on my collection from Quint, Mother, and Ivan" (Harrison 1984, 124–26). With this modest diary entry, Wilson established a century-long legacy of folklore scholarship and teaching at Western Kentucky.[1]

The same year as Wilson's earnest turn to studying local folklore in the far western Jackson Purchase region of Kentucky, Englishman Cecil Sharp, at the urging of Olive Dame Campbell, toured through eastern Kentucky collecting English ballads. While the work of Sharp and Campbell, inspired in part by the creation of the mountain settlement schools, is far better known, the establishment of the academic study of folklore in Kentucky developed to a large extent independently. In 1912, a cohort of scholars, mostly located in central Kentucky, came together to form the Kentucky branch of the American Folklore Society. Only three states—Missouri, Texas, and North Carolina—preceded Kentucky in forming statewide folklore societies (Wilgus 1957a, 394). A few months after the founding of the Kentucky society, the *Journal of American Folklore* noted:

> Kentucky is rich in folk-lore material. Some work has been done of late in this State, as is shown by the recently published results of investigations by Dr. H. G. Shearin of Transylvania University, and by Professor E. C. Perrow of the University of Louisville, but much remains to be done. Professor Perrow and Dr. Shearin have been very successful in collecting folk-songs, some of them old-country ballads. Since the recent organization of the Kentucky Folk-Lore Society, fresh impulse has been given to such work; and a number of people are now seeking one or another kind of folk-lore material in this State. (Thomas 1913, 90)[2]

Perrow, a former student of George Lyman Kittredge at Harvard, published a large collection of folk songs in the *Journal of American Folklore* from 1912 to 1915. Shearin, the new president of the Kentucky society, had already published *A Syllabus of Kentucky Folk Songs* in 1911 in collaboration with Josiah H. Combs. Only Combs provided a direct link to the settlement school movement. His study at the Hindman Settlement School led to his enrollment at Transylvania College and his subsequent work with Shearin. Eventually Combs would earn his doctorate at the Sorbonne, where he would write his thesis on folk songs of the United States (Wilgus 1956, 1957b; Clarke and Clarke 1974, 11–16).

Gordon Wilson came to folklore too late to be part of this early burgeoning of Kentucky folklore research that began in the years prior to the First World War. By 1920, several of the key scholars had left the state or passed away, and membership in the Kentucky Folklore Society dwindled to seven. In 1922, Wilson joined the society and subsequently played a leadership role for almost half a century. During the 1920s, Wilson also pursued doctoral work in English, becoming one of Stith Thompson's earliest folklore students at Indiana University (see Harrah-Johnson, this volume, for Thompson's role in establishing the folklore program at Indiana).[3] Thompson was also a Kentuckian by birth, and, while his research was international in scope, he maintained close ties to the commonwealth and was a frequent visitor and speaker at the Kentucky Folklore Society throughout his life.[4]

Wilson, unlike his mentor, always focused on Kentucky lore, although his interests in the state expanded from the far western "Purchase" to the Pennyrile region of south-central Kentucky, where the Western Kentucky State Normal School was located. Wilson pursued the study of local dialect as well as the folkways and "human ecology" of the Mammoth Cave area. In the mid-1930s, Wilson began to publish a column, "Tid-Bits of Kentucky Folklore," which ran in almost one hundred local newspapers. Throughout his life, he championed the study of the breadth of Kentucky folklore and not just Appalachia. The 1931 minute book of the Kentucky Folklore Society notes that Wilson "urged the young men and women of the state to accept the challenge offered by various sections of Kentucky, the Pennyrile, the Purchase, and the Bluegrass regions all being practically untouched in the field of collecting folklore."[5]

In 1928, Wilson became head of the English Department at Western Kentucky, a position he held until 1959. From this place of relative power, Wilson had the freedom to incorporate folklore into the curriculum, pursue his own folklore research, and ultimately lay the foundation for the development of a folklore program. Unfortunately, the decades of the 1930s and 1940s were not conducive to the expansion of faculty, and it was not until 1950 that Wilson was able to hire another specialist in folklore. That individual was a young ballad scholar finishing his doctorate at the Ohio State University. D. K. Wilgus's doctoral dissertation,

Fig. 13.1. Gordon Wilson as a young man, ca. 1935. Photograph courtesy of the Western Kentucky University Archives.

published as *Anglo-American Folksong Scholarship since 1898* (1959), became a landmark work in the discipline.

At midcentury, Kentucky once again became a powerhouse in academic folklore with three state universities leading the way. In 1949, William Hugh Jansen, who received his PhD in English and folklore at Indiana University, obtained a position in the Department of English at the University of Kentucky, where he would spend the next thirty years. Also in the late 1940s, Herbert Halpert, who had earned an MA in anthropology at Columbia University and a PhD in English at Indiana University, became a professor and head of the English Department at Murray State College in far western Kentucky. In 1955, Halpert was elected president of the American Folklore Society, the only Kentucky resident to serve in this role during the twentieth century.

With Wilgus, Jansen, and Halpert in the mix, the Kentucky Folklore Society grew in both size and prominence. Starting in 1951, the society began to meet twice a year, and in 1955, the *Kentucky Folklore Record* was established with

Wilgus as editor. At the same time, Wilson served as honorary president, Halpert as president, and Jansen as vice president. While academics took a firm lead in the society, membership included students and amateurs. As editor of the *Kentucky Folklore Record*, Wilgus struggled to find a balance between professional and amateur:

> One of the greatest weaknesses of regional journals has been their almost exclusive appeal to the learned, professional folklorist. Whatever their value as a means of communication between professional scholars, they have not succeeded in gaining the support of the average person interested in folklore, particularly the lore of his native region. At the other extreme is the attempt to gain popular support by watering down material—"popularizing" in the worst sense, dealing in fakelore instead of folklore.
>
> We believe that there is a middle way, that the amateur and the professional can find common ground, that there is a place in Kentucky for a folklore magazine that is popular without being cute or folksy, and scholarly without the trappings of erudition.[6]

The efforts for inclusivity paid off in the 1950s, as membership in the society grew to over three hundred. Western Kentucky had a folklore club, and the University of Kentucky sponsored a folk festival. The society also catered to public school teachers. In 1953, decades before "folklore and education" became a recognized specialty, the Kentucky Folklore Society sponsored a regional meeting of the American Folklore Society at Murray State College on the topic of "Folklore in the School." Attendees came from Ohio, Indiana, Illinois, and Tennessee, as well as Kentucky, to discuss how teachers could use folklore in the classroom.[7]

Along with editing the statewide folklore journal, Wilgus also worked formally to establish a folklore archive. While the early material consisted largely of work collected by Wilson and his students, Wilgus took credit for the formal founding of the archive:

> The Western Kentucky Folklore Archive is basically a manuscript collection brought together by D. K. Wilgus and housed in Cherry Hall at Western Kentucky State College. The archive was established in 1953 with a small nucleus of material collected by the students in the folklore classes of Gordon Wilson. The collection has grown through student contributions, field collection by its director, and deposits such as the manuscript collection of Josiah H. Combs and the songs collected by Herbert Halpert and his students at Murray State College. Though the materials represent a wide geographical area, the archive is important primarily as one of the two significant repositories of the collected folklore of western Kentucky. (Wilgus 1958, 3)

In 1971, the archive was transferred to the Helms-Craven Library, where it was renamed the Folklore, Folklife, and Oral History Archives. Today it is still administered by the professional library staff. Along with Wilgus's materials

Fig. 13.2. D. K. Wilgus, ca. 1955. Photograph courtesy of the Western Kentucky University Archives.

(some of which he moved to the University of California, Los Angeles) and the collections of Wilson, the archives include the papers of folklore professor Lynwood Montell and Sarah Gertrude Knott, founder and director of the National Folk Festival.[8]

Unfortunately, the heady days of academic folklore in Kentucky in the 1950s did not result immediately in the establishment of a graduate program in folklore in the commonwealth, though two prominent Kentucky folklorists would go on to help establish programs elsewhere. In the 1960s, Halpert founded a doctoral program in folklore at Memorial University in Newfoundland, Canada, and

Wilgus would play a key role in establishing graduate education in folklore at UCLA (see chapters by McNeill and Jones, this volume). Shortly before Wilgus left for California, he had begun to despair of the future of folklore in Kentucky. In 1962, membership in the Kentucky Folklore Society had dropped to about 185, and Wilgus bemoaned the loss of several key academic positions, expressing a sentiment still familiar to contemporary folklorists: "The fact that the college classrooms and educational organizations have been the greatest sources of members is indicative of another problem. An academic folklorist belongs necessarily to another discipline, and his replacement on a college faculty is chosen in terms of the OTHER discipline." Wilgus concluded, "One of the most important immediate tasks of the [Kentucky Folklore] Society is to contribute to the establishment of folklore study as a recognized discipline in all of the institutions of higher learning in the commonwealth" (1962, 6). The following year, Wilgus departed for UCLA.

The retired Wilson must have been sorely disappointed in losing his heir after more than three decades of folklore curriculum building in the English Department; however, working behind the scenes, he continued to pursue his dream. In 1964, Kenneth Clarke, who wrote his dissertation at Indiana University on folktales in West Africa, became part of the faculty at Western Kentucky. Clarke later recalled a bond he shared with the retired Wilson: "One of our first points of common interest was our discovery that our respective experiences as graduate students under Stith Thompson's direction had spanned our old professor's graduate faculty career: Gordon Wilson was among the first; I was among the last to have that privilege" (K. Clarke 1976, 11–12). Clarke would subsequently be joined by his wife, Mary Washington Clarke, who earned her PhD at the University of Pennsylvania, with her dissertation titled "The Folklore of the Cumberlands as Reflected in the Writings of Jesse Stuart" (M. Clarke 1960). Mary Clarke, the first woman folklorist hired at what was now called Western Kentucky University (WKU), in 1969 became the first recipient of the newly created University Award in Research and Creativity (Harrison 1987, 193).

That same year, Wilson helped summon back to WKU a former student now teaching at Campbellsville College. Monroe County native Montell had come under the spell of folklore while enrolled in a course taught by Wilgus. On finishing his BA, Montell, on the advice of Wilgus, enrolled in the folklore doctoral program at Indiana University. Montell completed his dissertation on an African American community in the Cumberlands of Kentucky, subsequently published as *The Saga of Coe Ridge* (1971), a pioneering work of oral history and folklore. Montell recalled that on his first day back at Western Kentucky, he encountered the retired Wilson on campus. Wilson reportedly exclaimed: "Lynwood, I can't tell you how many years I have been thinking about the fact that we need to have you here" (Puglia 2010, 20–21).[9]

By 1971, a proposal had been developed to create a master's degree in folk studies at WKU, and Richard M. Dorson, head of the Folklore Institute at Indiana University, was invited to visit campus to conduct an assessment. On October 18, Dorson wrote a glowing three-page endorsement, noting both the "luster of the tradition in folklore studies" represented by Wilson and Wilgus and the "impressive concentration of faculty" exceeded only by the doctoral programs at Indiana, the University of Pennsylvania, the University of Texas, and UCLA (Dorson 1971). With the subsequent hiring of Camilla Collins, an Indiana-trained folklorist who wrote her dissertation on occupational lore, the core faculty of a new Center for Intercultural Studies was established with Montell as center director. In 1972, the MA program was created. Following the trend established by Wilson, most of the folklore courses were initially based in the English Department, but other courses were cross-listed with anthropology (K. Clarke 1973, 47–48). The graduate program in Folk Studies awarded the first degree to David Sutherland in 1973 (Clarke and Clarke 1974, 93). Within two years, the program already had at least twenty students writing theses (Folk Studies Society 1974).

While doctoral education in folklore thrived during the 1970s at Indiana University, the University of Pennsylvania, and the University of Texas (see chapters by Harrah-Johnson, Miller, Zumwalt, and Bauman, this volume), Western Kentucky University carved out a niche at the MA level, preparing students for subsequent doctoral study and training students for the emerging profession of public and applied folklore. In fall 1974, Camilla Collins offered the first graduate seminar in Applied Folklore (later called Public Sector Folklore and then Public Folklore). The following year, a new course was added in Museum Procedures and Preservation Techniques taught by the Kentucky Museum director Bruce MacLeish, a graduate of the Museum Studies Program at Cooperstown (a program that also, at the time, offered a degree in folklore; see Bronner, this volume). In May 1975, faculty and eighteen students from Cooperstown visited Western Kentucky University, and later that year, WKU Folk Studies graduate student Ira Kohn became a staff member at the museum. Courses added in the mid-1970s included Folk Medicine, Women's Folklife, and Folklore Conversation and Communication.[10]

The prominence of WKU in teaching public folklore was later reflected in a speech by Archie Green, whose own heroic efforts led to the passage of the American Folklife Preservation Act in 1976: "This was the first school to recognize the field we now call public sector folklore—this is, trained folklorists working for federal agencies, state agencies, local agencies, the park service, the Smithsonian, the Library of Congress, recreation departments, school boards . . . this is the school that first recognized the necessity to train people for that responsibility . . . Lyn Montell and his colleagues . . . shaped a program to give students the vision that they might combine knowledge in a very esoteric field with service to the larger community" (Green 1984, 66–67).

In 1974, Folk Studies left the English Department and moved to Gordon Wilson Hall, renamed in honor of the founder of folklore at Western Kentucky who had passed away in 1970. As part of the reorganization, the center was renamed Intercultural and Folk Studies and in 1977 changed from being a freestanding center to the Department of Folk Studies and Intercultural Studies. Mary Clarke retired in 1975, followed two years later by her husband. They were replaced by two graduates of the University of Pennsylvania's folklore and folklife program: Burt Feintuch in 1975 and Robert Teske in 1977. Also in 1977, Marilyn White joined the faculty as director of the Afro-American Studies Program and an instructor in folklore.

As the program at Western Kentucky University grew, it increasingly dominated the Kentucky Folklore Society and *Kentucky Folklore Record*. In 1975, Camilla Collins became president of the organization, and in 1978 she took over editorship of the journal. With the appearance of volume 24, number 2, the journal annexed a subtitle: *A Regional Journal of Folklore and Folklife*. The content no longer focused primarily on Kentucky and became far more cognizant of current trends in the discipline. Volume 26 in 1980 included a special double issue on public sector folklore. The newly transformed *Kentucky Folklore Record* abandoned its chatty "News and Notes" and appealed more directly to a national audience of trained folklorists and less to the interested amateur. The journal ceased publication in 1987 with volume 33, a comprehensive index. Two years later, Western Kentucky University and editor Camilla Collins adopted the *Southern Folklore Quarterly*, which had not been published in several years, renaming it *Southern Folklore*.

By the end of the 1970s, Folk Studies was a well-established MA program with thesis and nonthesis tracks as well as a separate track in historic preservation.[11] However, its status as a stand-alone department was short-lived. With dramatic statewide cuts in higher education, in 1981 budgets were slashed at WKU and a number of restructurings took place, with smaller units eliminated or combined with other departments. Rather than return to English, Folk Studies merged with Modern Languages, creating the Department of Modern Languages and Intercultural Studies, and moved into the Ivan Wilson Fine Arts Center, where the program continues to be located today (Harrison 1987, 272). Significantly, however, since the late 1970s, the faculty of the Folk Studies Program have never held joint appointments in other departments or programs. Graduate students, while they may take electives in other departments, can also complete their programs through coursework only in folklore. The Department of Modern Languages and Intercultural Studies was twice headed by folklorists. In 1992–93, Montell came out of retirement to serve as interim head of the department. And later, Larry Danielson, who had previously spent much of his career at the University of Illinois and held a folklore degree from Indiana, served as head from 1993 to 1996 and then continued as a full professor of folk studies. In 1996, the small two-person anthropology program left sociology and joined the Department of Modern Languages and Intercultural Studies, setting the stage ultimately for the creation of the Department of Folk Studies and Anthropology in 2004. Michael Ann Williams served as head from 2004 to 2017.

During the 1980s and 1990s, several faculty joined the Folk Studies Program and served the department for two to three decades of their careers. In 1986, Williams, a graduate of the University of Pennsylvania, took over a position vacated by Jay Anderson—who had, in turn, taken over from Robert Teske when he left to work for the National Endowment for the Arts—teaching courses primarily in material culture, museum procedures, and historic preservation. A couple of years later, Erika Brady was hired, followed by Johnston A. K. Njoku, both with degrees from Indiana University. Brady specialized in folk medicine and belief, while Njoku was an ethnomusicologist and Africanist. With the retirement of longtime faculty member Camilla Collins in 1999, the program hired Tim Evans, who also had a PhD from Indiana as well as considerable public folklore experience.

The twenty-first century brought the first crop of WKU folk studies graduates back to faculty positions in the program, with the hiring of Chris Antonsen in 2001 and the employment of Ann Ferrell in 2010. Both Antonsen and Ferrell held MA degrees in folk studies from WKU and PhDs from the Ohio State University. Ferrell brought specific expertise in Kentucky, with her award-winning study *Burley: Kentucky Tobacco in a New Century* (2013), winner of the Wayland D. Hand Prize from the History and Folklore Section of the American Folklore Society. In 2014, another Ohio State graduate, Kate Parker Horigan, was added to the faculty. And in 2017, Tim Frandy, who holds a PhD from the University of Wisconsin, joined the Folk Studies Program.

Another major addition to the program came in 2012 when the Kentucky Folklife Program, formerly an interagency partnership between the Kentucky Historical Society and the Kentucky Arts Council, moved to WKU. Brent Björkman—who graduated from WKU in 1997 and formerly worked for the Kentucky Folklife Program, the American Folklore Society, and the Vermont Folklife Center—returned to Bowling Green to direct the program. In 2015, Björkman also became permanent director of the Kentucky Museum (while continuing to direct the Kentucky Folklife Program), and WKU graduate Virginia Siegel was hired as a folklife specialist for the Kentucky Folklife Program. In the past few years, closer ties to both the Kentucky Folklife Program and the Kentucky Museum have further enhanced the ability of the program to provide hands-on training for graduate students in folklore.

Throughout its forty-five-year history, the graduate program at WKU has remained thoroughly engaged in the field of folklore, including the American

Folklore Society. Collins, Brady, and Björkman all served on the executive board, and in 2014–15, Williams served as president. Montell, Brady, and Williams were also elected Fellows of the American Folklore Society, with Brady serving as president in 2016. The role of WKU's Folk Studies Program in editing *Southern Folklore* had ended in 2000, when the journal ceased publication. In 2015, WKU assumed editorship of the discipline's flagship journal, the *Journal of American Folklore*, with Ann Ferrell as editor in chief.

While other folklore programs have begun to emphasize applied training in the field, Western Kentucky University has done so since the inception of its graduate program. For more than forty years, WKU has placed students in key roles in public folklore as well as in museums and historic preservation positions. Not content, however, to play the role of the vocational school, WKU has also consistently prepared students for doctoral study, either in folklore or other fields. Approximately one-third of the graduates of the program go on to further academic study, while most of the rest enter professional positions.

Although the administrative organization of Folk Studies has changed over the years, academically trained folklorists who do not hold joint appointments in other departments define the program's curriculum. The autonomy of the program continues to be its strength and makes Folk Studies less vulnerable to the type of academic politics that Wilgus warned about in 1962. From a small core of faculty in 1972, the program at its largest, in 2012–15, included eight full-time faculty positions in folklore with six graduate faculty, one professor of practice, and one full-time instructor. Not all initiatives, of course, have been successful. In 2013, with strong support from the provost and the dean of arts and letters, the department proposed a doctoral program, emphasizing applied folklore. Although the curriculum was fully approved by the university senate, the statewide Council for Post-Secondary Education denied the proposal, citing the council's continued ban on PhDs at state schools other than the University of Kentucky and the University of Louisville. As a unique program in Kentucky with a strong reputation and the ability to attract graduate students nationally and internationally, the Folk Studies Program at Western Kentucky University continues as the largest stand-alone MA program of its kind in the United States.

Notes

1. As with many state schools, Western Kentucky changes names several times during the twentieth century. Although "Western Kentucky" is generally used to refer to the institution across the years, the proper names and relevant dates are: Western Kentucky State Normal School, 1906–22; Western Kentucky State Normal School & Teachers College, 1922–30; Western Kentucky State Teachers College, 1930–48; Western Kentucky State College, 1948–66; and Western Kentucky University, 1966–present.

2. Despite the *Journal of American Folklore*'s reference to the Kentucky Folklore Society, the minutes of the society reveal that the society referred to itself as "the Kentucky Branch of the American Folklore Society" rather than the Kentucky Folklore Society up until 1918.

3. Gordon Wilson's educational path was complex. He apparently earned AB degrees from three different institutions. Wilson first earned an AB from Clinton College, a small Baptist school, and then, dissatisfied with his education, in 1908 entered the newly created Western Kentucky State Normal School. In 1912, he made a quick transition from student to full-time teacher. However, taking leave from Western Kentucky, he also earned an AB from Indiana University (1919) as well as an MA (1924) and a PhD (1930) from the same institution. See Harrison (1988, 51).

4. While Stith Thompson left Kentucky as an adolescent and never lived there during his adult life, he is buried in Pleasant Grove Cemetery in Springfield, Kentucky. Other earlier members of his family bearing the same unusual first name are buried elsewhere in both Catholic and Protestant cemeteries in Nelson and Washington Counties.

5. Minute Book of the Kentucky Branch of the American Folk-Lore Society, Manuscripts and Folklife Archives, Manuscripts Small Collection 353, Western Kentucky University.

6. Unpublished manuscript, Manuscripts and Folklife Archives, Manuscripts Small Collection 353, Western Kentucky University.

7. A handwritten account of this meeting by D. K. Wilgus is found in the minute book of the Kentucky Folklore Society.

8. For a complete history of the Western Kentucky University Folklife Archives, see Puglia (2010).

9. Puglia's information on Montell's interaction with Gordon Wilson is based on Montell (2009).

10. Throughout the 1970s, the folk studies program produced the *Folk Studies Society Newsletter*. Information is drawn from issues available in the WKU archives dating from 1973 to 1979. The first three issues of volume 1 are not available. Copies of the newsletter have been digitized and are available at http://digitalcommons.wku.edu/stu_org.

11. The nonthesis track was later redesigned as the public folklore track.

References

Clarke, Kenneth. 1973. "Folk Studies at Western Kentucky University." *Kentucky Folklore Record* 19: 47–48.

———. 1976. "Stith Thompson, 1886–1976: Personal Recollection." *Kentucky Folklore Record* 22: 11–12.

Clarke, Kenneth, and Mary Clarke. 1974. *The Harvest and the Reapers: Oral Traditions of Kentucky*. Lexington: University Press of Kentucky.

Clarke, Mary Washington. 1960. "The Folklore of the Cumberlands as Reflected in the Writings of Jesse Stuart." PhD diss., University of Pennsylvania.

Dorson, Richard M. 1971. Letter to William Lynwood Montell, October 18, 1971. William Lynwood Montell Collection, Library Special Collections, Western Kentucky University, Box 72, Folder 4.

Ferrell, Ann K. 2013. *Burley: Kentucky Tobacco in a New Century*. Lexington: University Press of Kentucky.

Folk Studies Society. 1974. "Elective Courses Offered Spring 1974." *Folk Studies Society Newsletter* 1, no. 4.
Green, Archie. 1984. "Folklore and America's Future." *Kentucky Folklore Record: A Regional Journal of Folklore and Folklife* 30: 65–78.
Harrison, Lowell. 1984. "Gordon Wilson Turns to Folklore." *Kentucky Folklore Record* 3: 124–26.
———. 1987. *Western Kentucky University*. Lexington: University of Kentucky Press.
———. 1988. "Gordon Wilson's Normal Education: Western Kentucky State Normal School, 1908–1913." *Register of the Kentucky Historical Society* 86: 24–51.
Montell, Lynwood. 1971. *The Saga of Coe Ridge: A Study in Oral History*. Knoxville: University of Tennessee Press.
———. 2009. Tape-recorded interview conducted by David Puglia. Bowling Green, KY.
Puglia, David. 2010. "The Folklife Archives at Western Kentucky University: Past and Present." MA thesis, Western Kentucky University.
Thomas, D. L. 1913. "Local Meeting, Kentucky Branch." *Journal of American Folklore* 26, no. 99: 90.
Wilgus, D. K. 1956. "Leaders of Kentucky Folklore." *Kentucky Folklore Record* 2: 103–4.
———. 1957a. "The Kentucky Folklore Society." *Register of the Kentucky Historical Society* 55: 394.
———. 1957b. "Leaders of Kentucky Folklore: Eber C. Perrow." *Kentucky Folklore Record* 3: 29–31.
———. 1958. "The Western Kentucky Folklore Archive." *The Folklore and Folk Music Archivist* 1, no. 4: 3.
———. 1959. *Anglo-American Folksong Scholarship since 1898*. New Brunswick, NJ: Rutgers University Press.
———. 1962. "The Kentucky Folklore Society, 1912–1962." *Kentucky Folklore Record* 7: 6.

MICHAEL ANN WILLIAMS is University Distinguished Professor of Folk Studies and Anthropology Emeritus at Western Kentucky University. She is author of *Homeplace* and *Staging Tradition: John Lair and Sarah Gertrude Knott*.

14 Folklore at the University of Oregon

A History of Tradition, Innovation, and Pushing the Rock up the Hill

Sharon R. Sherman

Sisyphus, the king of Ephyra (now Corinth), according to mythological sources, was a man of great hubris and deceit. While no folklorists at the University of Oregon fit that description, the punishment for Sisyphus's deeds is metaphoric for the unending repetition of pushing the program up the hill, only to see it fall and need relifting.

Tradition and Innovation

Folklore studies at the University of Oregon began with Randall V. Mills (BA, University of California, Los Angeles; MA, University of California, Berkeley), an English professor who taught courses with folklore content as early as 1938. With interests in Pacific Northwest lore, Mills studied proverbs, popular beliefs, place names, steamboats, dialects, speechways, and railroad and hobo lore. He was the first president of the Oregon Folklore Society. When Barre Toelken established the folklore archives at the University of Oregon, he retained the name given by the library in honor of Mills and expanded it to the Randall V. Mills Memorial Archive of Northwest Folklore. Today it is one of the largest repositories of folklore in the West.

With the hire of Toelken in 1966, folklore as an area of emphasis in the English Department grew. Toelken never met Mills, but his papers were housed in Special Collections at the University of Oregon library, and Toelken thought the collection should be preserved in a folklore archive. Mills's wife donated additional items, including Mills's book collection. Other traditional materials augmented the holdings. Perhaps most notable is the Robert Winslow Gordon Collection of Folksong. Typical for the early days of collectanea, the combined collections housed primarily textual data. Mills's items include notebooks, card files, scrapbooks, manuscripts, and letters; the Gordon collection contains over one thousand folk songs, many of which are Child ballads.

Toelken's first influence in folklore scholarship was Arthur Brodeur, who had been an instructor at the University of Oregon, went on to a long career at UC Berkeley, and then returned to Oregon to teach after retiring from Berkeley. Brodeur had studied literary and oral-formulaic approaches at Harvard. He was drawn to Beowulf and ballads and had written about Gordon (1962). His book *The Art of Beowulf* (1959) became a classic, and his work was influential in fueling Toelken's interest in medieval literature when Toelken was a graduate student at the University of Oregon. Brodeur's emphasis on the ballad also appealed to Toelken, who had a background of singing as a child in a musical family. Although he never took a formal folklore class, Toelken eventually became one of the top folklorists in the world (Sharon R. Sherman Papers; Sherman 2006). Among the courses he taught were The Ballad, Introduction to Folklore, American Folklore, Fieldwork, Mythology, Beowulf, and Medieval Epic.

Toelken's personal experiences with the Navajo led him to teach courses on Native American folklore, and he made his academic mark with the publication of "The 'Pretty Languages' of Yellowman: Genre, Mode, and Texture in Navajo Coyote Narratives" (1969). For the rest of his career, Toelken reevaluated his conclusions about this publication and even published a "retranslation" (Toelken and Scott 1981) as well as articles on the ethics of representation.

Tales of the Faculty

Toelken has been a genuine inspiration for truth and integrity in humanistic work. Keeping the rock at the top of the hill was difficult during Toelken's time at Oregon. The university did not give a degree in folklore, and many in the Department of English did not value the work of folklorists. But Toelken had students who received degrees in English, specialized in folklore topics, and furthered the field: Chip Sullivan, Polly Stewart, Suzi Jones, and Susan Fagan received doctorates. Steve Siporin and Bob McCarl obtained MA degrees under Toelken's tutelage. For many, Toelken stands as an icon of folklore at the University of Oregon. Toelken wrote *The Dynamics of Folklore* (1979), widely used as an introductory text, during his time at the University of Oregon.

Next, I will provide some background about my time at the University of Oregon and my perspective. I was hired by the university in 1976. I had written my senior thesis at Wayne State in 1965 under Ellen Stekert on Child ballad collectors in the United States. In 1967, Stekert won a university-wide award to hold a symposium titled "The Urban Experience and Folk Tradition," an important step in folklorists' conceptions of who the folk were. Scholars who presented at the symposium included Roger Abrahams, D. K. Wilgus, and Richard Dorson. Soon after, I applied to UCLA based on Wilgus's talk. Like many folklorists of my generation, the folk song revival was an important impetus for my enthusiasm.

Fig. 14.1. Barre Toelken and Sharon Sherman following Barre's plenary address at the 2002 American Folklore Society annual meeting. Photograph by Carol Spellman.

While earning an MA in folklore and mythology from UCLA (1971) and a PhD in folklore from Indiana (1978), I had studied with Alan Jabbour, D. K. Wilgus, Robert Georges, Michael Owen Jones, and Richard Dorson. My interest in communicative events led me to a year in the Ethnographic Film Program (1969–70) and a year of film school (1971–72) while at UCLA. There I encountered Argentine ethnographic filmmaker Jorge Preloran, who would become a mentor and friend until his death in 2009. A theoretical stance that saw folklore as interaction, behavior, event, and performance convinced me that film was the means to study traditional behavior. Preloran taught me to be a filmmaker. He had made over sixty films, mostly on folkloric topics. At Oregon I created various films and videos of my own and turned film and folklore into a characteristic of the Folklore Program. Students eventually produced over one hundred films and videos at the University of Oregon. I also offered topics in mythology and narrative theory and courses such as Film and Folklore; American Popular Literature and

Culture; Magic, Myth, and Religion; Folklore Fieldwork; and Video Fieldwork. Thus, the program at Oregon took a direction that emphasized performance and event as well as literary studies and film.

After receiving a PhD in theater at the University of Oregon, Ed Coleman was hired in the English Department in 1971 to establish courses in African American literature. One of only three African American professors on campus when he joined the faculty, Coleman found the lack of faculty of color daunting. But he fought for diversity and the addition of new courses in ethnic literature and encouraged other departments, such as history, to add similar courses. As Coleman's interest in African American literature expanded to include folklore—especially the blues, the development of jazz, and the significance of work songs, toasts, and the dozens in a historical perspective—he realized the overlap his studies had with folklore, and he provided insights into a new world where folklore functions along with and within literature to illuminate the richness of folk culture. He developed a class in Afro-American folklore in 1988 that became an important part of the curriculum. Coleman took it upon himself, as an African American man in a predominately white world, to teach us to recognize the gifts and trials of minority cultures in the United States. Students learned what it meant to live the Black experience through Coleman's eyes.

Carol Silverman, who holds a PhD in folklore and anthropology from the University of Pennsylvania (where she had studied with Barbara Kirshenblatt-Gimblett, Dell Hymes, and Kenny Goldstein), arrived at the University of Oregon in 1981 on a grant from the Russian and East European Studies Center. She later acquired a tenure-track appointment in anthropology. Her courses in Balkan, Romani, feminist, and Jewish folklore enhanced the program. Because Silverman and I both had degrees in folklore but different appointments, the interdisciplinary nature of folklore became obvious. Regardless of departmental appointment of the faculty, folklore was a separate discipline with its own theoretical approaches, field methods, and subject matter. Everyone teaching in Folklore also had to satisfy requirements in a home department and teach courses under the rubric of their own department.

Roadblocks

In 1981, a university committee suggested that the Folklore Program be combined with Ethnic Studies, or the latter would be eliminated. Toelken was in Germany and I agreed to the merger in his stead, knowing that Toelken, Coleman, and others had worked hard to keep Ethnic Studies alive. Folklorists believed Ethnic Studies was an important linkage. A bonus was that we would get a half-time secretary. Much was made of the "white" folks taking over, despite keeping the budgets separate, and Ed Coleman being African American. As the only person trained in the social sciences, I agreed to teach the ethnic studies sequence as my colleagues requested. The class went well, but graduate students in sociology who had expected to teach it were incensed. Folklorists' definitions of ethnicity also did not meet that of those who insisted that ethnicity only applied to persons of color.

In the midst of this tense situation, other universities were wooing Toelken. When Toelken was offered the position to head the Folklore Institute in Bloomington, the University of Oregon did not jump to make him a counter offer. He was one of the lowest paid people in the English Department, but he decided to stay. When Utah State came calling, the folklorists assumed Toelken would not leave. A colleague from the dean's office met with us a few times to develop a strategy to urge Toelken to stay—even offering to move us all to anthropology. We were thus surprised that Toelken decided to return to Utah, where he had received his BA at Utah State and where his wife had relatives. William "Bert" Wilson had been urged by his church to move from Utah State to Brigham Young University, and he encouraged Toelken to take over his position in Logan. Utah State also provided a full-time folklore archivist.

When Toelken left in 1985, the rock slipped back to the bottom of the hill, and the remaining folklore faculty members (Ed Coleman, Carol Silverman, and I) were devastated. Ed Coleman directed Ethnic Studies; I became the director of Folklore, which was really an ad hoc program. After a history that is still too painful to discuss, the university hired a person from outside to take over Ethnic Studies.

The secretary stayed with the Folklore Program, because Ethnic Studies wanted to hire a person of color. A few years later, when the folklore secretary retired, we were told that Folklore would have no secretary. English took over the position (having had its own budget cut) and gave us a quarter of that position and a person who had to answer to English to a greater degree than to folklore. English later closed our office.

The upside is that the combined academic unit of Folklore and Ethnic Studies gained some autonomy for folklore. Ethnic Studies reported to the university president; Folklore reported to the dean of the graduate school. Whereas we had awarded a combined folklore and ethnic studies undergraduate certificate from 1981 to 1993, two separate certificates emerged. We had started to award folklore MA degrees under the rubric of the graduate school's individualized program and pushed forward until the graduate school in 1989 allowed a degree of Interdisciplinary Studies: Folklore. Students now entered the program without going through the English Department, admissions moved from the graduate school to Folklore itself, and the Folklore Program acquired its own designator: FLR. In 2011, Folklore became totally independent.

For over five years, we struggled to keep Toelken's slot alive. The rock was now precariously quivering near the bottom of the hill. Although the position was threatened with closure during cuts to faculty, we advertised and received numerous promising applications. None of the candidates seemed to satisfy English, and we became the butt of jokes in the wider folklore community. I feared we would never be allowed to hire anyone. At long last, in 1991, Daniel Wojcik, a graduate of the UCLA Folklore and Mythology Program, was appointed. At the same time, folklore welcomed Dianne Dugaw in an eighteenth-century slot in the English Department. Like Toelken, Dugaw grew up in a musical family. She put herself through university by singing during the 1960s–70s folk song revival and earned her PhD in English at UCLA with D. K. Wilgus, James Porter, and Robert Georges. Her emphases on British folklore and the ballad were solid additions to the folklore offerings, and she quickly became an impressive folklore faculty member, teaching two classes per year with folklore content.

The hire of Wojcik expanded the number of core classes offered, along with new courses on the Folklore of Subcultures, Folklore and Religion, and Folk Art and Material Culture. His work on neotribal body art, visionary art, apocalyptic movements, and the legend of famous runner Steve Prefontaine added to his professorial appeal. With more faculty members, student numbers increased dramatically. Wojcik's theoretical stance blended well with mine and complemented that of Dugaw and Silverman.

Many of our graduate students continued their careers as academic or public-sector foklorists. Revell Carr, Beth Dehn, Nathan Georgitis, Robert Glenn Howard, Elena Martinez, Michael Mason, Alysia McLain, Camilla Mortenson, Amy Mills, Carol Spellman, Jeannie Banks Thomas, Casey Schmitt, Emily West, and Ziying You are but a few.

In 2002, Anthropology hired Philip Scher, who held an MA in folklore and folklife and earned a joint PhD in anthropology and folklore from Penn in 1997, studying with Roger Abrahams and Regina Bendix. Scher's expertise in Caribbean folklore, heritage, cultural identity, and carnival enlarged the number of cultural areas covered by the program as well as added theoretical ideas about tourism and transnationalism. He later directed the Folklore Program and is now a divisional dean for the social sciences.

English never increased its number of folklorists, but my position was retained when I announced my retirement and Lisa Gilman was hired in 2005. Gilman received her MA and PhD in folklore at Indiana, where she studied with Beverly Stoeltje and Richard Bauman. Having lived in Malawi as a child, she specialized in African studies, gender issues, and politics and, like Wojcik, worked tirelessly to expand the number of affiliated faculty and promote folklore throughout the university. Gilman's husband, John Fenn III (who had studied with Bauman and Sue Tuohy for a folklore PhD from Indiana) taught in Arts and Administration and helped create a degree in public folklore. In 2017, he became the Head of the Research and Programs section at the American Folklife Center in the Library of Congress and moved to Washington, DC, with Gilman. This move once again left the rock teetering.

Riki Saltzman joined the faculty as director of the Oregon Folklife Network in 2012. Saltzman earned her PhD working with Roger deVeer Renwick and Richard Bauman at the University of Texas, where Anthropology and English then offered the folklore degree. Saltzman's long work as folklife coordinator for the Iowa Arts Council and other public agencies brought public-sector folklore into sharper focus. As of 2018, the University of Oregon had representation from four of what had been the major folklore degree-granting institutions in North America: UCLA, Penn, Indiana, and Texas. (See chapters by Jones, Hufford, and Bauman, this volume, for the demise of the folklore graduate degree at UCLA, Penn, and Texas and Harrah-Johnson, this volume, on Indiana.)

Doug Blandy became an important presence in recent years. Combining fieldwork with public programming, Blandy has expertise in public-sector folklore and folklore and education. He holds a PhD in art education from the Ohio State University and is the former senior vice provost at the University of Oregon. He became the director of the program.

In the wake of Gilman's and Fenn's departure, the dean canceled graduate admissions for 2017 for lack of faculty, but reopened them in 2018. On a positive note, Anthropology has recently hired Leah Lowthorp, a folklorist whose work engages art and social change, critical heritage studies, cosmopolitanism(s), and the online circulation of biopolitical narratives. Lowthorp studied with Alan Dundes as an undergrad at UC Berkeley and received her MA and PhD from the University of Pennsylvania, working with Mary Hufford, Dan Ben-Amos, and Roger Abrahams, as well as UC Berkeley's Charles Briggs. She earned a dual PhD in folklore and anthropology in 2013, the last folklore and folklife doctorate awarded at Penn.

In its five decades, the University of Oregon Folklore Program has had splendid milestones: planning the program for the 1987 American Folklore Society meeting in Albuquerque; hosting the 1993 American Folklore Society meeting in Eugene; and hosting, organizing, and lecturing for the United States Information Agency's Regional Culture Tour for Foreign Scholars for five years (1983–87). These groups visited author Ken Kesey, the Siletz nation, and met various folk artists from eastern, central, and western Oregon.

University of Oregon folklorists have served on the American Folklore Society and Western States Folklore Society executive boards, hosted the Western States Folklore Society meeting, given the Archer Taylor Memorial Lecture, and served as film and videotape editors for the *Journal of American Folklore* and *Western Folklore*. Films have won international awards and have aired on public broadcasting. Over the years, the program has sponsored talks by renowned

Fig. 14.2. *Left to right*: Daniel Wojcik, Doug Blandy, Sharon Sherman, and Riki Saltzman, some of the core folklore faculty at the University of Oregon, 2018. Photograph by Susan Fagan, courtesy of Sharon Sherman.

folklorists. Faculty have received Fulbright and Guggenheim awards, teaching awards, and grants. Toelken, Sherman, and Silverman are Fellows of the American Folklore Society.

The program is experiencing a moment of transition as it reformulates and reimagines itself with new faculty and administrative support. By the time this chapter is published, the program will be called Folklore and Public Culture (see Toelken 1998 on changing the name of folklore). As is the case elsewhere, folklore programs reflect the scholarly concerns of their founders and the subsequent professors who teach introductory folklore and classes in their special areas of interest. These scholars have fought to keep folklore alive as a discipline despite budget cuts and their colleagues' lack of awareness of folklore's cultural significance. We managed to build a large interdepartmental program with vast interdisciplinary threads.

Survival

Many problems faced by the Folklore Program at the University of Oregon seem to be endemic in the discipline at large. The first of these is recognition of folklore as a separate discipline. Richard Dorson had stressed this point in articles and public presentations (1963a, 1963b, 1967, 1971, 1972, 1973). He instilled this idea in those who studied with him, including Robert Georges and Michael Owen Jones, who expressed similar views (1995). Thus, in studying with Georges and Jones and then going to Indiana, I was deeply convinced that folklore is unique. Yet I was in a department that thought of folklore as a subdiscipline.

Serving two masters is something most folklorists learn to do. If they have graduate students in folklore, they must, at the same time, participate in committees and work with students in their home departments. Work in folklore generally went unappreciated (although that has been changing at the University of Oregon as a younger, more broad-based group of scholars has moved into administrative positions). Dorson was fond of a preliminary exam question asking students to explain how they would talk about folklore as a social science or as a humanities topic at a cocktail party (see Wilson 1988). Of course, such an explanation would also be useful in job interviews and teaching.

Another problem is that few universities grant a PhD in folklore. Most programs offer an MA or a PhD within an allied field. What does the future hold for folklore as a discipline? Although the Sisyphean task of continually pushing for folklore studies may continue, the future of folklore at the University of Oregon is secure at this time.

References

Brodeur, Arthur. 1959. *The Art of Beowulf.* Berkeley: University of California Press.
———. 1962. "The Robert Winslow Gordon Collection of American Folksong." *Oregon Folklore Bulletin* 1, no. 4: 1–2.
Dorson, Richard M. 1963a. "The American Folklore Scene." *Folklore* 74, no. 3: 433–49.
———. 1963b. "Should There Be a Ph.D. in Folklore?" *American Council of Learned Societies Newsletter,* 1–8.
———. 1967. "Letter from the President to the Members of the American Folklore Society." *Journal of American Folklore,* Supplement 80: 2.
———. 1971. *American Folklore and the Historian.* Chicago: University of Chicago Press.
———. 1972. *Folklore, Selected Essays.* Bloomington: Indiana University Press.
———. 1973. "Is Folklore a Discipline?" *Folklore* 84: 177–205.
Georges, Robert A., and Michael Owen Jones. 1995. *Folkloristics: An Introduction.* Bloomington: Indiana University Press.
Sharon R. Sherman Papers, Special Collections, University of Oregon Library.

Sherman, Sharon R. 2006. *Barry Lopez and Barre Toelken: A Conversation*. DVD. Randall V.Mills Archive of Northwest Folklore. Copies available from filmmaker. Contact srs@uoregon.edu.

Toelken, J. Barre. 1969. "The 'Pretty Languages' of Yellowman: Genre, Mode, and Texture in Navajo Coyote Narratives." *Genre* 2: 211–35.

———. 1979. *The Dynamics of Folklore*. Boston: Houghton Mifflin.

———. 1998. "The End of Folklore." *Western Folklore* 57: 81–101.

Toelken, J. Barre, and Tacheeni Scott. 1981. "Poetic Retranslation and the 'Pretty Language' of Yellowman." In *Traditional Literatures of the American Indian: Texts and Interpretations*, edited by Karl Kroeber, 65–116. Lincoln: University of Nebraska Press.

Wilson, William A. 1988. "The Deeper Necessity: Folklore and the Humanities." *Journal of American Folklore* 101: 156–67.

SHARON R. SHERMAN is Professor Emerita of Folklore and English at the University of Oregon and an independent filmmaker. She is author of *Documenting Ourselves: Film, Video, and Culture* and *Chainsaw Sculptor: The Art of J. Chester "Skip" Armstrong.*

15 From Ukrainian Studies to Folklore of the Prairies

The Kule Center for Ukrainian and Canadian Folklore, University of Alberta

Natalie Kononenko

The Folklore Center at the University of Alberta, currently the Kule Center for Ukrainian and Canadian Folklore, was the brainchild of Bohdan Medwidsky, who was born in Stanislaviv, Ukraine, in 1936. Because he had health issues, Medwidsky was sent to a sanatorium in Switzerland, where he spent the next ten years. That is where he developed his extensive linguistic competence—namely, a knowledge of both German and French and an ability to pick up additional languages with ease. With the start of the Second World War, Medwidsky was trapped in Switzerland and not reunited with his family until they left Ukraine and headed west. It was in Vienna in 1948 that Medwidsky saw his brother for the first time and also became aware that he did not know his native language. His mother then set about teaching him Ukrainian through folktales, thus creating for him a link between folklore and Ukrainian identity. As they escaped communist Ukraine, the family ended up in refugee camps. Medwidsky, although still a boy, participated in groups discussing Ukraine, its political situation, and its future. This experience, along with his family's rejection of Soviet rule, instilled in Medwidsky an intense Ukrainophilia.

Sponsored by a relative, the family moved to Toronto, Ontario, Canada, in 1949, where Medwidsky's parents ran an apothecary. In an interview recorded by Mariya Lesiv and Nadya Foty, Medwidsky recounts his disappointment with the lack of language knowledge and lack of interest in heritage among Ukrainian Canadians (Medwidsky 2009). As an example, he noted the speed with which they switched to English once they left events like a Ukrainian church service. Sensing a threat to Ukrainian identity in Canada and determined to preserve his Ukrainian heritage, Medwidsky matriculated at the University of Ottawa because that was where he could pursue Ukrainian studies. After earning his bachelor and master's degrees, he transferred to the University of Toronto, where he fought for the right to work on Ukrainian subject matter, even as the faculty pushed Medwidsky toward a more standard, Russian-focused curriculum. While his specialization was linguistics, Medwidsky urged the teaching of Ukrainian literature and, in the interview, mentions his fondness for Vasyl Stefanyk, whose use of colloquial Ukrainian became the subject of his dissertation.[1]

Medwidsky took on various temporary teaching positions at Carleton University in Ottawa. His sojourn in this city provided the opportunity to meet Robert Bohdan Klymasz, a folklorist trained at Indiana University and then employed at the Canadian Museum of Man (later the Canadian Museum of Civilization and currently the Canadian Museum of History). A prolific and enthusiastic fieldworker, Klymasz became Medwidsky's friend and encouraged his interest in folklore. In 1971, Medwidsky was offered a permanent position at the University of Alberta. While beginning his career at Alberta, he continued working on his PhD, earning the doctorate from the University of Toronto in 1977. Medwidsky's Alberta job required him to teach linguistics and Ukrainian and Russian language. All this he did, but he also promoted Ukraine and Ukrainian studies every way he could.

The path that he found was fund-raising and folklore. Medwidsky noticed that young people who attended summer camps that offered cultural activities were more willing to embrace their Ukrainian identity than other Canadian-born Ukrainians, and this gave him the idea that teaching folklore was the way to accomplish his goal of promoting Ukrainian studies. Getting a course in Ukrainian folklore approved by his department was not easy, but Medwidsky's lobbying efforts paid off, and folklore was first offered in 1977. Medwidsky started attending the meetings of the Folklore Studies Association of Canada and learned that there was more to folklore than the study of the verbal arts. This insight prompted him to expand his folklore offerings, and, with course expansion, the program grew.

The 1970s were an important period for establishing Ukrainian programs through community support. The Harvard Ukrainian Research Institute was founded in 1973, followed in 1976 by the Canadian Institute of Ukrainian Studies. Both were research institutes with a political purpose and both emphasized history and politics, with Harvard also including literature. Medwidsky decided that he would follow the model of these two institutions, but he would coordinate rather than compete. He would concentrate on teaching and cover something that was not covered elsewhere: folklore. Thus, folklore studies at the University of Alberta was a program born out a combination of ardent Ukrainophilia, a childhood connection between folklore and Ukrainian identity, the conviction that folklore was the way to promote Ukrainian studies, and opportunism.

Growing the program, adding graduate courses and graduate degrees, Medwidsky became keenly aware of the need for funding to hire another professor.

Fig. 15.1. Bohdan Medwidsky, 1913, founder of the Ukrainian Folklore Program at the University of Alberta. Photograph by permission of the Kule Center for Ukrainian and Canadian Folklore.

Conversations with the dean convinced him that raising money for an endowed chair was the solution. Medwidsky turned out to be an effective fund-raiser, and many of the publications put out by the center emphasize its fund-raising history. These publications and the interview granted to Lesiv and Foty describe how Medwidsky lobbied for funding, shepherded monies, and eventually secured a major donation from Erast and Lydia Huculak of Toronto, creating the Huculak Chair of Ukrainian Culture and Ethnography (Cipko and Kononenko 2009). Additional important funding from Wasyl and Anna Kuryliw helped support graduate students, as did contributions from other donors.

As Medwidsky told this author, he chose to use the money that he raised for the program rather than to promote himself. Thus, when he managed to establish an endowed chair, he did not take it himself but used the position to hire graduate student Andriy Nahachewsky, who was born in Saskatchewan and received his bachelor's degree from that province's university in 1979. Nahachewsky went on to earn a bachelor of fine arts in dance at York University and then joined the graduate program at the University of Alberta, earning a master's degree in

1985 and a doctorate in 1991. Nahachewsky's primary interest has always been dance. He wrote his dissertation on a dance type called the *kolomyika*. He published a book on Ukrainian dance (2012), and he taught a popular course on this topic. In addition to his work on dance, Nahachewsky produced a publication about Ukrainian folk architecture (1985), along with articles and other scholarly contributions. In 2003, with the help of his administrative assistant, Theresa Warenycia, Nahachewsky secured a major grant and launched the Local Culture and Diversity on the Prairies Project, documenting the pre-1939 daily life of Ukrainian, French, German, and English immigrants on the Canadian prairies (2005). This project received support from the University of Manitoba and other University of Alberta departments. It produced a book-length report and a DVD. Work on indexing the data collected during this project and compiling an online database continues. Nahachewsky did fieldwork in Canada and Ukraine, and with his interest in diaspora studies, he also worked in a number of other countries, most notably Brazil.

A major component of the Folklore Center at the University of Alberta is its archive. Archives were always of special interest to Medwidsky. He started preserving student folklore papers in 1977, encouraging students to do fieldwork in the community. As the archive grew, he donated a substantial sum of his own money toward its upkeep. The archive was renamed in his honor in 2003 and moved to a larger and more easily accessible space in 2009. The current archivist is Maryna Chernyavska. She earned master's degrees in folklore and in library and information studies. The electronic Bohdan Medwidsky Folklore Archives is currently accessible at http://archives.ukrfolk.ca.

The early 2000s were a golden age for Ukrainian folklore. The University of Alberta designated East European studies as an emerging field of excellence and, acknowledging the importance of folklore to the prominence of the East European field, created the Canadian Center for Ukrainian Culture and Ethnography in 2001. Nahachewsky added the position of center director to his title as Huculak chair. Enrollments grew, especially at the graduate level, as students from Canada were joined by applicants from abroad. Most of the international students came from Ukraine, but students from Korea, China, Turkey, Brazil, Croatia, the United States, and Russia also successfully completed the folklore program. As of this writing, forty people have received graduate degrees through the University of Alberta folklore program, and four of the PhDs hold academic appointments—three in Canada and one in South Korea.

When Medwidsky approached mandatory retirement age, he decided that he needed to maximize the effectiveness of the position that his departure would create. As he had done with the Huculak chair, Medwidsky worked tirelessly to endow another chair so that he could be replaced with a senior hire rather than an entry-level faculty member. Having another chair also guaranteed that his replacement would be a folklorist rather than a specialist in another area. Medwidsky convinced Peter and Doris Kule, whom he knew from both church and Ukrainian Canadian philanthropic and political organizations, to donate $1 million, and he negotiated to have this amount double-matched with provincial and university monies. Medwidsky's efforts resulted in the establishment of the Kule Chair in Ukrainian Ethnography. Natalie Kononenko was hired to be the first holder of this chair in 2004. Kononenko had already published an award-winning book on Ukrainian minstrelsy, based primarily on archival work. With the collapse of the Soviet Union and the independence of Ukraine, she began doing fieldwork in the Ukrainian countryside, gathering material on rites of passage such as the rituals of marriage, birth, and death. This work resulted in a number of articles, and Kononenko plans to incorporate these into a book. With her arrival in Canada, Kononenko's focus changed. She accepted the invitation to contribute to the Greenwood folklore series and completed *Slavic Folklore: A Handbook* (2007). She joined Serge Cipko in editing a book honoring Peter and Doris Kule called *Champions of Philanthropy: Peter and Doris Kule and Their Endowments* (2009).

Kononenko began work with John-Paul Himka and Frances Swyripa on Sanctuary: The Sacral Heritage Documentation Project, which aims to provide a record of all churches in Alberta and Saskatchewan where Ukrainians might have worshipped. This project began in 2009 and is nearing completion. The project takes photographs of all church and related buildings such as belfries. Unlike other documentation efforts, all items inside the churches, such as icons, banners, and vestments, are also photographed. Kononenko's contribution is conducting interviews with parishioners about ritual practice such as weddings, funerals, and baptisms and all holiday celebrations such as Easter and Christmas. The photographs and the sound files from this project will be available through the University of Alberta library. In addition to the research sites hosted by the library, a popular site with interview clips, artist profiles, and selected photographs has been started at http://livingcultures.ualberta.ca/sanctuary/. Kononenko has published two articles on the Sanctuary research (Kononenko 2018a, 2018b) and plans more articles and books, including a comparative study of ritual change in Canada, Ukraine, and among the Ukrainian diaspora in Kazakhstan, where Kononenko gathered data in 2011.

Following up on her work with Ukrainian minstrels (1998) and also responding to the needs of the Ukrainian diaspora, Kononenko completed a book of translations of Ukrainian epic and historical song (2019) set in the context provided by recent research on the history of the common people during the period described in Ukrainian historical verse. In an effort to serve the community, Kononenko has used her expertise in digital technologies to produce a series of popular and educational websites such as ukrainealive.ualberta.ca.

Fig. 15.2. Parishioners of the Saint Elias church, Luzan-Toporiwtsi, Alberta, singing folk songs after the service, 2014. Photograph by Natalie Kononenko.

Ever the fund-raiser, Medwidsky continued to be active in retirement. Monetary gifts came from Michael and Elsie Kawulych for graduate and other support. The Kules gave a major grant of an additional $2 million, and the center was renamed in their honor in 2006. They followed this gift with donations to the Folklore Center to be used for postdoctoral or graduate studies.

While, over the years, the program prospered financially, interest in Ukrainian studies waned. The number of undergraduate majors fell and both the Ukrainian major and the Ukrainian folklore major were canceled in 2015. The Ukrainian folklore minor remains, but it draws few students. The entire curriculum of the Modern Languages and Cultural Studies Department, which houses folklore, has been revamped at both the graduate and undergraduate levels. While language training is expected, no degree specifies the language in which the student specialized, a real blow to Medwidsky and his emphasis on specifically Ukrainian work.

Even before the downward turn began, Nahachewsky sensed the need for courses that were not specifically Ukrainian and created a general course in folkloristics. Kononenko took over this course shortly after she arrived, supporting the idea of more general folklore teaching and research. Having instruction that was not limited to Ukrainian subject matter facilitated the major donation from Peter and Doris Kule because the matching funds that the Kules demanded were easier to secure when interim dean Gurston Daks could hire a much-needed French professor as the university's contribution. Micah True was hired in 2010. His mandate was to devote 50 percent of his time to teaching folklore classes and the rest to teaching French. Obviously the two could be combined. True's work includes a book called *Masters and Students: Jesuit Mission Ethnography in Seventeenth Century New France* (2015).

Kononenko supported instruction in general folklore and created a survey of folklore genres to complement the course in folkloristics. As Ukrainian courses were canceled, she introduced additional general folklore offerings, including Folklore through Film and Folklore and the Internet. Nahachewsky introduced a course on graffiti. While the general folklore courses are very popular and grow every year, there is tension between the emphasis on Ukrainian, including Ukrainian language, and the emphasis on folklore, regardless of language or geographic ties. Kononenko has tried to respond to this by offering a course in Slavic folklore. Although the course is taught in English, it contains substantial Ukrainian content. Nahachewsky's course on Ukrainian dance also helps promote Ukrainian subject matter to a general audience.

The economic downturn of 2008 hit the University of Alberta hard and impacted the Kule Center for Ukrainian and Canadian Folklore. The university administration needed to preserve the economic well-being of the university and to ease the strain caused by deep budget cuts. Then president Indira Samarasekera decided to make a push to attract international students because these pay a considerably higher tuition than Canadian citizens. Samarasekera's particular emphasis was on recruiting Chinese students, and her efforts were successful. In the general folklore courses, as many as half of the students are Chinese. They find folklore to be an excellent way to learn about North America and the real lives of Canadians. They also appreciate the fact that Kononenko allows them to write about Chinese tales and Chinese rituals, applying the folklore concepts taught in her courses to material with which they are familiar. As a result, the current situation finds large folklore courses that contribute to university and department financial solvency and are not Ukrainian focused.

Student demand bodes well for increased recognition of folklore at the departmental and university levels and for the creation of a FOLK course rubric and a certificate in folklore studies. Emphasis on general folklore in undergraduate teaching has not taken away from the study of the Ukrainian subject matter that was central to Medwidsky's original plan. Graduate students are trained in Ukrainian studies, and both Nahachewsky and Kononenko focus on Ukrainian and Ukrainian diaspora topics in their research—a task that is facilitated by the endowments Medwidsky secured.

Recent developments at the Folklore Center include the retirement of Andriy Nahachewsky and the hiring of a new director. Nahachewsky chose to leave the position of center director in 2016 and to retire from the university in 2017. The director's position was assumed by Jelena Pogosjan, professor of Russian language, literature, and culture. She holds three degrees from the University of Tartu, Estonia, in Russian literature and philology. She has published three books in Russian, one of which was recently translated into English, plus numerous articles. Her current research project (funded by the Social Sciences and Humanities Research Council) focuses on Ukrainian architect and painter Ivan Zarudny, famous for his iconostases. This project led Pogosjan to study traditional Ukrainian iconostases and iconography. Recently, her interests have spread to Ukrainian Canadian religious art. A search to fill the faculty position vacated by Nahachewsky will take place shortly.

The new hire will teach Ukrainian as well as folklore, thus taking on a role similar to that of Medwidsky, the center's founder. Interest in Ukrainian icons is growing, as evidenced by a recent exhibit sponsored by the center and held in downtown Edmonton. Whether the center will realize its potential to work with the many new immigrants to Canada and to help them document their folklore remains to be seen.

Note

1. See Nahachewsky and Chernyavska (2014) for biographical information on Medwidsky.

References

Cipko, Serge, and Natalie Kononenko, eds. 2009. *Champions of Philanthropy: Peter and Doris Kule and Their Endowments*. Edmonton, Canada: Kule Endowment Group.

Kononenko, Natalie. 1998. *Ukrainian Minstrels: And the Blind Shall Sing*. Armonk, NY: M. E. Sharpe.

———. 2007. *Slavic Folklore: A Handbook*. Westport, CT: Greenwood.

———. 2018a. "Vernacular Religion on the Prairies: Negotiating a Place for the Unquiet Dead." *Canadian Slavonic Papers/Revue canadienne des slavists* 60, nos. 1–2: 108–35.

———. 2018b. "Children of Stone: Performing Self-Memorialization." In *Aspects of Performance in Faith Settings: Heavenly Acts*, edited by Andrey Rosowsky, 29–53. Cambridge, England: Cambridge Scholars Press.

———. 2019. *Ukrainian Epic and Historical Song: Folklore in Context*. Toronto: University of Toronto Press.

Medwidsky, Bohdan. 2009. Interview with Mariya Lesiv and Nadya Foty. Bohdan Medwidsky Ukrainian Folklore Archives: CA BMUFA 0090.

Nahachewsky, Andriy. 1985. *Ukrainian Dug Out Dwellings in East-Central Alberta*. Alberta Historical Sites Service.

———, ed. 2005. *Local Culture and Diversity on the Prairies: A Project Report*. Edmonton, Canada: Friends of the Ukrainian Folklore Center.

———. 2012. *Ukrainian Dance: A Cross-Cultural Approach*. Jefferson, NC: McFarland.

Nahachewsky, Andriy, and Maryna Chernyavska, eds. 2014. *Proverbs in Motion: A Festschrift in Honor of Bohdan Medwidsky*. Edmonton and Toronto: Canadian Institute for Ukrainian Studies Press and Kule Center for Ukrainian and Canadian Folklore.

True, Micah. 2015. *Masters and Students: Jesuit Mission Ethnography in Seventeenth Century New France*. Montreal: McGill-Queens University Press.

NATALIE KONONENKO is Professor and Kule Chair in Ukrainian Ethnography at the University of Alberta. She is author of *Ukrainian Minstrels: And the Blind Shall Sing* and *Ukrainian Epic and Historical Song: Folklore in Context*.

16 Engagement with Community in Distinctive Folklore Concentrations

University of Louisiana at Lafayette

Marcia Gaudet and Barry Jean Ancelet

THE FOLKLORE PROGRAM at the University of Louisiana (UL) at Lafayette derives from two main thrusts. Patricia Rickels began teaching folklore courses in the English Department in the early 1960s, when she was also working with Harry Oster, who was conducting fieldwork in Louisiana, and Barry Jean Ancelet began teaching folklore courses in the French Department in the 1970s, when he was also working on several fieldwork and festival projects in the area. Other faculty members have since participated in the evolution of the program. These two currents work together to coordinate folklore concentrations in both areas. Faculty members from both English and French regularly serve on graduate committees for students in both areas. In addition, students may take related courses in other programs such as anthropology, sociology, history, and ethnomusicology. These joint programs are connected to the Center for Louisiana Studies and its Archive of Cajun and Creole Folklore as well as to the School of Music's Endowed Chair in Traditional Music, named for Tommy Comeaux, who was a member of the group Beausoleil.

Folklore studies at UL Lafayette,[1] and in Louisiana in general, have evolved from the interest in folklore and culture by individual scholars in the state. When the Louisiana Folklore Society was founded in 1956 "to encourage the study, documentation, and accurate representation of the traditional cultures of Louisiana" (Louisiana Folklore Society 2020), there were no folklore programs nor, as far as we can determine, any folklore courses being taught at any university in Louisiana. There were, however, a number of college professors and cultural activists who were keenly interested in Louisiana folklore, culture, and cultural geography. Harry Oster was then a young faculty member in the English Department at Louisiana State University (LSU), and he pursued his interest and training in collecting folk music. At LSU, Oster got to know Patricia Rickels (then Patricia Vincent), who was a graduate student in English. Fred Kniffen, professor of cultural geography at LSU, was influential in promoting the study of material culture in Louisiana. George Reinecke, a native of New Orleans, returned in 1958 with a PhD in medieval literature from Harvard to become a faculty member at LSU New Orleans (now University of New Orleans). Along with others, including Milton Rickels, professor of American literature at UL Lafayette (then Southwestern Louisiana Institute), they incorporated folklore and folkloristics into their English and French department classes. In 1962, Milton Rickels began teaching a course in American humor, and shortly after, in 1964, Patricia Rickels began teaching English 432G, American Folklore, for upper-level undergraduates and graduate students. In the 1970s, she added a graduate Seminar in Folklore (English 632), with varying topics in folklore (regional, ethnic, historical, or literary surveys).

As a scholar, Patricia Rickels established a national reputation in the field of African American literature and coauthored with her husband, Milton, two books, *Richard Wright* (1970) and *Seba Smith* (1977). With her PhD in American literature, she was a student at the Summer Folklore Institute at Indiana University. Her folklore articles include "Martin Luther King as Folk Hero" (1980–81), "The Folklore of the Acadians" (1983), and "The Folklore of Sacraments and Sacramentals" (1965). Her article "Some Accounts of Witch Riding" (1961), first published in *Louisiana Folklore Miscellany* and later republished in two anthologies, is cited as an important study in folk belief.

Patricia Rickels was the Louisiana collector for the *Dictionary of American Popular Beliefs and Superstitions* project at the University of California, Los Angeles, with an index of more than five thousand items of Louisiana folklore. She was a founding member of the Louisiana Folklore Society and participated in the American Folklore Society until 1995. As a teacher and mentor, Rickels inspired generations of students, often shocking and entertaining them as well with her wit and her ability to say anything with impunity, even to university administrators. The university ultimately responded by naming Judice-Rickels Hall, which houses the university's honors program, for Patricia and Milton Rickels.

A 1968 article in the university's weekly student newspaper, *The Vermilion*, about the Louisiana Folklore Society meeting in Baton Rouge reports, "Miss Elaine Abboud and Darrell Bourque, both USL graduate students, read papers which they had done as part of a project for American Folklore (432), a class conducted by Dr. Patricia Rickels. This course is the only one of its kind to be found in any state college or university in Louisiana." The article goes on to say that Abboud's paper was titled "Some Syrian-Lebanese Superstitions Collected in New Orleans." Bourque's paper, "Cauchemar and Feu Follet," "dealt with the Acadian belief in two evil spirits." Elaine J. Abboud completed her MA in English in 1969. Her thesis, "Syrian-Lebanese Folklore in Louisiana, Particularly New Orleans," was directed by Patricia Rickels.[2]

In his 1985 essay, "A History of Folklife Research in Louisiana," Frank de Caro writes that in January 1964, Ralph Rinzler contacted Patricia and Milton Rickels and other folklore collectors and promoters in Louisiana regarding the identification of Louisiana French musicians for the Newport Folk Festival. This resulted in the Louisiana Folk Foundation and additional support for folklore studies at UL Lafayette (then the University of Southwestern Louisiana [USL]):

> The Louisiana Folk Foundation (which existed until 1974) found support at the University of Southwestern Louisiana in Lafayette; not only were there interested faculty members, but a major festival was held on the campus in fall of 1966, sponsored jointly by the Newport and Louisiana foundations and the university itself. This reflects the interest in folklore gradually growing through the 1960s and accelerating in the 1970s at the state's colleges and universities. A course in American folklore was established at USL in the mid-sixties by Patricia Rickels, who had joined the English faculty there in 1957. This popular course generated both student interest in folklore and student fieldwork (as did another course on American humor, taught by Milton Rickels, an authority on the humor of the old Southwest) and helped to lay a strong foundation for the development of folklore at USL, a development which really began to blossom in the mid-seventies with the establishment of the Center for Acadian and Creole Folklore.
>
> Established by USL in 1974 this center was first headed by archivist Otis Hebert, until his untimely death. It was then taken over in 1977 by Barry Jean Ancelet, also a native speaker of Cajun French and a folklore MA from Indiana University. Ancelet also received practical training in folklore from the American Folklife Center and the Smithsonian's Festival of American Folklife. In 1977, he was successful in obtaining grant funding from the Rockefeller Foundation, and under his direction the center became an active focus for field collecting and an important archival depository. The center existed until 1980 with Ancelet moving to the Center for Louisiana Studies at that time and continuing his field research under their auspices and with the Center's existing collections being moved to the USL Library. (de Caro 1985, 26)

The graduate folklore concentration in Francophone Studies emerged from the development of the Center for Acadian and Creole Folklore in 1977. The Center was established to conduct and collect research on the traditional Cajun and Creole cultures of French Louisiana. In addition to the original fieldwork done by Ancelet, with grant support from the Rockefeller Foundation, from January 1977 to May 1978, the center also began to gather copies of previous fieldwork collections from scholars such as John and Alan Lomax, Ralph Rinzler, Harry Oster, William Owens, Elizabeth Brandon, and Corinne Saucier. The center developed an active outreach program, working in the community to produce special events, such as the annual Festivals Acadiens et Créoles, as well as special concerts, storytelling events, radio and television programs, and museum exhibitions. In a report to the Rockefeller Foundation, Roger Abrahams wrote that USL was to be commended for "willingly coming down out of the ivory tower to engage itself meaningfully in the community that surrounded it" (quoted in University of Southwestern Louisiana 1996, 9). In 1984, the folklore archives became a branch of the university's Center for Louisiana Studies.

Ancelet had already begun teaching undergraduate-level classes on Louisiana French folklore, Cajun and Creole music, and Louisiana French fieldwork. In 1984, he earned a doctorate in *Études Créoles* (anthropology and linguistics) from the Université de Provence (Aix-Marseille I). In 1985, he joined the faculty of the Department of Foreign Languages (now the Department of Modern Languages) and began developing graduate-level courses that address the folklore of French Louisiana and the Francophone world in such areas as oral tradition, folk song, the carnivalesque, sociolinguistics, and dialectology. This resulted in several MA theses on various aspects of Louisiana French folklore. In 1994, the university established a PhD program in Francophone Studies, which includes a concentration in folklore. Since then, students have produced dissertations on issues ranging from folk medicine and traditional wedding practices to oral tradition, carnival, and folk song in various parts of the Francophone world. Copies of student research projects are housed in the Center's archival collection, which has grown to include photographs, video and film footage, and digital and analog audio recordings.

Patricia Rickels and Barry Ancelet worked together to promote folklore research and folklore studies at UL Lafayette. One such project was a 1978 oral history of the civil rights movement in Louisiana titled, "No Gains without Pains: An Oral History of the Civil Rights Movement in Louisiana," which resulted in the J. Carlton James Collection.

In the early 1980s, Rickels became director of the university honors program, but she continued to teach the American Folklore course and to mentor students. Rickels and Ancelet also instituted a Louisiana Folklore Fieldwork course in which students could register for credit in either English or French.

Given its origins and its sources of inspiration, including Rinzler, Oster, and Lomax, it is easy to see how the folklore program at UL Lafayette was influenced by the civil rights and counterculture movements and what Lomax described in his "Appeal for Cultural Equity" (1977). Folklore was a way to address issues of social and linguistic equity as well, giving attention to segments of the community that did not have a history of inclusion in the academic realm. In addition to studying the cultural heritage of south Louisiana's Cajuns, Creoles, and others, folklorists found ways to present and celebrate this heritage through festivals, concerts, exhibitions, and other special programs. Storytellers, such as Ben Guiné and Evelia Boudreaux, became regular presenters in newly developed courses that included oral tradition in the consideration of Louisiana French literature.

Fig. 16.1. Barry Jean Ancelet (*center, foreground*) with Patricia Rickels (*right*) and Matt Schott (*left*) in the sound editing room at La Louisianne Studios in Lafayette, working on the "No Gains Without Pains" oral history project on the civil rights movement in Louisiana, 1978. Photograph by Elemore Morgan Jr.

Legendary musician Dennis McGee was named honorary dean of Cajun music, and Dewey Balfa and Canray Fontenot were named honorary professors of Cajun and Creole music. Michael Doucet and Kristi Guillory are among the traditional musicians who have taught versions of the Cajun and Creole music appreciation course. Tommy Comeaux Chair Professor Mark DeWitt regularly involves a host of Cajun and Creole musicians in the traditional music courses he teaches in the School of Music and Performing Arts and serves on folklore-related graduate student committees in English and Francophone Studies.

In the 1980s, Marcia Gaudet, who had earned her PhD in English at USL with Pat Rickels as her advisor, began teaching an undergraduate course on Louisiana folklore and literature as an adjunct instructor, although she left to become an assistant professor in English at Arkansas State University. In 1986, Eric Montenyohl, a PhD in folklore from Indiana University, joined the UL Lafayette English Department as an assistant professor. He expanded the folklore course offerings in English considerably, adding an undergraduate course in Folklore Genres as well as graduate seminars in Folklore in Culture (varying topics), Festivals and

Fig. 16.2. Michael Doucet (left) and Dennis McGee playing fiddles in the Louisiana French Folklore course at the University of Southwestern Louisiana (now the University of Louisiana at Lafayette), 1978. Photograph by Philip Gould.

Celebrations, and Readings in Folklore. Montenyohl added a strong folklore theory element to the Seminar in Folklore, and he established an official concentration in folklore for the MA in English. In 1992, Montenyohl received a $110,000 grant from the Louisiana Education Quality Support Fund to "further improve the ability of USL to collect, preserve and study examples of Cajun and Creole folk life" (*The Advertiser* 1992). The interdisciplinary team named in the grant consisted of Ancelet, Sherri Condon (sociolinguistics), Gaudet, Montenyohl, and Pat Rickels.

Gaudet returned to the UL Lafayette faculty in 1991, adding to the folklore presence along with Rickels, Montenyohl, and Ancelet. Montenyohl left in 1994, and Patricia Sawin was hired as an assistant professor in English in 1995. While Gaudet taught seminars in African American Folklore, Narrative Folklore, Festivals and Celebrations, and Folklore and Literature, Sawin added to the program with her Women and Folklore seminar as well as her expertise in performance studies and folklore theory. Gaudet and Sawin established folklore as an official concentration for a PhD in English in 1996. Particularly active during this time was the UL Lafayette Folklore Organization, presenting programs and facilitating student research. Folklore faculty members presented public programs with students on various topics, including Mardi Gras in February of most years. In a 1996 report to the Louisiana Board of Regents awarding fellowships in folklore, four out-of-state consultants praised the "distinctive concentration in folklore studies" (University of Southwestern Louisiana 1996, 8).

In 1998, Sawin left UL to accept a position at the University of North Carolina at Chapel Hill. John Laudun, another Indiana University PhD in folklore, was hired as an assistant professor of English in 1999. Laudun, a native of Lafayette, Louisiana, has brought his knowledge of Louisiana folklore as well as his expertise in material culture and digital humanities to the program. He continues the graduate seminar in folklore theory.

In 2012, Shelley Ingram, a PhD from the University of Missouri with a concentration in folklore, joined the English Department as an assistant professor, replacing Gaudet. Ingram has not only been a major contributor to the program in directing dissertations but also helped establish an undergraduate submajor in folklore in the English Department and the College of Liberal Arts that draws on a group of undergraduate folklore courses in English. In the last five years, the graduate concentration in folklore in the English Department has consciously gone in the direction of folklore and literature, with most of the dissertations in that area.

The concentration in folklore in the Francophone Studies PhD program at UL Lafayette continues to be a strong presence as well. Despite Ancelet's official retirement in 2015, he continues to teach classes and to direct graduate student work in folklore and Francophone studies in his capacity as professor emeritus. In his "Last Lecture" presentation (an invited address by a retiring faculty member in the College of Liberal Arts), he said:

> Why folklore? I didn't know that there was such an academic discipline until I arrived at Indiana University in 1974. I actually went there to pursue graduate studies in French. But I had already come to understand, through my experiences in Louisiana, that the language was inseparable from the content. To study the French language of Louisiana, one had to study the culture that it expressed. Another thing that was obvious was that very little of this could be found on the library shelves. Ultimately, getting at Louisiana's French language and culture was going to require an improvised, hybrid approach. That approach turned out to be folklore. (Ancelet 2015)

In 2018, UL folklore concentration graduate Joshua Caffery came back to the university as director of the Center for Louisiana Studies. Among other tasks, he oversees the activities of the center's Cajun and Creole Folklore Archive. Staff members, including John Sharp and Christopher Segura, organize, catalog, and preserve the collection. The archive also serves as a laboratory for graduate and undergraduate student interns.

Folklore studies at the University of Louisiana at Lafayette have gone well beyond an academic exercise. People in both the academic and local communities have been genuinely excited about and engaged with the festivals and exhibits that draw on the work done by folklorists and students. It was and still is truly fieldwork and education that have made a difference. The focus has been consistently driven by the practical—starting with fieldwork and finding out what is there—but the program also has been informed by current methodology and theory in folklore. Perhaps most importantly, students learn how to read a community. In a 1984 review of the program, consultants wrote, "It is possible to achieve national distinction through regionally oriented excellence" (University of Southwestern Louisiana 1996, 7). Folklore studies at UL Lafayette have continually shown this premise to be true.

Notes

1. The institution has had several names: starting in 1900, Southwestern Louisiana Industrial Institute; in 1921, Southwestern Louisiana Institute; in 1960, University of Southwestern Louisiana; and in 1999, University of Louisiana at Lafayette.
2. Milton and Patricia Rickels Papers, Edith Garland Dupré Library, University of Louisiana Lafayette, Box 19-A Folklore, Folder 27.

Archive Consulted

Rickels, Drs. Milton Henry (1920–97) and Patricia Kennedy (1927–2009) Papers, 1950–2007. University Archives, Edith Garland Dupré Library, University of Louisiana Lafayette, Collection 307, Box 19-A Folklore, Folder 27.

References

The Advertiser. 1992. "USL Gets Major Grant to Study Cajun Lifestyle." February 24, 1.

Ancelet, Barry Jean. 2015. "The Theory and Practice of Activist Folklore: From Fieldwork to Programming." The Last Lecture invited presentation, University of Louisiana Lafayette College of Liberal Arts.

de Caro, F. A. 1985. "A History of Folklife Research in Louisiana." In *Louisiana Folklife: A Guide to the State*, edited by Nicholas R. Spitzer, 12–34. Baton Rouge: Louisiana Folklife Program, Office of Cultural Development. http://www.louisianafolklife.org/LT/Virtual_Books/Guide_to_State/decaro.html.

Lomax, Alan. 1977. "Appeal for Cultural Equity." *Journal of Communication* 27: 125–38.

Louisiana Folklore Society. 2020. Home page. www.louisianafolklore.org.

Rickels, Milton, and Patricia K. Rickels. 1970. *Richard Wright*. Boston: Twayne.

———. 1977. *Seba Smith*. Boston: Twayne.

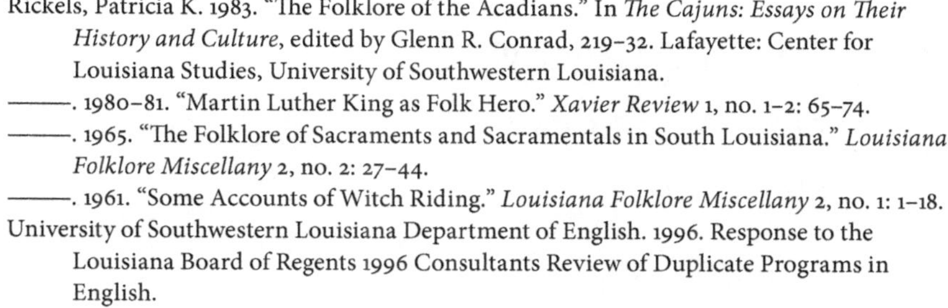

Rickels, Patricia K. 1983. "The Folklore of the Acadians." In *The Cajuns: Essays on Their History and Culture*, edited by Glenn R. Conrad, 219–32. Lafayette: Center for Louisiana Studies, University of Southwestern Louisiana.

———. 1980–81. "Martin Luther King as Folk Hero." *Xavier Review* 1, no. 1–2: 65–74.

———. 1965. "The Folklore of Sacraments and Sacramentals in South Louisiana." *Louisiana Folklore Miscellany* 2, no. 2: 27–44.

———. 1961. "Some Accounts of Witch Riding." *Louisiana Folklore Miscellany* 2, no. 1: 1–18.

University of Southwestern Louisiana Department of English. 1996. Response to the Louisiana Board of Regents 1996 Consultants Review of Duplicate Programs in English.

MARCIA GAUDET is Professor of English Emerita at the University of Louisiana at Lafayette. She is author of *Carville: Remembering Leprosy in America*.

BARRY JEAN ANCELET is Professor Emeritus of Francophone Studies and Center for Louisiana Studies Research Fellow at the University of Louisiana at Lafayette. He is author of *Cajun and Creole Folktales: The French Oral Tradition of South Louisiana* and *Cajun and Creole Music Makers*.

17 The Fife Legacy

Fifty Years of Folklore at Utah State University

Randy Williams

WITH CHARISMATIC CHARM and evangelist-like determination, Austin Edwin Fife and Alta Stevens Fife built a notable folklore kingdom at Utah State University (USU). This kingdom includes a rich heritage of fieldwork and important archival collections as well as a strong tradition of ethics, scholarship, teaching, mentoring, and influential summer workshops and field schools. But perhaps the Fifes' most important legacy was the genius to continutally proselytize for folklore to keep the collections and program relevant and strong for over fifty years. The founders, however, came to the folklore profession circuitously. Following Austin's mission to France for The Church of Jesus Christ of Latter-day Saints (Mormon), the couple met at USU in 1932 (Wilson 2004, 41).[1] From there, Austin relocated to Palo Alto, California, to complete his undergraduate degree at Stanford. Alta soon joined him, and the couple married in 1934. Austin began graduate work under renowned folklorist Aurelio Espinosa Sr. in the Department of Romanic Languages. He earned an MA in 1935 and a PhD in 1939 (Wilson 2004, 41; Alta Fife 1988, xiii).

Significantly, Austin's graduate work focused on the sacredness of bees, honey, and wax in Christian popular tradition (1939, 15). Following his father's death, Austin worked high school summers as a beekeeper's assistant (Hatch 1990, 11). Furthermore, bees and beehives factored prominently in the worldview of Austin and Alta, both westerners raised in the heart of Mormon country. It was this connection that inspired Espinosa to suggest that Austin "apply what he had learned about the uses of folklore to his own background . . . in the Mormon field" (Hatch 1990, 11).

Armed with notepad and pencil, a camera, and later a portable Wilcox-Gay Recordio, the Fifes set out in their camp trailer to collect Mormon folklore (Austin Fife 1948, 299; Hatch 1990, 12–13; Rudy 2002, 44; Toelken 1988, x). From 1939 through the early 1950s, they collected, categorized, and preserved over a thousand entries of Mormon folklore, which became the Fife Mormon Collection (Austin Fife 1948, 299; Fife and Fife 1986, xii).

Fig. 17.1. Austin and Alta Fife with fieldwork equipment and camping trailer on a fieldwork trip, Moab, UT, 1954. Photograph by Austin Fife, by permission of Fife Folklore Archives, Utah State University.

Their paths crossed with others collecting Mormon folklore, including Wayland Hand and Hector Lee. A common interest was the Three Nephites legend. These stories involve two-millennia-old characters from the *Book of Mormon* who live covertly on earth and come to the aid of Church of Jesus Christ members in need. All three scholars published on this distinctive legend, and owing to this shared connection, David Stanley wrote, the trio "were jokingly called the

'The Three Nephites' by friends" (2004, 9). With all three teaching at institutions in the Los Angeles area, they frequently got together at Austin and Alta's home for dinner and to discuss folklore (Hatch 1990, 22). This social and intellectual contact was important for the Fifes, who came from outside the folklore academy and benefited from peer synergy (Rudy 2002). Espinoza's mentoring and the collegiality between the Fifes, Lee, Hand, and others helped build a foundation for the Fifes' folklore pursuits.

In 1960, the Fifes left California after Austin accepted a position at USU to teach French language and literature (Wilson 1986, 288; 2004, 42). At USU, the Fifes began organizing events to promote folklore. Austin chaired two conferences: Folklore in the American West in 1963 and the 1968 regional meeting on material culture and customs with Henry Glassie (Utah State University 1963; Glassie 1969, 2). These conferences, which were sponsored by the Folklore Society of Utah (which the Fifes had helped to found) and the American Folklore Society, put folklore on the map at USU (Wilson 1986, 288–90; 2004, 47; Williams 2004). The 1968 conference followed a weeklong course, American Folk Cultures and Their Crafts, and led to *Forms upon the Frontier: Folklife and Folk Arts in the United States*, published by USU Press.[2]

In 1964, responding to Austin's spirited proposal that the Fifes' fieldwork collection be housed in the USU library, university librarian Milton C. Abrams wrote Austin Fife confirming that the "library would accept custody at any time it pleases you" (Abrams 1964). The Fifes began depositing their extensive fieldwork collection in 1966 (Abrams 1967).[3] In 1972, the library established the Austin and Alta Fife Library of Western American Folklore, renamed the Fife Folklore Archives, in Special Collections and Archives (Simmonds 1972).

Austin and Alta championed the idea of hiring a folklorist to manage the collection and to teach folklore. Library director Max Peterson remembers that their gift was not easy because the Fifes wanted to have hands-on oversight of the collection and there was no precedent for this in the library. Peterson recalls that because of the Fifes' wishes, the politics of the donation were "intense . . . [both] in-house and across campus." But he explains how Austin did a "wonderful job of taking me in . . . , teaching me about folklore."[4]

During summer 1970, Austin arranged for Hector Lee to teach the first non-workshop folklore course. A year later, after stepping down as head of the Department of Languages and Philosophy, Austin also began teaching folklore. "Throughout Austin's professional career as a language and literature teacher and administrator," William A. Wilson notes, "he and Alta followed a second career in folklore research—collecting, documenting, archiving, and publishing the folklore of the West" (1986, 288). In 1971, Austin's name was added as a full professor in the English Department (Utah State University, 1971–72). Fife required students to collect folklore and deposit the items in the Fife Folklore

Archives (FFA). From this time forward, folklore courses have been taught at USU.

Austin retired from USU in 1975, but he and Alta continued championing the idea of an in-house folklorist to curate folklore collections and to create a folklore program. Their dream was realized in 1978, when William A. "Bert" Wilson left Brigham Young University (see Rudy, this volume) to teach folklore courses and manage the FFA at USU. A tireless folklore advocate, Wilson presented at conferences, spoke to community groups, published, and served as a board member for professional organizations. With Wilson at the helm, the university set out to establish a premier folklore program and archive.

Wilson and Peterson (Austin's protégé in the library) created a blueprint for USU's folklore program and archive. Peterson recalls a trip that he and Wilson made to look at folklore programs and archives. "Alan Jabbour was our host in DC," Peterson recounted, "he showed us the American Folklife Center at the Library of Congress. It was a perfect pattern, because it was sitting in the library."[5]

Wilson was not only a determined promoter of folklore to the local community and university administrators but also a gifted and admired teacher. Like Fife, Wilson required his students to collect and deposit folklore in the FFA. During his graduate work at Indiana University, Wilson conducted research in the Finnish Folklore Archives. The Finnish model served as a guide for Wilson and his graduate assistant and later colleague, Barbara Walker Lloyd, to create the archiving system for the student folklore collection. Today, due to Austin's and Wilson's founding efforts, the USU Student Folklore Collection includes thousands of examples of folklore.

In summer 1978, Wilson, English professor Patricia Gardner, and others organized the second Fife Folklore Conference on Western American Folk Culture (Williams 2008). The workshop boasted a faculty of eight folklorists, including the aforementioned "Three Nephites" as well as Barre Toelken, who taught a diverse audience of university students, schoolteachers, and community members. A steak fry in Logan Canyon brought together university deans and department heads with prominent US folklorists. Under Wilson's and Lloyd's direction, the Fife Folklore Conference became a premier event. Elaine Thatcher, USU's first folklore graduate student, remembered the importance of the conference to her education: "All these people came, so even though you were a one-person department [speaking to Wilson] . . . we were exposed to all these other folklorists" (Thatcher 2013, 26).

Selected to deliver the twenty-fifth annual Fife Honor Lecture in 2001, Lloyd asked Wilson for his impressions of the conference: "It was a helluva lot of work, especially for a paranoid person like me . . . but work that enriched my life immeasurably. I was always thrilled to be able to honor Austin and Alta Fife with a conference named after them. I took great pleasure in helping open up the world of folklore to public school teachers, librarians, local historians, folklore students from other universities, senior citizens who drifted in, and just about anyone with a zest for learning" (Lloyd 2004, 234). The conference gained a national reputation that Wilson took pains to preserve. "I had people coming up and asking me if they could teach," he later related, "but I was very selective in who I would let teach, because some . . . were dry as dust folklorists, and I didn't want them destroying it" (Thatcher 2013, 26).

Lloyd codirected the conference, served as the associate director of the folklore program, and managed the Fife Folklore Archives. With input from the Fifes, she expertly oversaw their materials and, during her tenure, added twenty more collections. In 1993, she received a National Historical Preservation and Records Commission grant to transfer the Fifes' fieldwork acetate discs and reel-to-reel tapes to archival Mylar reel-to-reel tapes. (In 2016, funding from the Utah Department of Heritage and Arts allowed digitization of the collection.)

After Brigham Young University enticed Wilson to return, USU hired Barre Toelken in 1985 to lead its folklore endeavors. Toelken had directed the folklore program at the University of Oregon (see Sherman, this volume). Toelken, like Austin Fife, traveled a winding road to the profession. As a forestry student at USU during the 1950s, Toelken took a class from King Hendricks, the larger-than-life head of the English Department. The course, titled Floating Poetry, was described as "poetry that has lived in oral tradition since medieval times" (Utah State University 1964–65). Toelken grew up singing ballads, and the class whetted his academic appetite for balladry. He promptly changed his major to English (Williams 2011, 15–16). Toelken often incorporated folk songs into classroom lectures and community presentations. Peterson recalls going with Toelken to eastern Utah on a networking trip. When they were leaving Logan, Toelken cried, "Wait, let me get my guitar. If things go bad, I can always sing and make it better."[6]

Toelken's charismatic personality and engaging teaching style attracted graduate students to USU from across the country and around the world, and the program grew significantly. During his tenure (1985–2002), he served as the director of the folklore program and codirector (with Lloyd and then Randy Williams) of the Fife Folklore Conference. Like Wilson, Toelken worked to raise the national presence of the program. Toelken and Lloyd, with support from the USU library, submitted the successful proposal to the American Folklore Society for USU's Special Collections and Archives to become the official repository of the society's papers.

Toelken worked with the American Folklore Society to create a two-week public-sector residency at USU. A Folklore Fellow, he kept his collegial bonds throughout the world strong and mentored junior colleagues and graduate students. He nurtured connections with USU's history and anthropology departments and strengthened ties with USU Special Collections and Archives. He used his political savvy and people skills to make and keep campus and community friends. Hal Cannon, founding director of the Western Folklife Center and early Fife Folklore Conference collaborator, wrote,

> Barre Toelken is one of my great heroes. It's more than the fact that he's an esteemed folklorist who younger folklorists look up to. It's more than his wonderful books on folklore, or the hundreds of songs he knows. It's really the way he conducts his life with courage and individuality that makes him a hero. . . . A few years ago he asked me if I wanted to travel to Navajo country to visit his family. . . . As he conversed in Navajo I realized he was not just a folklorist, curious about exotic traditions that were far from what he grew up with. With time, he had become a trusted keeper of the family history, a respected elder. (Cannon 2009)

Toelken joked that it took three people to replace Wilson, referring to Steve Siporin, Jay Allan Anderson, and himself. Siporin's and Anderson's faculty positions were a tribute to the Fifes' groundwork and to Wilson's and Toelken's efforts to secure funding. Siporin, an outstanding student of Toelken's at the University of Oregon, received his PhD from Indiana University and worked as a state folklorist in Idaho and Oregon. In 1989, when Siporin joined the USU faculty, the university acquired a seasoned public folklorist who helped cultivate the folklore program's new public-sector emphasis. He taught an array of folklore courses, continued Fife's and Wilson's tradition of teaching Mormon folklore, and introduced Jewish folklore. Siporin successfully served as director of the folklore program from 2008 to 2013, during the US economic downturn, carefully shepherding the program through this difficult time when other programs were closing. A thoughtful educator and mentor, Siporin nurtured many important public folklorists. Steven Hatcher recollects, "Twenty years after graduate school, and now as the state folklorist of Idaho in the same chair that Steve occupied many years before, I feel both influenced by his mentorship in Utah and inspired by his legacy as a civil servant."[7] Siporin retired in 2016.

An outdoor museum specialist, Anderson came to USU to direct the Jensen Historical Farm Museum and establish an MA program in outdoor museum administration (Jones and Carter 2011). Jointly appointed in history and English, his course offerings included historic preservation and foodways. During Anderson's tenure (1985–99), outdoor museum students participated in hands-on projects at the Ronald V. Jensen Living History Farm, a Mormon pioneer farm that includes a museum that Austin Fife helped plan in the 1960s.

With Toelken at the helm, the 1990s brought steady gains for folklore with increased library space, outreach endeavors, and two new positions. In 1993, Randy Williams, a public-sector MS from USU, came on board to assist with the FFA and Fife Folklore Conference; shortly after, she was appointed university folklorist, focused on outreach. In 1996, when Lloyd left for a position in Ohio, Williams became director (now curator/library faculty) of the Fife Folklore Archives, assistant director of the folklore program (until 2003), and archival liaison for the American Folklore Society. As the codirector of the Fife Folklore Conference, Williams continued Wilson's commitment to include tradition bearers as conference faculty, and she hosted several teacher tracks at the conference.

Following in the Fifes' fieldwork footsteps, in 2003, Williams launched Northern Utah Speaks, a bold FFA oral history initiative focused on gathering, preserving, and presenting the voices of the people and heritage of the Intermountain West, especially the historically excluded. A hallmark of these efforts is deep collaborations with community stakeholders, and results include the Cache Valley Drug Court Oral History Project and the award-winning Latinx Voices Project. In 2010, with Timothy Lloyd and Michael Taft, Williams created Collecting Memories: Oral Histories of American Folklorists. Partnering with the USU folklore faculty, she strives to make the Fife Folklore Archives a lab for folklore students, including hosting graduate interns, shepherding digital exhibit curation, and teaching cultural documentation. During her tenure, fifty collections were added to the FFA. In 2017, Williams was appointed to the Utah Humanities Board.

In 1998, Jeannie Thomas, MA from USU and PhD from the University of Oregon, joined the folklore faculty. On her arrival, she created a folklore minor. Thomas quickly moved into administrative duties when Toelken suffered a major stroke in 2002. Thomas served as interim director (2002–4) and director (2004–8) of the folklore program, and from 2009 to 2020 as the department head of English. "I followed Barre Toelken," Thomas noted, "as the director of the program; he is a very charismatic personality and a hard act to follow."[8] She put a structure in place that would see the program survive and grow past any one director. Of this she said: "One way we did that was to make sure the curriculum was strong, that it was important to the mission of the English Department. We began to offer courses online, using the Regional Campuses and Distance Education model, and we made money, which is always important to a department. So, we made folklore profitable to the department in both curricular offerings and funding."[9]

Thomas focused on program building and security, along with obtaining financial support for students. During her tenure as program director, she obtained funding for a folklore graduate fellowship. Shortly after the economic downturn, she secured a $2.5 million gift from Janice Dee; this endowment supports undergraduate and graduate students, including folklore students. Thomas partnered with the American Folklife Center to create an internship for USU folklore students. And she worked to "make folklore a necessary part of the department curriculum, so that as folklorists retire, their vacated lines will be replaced with other folklorists, and the program at USU will continue."[10]

This came to pass in 2004, when Lisa Gabbert, PhD from Indiana University, joined the folklore faculty upon Toelken's retirement. A dedicated educator and mentor, Gabbert served on the American Folklore Society board (2011–13) and as the director of the folklore program from 2013 to 2019. As director, she worked to revitalize and integrate public-sector opportunities for students and to integrate the folklore program more closely with the FFA. She worked with folklorist Elaine Thatcher to host a joint meeting of the Western States Folklore Society and the Association of Western State Folklorists in Logan that served to broaden USU students' exposure to folkloristics.

Gabbert also expanded the scope of the program's fieldwork component by making the fieldwork course required for all folklore graduate students and, working closely with Williams, including significant public-sector and archiving fieldwork components. Together they hosted two Library of Congress Field Schools for Cultural Documentation, keeping alive the strong fieldwork tradition started by the Fifes. Gabbert and Williams, along with library dean Brad Cole, created a graduate certificate in archiving and public programming that cemented the folklore program's new direction toward a greater emphasis in libraries and archiving. This emphasis is expanded by the study of digital culture brought about by the Digital Folklore Project and new technologies in digital exhibits and archiving.

The 2015 field school heralded the movement away from the financial crunch brought on by the economic recession that had hit the folklore program, including the loss of "support/alliance with the USU Mountain West Center for Regional Studies" that Thatcher directed before the position was lost.[11] Under Gabbert's thoughtful care, the program "stayed vibrant by focusing on strengths and by moving in new directions with online classes."[12] This led the way for a full online major and allowed the program to grow and reach a broader audience.

In 2009, Lynne McNeill was hired as an adjunct professor; in 2016, following Siporin's retirement, she assumed a tenure-track position. A specialist in digital culture, legend, and belief and a brilliant scholar and student advocate, McNeill holds an MA from USU and a PhD from Memorial University of Newfoundland. With Thomas, she cofounded and codirects the Digital Folklore Project that tracks annual digital trends. She founded the online folklore minor and worked with Williams and Dylan Burns, former USU digital scholarship librarian, to facilitate online folklore collecting. A tireless promoter of folklore, McNeill mentors students in creative and innovative ways, including serving—as did Austin Fife, Wilson, Toelken, Williams, and Gabbert—on the Folklore Society of Utah Board. She is the current director of the folklore program.[13]

Today the faculty of the Fife Folklore Archives and the folklore program at Utah State University work hand-in-hand, sometimes like evangelists, but more often just diligently and intelligently, to preserve folk culture at the archives,

Fig. 17.2. 2017 Utah State University/University of Wyoming Library of Congress Field School for Cultural Documentation students and faculty at the historic Bar BC Ranch, Grand Teton National Park. *Left to right:* Andrea Graham, Bethany Budge, Rebecca Westrup, Carol Nicholas, Jessica Cushenberry, Shelley Jones, Anthony Ross Garner, Liz Setterburg, Randy Williams, Guha Shankar, Amelia Mathews-Pett, Kylie Schroeder, Rebecca Goodson, Lisa Gabbert, Maggie Kruesi, Alexander Hodel, Lori Hyde, Jeannie Banks Thomas, and CJ Guadarrama. Photograph by permission of Fife Folklore Archives, Utah State University. Photographer: Jeannie Banks Thomas.

pursue new trends, publish, and present folklore to the next generation of folklorists. Thus, today Utah State University has a thriving folklore program and the strong and relevant Fife Folklore Archives that continue in the spirit of inquiry, preservation, and presentation of folk culture established by the indomitable Austin and Alta Fife, shepherded by devoted and passionate folklorists for over fifty years.

Notes

1. In August 2018, The Church of Jesus Christ of Latter-day Saints issued a new naming style guide, requesting that the use of the word *Mormon* be discontinued with exception for proper names, such as the Fife Mormon Collection, or as an adjective in historical expression, such as Mormon folklore.

2. This began a fruitful publishing relationship between folklorists and USU Press. Today, folklore is a major publication focus.

3. The collection grew to include acetate discs and reel-to-reel field recordings, sixty-seven bound volumes of field notes and transcriptions, an extensive slide collection, and the Fifes' folklore book and record collection.

4. Max Peterson, phone conversation and email exchange with the author, March 19, 2016.

5. Ibid.

6. Ibid.

7. Steven Hatcher, email to the author, January 15, 2018.

8. Jeannie Thomas, phone conversation and email exchange with the author, March 15, 2016.

9. Ibid.

10. Ibid.

11. Lisa Gabbert, email to the author, March 17, 2016.

12. Ibid.

13. Over the years, others helped to shape folklore at USU. I would be remiss not to mention the following people: Glenn Wilde, Patricia Gardner, Jan Roush, Karen Krieger, Patricia Gantt, Elaine Thatcher, Star Coulbrooke, Claudia Schwabe, Heidi Williams, Eric Morales, and many graduate interns and student workers.

References

Abrams, Milton C. 1964. Letter to Austin Fife from Milton C. Abrams, April 15, 1964. USU Special Collections and Archives. Fife, Austin and Alta Donor File.

———. 1967. Letter to Austin and Alta Fife from Milton C. Abrams, University Librarian, June 7, 1967, USU Special Collections and Archives. MSS Collection 281. The Papers of Austin E. and Alta S. Fife. Box 1, Folder 13.

Cannon, Hal. 2012. "Barre Toelken Is One of My Great Heroes." Western Folklife Center. https://westernfolklifecenter.wordpress.com/2012/01/09/barre-toelken-is-one-of-my-great-heroes/.

Fife, Alta. 1988. Preface. In *Exploring Western Americana*, by Austin E. Fife and edited by Alta Fife, xiii. Ann Arbor, MI: UMI Research Press.

Fife, Austin E. 1939. "The Concept of the Sacredness of Bees, Honey and Wax in Christian Popular Tradition." PhD diss., Stanford University.

———. 1948. "Collectors and Collections." *Western Folklore* 7, no. 3: 299–301.

Fife, Austin E., and Alta Fife. 1986. Preface. In *Fife Mormon Collection*, xii–xiii. Logan: Utah State University Special Collections, Folk Coll 4 no. 1, Series I.

Glassie, Henry. 1969. Introduction. In *Forms upon the Frontier: Folklife and Folk Arts in the United States*, edited by Austin and Alta Fife and Henry Glassie, 1–7. Logan: Utah State University Press.

Hatch, Anne F. 1990. "An Interview with Alta Fife." Fife Folklore Archives. Folk Coll 8, Grad, Box 9, 90-012, 11.

Jones, Zach, and Andrea Carter. 2011. History. The Jensen Historical Farm Research Collection, 1961–93. Utah State University Special Collections and Archives, MSS 236. http://archiveswest.orbiscascade.org/ark:/80444/xv57568.

Lloyd, Barbara. 2004. "Lessons of Summer: The Fife Folklore Conference." In *Folklore in Utah: A History and Guide to Resources*, edited by David Stanley, 230–39. Logan: Utah State University Press.

Rudy, Jill Terry. 2002. "'Rather Out of the Center of Things': Contributions of Alta Fife to American Folklore Scholarship." *Western Folklore* 61, no. 1: 43–62.

Simmonds, Andrew J. 1972. Letter from Austin Fife to Simmonds, March 11, 1972. USU Special Collections and Archives. Fife, Austin and Alta Donor File.

Stanley, David. 2004. "Folklore Work in Utah: A Historical Survey." In *Folklore in Utah: A History and Guide to Resources*, edited by David Stanley, 6–19. Logan: Utah State University Press.

Thatcher, Elaine. 2013. William A. Wilson Interview. *Collecting Memories: Oral Histories of American Folklorists*. Utah State University. https://digital.lib.usu.edu/digital/collection/AFS/id/365/rec/1.

Toelken, Barre. 1988. Foreword. In *Exploring Western Americana*, by Austin E. Fife and edited by Alta Fife, x. Ann Arbor, MI: UMI Research Press.

Utah State University. 1963. Folklore in the American West. Brochure. USU Special Collections and Archives, Utah State University Library, Folk Collection 31, Box 1, Folder 2, item 1.

———. 1964–65. Course Catalog: English. Logan: USU Publication. University Archives, 9.5/1, Box 13. USU Special Collections and Archives, Utah State University Library, 214.

———. 1971–72. Course Catalog: English. Logan: USU Publication. University Archives, 9.5/1, Box 15. USU Special Collections and Archives, Utah State University Library, 171.

Williams, Randy. 2004. *Folklore Society of Utah Records, 1958–2015*. Special Collections and Archives, Utah State University Library. http://archiveswest.orbiscascade.org/ark:/80444/xv90362.

———. 2008. *The Fife Folklore Conference Collection, 1977–2015*. Special Collections and Archives, Utah State University Library. http://archiveswest.orbiscascade.org/ark:/80444/xv88607.

———. 2011. John Barre Toelken Interview. *Collecting Memories: Oral Histories of American Folklorists*. Utah State University. https://digital.lib.usu.edu/digital/collection/AFS/id/433/rec/1.

Wilson, William A. 1986. "In Memoriam: Austin E. Fife, 1909–86." *Utah Historical Quarterly* 54, no. 3: 288–90.

———. 2004. "Austin and Alta Fife, Pioneer Folklorists." In *Folklore in Utah: A History and Guide to Resources*, edited by David Stanley, 41–48. Logan: Utah State University Press.

RANDY WILLIAMS retired at the end of 2019; she is emerita faculty and former Fife Folklore Archives Curator and Oral History Specialist at Utah State University Library's Special Collections and Archives.

Part III

Newer Programs and Innovations

18 Folklife in the Nation's Capital

The George Washington University Experience

James I. Deutsch

The George Washington University in Washington, DC, offered courses on folklore as early as the 1890s. Taught by Otis T. Mason, an anthropologist and curator at the Smithsonian Institution, the following offerings were included in the anthropology curriculum: The History of Culture, The Races of Man, and The History of the Past as Revealed in the Sciences of Archaeology and Folk-Lore (Vlach 1987, 4–5). Mason had served in 1891 as the third president of the American Folklore Society and remained a part-time faculty member at GWU (known as Columbian University from 1873 to 1904) for most of his professional life. He also arranged for the American Folklore Society to hold its annual meeting at Columbian University in 1891.

So far as can be determined, folklore courses were not offered at GWU in any systematic way until the mid- to late 1970s, when once again curators from the Smithsonian Institution served as part-time faculty members through the American Studies Program. One impetus for the return of folklore to the curriculum was the Smithsonian's Festival of American Folklife, which began in 1967 on a relatively modest scale. However, in conjunction with the American Bicentennial in 1976, the Folklife Festival lasted twelve weeks, from June 16 through September 6, 1976, occupying much of the National Mall of the United States. As noted by Richard Kurin, former director of the office that produces the festival, "The Bicentennial Festival illustrated in the strongest terms the living nature of folk culture throughout the United States and the world. Rather than dying in the Industrial Revolution or having been smothered by the influence of mass culture, community-based grassroots cultural traditions were still practiced, still meaningful in the contemporary lives of Americans and other people of the world" (1998, 132). With the immense visibility that the festival generated for American folklife, the GWU American Studies Program felt it was time to incorporate folklife into its curriculum.

Based on correspondence in the GWU Archives, Ralph Rinzler, who had cofounded the Folklife Festival and who directed the Office of Folklife Programs at the Smithsonian, wrote to Bernard Mergen, professor of American studies, on August 8, 1977, to offer several Smithsonian staff members to teach folklore at GWU. As envisioned by Rinzler, Jack Santino and Steve Zeitlin (both of whom had worked on Folklife Festival programs in 1975, 1976, and 1977) would take the lead in designing both undergraduate and graduate courses at GWU, with the help of occasional lecturers from the Office of Folklife Programs. Rinzler identified Susan Kalčik as a specialist in ethnic lore, Tom Vennum in ethnomusicology, Robert Byington in occupational folklore, and Rinzler himself in British and American folk music. The Smithsonian would pay the salaries for Santino and Zeitlin but would expect to receive in return half of the tuition revenue that students in these courses would pay (Rinzler 1977).

Santino and Zeitlin continued to lead the folklife offerings at GWU for the next four years and taught a variety of courses, with Introduction to Folklore and The Uses of Folklore in the Modern World the most frequently offered. As Santino recalled,

> Ralph Rinzler used to allow us release time. He thought it was good to have a professional relationship with GWU, and we taught different courses, which were always cross-listed with American Studies and Anthropology. There was one that we did where we brought in people from museums and government offices, possibly leading to internships for students. So we had this course where we brought in different folklorists, Joe Hickerson [director of the Archive of Folk Culture at the Library of Congress], Ralph Rinzler, Alan Jabbour [director of the American Folklife Center at the Library of Congress], and Rusty Marshall [also at the American Folklife Center]. They were regulars, once a year or once a semester, to talk about their expertise and their institution. This went on for a while, and I was even full-time for one academic year. . . . We were supposed to be developing interest among students, so they wanted to build a program within the American Studies Department.[1]

The American Studies Program at GWU became the Department of American Studies in 1998.

Seeking to provide a firmer foundation for its folklife courses, the American Studies Program at GWU applied in July 1979 to the National Endowment for the Humanities (NEH) for $83,952 in support of developing a graduate program in American Folklife Studies. The funds would be used to hire a program director for the period from July 1, 1980, through June 30, 1983 (Solomon 1979). However, on November 30, 1979, the NEH informed Henry Solomon, dean of the GWU Graduate School of Arts and Sciences (who had formally submitted the application on behalf of American Studies) that the proposal was not recommended for funding (Duffey 1979).

Nevertheless, GWU persisted in seeking to develop a folklife program through American Studies, largely through the efforts of faculty members Howard Gillette (who was serving as American Studies chair), Bernard Mergen (whose own interests in play and material culture resonated with folklife offerings), and Robert Walker (who was the senior member in GWU's American Studies Program and former president of the American Studies Association in 1970–71). As Gillette recalled, "American Studies [at GWU] owed much to the idea that when disciplines rubbed up against each other, new insights emerged. Bob Walker was very much a part of that, and he had the good sense to figure out that GW could gain distinction through external affiliations—at the LC [Library of Congress] and the Smithsonian. My role was to extend that sense of radiation by adding the programs in preservation and folklore. In fact both programs owed much to Walker, because he laid the groundwork."[2] Less than seven months after receiving notification that its NEH proposal was rejected, the GWU American Studies Program received notification from the university provost that its request for a folklorist at the rank of associate professor was approved, effective for the 1981–82 academic year (Bright 1980).

Word spread quickly that GWU would be hiring a folklorist. Richard Dorson, director of the Folklore Institute at Indiana University, wrote to suggest that IU doctoral students who pursued the combined degree of folklore and American studies might be strong candidates for the new position (1980). Alan Jabbour, director of the American Folklife Center at the Library of Congress, wrote to advise on the job description's wording and to suggest that the upcoming American Folklore Society meeting in Pittsburgh might be a good opportunity for interviewing potential candidates (1980).

GWU received applications from many candidates and ultimately selected John Michael Vlach from the University of Texas at Austin to fill the position. Vlach had completed his PhD at Indiana University in 1975, writing a dissertation (co-supervised by Henry Glassie and Warren Roberts) titled "Sources of the Shotgun House: African and Caribbean Antecedents for Afro-American Architecture." He had also recently published *The Afro-American Tradition in Decorative Art* (1978) as an exhibition catalog for the Cleveland Museum of Art, covering the traditions of architecture, basketry, blacksmithing, boatbuilding, graveyard decoration, musical instruments, pottery, quilting, and woodcarving among African Americans in the United States. Vlach's strengths in material folk culture undoubtedly appealed to GWU's American studies faculty, which could assert that "The George Washington faculty is particularly strong in the areas of material culture and ethnohistory and programs in museum studies and historic preservation provide a public sector compliment [*sic*] to the usual folklife offerings" ("Folklife Program"). Many of the graduate students in these concentrations—especially material culture and historic preservation—were already working in

A FOLKLIFE PROGRAM IN THE NATION'S CAPITAL

The George Washington University announces the creation of a graduate program in folklife study in the American Studies Program and the Anthropology Department. This program is being developed in cooperation with the Smithsonian's Folklife Program and the American Folklife Center at the Library of Congress. Students can pursue an MA in American Civilization with a concentration in folklife or may select folklife for one or two fields in a four field Ph.D. program in American Civilization. It is also possible to earn an MA in anthropology with a concentration in folklife. The George Washington faculty is particularly strong in the areas of material culture and ethnohistory and programs in museum studies and historic preservation provide a public sector compliment to the usual folklife offerings.

Much of each student's course of studies can be tailored to suit individual interests and needs. Independent study courses can be arranged with the many folklife specialists who reside in the Washington area; internships for course credit at the Smithsonian, Library of Congress, or other cultural agencies are also available. Students will find a tremendous range of resources in the region including museums, libraries, other colleges and universities, and many preservation, local history, and federal agencies. Exciting opportunities exist for fieldwork on urban lore as well as on the maritime and agricultural life of the greater Chesapeake-Potomac region.

Listed below are the George Washington faculty who offer folklife and folklife-related courses and some of local Washington area folklorists who are available to students.

George Washington Faculty

Catherine Allen, symbolic anthropology, religion
Pamela Cressy, historical archaeology
Marcus Cunliffe, history of ideas
Howard Gillette, urban lore
Victor Golla, linguistic anthropology, Native American culture
Frank Grubar, folk art
James Horton, Afro-American culture
Robert Humphrey, ethnohistory
Ruth Krulfeld, peasant society, art and aesthetics
Bernard Mergen, labor lore, oral history, play
Clarence Mondale, regionalism
Phyllis Palmer, women's studies
John Pearce, historic preservation, architectural history
Michael Shapiro, museum studies
Colin Turnbull, cultural anthropology
John Vlach, American folklife, folklore theory
Robert Walker, cultural history
Wilcomb Washburn, material culture

Selected Folklife Associates

Charles Camp, Maryland State Arts Council
Bess Lomax Hawes, National Endowment for the Arts
Joseph Hickerson, Archive of Folksong
Richard Hulan, National Council for the Traditional Arts
Alan Jabbour, American Folklife Center
Gerald Parsons, Archive of Folksong
Barry Lee Pearson, University of Maryland
Jo Radner, American University
Ralph Rinzler, Smithsonian
Peter Seitel, Smithsonian
Robert Teske, National Endowment for the Arts
Thomas Venum, Smithsonian
Sally Yerkovich, National Endowment for the Humanities

For further information write:

Dr. John Michael Vlach
Director of the Folklife Program
American Studies Program
George Washington University
Washington, D.C. 20052

Fig. 18.1. Flyer announcing the inauguration of the George Washington University folklife program, undated, probably 1981. Courtesy of James Deutsch.

these fields and found GWU's American Studies Program particularly amenable to their work schedules. Most of the graduate seminars took place in the late afternoon or early evening, and faculty-directed independent studies were readily available for graduate credit.

When Vlach arrived at GWU in fall 1981, he was expected to formalize the folklife program at the university. Of course, Santino and Zeitlin, through their course offerings and contacts at the Smithsonian, had already attracted a small group of graduate students who were interested in pursuing folklife studies at GWU. Vlach's primary task was to promote the materials and methods of folkloristic research within the larger framework of American studies. He needed to entice students already enrolled in GWU's American Studies Program to folklife while also attracting new students interested in folklife to pursue a graduate degree in American civilization.[3] GWU students could pursue "a concentration in folklife" through an MA degree either in American civilization or in anthropology; or they could "select folklife for one or two fields in a four field Ph.D. program in American Civilization" ("Folklife Program").

Vlach's tasks were aided immeasurably by the graduate students who established the GW Folklife Association not long after he arrived. Publishing the first *GW Folklife Newsletter* in spring 1982, these students proclaimed, "Now that we are a full-fledged folklife program, it's time to announce our existence to a larger audience of folklorists, students, and institutions around the country. . . . For the moment, the purpose of the Association is to issue the newsletter, but as the program grows, we plan to schedule lectures, informal discussion groups, concerts, and student folklife conferences" (Maguire 1982, 1). Publication of the *GW Folklife Newsletter* continued for the next ten years, usually semiannually, through fall 1991. The newsletter reappeared briefly with two issues in 1997 but has not been published since.

Regular stories throughout the 1980s included a report from Vlach titled "Director's Column"; news about GW Folklife Association members; reports on current student activities; and a "featured folklorist" working in one of the nearby federal agencies, such as the Library of Congress, Smithsonian Institution, or National Endowment for the Arts. Special issues appeared on such topics as folk art, women's folklore, and urban folklore. The *GW Folklife Newsletter* provides one of the best glimpses into the health of the GW Folklife Program for the first ten years of its existence.

Many of the most active members of the GW Folklife Association worked regular nine-to-five jobs, including Beverly Brannan, Catherine Hiebert Kerst, and Marsha Maguire at the Library of Congress; Olivia Cadaval at Centro de Arte; and Claudine Weatherford at the Alexandria Archaeological Research Center. Accordingly, the group held its biweekly meetings over breakfast, starting at 7:30 a.m. in Reeves Bakery and Restaurant in downtown Washington, DC. As described in the newsletter: "Each breakfast meeting is devoted to a particular topic presented by one of the students, followed by a general discussion. Since January presentations have included: Karen Pataky on folk healing and folk medicine; Claudine Weatherford on Virginia genre painter Queena Stovall; Darcie MacMahon on town planning in St. Augustine, Florida; and Barbara Fertig on barbecue" (Deutsch 1983, 3). Other highlights in the 1980s and early 1990s included hosting two meetings of the Middle Atlantic Folklife Association, first

Fig. 18.2. Members of the GW Folklife Association meet for an early-morning breakfast at Reeves Bakery and Restaurant on September 6, 1988. Photograph courtesy of James Deutsch.

in April 1986 and then in March 1991; assisting with the National Endowment for the Arts's National Heritage Fellowships awards ceremony when it moved to Lisner Auditorium on the GWU campus in 1986; and sponsoring a blues house party in May 1986, which raised some $500 for the association.

Vlach regularly taught graduate seminars on American folklife and American folklore theory as well as special topics that included folklife and federal policy, folk art, and vernacular architecture. For undergraduates, he regularly taught Introduction to Folklore and Folk Arts in America. Vlach supervised doctoral dissertations on topics ranging from folklife festivals, folk schools, folk dance, folk music, and folk potters to African American folklore, Portuguese American feasts, and Jewish foodways. Although a one-person program in folklife presented obvious limitations, GWU occasionally hired additional faculty members—such as LeeEllen Friedland, Barry Lee Pearson, and Robert Teske—to supplement Vlach's focus on material folk culture.

When Vlach retired suddenly in fall 2012 due to health issues, his graduate seminars on American folklife and folklore theory were taught respectively by Stephen Winick from the American Folklife Center and James Deutsch from the Smithsonian Center for Folklife and Cultural Heritage. However, by fall 2014, the Department of American Studies was no longer offering folklore courses, and the Folklife Program had effectively ceased. In spring 2019, Deutsch once

Fig. 18.3. John Michael Vlach and his wife, Beverly Brannan, at a retirement celebration sponsored by the George Washington University American Studies Department, February 28, 2013. Photograph by Abby Greenawalt.

again taught a graduate seminar on folklore theory, but the future of such courses remains uncertain. Gayle Wald, chair of the American Studies Department, has indicated that

> Folklore/folklife studies have long been a part of GW's American Studies Department. In the 1980s we had particular strength in this area, but over the years the field of American Studies has shifted, and in many ways folklore studies, as traditionally conceived, is no longer as central to undergraduate and graduate training. But folklore studies remains crucial, and finds expression in new fields such as "object studies" (a version of material culture studies), as well as in work on cultural sustainability, ethnography, popular music studies, and other fields. We're currently exploring a reboot of our "Museums and Material Culture" MA track—a kind of Folklore/Material Culture 2.0.[4]

Through the ups and downs of the Folklife Program at GWU since the mid-1970s, its most distinguishing feature has been its advantageous location in the nation's capital, which, as Vlach once wrote, "is probably the 'folklore capital' of the country, with upwards of fifty degree-holding folklorists and specialists in related disciplines" who work in the American Folklife Center, the Folk and

Traditional Arts division of the National Endowment for the Arts, and the Smithsonian Center for Folklife and Cultural Heritage (Vlach 1983, 1). The Folklife Program at GWU not only utilizes these individuals as consultants and part-time faculty members but also has helped to augment their ranks with graduates of the program for nearly forty years.

Notes

1. Jack Santino, personal communication with the author, March 12, 2019.
2. Howard Gillette, personal communication with the author, March 7, 2019.
3. The American Studies Program at GWU awarded the degree in American civilization, not in American studies.
4. Gayle Wald, personal communication with the author, April 1, 2019.

References

Bright, H[arold] F. 1980. Letter to Howard Gillette, June 23. Record Group 82, Series 3, Box 1, George Washington University Archives (GWU Archives), Washington, DC.

Deutsch, Jim. 1983. "Folklife Association Breakfast Meetings." *GW Folklife Newsletter* 2, no. 1 (Fall): 2–3.

Dorson, Richard M. 1980. Letter to Howard Gillette, June 27. Record Group 82, Series 3, Box 1, GWU Archives, Washington, DC.

Duffey, Joseph D. 1979. Letter to Henry Solomon, November 30. Record Group 82, Series 3, Box 1, GWU Archives, Washington, DC.

"A Folklife Program in the Nation's Capital." [1981?]. Courtesy of the author.

Jabbour, Alan. 1980. Letter to Howard Gillette, July 11. Record Group 82, Series 3, Box 1, GWU Archives, Washington, DC.

Kurin, Richard. 1998. *Smithsonian Folklife Festival: Culture Of, By, and For the People.* Washington, DC: Smithsonian Institution.

Maguire, Marsha. 1982. "G.W.U. Folklife Association." *GW Folklife Newsletter* 1, no. 1 (Spring): 1.

Rinzler, Ralph. 1977. Letter to Bernard Mergen, August 7. Record Group 82, Series 4, Box 1, GWU Archives, Washington, DC.

Solomon, Henry. 1979. "Development of a Graduate Folklife Program," July 27. Record Group 82, Series 3, Box 1, GWU Archives, Washington, DC.

Vlach, John Michael. 1983. "Director's Column." *GW Folklife Newsletter* 2, no. 1 (Fall): 1.

———. 1987. "Director's Column." *GW Folklife Newsletter* 5, no. 2 (Spring): 4–5.

JAMES I. DEUTSCH is Curator and Editor at the Smithsonian Institution's Center for Folklife and Cultural Heritage and Adjunct Professor in the Department of American Studies at George Washington University.

19 The University of Wisconsin–Madison's Folklore Program and the Wisconsin Idea

Christine J. Widmayer and
B. Marcus Cederström

Most clearly articulated by and often attributed to former University of Wisconsin–Madison president Charles Van Hise, the Wisconsin Idea suggests "that the boundaries of the university should extend to the boundaries of the state, and, therefore, the research and teaching at the university should be used to improve the welfare of all Wisconsin citizens" (Garlough and Pryor 2011, 244). The Wisconsin Idea—an ethos and tradition practiced by faculty and students at the University of Wisconsin–Madison—as the university itself describes it "has come to signify more broadly the university's commitment to public service" (University of Wisconsin–Madison 2017). For folklorists at UW–Madison, the Wisconsin Idea has fostered a socially engaged research environment that, as Janet Gilmore, a professor of landscape architecture and folklore at UW–Madison, suggests, can work in many directions: "A mischievous public folklorist twist [to the Wisconsin Idea] encourages a reverse flow of knowledge from outside the classroom into the classroom, which then loops back out again, affording a greater sense of exchange, collective knowledge-building, and social equity between the state's people and the University" (2011, 257). That exchange, that knowledge building, that constant striving for social equity, is what has sustained folklore at the University of Wisconsin–Madison.

Despite the formal academic program in folklore studies being relatively young compared to many of the programs detailed in this volume, folklore has a long history at UW–Madison. From at least 1868, folklorists have been in residence at the university (Leary 1998, 16). James P. Leary's overview of the work conducted by several of these individuals in his book *Wisconsin Folklore* (1998) is but a brief glimpse into the work UW–Madison folklorists have undertaken since the late nineteenth century.

Despite those early scholars, it was not until 1982 that folklorists at the university from various area studies departments recognized the preponderance of folklore-oriented researchers present and chose to form the Folklore Program. What started as an effort to unify a dispersed set of scholars has since spawned graduate and undergraduate degree options and curricula, a regional Center for the Study of Upper Midwestern Cultures, well-respected archival holdings, and a continued engagement with the Wisconsin Idea by focusing on public folklore in the Upper Midwest and beyond. This chapter examines how the UW–Madison Folklore Program developed by committing to a public approach to folklore, especially through area studies, and a reliance on the Wisconsin Idea, which has been the program's sustaining force.

The Wisconsin Idea: The Folklorist's Imperative Today

As a public, land-grant institution since 1848, UW–Madison has long played a central role in the state. Former Wisconsin governor Robert La Follette credits his professor, John Bascom, who served from 1874 to 1887 as the fifth president of the university, with originating the Wisconsin Idea (Hoeveler 1976, 285). Bascom reportedly argued that university students and faculty had a moral responsibility to share their knowledge with Wisconsin residents (Garlough and Pryor 2011; Gilmore 2011). His successor, Thomas Chamberlin, expressed similar sentiments in a speech at the University of Nebraska in 1890, saying, "Scholarship for the sake of the scholar is simply refined selfishness. Scholarship for the state and the people is refined patriotism" (1890, 10).

These early attitudes were later summarized by Charles Van Hise, who, in a 1905 speech, suggested he would "never be content until the beneficent influence of the University reaches every family of the state" (University of Wisconsin–Madison 2017). Van Hise continued to clarify the Wisconsin Idea, and his 1905 speech is often cited as the inspiration for the university's long commitment to this ethos.

In 2011, Christine Garlough and Anne Pryor, both affiliates of UW–Madison's Folklore Program, edited a special issue of *Western Folklore* dedicated to folklore and the Wisconsin Idea. In their introduction, Garlough and Pryor describe three common themes shared among Wisconsin folklorists and informed by the Wisconsin Idea: first, inclusivity, both "of the state of Wisconsin and whatever local community and institutions it is serving"; second, civic engagement, which, through its connection to the community, "holds the potential to foster engagement, in terms of community service, social justice, activism, and community pedagogy"; and, finally, "locatedness" in terms of both "geographic space and the context of community" (2011, 247–48). The Wisconsin Idea, therefore, informs the way folklorists approach the communities with which they work and their

Fig. 19.1. Plaque celebrating the Wisconsin Idea set into a rock at the top of UW–Madison's Bascom Hill. Photograph by Marcus Cederström, April 19, 2017.

methods of engaging with those communities, and it brings to the fore their commitments to social justice, ethical practice, and reciprocity. The state's communities are recognized for their expertise, and folklorists amplify those voices through their public work. Of course, folklore has long claimed to embrace such an approach, but at UW–Madison that approach is encouraged, institutionalized, and very nearly carved in stone. Charles Van Hise's words from 1905 are etched in a plaque affixed to a stone at the top of Bascom Hill. Despite this lofty ideal, the Folklore Program at UW–Madison began not through public engagement but through area studies scholars' affinity for narrative-focused folklore.

Area Studies: The Folklore Program's Origins

In the 1980s several faculty members organized in an attempt to institutionalize folklore as a university-recognized program. At the time, folklore was both studied and occasionally taught by faculty members largely concentrated in area studies departments. Thomas A. Dubois, professor of Scandinavian studies and folklore at UW–Madison, described this factor as especially important to the development of the Folklore Program, saying that "an important thing [in the formation of the program] is area studies, and the way that so much of what folklore—the way it grew up at this university in particular—was out of area studies departments" (Dubois 2017). Folklore's place for Scandinavian scholars and the many other area studies scholars in Madison was often at the root of their studies, wrapped up in their understandings of their area's languages, history, and culture.

The Folklore Program was built by area studies scholars who recognized the place of folklore in higher education. Niels Ingwersen, a Scandinavian studies professor who chaired the Folklore Program in its beginnings, describes those early days: "Three people contacted me: Jim Bailey from Slavic, Harold Scheub from African, and Narayana Rao from Southeast Asian Studies, and they were toying with the idea of starting a Folklore Program, and they wondered if I would be interested. And I said 'Yes, of course.' So, together we started this Folklore Program" (Ingwersen 2006). If only it were that easy. Of course, Ingwersen leaves out countless meetings, committee work, a detailed proposal, a new curriculum, and letters of support to the deans of the college. Though folklore courses had been taught prior to the formation of the program, the lack of a central home or a defined curriculum for these courses had its drawbacks. The original proposal for the Folklore Program (UW–Madison Folklore Program 1983) reads, "Even though the University of Wisconsin currently offers a number of courses focused on the folklore of a particular area or limited to specific aspects of folklore, the University does not have any general courses on the subject. Because of this gap in coverage, faculty members and students, who are interested in folklore, are working in relative academic isolation." This statement from 1983 is reminiscent of Gilmore's words nearly thirty years later as she encourages "a greater sense of exchange" and "collective knowledge-building" (2011, 257). Instead of faculty and students working in isolation, the Folklore Program promised stability for the faculty and instructors, a broader comparative emphasis for the students, and an opportunity for exchange and knowledge building.

The proposal was officially accepted in 1983, with professors V. Narayana Rao (South Asian studies), James Bailey (Slavic languages), Niels Ingwersen (Scandinavian studies), Kari Lokke (comparative literature), Emiko Ohnuki-Tierney (anthropology), and Harold Scheub (African languages and literature) forming the initial executive committee. Over four dozen faculty members, mostly in other area studies and language departments, became affiliates. That same fall, UW–Madison began offering courses under the Folklore Program heading, beginning with Introduction to Folklore, The Folk Tale, The Folk Epic, and Myth (UW–Madison Folklore Program 1983). A 1983 press release from UW News billed the new program as an opportunity for students to get "a look at life as seen through the eyes of common people" (UW News 1983). According to Ingwersen, students responded positively to the new program. "Courses were very popular," he said, "people streamed to folklore. Students took a liking to it right away" (Ingwersen 2006).

At home, the program succeeded in establishing a student base; nationally, it earned recognition through a 1987 grant from the National Endowment for the Humanities (NEH). James Bailey, director of the Folklore Program at the time, wrote to his colleagues, "We received the news that NEH has given the Folklore Program $153,000 for a three-year grant to improve the program" (Bailey 1986). Improvement meant additional folklore hires, new courses, and expanding the university's archives. James Leary, who, as a visiting faculty member, first taught a course on Wisconsin folklore in the summer of 1984, was hired with NEH funds to teach a folklore course each semester. The federal funds also allowed the Folklore Program to bring folklorists from neighboring institutions. Richard Bauman visited in 1987 and advised on the program and its future direction. "In these lean times," Bauman wrote to Leary on August 3, 1987, "it's especially heartening to see a new Folklore Program get going" (Bauman 1987). While the lean times may have delayed its growth, grow it did.

The late 1980s and early 1990s saw new courses offered in American folklore and new instructors join the program. As the program expanded, so, too, did the opportunities for students. By the mid-1990s, the program offered a special committee PhD allowing graduate students to form a PhD committee made up of folklore-affiliated faculty. In 1999, Scott Mellor became the first student to graduate with a PhD in folklore from the University of Wisconsin–Madison. "My degree wasn't in Scandinavian Studies. It was a committee degree that had mostly folklore components. And I was looking at that interplay between oral and written story and narration, and therefore I was taking a lot from the folklorists and their way of looking at things, and I was taking some things from the literature people and how they did some things" (Mellor 2017). The Folklore Program's new special committee degree allowed Mellor and other students to examine and engage with folklore studies directly.

The same year that Mellor became the first PhD in folklore, the program expanded its offerings to undergraduate students, giving them the option to earn a folklore certificate in conjunction with their majors. In doing so, the university and the Folklore Program further strengthened the reverse flow of knowledge that Gilmore described. A folklore certificate legitimized the folkloristic expertise of the students, making space for them to share that expertise, to learn from others, and to strive for some sense of equity between the university situated in the state's capital and the people from across the state and region.

Expanding the Program: A Public Twist

As the Folklore Program continued to grow its student base, faculty and staff looked for new ways to expand the program. Leary, who had served as academic staff in the program for over a decade, became director of the Folklore Program in 1998. The next year, he was advanced to full professor. Leary describes the time as ripe for expansion. The university had started a cluster initiative to hire scholars who shared a discipline or research interests and to place them in departments across campus. With Professor Joe Salmons, a linguist working with languages of the Upper Midwest, Leary proposed a cluster hire for three new faculty members researching the language and folklore of the Upper Midwest. That same year, the NEH announced a program to fund the creation of regional humanities centers around the country. The two joined with Dr. Ruth Olson—then adjunct lecturer of folklore—to create a plan to leverage the institutional funding available for new hires alongside the federal funding for a regional humanities center. Leary recalls, "We were able to get the NEH and the university to recognize those cluster positions as being backed up by the endowment, so we had a match. So we got this grant from the NEH to establish the Center for the Study of Upper Midwestern Cultures" (Leary 2005).

Olson, hired as the assistant director of the Center for the Study of Upper Midwestern Cultures (CSUMC), explains, "The Center is meant to sustain and disseminate information about the cultures and languages of the Upper Midwest. And so we do that in a number of different ways. We emphasize this kind of outreach working collaboratively with communities and with classrooms so that they can explore . . . the varied identities within all these different communities in the Upper Midwest. Another way we do that is through production of materials" designed to be useful beyond the university (Olson 2017). Olson continues, "We received some money from [UW–Madison's] Continuing Studies to work on a project called 'Cultural Maps, Cultural Tours,' and that allowed us to work with some classroom teachers to take kids out to explore Wisconsin communities. . . . And then the kids developed material that was put into websites that emphasized, for example, Dane County. That cultural tour. We did a Hmong cultural tour in collaboration with the Madison Children's Museum for a major exhibit on Hmong culture that they had. And that tour took a class of 4th graders all around the state to different Hmong population centers" (Olson 2017).

Public work was instrumental in the formation of the Folklore Program and, with the formation of CSUMC, folklore at UW–Madison truly committed to the Wisconsin Idea. Gilmore, Leary, Olson, and others partnered with ethnic and indigenous communities, archives, museums, and arts organizations as well as with folklorists employed outside the university, such as Mark Wagler from Randall Elementary School in Madison, Wisconsin, and Anne Pryor and Richard March of the Wisconsin Arts Board. Pryor, for example, organized the Wisconsin Weather Project, which brought together UW–Madison folklorists, meteorologists, K–12 Wisconsin classroom teachers, and folklore and atmospheric science students to create a curriculum for science, language arts, and social studies in Wisconsin public schools. With CSUMC, the Folklore Program at UW–Madison heeds Charles Van Hise's words to "never be content until the beneficent influence of the University reaches every family of the state" and expands the scope to the entire Upper Midwest.

Around the same time that CSUMC was created, Thomas Dubois was hired in the Department of Scandinavian Studies and soon became an affiliate of the Folklore Program. Reflecting on the importance of CSUMC, Dubois noted the clear connection between CSUMC and the Wisconsin Idea as well as the value the center offered toward validating the Upper Midwest as a cultural region. "CSUMC gave a very concrete way in which public folklore could be done and be profiled at the University as valid research," he says. Further, he argues that the integration of CSUMC into the university is "a model for how the humanities should be done at the university" (Dubois 2017).

As part of the new cluster hires for the NEH grant, the Folklore Program hired Theresa Schenck, an American Indian specialist; Janet Gilmore, whose public folklore work with Upper Midwestern European immigrant communities was well established; and Christine Garlough, who would work with new immigrant communities in the Upper Midwest. A new breadth of diverse folklorists in secure positions within the university allowed the program to flourish. Enrollments grew and new courses were established. Mellor, who stayed on as a lecturer for the Folklore Program and Scandinavian Studies after he received his PhD, notes changes in the Program's focus: "I thought our Scandinavian Department, and even the old Folklore Program, was very narrative-based, the way I remember it in 1992, moving to 2000 . . . and I'm really glad that, in the last sixteen, seventeen years, it's moved from narrative to be more inclusive" (2017). As the program engaged more with public folklore, it began to expand beyond its narrative orientation to look at other folkloristic genres.

The influx of new faculty also led to an expansion beyond the Folklore Program's origin in area studies. The program made new efforts to encourage graduate enrollments in folklore courses. First, the Department of Scandinavian Studies created a folklore track as part of its graduate program, allowing students to specialize in Scandinavian folklore. Dubois, who was chair of Scandinavian Studies when the track was developed, noted that while it was helpful to students studying Scandinavia, this option did not appeal to students working in folklore outside the Scandinavian region. "There were these area studies places where people could study at the university . . . but there really wasn't any place to take in students who wanted to do an Americanist thing and/or a public folklore thing" (Dubois 2017). In hopes of attracting a more varied student body, the program merged with comparative literature to create the Department of Comparative Literature and Folklore Studies (CLFS). Despite the department being relatively short-lived, CLFS successfully brought new graduate students to UW–Madison, all of whom have continued to work in the public and collaborative spirit of the Wisconsin Idea.

Looking to the Future: Collaborative Efforts, Future Success

Following an administrative transition, the Folklore Program has moved to the Department of German, Nordic, and Slavic (GNS), returning, in some ways, to its roots at UW–Madison. In GNS, we trust that the program will continue to succeed in large part because of how it so purposefully and successfully engages with the Wisconsin Idea. UW–Madison's Folklore Program has become a collaborative space for folklorists of all sorts to work together. Public folklorists and academic folklorists, students and faculty, scholars and community members all come together at UW–Madison to collaborate with communities in the Upper Midwest and beyond. Dubois describes this as "learning with instead of from" each other. "What folklore [at UW–Madison] has done over the years—all the time that Jim [Leary] and Janet [Gilmore] and Ruth [Olson] and I and others, have done—has been to try to make a place for team scholarship and help students understand that that's something that they could get involved with and that that's actually the model for how the Humanities can go forth" (2017). Dubois believes that this collaboration, which he links to the Wisconsin Idea, is valuable for the field of folklore as a whole. And so do we. It is clear through the history of the Folklore Program at UW–Madison that folklore studies thrive when public and academic approaches to the field are merged; that folklorists, no matter their background, collaborate with the communities with which they work; and that we all will "never be content until the beneficent influence of the university reaches every family of the state." No matter the university. No matter the state.

References

Bailey, James. 1986. Letter to Folklore Program colleagues, March 11. University of Wisconsin–Madison Folklore Archive.

Bauman, Richard. 1987. Letter to Jim Leary, August 3. University of Wisconsin–Madison Folklore Archive.

Chamberlin, Thomas. 1890. *The Coming of Age of the State Universities.* University of Nebraska Charter Day, February 15. Lincoln, Nebraska.

Dubois, Thomas. 2017. Interview by Christine J. Widmayer and B. Marcus Cederström. November 9. University Archives and Records Management Services, University of Wisconsin–Madison.

Garlough, Christine, and Anne Pryor. 2011. "'Sifting and Winnowing': Folklore and the Wisconsin Idea." *Western Folklore* 70, no. 3/4: 243–53.

Gilmore, Janet C. 2011. "Teaching Practice through Fieldwork Course Design." *Western Folklore* 70, no. 3/4: 255–85.

Hoeveler, J. David Jr. 1976. "The University and the Social Gospel: The Intellectual Origins of the 'Wisconsin Idea.'" *Wisconsin Magazine of History* 59, no. 4: 282–98.

Ingwersen, Niels. 2006. Interview by Robert Lange. November 6. Digital audio file. OH #0825. University Archives and Records Management Services, University of Wisconsin–Madison.

Leary, James P. 1998. *Wisconsin Folklore*. Madison: University of Wisconsin Press.

———. 2005. Interview by Robert Lange. December 2. Digital audio file. OH #0736. University Archives and Records Management Services, University of Wisconsin–Madison.

Mellor, Scott. 2017. Interview by Christine J. Widmayer and B. Marcus Cederström. September 25. University Archives and Records Management Services, University of Wisconsin–Madison.

Olson, Ruth. 2017. Interview by Troy Reeves. September 28–29. OH #1630. University Archives and Records Management Services, University of Wisconsin–Madison.

University of Wisconsin–Madison. 2017. "The Wisconsin Idea." *University of Wisconsin–Madison*. https://www.wisc.edu/wisconsin-idea/.

UW–Madison Folklore Program. 1983. "Proposal for a Folklore Program at the University of Wisconsin Madison." UW–Madison Folklore Program Archive.

UW News. 1983. "Folklore Program Begins This Fall at UW–Madison." August 22. UW–Madison Folklore Program Archive.

CHRISTINE J. WIDMAYER is PhD candidate in folklore studies at the University of Wisconsin–Madison.

B. MARCUS CEDERSTRÖM is the Community Curator of Nordic-American Folklore in the Department of German, Nordic, and Slavic at the University of Wisconsin–Madison.

20 Folklore at Brigham Young's Universities

Four Generations of Inter(con)textual Studies of Region, Religion, and Beyond

Jill Terry Rudy

The more I learn the more I discern an eternity of knowledge to improve upon.

—Brigham Young

WHILE FOLKLORE INSTRUCTION at Brigham Young University (BYU) in Provo, Utah, institutionally depends on historical associations with English departments, the practice of teaching and scholarship at BYU and at BYU-Hawai'i (BYUH) in La'ie hinges on the pivoting arcs afforded by ways that folklore invites thinking with and incorporating literary and cultural studies. A unique feature of folklore at Brigham Young's universities remains the affiliation with The Church of Jesus Christ of Latter-day Saints (LDS) as institutional sponsor and pervading cultural influence. Along with other belief-based groups, members of the church occupy a noticeable spot in American folklore scholarship. Mormon folklore originally was framed regionally but also must be considered globally and religiously. Far from delimiting how professors and students study, an ethos and worldview rooted in The Church of Jesus Christ of Latter-day Saints suffuses folklore studies at BYU and BYUH with a vast perspective. The result for students and faculty involves studying traditional expression as eclectic stability in the BYU English Department and as core experimentation at BYUH. Folklore as literary and cultural learning that spans generations contributes to both institutions' founding mandates to forge intellectual challenge and spiritual strength with leadership and character. This educational endeavor affords expansive opportunities to achieve community service, meaningful work, and eternal learning.

Folk Song, Thomas Cheney, and First-Generation Mormon Folklore Studies

Folklore at BYU started with the literary study of traditional song connecting with Mormons as a religious group centralized in the Intermountain West. The BYU English Department acquired a folklore-related class through Thomas Cheney, who came to folklore in a most historical way—as a British romanticist interested in folk song. English departments and literary folkloristics developed together, both emerging at Harvard University with philological study and Francis James Child's English and Scottish ballads scholarship (Graff 1987; Zumwalt 1988; Bauman 2008). Before teaching at BYU, Cheney received a master's degree from the University of Idaho, where he took a ballad course with Child's student George Moray Miller. Cheney collected seventy-five ballads for his thesis, comparing them with Child ballads. As an initial folkloristic offering, P. A. Christensen, the BYU English Department chair, encouraged Cheney to offer a ballad course, which became quite popular (Shoemaker 2004b, 55). With summer grants and support of the American Folklore Society publication series, Cheney expanded his folk song collection to over 250 tape-recorded songs, published as *Mormon Songs from the Rocky Mountains* (Shoemaker 2004b, 56). Cheney published other books on Mormon folklore and helped found the Folklore Society of Utah. When William A. "Bert" Wilson, his junior colleague, returned from doctoral study at Indiana University (IU), Cheney allowed his ballad course to morph into the Introduction to Folklore and American Folklore courses taught by Wilson.

Mormon scholars, including Cheney and Wilson, were drawn to study folk song, historical legends, and Three Nephite stories—supernatural legends of Book of Mormon disciples similar to the Wandering Jew cycle. With this literary impetus, decades of American folklore scholarship have pinpointed region and heritage as the Mormon contribution to folklore studies. These studies coalesced in the 1930s and 1940s around scholars from the region who found folklore amenable to their interests in languages and literature. Wayland Hand received his degree in German from the University of Chicago; Hector Lee received his in English and American studies and civilization from the University of New Mexico; and Austin Fife's PhD was in French and Spanish from Stanford University (Stanley 2004). Hand, Lee, and Fife and his wife and collaborator, Alta, published books and articles and founded folklore societies in California and Utah. (For the Fifes, see R. Williams, this volume.) Cheney at BYU and Lester Hubbard at the University of Utah also contributed to the study of Mormon folk song as an extensive side note to their English literary training (Cannon 2004). Scholars more distant from the area and culture, such as Richard Dorson, then presented Mormon folklore as a regional representation of distinctly American traditions

Fig. 20.1. Brigham Young University students in a bucket brigade for the tradition of whitewashing the block Y, September 13, 1975. Photograph by Mark A. Philbrick. Copyright BYU Photo 2014. Courtesy of BYU Photography.

(Eliason and Mould 2013, 2). American folkloristics has appreciated Mormonism for its unique founding, communalism, and migratory history across the United States, while folklore studies has appealed to scholars with Mormon backgrounds and humanistic inclinations for these same reasons and others to be discussed below.

The English Department hosts folklore teaching and scholarship at BYU because of this long-standing literary interest in traditional expression that unites with cultural concerns. Students make connections with the Mormon experience because of ways folklore encapsulates and perpetuates the religious and cultural values of this people. Because of doctrinal beliefs about agency, health practices, eternal family relationships, and gender roles, social issues and practices take on a unique inflection noticeably expressed in customary practices and informal, as well as official, beliefs. Since most students and faculty are church members, teaching and publishing about this tradition remains an ongoing component of folklore at BYU, yet there is not a dedicated course on Mormon folklore in the curriculum. Additionally, thousands of BYU and BYUH students have learned folkloristic concepts and methodologies, but there is no degree-granting program nor an official folklore department at either university. Rather, folklore studies happen within the BYU English Department, in association with the

Wilson Folklore Archives, and within the curricular experimentation of international cultural studies and related programs at BYUH.

Folklore Archives, Bert Wilson, and Second-Generation Commitment to the Future

Wilson assured that folklore studies would receive recognition and thrive into the future. Like Cheney, Wilson began teaching at BYU with a master's degree but serendipitously found a more professionalized path. George Shoemaker reports that Wilson was encouraged by a BYU colleague, also a former Finnish missionary, to pursue doctoral studies at IU because of fine programs in language and folklore (2004a, 79–81). At IU, Dorson encouraged Wilson's study of Finnish nationalism and Mormon lore. Wilson became an accomplished scholar in both areas, with his *Folklore and Nationalism in Modern Finland* (1976) making important connections and critique and his collected essays highlighting work on folklore in the academy, Mormon folklore, and folklore and nationalism (2006).

When Wilson returned to BYU from doctoral studies, while continuing to finish his dissertation and battling thyroid cancer, he convinced colleagues to add new courses that required, and archived, student collecting projects. He left BYU from 1978 to 1984 to consolidate folklore work with the MA program, Fife Archives, and other opportunities at Utah State University. He then returned to chair the English Department at BYU and directed the Charles Redd Center for Western Studies before his retirement in 1997.

Wilson's scholarship, teaching, and extensive promotion of the field stems from his vision of folklore as a key to understanding human experience—bridging the cultural and literary aspects inherent in folkloristics. At an Indiana University conference, he summarized his reasons for institutionalizing folklore studies: "If in the process [of building folklore programs] we find the means to give voice to the carriers and performers of the traditions we study and value, then our work will also prove suitable" (2006, 31). His programmatic commitment involved conducting scholarship, creating courses, directing theses, editing *Western Folklore* (1979–83), serving in folklore societies and on local and national arts boards, and practicing what he called "hallology" by advocating folklore at every opportunity with colleagues.

Archiving became important to Wilson through the examples of Fife and Hand and additionally through the extensive archiving tradition in Finland. Saving student projects started with his classes in the 1960s, and he prioritized developing the BYU Folklore Archives after formalizing the Fife Archives at Utah State University. Before his retirement, he assured the transfer of the collections from two small rooms in the campus library to the L. Tom Perry Special Collections. He tried to mitigate trading of autonomy for security by assuring that Kristi

Fig. 20.2. William A. "Bert" Wilson, 1985. Photograph and permission courtesy of Sven Wilson and the Wilson family.

Young Bell, a former student, was the curator. Special collections in the Harold B. Lee Library has supported several archive outreach events, including an archives conference, two American Folklife Center field schools (2004–5), and the Utah Heritage Project (Rudy and Bell 2004). This research emphasized the local landscape surrounding BYU by including agricultural and recreational traditions.

Folklore studies at BYU, and extending to BYUH, thus may seem to begin with Utah and the Intermountain West but actually employs a complex geographic configuration that involves the global Church Educational System and the international sweep of LDS settlement patterns, missionary endeavors, and membership. Despite the regional impetus of early Mormon folklore, Wilson insisted that the religious component of Mormonism be the focus: "We must turn our eyes from . . . the West in general to the faith and commitment that give unity and direction to Mormon life" (2006, 180). Exemplifying this approach, Eric Eliason and Tom Mould's anthology surveys the past but also plots the trajectory that Wilson foresaw for Mormon folklore studies (2013). They propose that these groups go together because of a religious commitment to record keeping, spiritually inflected narratives, and an organization that depends both on lay members for local leadership and a distinctive church-wide hierarchy of leaders accepted as prophets (2013, 13–19). Similar to other high-context groups, members of The Church of Jesus Christ of Latter-day Saints perpetuate beliefs through formal and informal traditions and, as Christians, emphasize the significance of serving the needy and maintaining family relationships that may be perpetuated beyond mortal life. Wilson valued recognizing common ground and advocating folklore as a way to appreciate human aspirations for self-awareness and the collective struggle to endure and prevail (2006, 22).

BYUH and the Sociology of Folklore at the Core of Institutional Experimentation beyond the Third Generation

Folklore's involvement at BYU primarily centers in the English Department, and the Anthropology Department shares some interest in folklore studies with visiting faculty such as Tom and Pamela Blakely and past folklore-friendly hires such as Julie Hartley-Moore (2007). Phillip McArthur and I both were beneficiaries of the Blakelys' time at BYU. Pamela taught folklore courses, and their anthropological studies resonated with McArthur's Latter-day Saints mission experiences in the Marshall Islands and encouraged his doctoral work at Indiana. In the late 1990s, McArthur designed an international cultural studies program that enacts the intellectual connections and practical benefits of folkloristic theories, and thus his work at BYUH stands as the anthropological counterpoint to the literary precedents of BYU folklore. In this case, students do not take folklore courses, but their study programs, and McArthur's scholarly and administrative contributions, resonate with folkloristic perspectives at the core of programmatic and conceptual creativity (McArthur 2008, 2004).

McArthur's program offered tracks in comparative humanities, cultural anthropology, communications and culture, and international peace building; he later served as the first dean of the College of Language, Culture, and Arts. This program and the college supporting it currently are being redesigned to distribute key concepts and learning practices across campus. McArthur describes how these core components relate with folklore studies and theories in a March 2016 email communication to me: "I attribute the breadth of this perspective to my training in folklore, not just in terms of the theory, but in a disposition to think about and incorporate ideas beyond parochial disciplinary boundaries." His proclivities for reading culture and social structures in situated expressivity enhance his leadership abilities: "Folklore has provided me sensibilities to institutional discursive practices, structures of power and rhetoric, as well as the significance of narrative constructions in motivation and persuasion." In other words, McArthur sees and adapts curricular programs and administrative social relationships through folklore studies training.

Folklore at BYUH demonstrates that administrative work, astutely conceived and collaboratively implemented, allows folklore teaching, research, and scholarship to be applied in the academy and beyond. Because of the university's size, McArthur does not have course releases, so his administrative work is informed by constant classroom engagement with students. Graduates of the international cultural studies program come from numerous countries, including China, Japan, Korea, Tonga, the United Kingdom, and the United States. Speaking of the power of folklore methods, McArthur writes: "We can see this working at two ends of time: a) the immediate social interactions of our lives; b) the history of a text (and often deep history) and its relationship to other texts. We [folklorists] are not just good intertextualists long before this term came into vogue, but we are also very good inter-contextualists, carefully observing how texts move in and out of contexts." Thus, he has developed a "sociology of folklore" to describe the scrutiny of texts and cultures that informed the cultural studies program and his work as dean, teacher, and scholar.

McArthur's scholarship spans and connects the possibilities of literary and cultural analysis by putting folklore at the core of curricular and programmatic educational experimentation and vocation. He writes, "I continue to pursue . . . how social relationships are embedded in and made manifest through text and performance and conversely, how text and performance generate social relationships at a full range of ever-increasing social complexity, from the intimate face-to-face and familial through the nation-state and transnational relations." The founding vision of BYUH—"to produce leaders committed to building the kingdom of God and establishing peace internationally"—matches this folkloristic attentiveness to intimate situated communication and transnational literary and cultural representation (About BYU–Hawai'i 2019). The fourth generation of Mormon folklore at BYUH continues with Caryn Lesuma, who grew up in La'ie and received degrees from Stanford and BYU and a PhD from the University of Hawai'i at Manoa in 2018.

Next Generations from BYU and the Eclectic Stability of Cultural Study in English

Wilson's groundwork at BYU and McArthur's experimentations at BYUH exemplify how astute administrative communication and folklore coursework spark educational and institutional decision making. Wilson might never have retired without the commitment that folklorists be hired in his stead. In fall 1996, Jackie Thursby and I joined him in his last year at the university. When I was an MA student, Wilson had mentioned that I could pursue a folklore PhD at Indiana University, a surprising possibility to me. Thursby was hired at BYU primarily to teach English education, but she trained in folklore during her MA at Utah State and completed her PhD in popular culture from Bowling Green State University. Because Thursby's primary appointment was not in folklore, the department hired Eric Eliason with his University of Texas PhD in 1997.

With projects that merit BYU's generous research support, including travel funding, research assistants, a digital humanities program, and a superb library, folklorists are the most prolific scholars in the English Department. Our topics exemplify the eclectic possibilities afforded by folklore studies and BYU's distinctive support. Eliason's books range from a continuation of his doctoral research on Mormon lore and religious studies (2004, 2007) to ethnographic studies of hunting lore (Cutchins and Eliason 2009; Eliason 2015), military lore (Eliason and Tuleja 2012), and *Black Velvet Art* (2011). My training and research interests include folklore's history in English departments, Mormon lore, foodways, and folk narrative. Another turn to my research emerged from a casual question I posed to Pauline Greenhill at the American Folklore Society meeting: Would she be following up her book, coauthored with Sidney Eve Matrix, on *Fairy Tale Films* (2010)? She initially responded no but quickly changed her mind and asked me to join her on the project. This yielded the co-edited volume, *Channeling Wonder: Fairy Tales on Television* (2014) and collaborations from her SSHRC Partnership Development Grant, including a special issue of *Marvels & Tales* (2017) and *The Routledge Companion to Media and Fairy-Tale Cultures* (Greenhill et al. 2018). Thursby published her dissertation on Basque lore with Utah State University Press (1999), and other books include *Funeral Festivals in America* (2006a), handbooks on *Story* (2006b) and *Foodways* (2008), a family relationship guide for an LDS audience (2004), and an extensive project on Maya Angelou (2011).

Since Wilson's retirement, we have taught over a thousand folklore students, with several continuing their formal studies in the field and others using folklore to branch out into consulting, historic sites, information technology, fantasy writing, and even creating The Color Run, a 5K race influenced by the Indian Holi spring festival where participants are showered by colorful chalk at intervals. Two of Wilson's last students, Jill Hemming Austin and Danille Christensen, received PhDs from Indiana, and Curtis Ashton, Meghan McGrath, and Jessie Riddle also completed graduate degrees there. David Allred emphasized folklore in his University of Missouri PhD and chairs the English Department at Snow College. Former Wilson Folklore Archives employee Julie Swallow is an administrator at the BYU–Salt Lake Center and is preparing Wilson's Three Nephite collection for publication. A number of LDS folklorists who started studies at Brigham Young and Utah State have conducted folklore doctoral work in the Penn State Harrisburg program, including Spencer Green, Brant Ellsworth, Kathryn Holmes, Jared Rife, David Giles, and Raven Hammond. Green, Ellsworth, and Holmes contributed to a *Folklore Historian* special issue honoring Wilson (Rudy 2017).

BYU and the Church Educational System exist because of LDS doctrine and members' personal commitments to gaining knowledge and serving others, for lifelong learning and eternity. The church system, through tithes of its members, supports three universities—BYU, BYUH, and BYU-Idaho—and several other educational entities. In my folklore classes, I emphasize the functional and representation aspects of folklore performance, ways that a proverb may obliquely offer wisdom and solve problems and how a cultural performance such as a spontaneous shrine or rite of passage may explicitly display cultural values and social structures. The deliberate decisions involving folklore performance, study, and institutionalization lead to significant continuities through the myriad repetitions afforded by traditional expressivity. The BYUH newsletter, *Hoʻomau*, which derives its name from the Hawaiian language and means "to persevere and persist,"[1] connects folklore at BYU and BYUH with Henry Glassie's definition of tradition as "the creation of the future out of the past" (2003, 176). Commitment to tradition and generations at BYU and BYUH enacts Christian faith and encourages learning that strives to continue.

Acknowledgments

The Brigham Young quotation in the epigraph is from *Discourses of Brigham Young*, 2nd ed., selected and arranged by John A. Widstoe (Salt Lake City: Deseret, 1926), 384.

Note

1. See PBS Hawaiʻi, "HIKI NŌ: Hoʻomau, Hawaiian Values Compilation," December 22, 2016, https://www.pbshawaii.org/tag/hoomau/.

References

About BYU–Hawaiʻi. 2019. Accessed May 2, 2019. https://about.byuh.edu/.

Bauman, Richard. 2008. "The Philology of the Vernacular." *Journal of Folklore Research* 45, no. 1: 29–36.

Cannon, Hal. 2004. "Lester Hubbard and the Folksongs of Utah." In *Folklore in Utah*, edited by David H. Stanley, 49–53. Logan: Utah State University Press.

Cutchins, Dennis, and Eric A. Eliason, eds. 2009. *Wild Games*. Knoxville: University of Tennessee Press.

Eliason, Eric A. 2004. *Celebrating Zion*. Provo, UT: Brigham Young University Press.

———. 2007. *The J. Golden Kimball Stories*. Urbana: University of Illinois Press.

———. 2011. *Black Velvet Art*. Jackson: University Press of Mississippi.

———. 2015. *To See Them Run*. Jackson: University Press of Mississippi.

Eliason, Eric A., and Tom Mould, eds. 2013. *Latter-Day Lore*. Salt Lake: University of Utah Press.

Eliason, Eric A., and Tad Tuleja, eds. 2012. *Warrior Ways*. Boulder: University Press of Colorado.

Glassie, Henry. 2003. "Tradition." In *Eight Words for the Study of Expressive Culture*, edited by Burt Feintuch, 176–97. Urbana: University of Illinois Press.

Graff, Gerald. 1987. *Professing Literature*. Chicago: University of Chicago Press.

Greenhill, Pauline, and Sidney Eve Matrix. 2010. *Fairy Tale Films*. Logan: Utah State University Press.

Greenhill, Pauline, and Jill Terry Rudy, eds. 2014. *Channeling Wonder: Fairy Tales on Television*. Detroit: Wayne State University Press.

Greenhill, Pauline, Jill Terry Rudy, Naomi Hamer, and Lauren Bosc, eds. 2018. *The Routledge Companion to Media and Fairy-Tale Cultures*. New York: Routledge.

Hartley-Moore, Julie. 2007. "The Song of Grydon." *Journal of American Folklore* 120, no. 476: 204–29.

McArthur, Phillip. 2004. "Narrative, Cosmos, and Nation." *Journal of American Folklore* 117, no. 463: 55–80.

———. 2008. "Ambivalent Fantasies: Local Prehistories and Global Dramas in the Marshall Islands." *Journal of Folklore Research* 45, no. 3: 263–98.

Rudy, Jill Terry, ed. 2017. *Folklore Historian* 33: 10–62.

Rudy, Jill Terry, and Pauline Greenhill, eds. 2017. *Marvels & Tales* 31, no. 1.

Rudy, Jill Terry, and Kristi Bell, eds. 2004. *Folklore Forum* 35, no. 1/2.

Shoemaker, George H. 2004a. "'On Being Human': The Legacy of William A. Wilson." In *Folklore in Utah*, edited by David H. Stanley, 78–85. Logan: Utah State University Press.

———. 2004b. "Thomas Cheney and the Dilemmas of Mormon Folklore." In *Folklore in Utah*, edited by David H. Stanley, 54–59. Logan: Utah State University Press.

Stanley, David H., ed. 2004. *Folklore in Utah*. Logan: Utah State University Press.

Thursby, Jacqueline S. 1999. *Mother's Table, Father's Chair*. Logan: Utah State University Press.

———. 2004. *Begin Where You Are*. Salt Lake City: Deseret.

———. 2006a. *Funeral Festivals in America*. Lexington: University Press of Kentucky.

———. 2006b. *Story*. Westport, CT: Greenwood Press.

———. 2008. *Foodways and Folklore*. Westport, CT: Greenwood Press.

———. 2011. *Critical Companion to Maya Angelou*. New York: Facts on File.

Wilson, William A. 1976. *Folklore and Nationalism in Modern Finland*. Bloomington: Indiana University Press.

———. 2006. *The Marrow of Human Experience*, edited by Jill Terry Rudy. Logan: Utah State University Press.

Zumwalt, Rosemary Lévy. 1988. *American Folklore Scholarship: A Dialogue of Dissent*. Bloomington: Indiana University Press.

JILL TERRY RUDY is Associate Professor of English at Brigham Young University. She is editor of *The Marrow of Human Experience: Essays on Folklore* by William A. Wilson and (with Pauline Greenhill, Naomi Hamer, and Lauren Bosc) *The Routledge Companion to Media and Fairy-Tale Cultures*.

21 The Mason Idea

Debra Lattanzi Shutika

Creating a new academic program requires time and dedication and a scholar who is willing to commit her career to program building and seizing opportunities. It also demands a steadfast resolution to a long-term goal. A successful new program should have institutional roots that survive beyond the legacy of the founding scholar. Perhaps most importantly, the program should match the institutional culture and vision. In all respects, the history of folklore studies at George Mason University fits this ideal. Folklore at Mason was the lifelong project of Margaret "Peggy" Yocom and the coalitions she developed to institutionalize folklore at Mason. The folklore program is at once a product and a reflection of the Mason Idea, the core values of the institution.

George Mason University was founded in 1957 as a two-year branch campus of the University of Virginia and then became a four-year college in 1966.[1] In the early 1970s, Ralph Baxter, a specialist in professional writing and editing, taught American folklore in the English Department. Folklore was Baxter's avocation; he was particularly interested in naming traditions and named many of the roads on Mason's Fairfax campus after state landmarks. Baxter's love of folklore was fortuitous: he provided a path that gave rise to the recruitment of Mason's first tenure-track folklorist.[2]

Mason became an independent university in 1972, the same year Yocom was hired. Yocom was a graduate student at the University of Massachusetts Amherst under the tutelage of Professors George Carey and Rayna Green when she applied for one of the five "open specialization" positions. During her interview, Yocom successfully highlighted the benefits that a folklorist would offer the growing university. She began teaching American folklore along with courses in freshman writing and popular culture. That same year, Yocom created the Northern Virginia Folklife Archive, a depository of student fieldwork projects from her classes. After earning tenure in 1983, Yocom dedicated herself to institutionalizing the folklore studies program from the one folklore course a year to the undergraduate and graduate programs it is today.[3]

The Department of English at George Mason University is a distinct multidisciplinary department, offering a rich context for folklore studies to flourish.

Fig. 21.1. Margaret "Peggy" Yocom at her office at George Mason University, ca. 2001. Photograph by George Mason University Creative Services.

As in most English departments, literature and literary studies composed the central mission of the department, along with general education courses in composition and rhetoric. The department was also home to the study of linguistics. In 1980 a new MFA in creative writing was added, followed by film and media studies a decade later. This distinct multidisciplinary structure, which more closely mirrors a small college than an academic department, evolved into a unique intellectual community that today houses faculty in seven academic disciplines: creative writing, cultural studies, film and media studies, folklore, linguistics, literature, and writing and rhetoric.

When the English Department reorganized into a collection of concentrations in the mid-1990s, Yocom proposed the folklore, mythology, and literature (FML) concentration, a move that was opposed by many in the department's senior leadership. To address this opposition, she formed a coalition with department colleagues who were folklore-friendly and who agreed to support and, more importantly, to speak in favor of the FML proposal in department meetings. With strong support, the FML concentration was ultimately approved, but not before Yocom was asked to submit extra supporting evidence of student demand and faculty willingness to list courses as part of the program.

The FML concentration was quite successful and attracted increasing numbers of students to folklore courses among the large English major. Yocom's next strategic move was to build coalitions with colleagues from across the (then) College of Arts and Sciences to establish the folklore and mythology interdisciplinary minor. This required support for folklore across the university, including faculty from the Departments of Modern and Classical Languages, History, Religious Studies, and Art History. Yocom recruited an art history professor, Carol C. Mattusch, to codirect the program, introducing folklore to a wide constituency of university faculty. Establishing the minor also moved support for the folklore programs from the department to the college level and allowed students majoring in other academic disciplines to acquire a credential in folklore studies.

As a young institution, Mason has grown substantially in the last thirty-five years; it is now the largest state university in the Commonwealth of Virginia.[4] As other parts of the university grew, Yocom contributed to those programs where she thought folklore should play a leading role, most notably in Women's Studies, Native American Studies, Study of the Americas (which later became Latin American Studies), African American Studies, LGBTQ Studies, and the interdisciplinary PhD program in Cultural Studies. She served on committees, especially the curriculum committees of these groups, seeking to cross-list folklore courses, include folklore materials in introductory-level syllabi, and invite folklorists as guest speakers. What is particularly significant about her work through the 1990s was her ability to make folklore known to the university community using available resources and opportunities. For instance, in 1999, she organized a university-wide Text and Community event featuring the Grimm Brothers' fairy tales.[5]

This persistent promotion of folklore and Yocom's coalition building bore fruit in two vital achievements. First, in the spring of 2000, one of Yocom's English colleagues, Cóilín Owens, an Irish literature specialist, showed her how she could argue for a hire in folklore. A new university computer software program, he said, made it possible to count the number of students who attempted but were unable to enroll in folklore courses. Using these data, Yocom composed a proposal to convince her colleagues to hire a second folklorist. In fall 2001, I was hired as Mason's second tenure-track folklorist after completing my PhD in folklore and folklife at the University of Pennsylvania.

Second, with two full-time folklorists and the growth of interest in graduate folklore classes, Yocom proposed a master's degree in folklore under the umbrella of the master of arts in interdisciplinary studies (MAIS). In 2004, the MAIS in folklore studies admitted its first student, Kristina Downs, who completed her MA at Mason and went on to finish her PhD in folklore and ethnomusicology at Indiana University in 2017. Other Mason folklore students have pursued terminal degrees in folklore at Indiana (Paulina Guerrero), Ohio State University (Brittany Warman and Sarah Cleto), the University of Missouri (Jennifer Spitulnik), and other MA programs, including the Arts Management Program at Mason (Kerry Kaleba).

George Mason is a dynamic university unburdened by entrenched practices. New initiatives are valued and encouraged, particularly those that connect the university to the northern Virginia community. This creative atmosphere fosters a rich intellectual environment for faculty and students. Building on the foundation that Yocom established, I initiated a number of programs that highlight the distinctiveness of the program and sense of place. In 2004, I became the director of the Mason Project on Immigration—now the Institute for Immigration Research—and developed an undergraduate major in immigration studies that featured courses in folklore, ethnicity, and migration.[6]

Mason folklore forged a collaboration with the American Folklife Center at the Library of Congress in 2011, establishing a Field School for Cultural Documentation, which has been offered every summer since. The field school has led to professional documentation opportunities for students and faculty, including a National Endowment for the Arts–funded ethnographic collection of Bolivian folk dance troupes in northern Virginia; a community documentation of the Columbia Pike neighborhood in Arlington, Virginia; an occupational study of Arlington National Cemetery; a community study of Morgan County, West Virginia; a study of the pre-revitalization of the Alexandria waterfront; and the impact of community gardens in Arlington County. In 2017, the field school completed a large-scale ethnographic study of national parks in Washington, DC, and the legacy of the National Park Service's Summer in the Parks program under a grant from the National Park Service.

The benefit of the field school experience is to combine the real-world work of a professional folklorist in a community-based classroom. The projects have been housed in the Mason Folklore and Ethnography Archive, a series of special collections that build on Yocom's Northern Virginia Folklife Archive. Partnering with the American Folklore Society and the National Folklife Archive Initiative (NFAI), Mason folklore graduate students digitized and moved all collections to the NFAI website. We also created distinct collections based on faculty-student fieldwork. The Mason Folklore and Ethnography Archive houses all the materials from the field schools plus special projects, including the Northern Virginia Civil Rights Oral History Archive and video oral histories.[7]

Among the many intellectual connections that the Mason Folklore Studies Program has established, those bridging folklore and creative writing stand out. No other folklore program has the substantial, programmatic links between folklore studies and the MFA in creative writing. Yocom forged these multiple links with Mason's nationally recognized MFA program early in her career. She

Fig. 21.2. Debra Lattanzi Shutika (*front row, second from right*) with students at the state capitol in Charleston, WV, during the 2018 Folklife Field School. Photograph courtesy of Debra Lattanzi Shutika.

designed a new graduate course, Living Words: Folklore and Creative Writing, especially for folklore students and for creative writing students to introduce the practices of both. She also redesigned most of her folklore courses to include semester portfolios as options for MFA final course projects, and with Mason poet Susan Tichy, she team-taught Traditional Ballad: Folklore and Creative Writing. Several folklore students have published their creative writing, and students regularly select Mason's MFA program because they also want to study folklore. This work has also shaped the American Folklore Society: Yocom and Amy Skillman founded the creative writing section of AFS and requested the inclusion of creative writing in the *Journal of American Folklore*.

George Mason University is home to the oldest literary festival in the Washington, DC, region, Fall for the Book, and the Folklore Studies Program has been a steadfast supporter and participant in the festival since its early years.[8] The faculty invite folklorists who also are creative writers, such as Kirin Narayan and Norma Cantú, and poets who also work in folklore, such as Scotland's Tom Pow. The program also brings academic colleagues to share their work and ethnographic research experience, including Lisa Gabbert, Diane Goldstein, Montana Miller, Margaret Mills, Tom Mould, Dorothy Noyes, Kent Ryden, and Pravina Shukla.

The growth and varied student opportunities from the Folklore Studies Program resulted in a third tenure-track line to folklore; in fall 2011, Joy Fraser, a graduate of Memorial University of Newfoundland, joined the faculty, followed by Benjamin Gatling (Ohio State) in 2013, Lisa Gilman (Indiana) in 2018, and Lijun Zhang (Indiana) in 2019.[9] George Mason University underwent a significant transformation when the university's sixth president, Ángel Cabrera, took office on July 1, 2012. Six months later, I was elected chair of the English Department. Cabrera was tasked with creating a new vision to guide the university into the future, while I was reshaping the path forward for the department and folklore studies. My first act as chair was to restructure the leadership of the department, offering a seat on the chair's advisory committee to a representative of every discipline in the department. This move would ensure that folklore would have a permanent voice in departmental governance.

When Mason unveiled its strategic vision, the Mason Idea, it emphasized four core institutional characteristics: innovative, diverse, entrepreneurial, and accessible.[10] The values emerged through a series of town hall meetings and working groups with a goal of consensus and self-discovery. Through this process, it became clear that the Mason Folklore Studies Program is an organic part of the university environment and the faculty recruited to build the program. Mason folklore has demonstrated innovation and an entrepreneurial spirit in its work to build a new type of undergraduate and graduate education with an emphasis on public folklore that is informed by ethnographic practice (the field school) and a strong knowledge of the history of the field, taking full advantage of the Washington, DC, region and all it offers. Mason folklore students are a diverse group who fan out in the larger Fairfax community to document their local traditions. Many of the undergraduates are first-generation college students and immigrants, and this work has greatly benefited the program and archival collections. Finally, the work that Yocom began has made folklore studies accessible to generations of students in northern Virginia and the Washington, DC, region.

The Mason Folklore Studies Program celebrated its fortieth anniversary in 2017. At the time of this writing, it is home to four tenure-track faculty, reflecting the deep roots of folklore studies at George Mason University and a secure future for the discipline in the region.

Notes

1. George Mason University Libraries, "George Mason University: A History," http://ahistoryofmason.gmu.edu/.
2. Margaret Yocom, Mason Folklore History, n.d. Unpublished manuscript housed in the Mason Ethnography Archive, https://ethnography.gmu.edu/.
3. Ibid.
4. George Mason University Libraries, "George Mason University."
5. George Mason University, Text and Community Committee, "Text and Community Programs Presents Fairy Tales," http://nmge.gmu.edu/textandcommunity/1999/index.html.
6. Institute for Immigration Research, https://iir.gmu.edu.
7. George Mason University, Mason Folklore and Ethnography Archive, http://ethnography.gmu.edu.
8. Fall for the Book, http://fallforthebook.org.
9. Fraser left George Mason University in May 2018 and is currently employed at Memorial University of Newfoundland.
10. George Mason University, "Mason Idea," https://masonidea.gmu.edu/.

DEBRA LATTANZI SHUTIKA is Chair of the Department of English and Associate Director of the Folklore Studies Program at George Mason University. She is author of *Beyond the Borderlands: Migration and Belonging in the United States and Mexico*.

22 Folklore and Interdisciplinarity at the Ohio State University

Patrick B. Mullen and Amy Shuman

Folklore at the Ohio State University (OSU) has always been an interdisciplinary enterprise, both in the decades before and after an actual designated folklore program was created. Many shared research areas bring OSU folklorists into conversation with colleagues in other fields, especially the intersections between ethnographic research on narrative and ritual and broader ideological and institutional frameworks. In the absence of a department of folklore, the program is affiliated with various departments, and although some of the students describe themselves as folklorists, others have little prior folklore experience when they enroll in the courses. Nonetheless, the program has sustained a cohort of folklore faculty and graduate students who work in a wide range of research topics, geographical areas, and theoretical approaches. OSU folklorists have forged strong connections with scholars outside the discipline and thus have extended knowledge of the field, created allies, and demonstrated folklore's value to other disciplinary enterprises. This interdisciplinary, interdepartmental, and international model requires constant, ongoing efforts to sustain and create new collaborations. Although this framework does place the folklore program in a position of institutional precarity, it is hard to say whether the program is more or less vulnerable to budget cuts than stand-alone folklore programs. Intellectually, maintaining and forging connections across disciplines has been a source of the program's vitality.

People and Interdisciplinary Connections

Although the folklore program at OSU did not receive institutional recognition until 1991, it was a thriving, interdisciplinary, academic program from the time that Francis Lee Utley joined the Department of English in 1935. Utley received his PhD in 1936 at Harvard, where Professor George Lyman Kittredge influenced his interest in folklore and medieval literature. Utley began his first teaching job in 1935 at OSU, and he became professor of English and folklore in 1973. The wide range of Utley's folklore scholarship is indicated by the titles of some of his most significant publications (1961, 1963). Utley was equally at home in folklore, literature, anthropology, and linguistics. The breadth of his scholarship was a foundation for the teaching of folklore and the creation of new courses in the English Department. Several of Utley's graduate students went on to illustrious academic careers, including D. K. Wilgus at the University of California, Los Angeles, and Bruce Rosenberg at Brown University.

Like many other programs in North America in the second half of the twentieth century, folklore at OSU located textual studies (such as ballad and folktale) in English and ethnographic research in the Department of Anthropology. Faculty in English in the 1970s included Patrick B. Mullen, Daniel R. Barnes, Jean McLaughlin, and William Lightfoot. E. Ojo Arewa and John Messenger held faculty positions in Anthropology. Steven Swann Jones taught folklore as a faculty member in the Department of Comparative Studies.

Although divided between the Departments of English and of Anthropology, the field of folklore provided intersections and sustained interdisciplinary dialogue. Medievalists like Utley and, later, Richard Firth Green and nineteenth-century Americanist and folklorist Barnes studied connections between folklore and literature. The anthropologists used ethnographic methods and often focused on African rather than European collections, though Messenger worked in both Africa and Ireland. However, the lines between textual and ethnographic approaches were not strictly drawn. Barnes, Arewa (1970), and Messenger (1959) all studied the proverb, and the faculty today includes a prominent African and African American literature and proverb scholar, Adélékè Adéẹ̀kọ́ (1998).

In response to the increasing interest in ethnographic field research in folklore studies in the 1960s and 1970s, Utley hired Mullen as an assistant professor in 1969. Mullen's PhD was in English from the University of Texas, but his dissertation was based on ethnographic fieldwork that yielded his first book (1988). Mullen taught folklore and American literature in the English Department for forty years. During that time, he introduced many students to African American folklore (Abernethy and Mullen 1996; Mullen 2008). Valerie Lee—one of Mullen's students, who later became a faculty member in the Department of English; chair of the Department of Women's, Gender, and Sexuality Studies and of African American and African Studies; and vice provost of the Office of Diversity and Inclusion—said that her first encounter with African American literature was in one of Mullen's courses. She remembers reading Alan Dundes's *Mother Wit from the Laughing Barrel* (1973), which, Lee was surprised to discover, included African American traditions from her own childhood. Lee became hooked (1996). Along with John W. Roberts, Trudier Harris, and Aaron Oforlea, Lee was one of the many scholars of African American folklore who had studied with Mullen. Like Lee, Roberts also returned to teach folklore in the English Department at

Fig. 22.1. *Left to right:* Daniel Barnes, Amy Shuman, and Patrick Mullen, August 2013. Photograph by Cassie Patterson. Courtesy of Ohio State University Archives.

OSU, later chairing the Department of African American and African Studies and serving as dean of the Division of Arts and Humanities.

Barnes, who began teaching in the English Department in 1968, was especially known for his articles on American legend, proverbs, and the relationship of folklore and American literature (1966, 1970, 1972, 1996). He was the author of over a hundred scholarly papers in numerous European and American academic journals. He founded *Motif: International Review of Research in Folklore and Literature* in 1981 and served as editor for nine years. He also served as one of the editors of *Proverbium*, an international journal of the study of the proverb. At OSU, Barnes was known as a brilliant teacher able to engage students with complex intellectual ideas while also entertaining them with his sharp sense of humor.

Amy Shuman was hired as a faculty member in the English Department in 1981, the year she received her PhD from the University of Pennsylvania, where she studied with Barbara Kirshenblatt-Gimblett, John Szwed, and Dan Ben-Amos. Szwed, had received his PhD at OSU in 1965 in anthropology under the direction of Professor Erika Bourguignon, who then served as a mentor to Shuman. Shuman is the author of two books on personal narrative (1986, 2005) and two books on political asylum coauthored with Carol Bohmer (Bohmer and Shuman 2007, 2018).

She has co-edited a special issue of *Western Folklore* with Charles Briggs (Briggs and Shuman 1993) and co-edited volumes with Diane Goldstein (Goldstein and Shuman 2016) and Bridget Haas (Haas and Shuman 2019).

Sabra Webber, who had studied with Alan Dundes at the University of California, Berkeley, and with Richard Bauman and Elizabeth Warnock Fernea at the University of Texas at Austin, joined the OSU faculty in 1983 with a joint appointment in the Department of Near Eastern Languages and Cultures and of Comparative Studies. Her appointment represented a shift in the structural organization of folklore studies at OSU. Professor Marilyn Waldman, chair of Comparative Studies, had been working with Mullen, who created for Comparative Studies four core, upper-level folklore courses covering folk arts and material culture (subsequently team-taught for many years by Mullen and Webber), ritual and festival, and verbal art—all areas that were considered to be outside the purview of the English Department. In her book *Romancing the Real* (1991), Webber addressed the complex political heritage of folklore scholarship—an approach that became central to the graduate program. In an examination of local history narratives, Webber outlined some of the tensions between tradition and change—tensions evident in the work of several OSU scholars who were taking on studies of lore somewhat marginal to the field of folklore at the time.

Others who have taught folklore at OSU include Inez Cardozo-Freeman and Terry Long at the Newark campus; John Moe, a graduate in folklore from Indiana University; and Martha Sims, who teaches folklore and composition on the Columbus campus while pursuing her PhD in folklore. Before retiring, Cardozo-Freeman developed courses in Hispanic folklore and folklore research with prisons and prisoners (Cardozo-Freeman et al. 1984). Long came to his teaching of folklore through his study of Granville Hicks, one of the early Marxist literary theorists.

Dorothy Noyes joined the English Department as a folklorist in 1996. A graduate of the University of Pennsylvania, where she studied with Roger Abrahams, Noyes conducted extensive ethnographic research on a Corpus Christi festival in Berga, a province of Catalonia, resulting in her book, *Fire in the Plaça* (2003). She has published widely on topics including heritage culture, the concept of the group (of central importance to folklorists), festival, and the fairy tale. She collected her reflections on folklore's particular perspective on social interaction in *Humble Theory* (2016) and co-edited *Sustaining Interdisciplinary Collaboration* (Bendix, Bizer, and Noyes 2017). As director of the Center for Folklore Studies from 2005 to 2014, Noyes led the development of a core graduate curriculum and created the graduate interdisciplinary specialization in folklore.

Ray Cashman joined the English Department as a folklorist in 2006. He is a graduate of Indiana University, where he studied with Henry Glassie and Richard Bauman. His 2008 book, *Storytelling on the Northern Irish Border*, offers an ethnographic study of the community of Aghyaran, a mixed Catholic-Protestant border community in Northern Ireland. His second book, *Packy Jim* (2016), continued his study of narrative, local character, and Irish folklore. During Cashman's tenure as director of the Center for Folklore Studies, he created two graduate fellowships in folklore, a significant development in the establishment of folklore at OSU.

Merrill Kaplan, who received her PhD from UC Berkeley as a student of Alan Dundes, also came in 2006. She holds joint appointments in the Department of English and the Department of Germanic Languages and Literatures. She is a specialist in Old Norse-Icelandic literature and folklore and nineteenth century Norwegian literature and culture as well as a scholar of internet folklore. Kaplan's book *Thou Fearful Guest* (2011) represents her extensive research on the medieval Icelandic saga.

In 1999, the OSU Newark campus hired Katherine Borland for a folklore position in Comparative Studies. She was assistant dean of that campus until becoming a faculty member at the main campus in 2006. She received her PhD from Indiana University, where she studied with Richard Bauman. Borland has conducted extensive research in Central American and US Latina/o communities (2001), including in her book *Unmasking Class, Gender, and Sexuality in Nicaraguan Festival* (2006).

Mark Bender, who received his PhD at OSU and currently chairs the Department of East Asian Languages and Literatures, has taken OSU students to do fieldwork in China and has brought a constant stream of excellent folklore students from China. Bender's research focuses on Chinese professional storytelling (2003). For several years, the Performance Theory course was offered collaboratively by scholars specializing in Japanese, Korean, and Chinese performances—a framework that had the advantage of introducing students to a foundational folklore paradigm through the lens of particular, non-Western cultural practices. Georgios Anagnostou received his PhD at OSU, with Webber as a co-adviser, and teaches in the Department of Greek and Latin. Like many of the folklorists at OSU, Anagnostou also studies folklore and social justice (2006).

Hiring folklorists in language departments was not without its challenges. Some literary scholars dismissed ethnographic research and the study of performance of verbal arts in everyday life. Others, however, welcomed the opportunity to expand the conception of textual studies. By the time that Margaret Mills was hired to chair Near Eastern Languages and Cultures in 1998, many in the literature and language departments appreciated folklorists' understanding of a variety of cultural knowledge extending beyond the canons of literature. Mills and Roberts had been core faculty in the Department of Folklore and Folklife at the University of Pennsylvania. Mills's courses on Persian folklore and Webber's courses on folklore in North Africa helped the program at OSU to recruit a generation of excellent international students working in Arabic, Turkic, and Persian traditions. Also, both Mills (1991) and Weber offered courses in orality and literacy that drew students from across campus, both folklorists and nonfolklorists.

The Creation of a Center and a Program of Coursework

From Utley's day until Barnes and Mullen joined the English Department in the late 1960s, OSU offered only one folklore course, which could be taken for advanced undergraduate or graduate credit. The courses were expanded in the early 1970s into separate undergraduate and graduate courses.

Created in the 1960s, Ohio State's folklore archive is one of the oldest in the country. Utley developed a record collection that included more than six thousand LPs from all over the world and a collection of over twenty thousand books, now housed in the OSU library and forming one of the largest collections of folklore texts in the world. With the initiation of the undergraduate Introduction to Folklore class in the 1970s, Mullen began adding the research projects undertaken by the students. Over the years, several scholars donated materials to the archive, including Rosemary Joyce, who received her PhD in English, and John Stewart, a faculty member in English who was hired as a creative writer and who was also a distinguished Trinidadian anthropologist and folklorist (1986). Stewart arranged for the donation of material collected by Professor Priscilla Tyler of the University of Missouri—a collection that includes over four thousand items of African and Caribbean folklore and literature. Also included are Mullen and Tim Lloyd's documents from the Lake Erie Fisherman Project, projects contracted by Lloyd through the Ohio Arts Council, Elena Foulis's video oral history interviews of Latina/os in Ohio, and newer collections, such as OSU PhD Sheila Bock's ongoing documentation of graduation cap traditions. The images of mortar boards demonstrate both students' sense of their identity and critiques of contemporary political issues such as student debt. The archive holds the slang journal project developed by linguistic anthropologist Gabriella Modan in 2011 (who also served as acting director of the Center in 2019). The slang journals provide evidence of first usages of terms and of how words cycle through different groups and change over time.

With the creation of field schools, OSU's folklore program continues to rethink the archive's role in the program, in the coursework, and in the field as a means of developing relationships between student learning and community engagement. The field school materials are held not only at OSU but also in the local communities where the material was collected. For the earliest projects in the archive, a student typically collected a genre of folklore and provided a brief statement about the context. By the 1980s, the assignment was reversed, and students wrote more about the cultural context of the performers and performances. Still, for decades, although these projects accumulated in the archive, few scholars used them as a resource. Dell Hymes described the ethnography of communication as "concrete, yet comparative, cumulative, yet critical" (1996, 63). Although the archive represented the cumulative research of decades of folklore students, it was regarded, for the most part, as a repository rather than a complex record of the development of the field, and over time, its usefulness for scholarship became less articulated if not entirely ignored. In part, the archive serves a philological research methodology mostly abandoned by ethnographic researchers. The archives are not quite old enough, nor are their contents carefully enough collected, to serve the function of something like the European archives of eighteenth-century folktales. However, the arbitrariness of the collections, the generalized rather than specified collection of just about anything that could qualify as folklore, makes them a source for research about what was collected and about particulars (such as first usages of slang).

In 1991, Mullen and Shuman created the Center for Folklore Studies. The center provided an opportunity to consolidate the program across departments, to coordinate the admission of doctoral students, and to invite visiting international scholars. When OSU initiated graduate interdisciplinary minors, we created a specialization in folklore and designed a core curriculum that we believe represents the knowledge and methods that would best prepare graduate folklore students. During her term as center director, Noyes proposed dividing the core courses into two areas: tools and theory. The tools sequence comprises two courses: (1) an introduction to folklore genres and to the history of the discipline and (2) a course on fieldwork and the ethnography of communication. The theory sequence comprises three courses: Tradition and Transmission; The Ethnography of Performance; and Differentiation, Identification, and the Folk. In addition to these core courses, several topical courses are offered, including Folklore, History, and Memory; Tourists, Travelers, and Tricksters; Cultures of Waste and Recycling; Theories of Myth; Chinese Performance Traditions; Discourse, Space, and Place; Folklore in the History of Disciplines; Orality and Literacy; Folklore and Gender Politics; Public Practice in Folklore and Ethnomusicology; Play and Children's Folklore; and The Frankfurt School. We also teach courses that are not exclusively about folklore but that bring a folkloristic perspective to the study of disability, refugees, narrative, popular culture, area studies, development studies, and cultural diplomacy.

The folklorists at Ohio State have made a strong commitment to undergraduate teaching. Sims and Martine Stephens wrote *Living Folklore*, an introductory text that builds on earlier introductions and is designed to provide students with the methods and frameworks they need to conduct their own research (2005). Webber's *Folklore Unbound* introduces students to many of the central issues in folklore research and opens up new areas of inquiry (2015). At OSU, where few students major or minor in folklore, undergraduate students are often unfamiliar with the field. Our goal has been to teach methods. Both *Living Folklore* and *Folklore Unbound* guide students in their own inquiries. In addition, the undergraduate courses provide important approaches to the study of diversity, whether in terms of race, class, gender, sexuality, or ability.

The creation of the center allowed us to connect our small core faculty to a wide community of faculty affiliates and to serve students across the humanities, arts, education, and social sciences. A typical graduate seminar in folklore assembles students from up to a dozen departments, and while this makes for labor-intensive discussion, it also helps spread awareness of the field. All of the folklore faculty serve individually on graduate committees across a range of disciplines, from classics to dance.

As director of the center, Mullen had coordinated a yearly exchange with folklorists at Western Kentucky University. When Shuman became director, she was able to procure funds for a more formal conference in 1999 titled "Going Native: Recruitment, Conversion, and Identification in Cultural Research." The executive offices of American Folklore Society came to OSU in 2001. Tim Lloyd served as executive director of the society, and Barbara Lloyd joined the center as the first assistant director. Having an assistant director with a degree in folklore moved us to a new level of productivity, engagement, and vitality. We created a Folklore Student Association and built a strong cohort of graduate and undergraduate students. Under Noyes's directorship, the Indiana/OSU Folklore Graduate Student conference was created. The current assistant director, Cassie Patterson, has a PhD in folklore from OSU and, with Borland, the current director, has been able to further develop the center's archive and community engagement.

The international character of the research interests and student base fostered an emphasis in OSU's folklore program on the political force of cultural traditions. Several of the folklore faculty (Noyes, Mills, Borland, and Shuman) have become affiliates of the Mershon Center for International Security, where folklore has relevance for the study of on-the-ground experiences, cultural practices, and cultural representations in situations of war and violence. Notably, in 2005, Mills and an OSU colleague coordinated a conference, "Afghan Women Leaders Speak," that brought Afghan women activists from nongovernmental organizations and governmental agencies to OSU. Noyes similarly created several Mershon conferences, including "Culture Archives and the State: Between Nationalism, Socialism, and the Global Market" and "Sustainable Pluralism: Linguistic and Cultural Resilience in Multiethnic Societies." Noyes's work on UNESCO heritage designations, Borland's work on Nicaragua, and Shuman's work on refugees and asylum seekers all use foundations of folklore research

Fig. 22.2. Folklore students and faculty at the Ohio State University, October 2017. *Clockwise from left*: Sydney Varajon, Sabra Webber, Nancy Yan, Sarah Craycraft, Dorothy Noyes, Gregg Vaillancourt, Mariah Marsden, Tessa Jacobs, Madeleine Smith, and Katey Borland. Photograph by Patrick Mullen.

methods and analysis but also resonate with the work of scholars in international studies (although the exchange is not always easy).

Folklore at OSU did not experience the divide between applied and academic folklore that resulted in heated debates at the annual meetings of the American Folklore Society in the 1980s. As Barbara Kirshenblatt-Gimblett observed in "Mistaken Dichotomies," the discipline is intertwined with the political and cultural conditions that sustain and change the production of knowledge in the academy (1988); and folklore at OSU has engaged in ongoing relationships with community partners. Mullen's work for the Smithsonian festival on Ohio in 1977 integrated his research and public folklore exhibition—an approach that is also represented in his work on the elderly (1992). Jack Shortlidge, a student of Mullen's, became a program officer at the Ohio Humanities Council, where he fostered programming for many community groups. Anne Grimes, a folksinger and collector of folk songs in Ohio, worked closely with the OSU folklore faculty in the 1950s, and Joyce engaged in research on material culture (Stump and Joyce 1989). Mullen and Tim Lloyd conducted research with Ohio fishermen (Lloyd and Mullen 1990), and, while Barbara Lloyd served as assistant director of the Center for Folklore Studies, she developed Appalachian folklore programs in Meigs County, Ohio, followed by her replacement, Patterson, who cultivated and continues to shepherd the lively Appalachian Studies Network@OSU. More recently, as current director of the Center for Folklore Studies, Borland has been conducting research in Latina/o communities in central Ohio and, with Patterson, has developed field schools in southern Ohio.

Moving Forward

The four hallmarks of the folklore program at OSU are (1) a strong theoretical program that continues to reconsider the ways that tradition and heritage are reconceptualized in discourses of the present; (2) the integration of ethnographic and textual research methodologies; (3) international, postcolonial, and interdisciplinary research on a wide range of groups often marginalized by race, class, gender, and/or ability; and (4) community engagement. Although the Ohio State University was barely mentioned in Baker's accounts of folklore programs (1971, 1986), today it has a substantial, thriving program, and typically about two dozen faculty and students attend meetings of the American Folklore Society. Several of the folklore faculty are fellows of the American Folklore Society: Utley was a founding member; and Mullen, Mills, Noyes, and Shuman are fellows currently. Presidents of the American Folklore Society include Utley (1951–52), Roberts (1997–78), and Noyes (2018–19). During most of his tenure as executive director of the society, Lloyd was located at OSU.

Folklore at OSU has moved far from the early divide between textual and ethnographic approaches to folklore. Being part of multiple departments helped fund conferences, bring visiting scholars and lecturers, and attract students who might not have otherwise considered studying folklore. The program has been able to increase faculty in part because foreign language departments were interested in hiring folklorists, who were fluent in the language and, importantly, could offer culture courses, enhancing enrollment numbers. As wonderful as these opportunities were for creating a strong folklore faculty, they are no guarantee of sustainability. Mills and Webber both retired and, thus far, have not been replaced by folklorists. Roberts and Lee were replaced by African American literature scholars, and the Department of English is not currently offering courses in African American folklore. Cashman, hired as a folklorist, left for Indiana University in 2015 and has not been replaced, though we anticipate hiring more folklorists by the time this essay is published.

Like folklorists everywhere, both in the academy and in public programs, OSU folklorists try to find ways to articulate what we do to people not yet familiar with the field. However, the goal of the folklore faculty at OSU has not been to articulate what we do as distinct but instead to demonstrate what it brings to a conversation. Folklorists are not the only ones with an interest in the vernacular, though the field does have a particular historical legacy, tinged by nationalism, sometimes racism, and often disparaging attitudes toward the people we study, and through attention to this legacy, we offer significant and relevant critiques. Folklorists contribute to and benefit from the many intersecting conversations that contribute to the work of the field. OSU's folklore program has been a story of developing relationships with fellow travelers. Having allies in other departments who value folklore methods and collaborations with folklorists has been a key to maintaining a strong presence at the university. In addition, and perhaps even more importantly, interdisciplinary connections have played a role in how folklorists deal with the Romantic legacy of the discipline. Folklore is as relevant today as it ever was, whether in questions of what counts as cultural heritage and to whom it belongs or how concepts of the folk are deployed to establish legitimacy of one kind or another.

References

Abernethy, Francis Edward, and Patrick Mullen. 1996. *Juneteenth Texas: Essays in African-American Folklore*. Denton: University of North Texas Press.

Adéẹ̀kọ́, Adélékè. 1998. *Proverbs, Textuality, and Nativism in African literature*. Gainesville: University Press of Florida.

Anagnostou, Georgios. 2006. "Metaethnography in the Age of 'Popular Folklore.'" *Journal of American Folklore* 119, no. 4: 381–412.

Arewa, E. Ojo. 1970. "Proverb Usage in a 'Natural' Context and Oral Literary Criticism." *Journal of American Folklore* 83, no. 330: 430–37.

Baker, Ronald L. 1971. "Folklore Courses and Programs in American Colleges and Universities." *Journal of American Folklore* 84, no. 332: 221–29.

———. 1986. "Folklore and Folklife Studies in American and Canadian Colleges and Universities." *Journal of American Folklore* 99, no. 391: 50–74.

Barnes, Daniel R. 1966. "Some Functional Horror Stories on the Kansas University Campus." *Southern Folklore Quarterly* 30, no. 3: 312–31.

———. 1970. "Folktale Morphology and the Structure of *Beowulf*." *Speculum* 45, no. 3: 416–34.

———. 1972. "The Bosom Serpent: A Legend in American Literature and Folklore." *Journal of American Folklore* 85, no. 336: 111–22.

———. 1996. "Interpreting Urban Legends." In *Contemporary Legend: A Reader*, edited by Gillian Bennett and Paul Smith, 1–16. New York: Garland.

Bender, Mark. 2003. *China's Suzhous Chantefable Tradition*. Urbana: University of Illinois Press.

Bendix, Regina, Kilian Bizer, and Dorothy Noyes, eds. 2017. *Sustaining Interdisciplinary Collaboration: A Guide for the Academy*. Urbana: University of Illinois Press.

Bohmer, Carol, and Amy Shuman. 2007. *Rejecting Refugees: Political Asylum in the 21st Century*. New York: Routledge.

———. 2018. *Political Asylum Deceptions: The Culture of Suspicion*. London: Palgrave.

Borland, Katherine. 2001. *Creating Community: Hispanic Migration to Rural Delaware*. Wilmington: Delaware Heritage.

———. 2006. *Unmasking Class, Gender, and Sexuality in Nicaraguan Festival*. Tucson: University of Arizona Press.

Briggs, Charles, and Amy Shuman. 1993. "Theorizing Folklore: Toward New Perspectives on the Politics of Culture." Special Issue, *Western Folklore* 52, no. 2/4.

Cardozo-Freeman, Inez, Eugene P. Delorme, David W. Maurer, Robert A. Freeman, and Simon Dinitz. 1984. *The Joint: Language and Culture in a Maximum Security Prison*. Springfield, IL: Charles C. Thomas.

Cashman, Ray. 2008. *Storytelling on the Northern Irish Border: Characters and Community*. Bloomington: Indiana University Press.

———. 2016. *Packy Jim: Folklore and Worldview on the Irish Border*. Madison: University of Wisconsin Press.

Dundes, Alan. 1973. *Mother Wit from the Laughing Barrel: Readings in the Interpretation of Afro-American Folklore*. Englewood Cliffs, NJ: Prentice Hall.

Goldstein, Diane E., and Amy Shuman, eds. 2016. *The Stigmatized Vernacular: Where Reflexivity Meets Untellability*. Bloomington: Indiana University Press.

Haas, Bridget M., and Amy Shuman, eds. 2019. *Technologies of Suspicion and the Ethics of Obligation in Political Asylum*. Athens: Ohio University Press.

Hymes, Dell. 1996. *Ethnography, Linguistics, Narrative Inequality: Toward an Understanding of Voice*. Bristol, PA: Taylor & Francis.

Kaplan, Merrill. 2011. *Thou Fearful Guest: Addressing the Past in Four Tales in Flateyjarbók*. Suomalainen, Finland: Tiedeakatemia.

Kirshenblatt-Gimblett, Barbara. 1988. "Mistaken Dichotomies." *Journal of American Folklore* 101, no. 400: 140–55.

Lee, Valerie. 1996. *Granny Midwives and Black Women Writers: Double-Dutched Readings*. New York: Routledge.

Lloyd, Timothy Charles, and Patrick B. Mullen. 1990. *Lake Erie Fishermen: Work, Identity, and Tradition*. Urbana: University of Illinois Press.

Messenger, John C. Jr. 1959. "The Role of Proverbs in a Nigerian Judicial System." *Southwestern Journal of Anthropology* 15: 64–73.

Mills, Margaret Ann. 1991. *Rhetorics and Politics in Afghan Traditional Storytelling*. Philadelphia: University of Pennsylvania Press.

Mullen, Patrick B. 1988. *I Heard the Old Fishermen Say: Folklore of the Texas Gulf Coast*. Logan: Utah State University Press.

———. 1992. *Listening to Old Voices: Folklore, Life Stories, and the Elderly*. Urbana: University of Illinois Press.

———. 2008. *The Man Who Adores the Negro: Race and American Folklore*. Urbana: University of Illinois Press.

———. 2018. *Right to the Juke Joint: A Personal History of American Music*. Urbana: University of Illinois Press.

Noyes, Dorothy. 2003. *Fire in the Plaça: Catalan Festival Politics after Franco*. Philadelphia: University of Pennsylvania Press.

———. 2016. *Humble Theory: Folklore's Grasp on Social Life*. Bloomington: Indiana University Press.

Shuman, Amy. 1986. *Storytelling Rights: The Uses of Oral and Written Texts by Urban Adolescents*. Cambridge: Cambridge University Press.

———. 2005. *Other People's Stories: Entitlement Claims and the Critique of Empathy*. Urbana: University of Illinois Press.

Sims, Martha, and Martine Stephens. 2005. *Living Folklore: An Introduction to the Study of People and Their Traditions*. Logan: Utah State University Press.

Stewart, John. 1986. "Patronage and Control in the Trinidad Carnival." In *The Anthropology of Experience*, edited by Victor W. Turner and Edward M. Bruner, 289–315. Urbana: University of Illinois Press.

Stump, Dwight, and Rosemary O. Joyce. 1989. *A Bearer of Tradition: Dwight Stump, Basketmaker*. Athens: University of Georgia Press.

Utley, Francis Lee. 1961. "Folk Literature: An Operational Definition." *Journal of American Folklore* 74, no. 293: 193–206.

———. 1963. "The Linguistic Component of Onomastics." *Names* 11, no. 3: 145–76.

Webber, Sabra Jean. 1991. *Romancing the Real: Folklore and Ethnographic Representation in North Africa*. Philadelphia: University of Pennsylvania Press.

———. 2015. *Folklore Unbound: A Concise Introduction*. Long Grove, IL: Waveland.

PATRICK B. MULLEN is Professor Emeritus of English at the Ohio State University. He is author of *The Man Who Adores the Negro: Race and American Folklore*; *Listening to Old Voices: Folklore, Life Stories, and the Elderly*; *I Heard the Old Fishermen Say: Folklore of the Texas Gulf Coast*, and *Right to the Juke Joint: A Personal History of American Music*.

AMY SHUMAN is Professor of Folklore in the Department of English at the Ohio State University. She is author of *Other People's Stories: Entitlement Claims and the Critique of Empathy* and (with Carol Bohmer) *Political Asylum Deceptions: The Culture of Suspicion*.

23 Show Me Folklore

The Folklore, Oral Tradition, and Culture Studies Program at the University of Missouri

Claire Schmidt

THE STUDY OF folklore at the University of Missouri has thrived through collaboration with public folklore organizations, formal and informal societies, folk musicians and artists, and what Lisa Higgins of the Missouri Folk Arts Program calls "ordinary citizens of genius." Thus, while this chapter is about the ways folklore has been collected, theorized, researched, and taught at the University of Missouri, it is also a story about the Missouri Folklore Society, the Missouri Cultural Heritage Center (later the Missouri Folk Arts Program), the University of Missouri Press, and the people behind those organizations. From its origins to the present day, the Mizzou Folklore Program has emphasized collaboration among student, academic, public, and amateur folklorists, and the need to theorize new ways of knowing that challenge unequal power structures to build a better, more ethical field.[1]

Beginnings

The study of folklore at the University of Missouri was inaugurated by Henry M. Belden, who, after receiving his PhD from Johns Hopkins University and spending a year in Nebraska, where he worked with Louise Pound, joined the faculty in 1895. Belden was elected president of the American Folklore Society in 1910 and 1911 and was one of the early "literary" presidents of the society (Zumwalt 1988, 36). An Anglo-Saxonist and ballad scholar, Belden founded the English Club at the University of Missouri in 1903. In addition to sharing original creative and critical work, the members of the English Club researched Missouri folklore, specifically ballads and folk songs.

Beginning with Belden's ballad collection and research, the study of folklore at the University of Missouri has been marked by significant contributions from undergraduate and graduate students. According to a 1903 campus newspaper, "The club hopes this summer to make a collection of Missouri songs—unpublished songs that live from mouth to mouth in different localities—songs that have grown from some far-off ballad or been 'gotten up' to commemorate some murder or famous happening in the neighborhood in days gone by" (quoted in Pentlin and Schroeder 1986–87, 2). Under Belden's supervision, students recorded and classified ballads and folk songs for Belden's proposed master collection. Drawing on the students' contributions to the collections, Belden published articles in *Modern Philology* (1905) and the *Journal of American Folklore* (1906) arguing for the importance of preserving English ballads in current circulation in Missouri.

The English Club changed its name to the Missouri Folklore Society in 1906 and by 1907 had more than forty members, some of whom worked at museums and universities and colleges around the state and others who might now be called independent folklorists or amateurs.

Belden's scholarship drew undergraduate and graduate students to the field of folkloristics.[2] Belden regularly taught The Popular Ballad at the University of Missouri beginning in 1918 until his retirement in 1937, when Edward Weatherly took over the course. Belden deposited his manuscript at Harvard in 1917, and *Ballads and Songs of the Missouri Folk-Lore Society* was finally published by the University of Missouri Press in 1940, reissued with updates in 1955, and again in 1973.

While individual faculty at the university maintained an interest in Missouri traditions and cultures, the Missouri Folklore Society gradually ceased activity. After Belden's retirement, the university produced little folklore scholarship until the mid-1970s, although faculty in German, Art History, and other departments conducted ethnographic, narrative, and material culture research. John Neihardt became poet in residence and lecturer in 1948, and his presence on campus (and donation of his collected materials and books) contributed to ongoing interest in ethnographic study, particularly in oral traditions. Neihardt's focus on epic poetry—he taught American Epic: The Twilight of the Sioux and American Epic: The Mountain Men between 1966 and 1974 (University of Missouri 1966–74)—foreshadowed John Miles Foley's work to make the University of Missouri a hub for the study of oral epic.

Although academic folklore study was quiescent between the late 1940s and early 1970s, beginning in 1964, the Chez Chandelle Coffee House at the First Presbyterian Church served as an important locus for undergraduate and graduate students. Here old-time musicians performed, including Taylor McBaine and other traditional musicians who featured prominently as master artists in the Traditional Arts Apprenticeship Program at the Missouri Cultural Heritage Center (Howland 2014). Cathy Barton Para and Dave Para, folk musicians and educators and longtime leaders in the Missouri Folklore Society, met at the Chez.

Dave, who moved into the Chez in 1975, was in charge of booking acts for the free entertainment every Friday and Saturday night. The Chez was frequented by many other musicians and collectors who became leaders in Missouri folklore, such as Howard Marshall and Gordon McCann.

The Rebirth of Mizzou Folklore

Reflecting the national interest in folklore and folk culture, in 1975, the English Department at the University of Missouri renewed its historical emphasis on folklore studies by hiring a full-time faculty member in folklore. Ellen Monica Pharr (later Gibb), whose PhD adviser was Barre Toelken, taught the first Introduction to Folklore class at the University of Missouri in the fall of 1975. Pharr also taught Folklore and Mythology (University of Missouri Department of English 1975). When Pharr left in late 1976, the English Department hired John W. Roberts (PhD, Ohio State) (University of Missouri 1977), which led to an upswing of folklore study. Under Roberts's purview, the university offered several popular sections of Introduction to Folklore and African American Folklore each semester (University of Missouri 1983). Roberts encouraged his undergraduate folklore students to engage with the collection, analysis, and interpretation of their own cultural traditions.[3]

With the resumption of folklore courses came the revitalization of the Missouri Folklore Society (MFS). Roberts, Don Lance, and Adolf E. and Rebecca B. Schroeder led the movement and, with a group of about forty members, officially restarted the MFS in March 1977 (Pentlin and Schroeder 1986–87, 28).[4] Since 1977, the MFS has held annual meetings bringing together academic, public, and amateur folklorists to share research and promote the study of folklore statewide. Between 1977 and 2017, MFS presidents have included Roberts, Adolf Schroeder, Barry Bergey, Erika Brady, Elaine Lawless, and Adam Davis. The society launched the *Missouri Folklore Society Journal* in 1977 under Roberts's editorship.

The revitalized MFS reflects the goals of Belden's ballad and folk song project. The Society provides a platform to support the study of folklore in Missouri, and for many this study centers on the role of traditional music in Missouri cultures. R. P. Christeson's work to collect old-time fiddle tunes played a significant role in maintaining the vibrant fiddling community into the twenty-first century, and Loman Cansler and Max Hunter have been recognized for their contributions to the documentation and study of folk song in Missouri (Pentlin and Schroeder 1986–87, 32).[5]

The Missouri Heritage Readers series published by the University of Missouri Press also brought Missouri folklore to a wide readership, emphasizing accessible prose for new adult readers. Rebecca Schroeder edited this series, and renowned storyteller and active member of MFS Gladys Coggswell contributed a volume.[6]

Furthering the partnerships between the university, the state, community scholars, and amateur folklorists, the Missouri Cultural Heritage Center was established as the Missouri Cultural Research Center in 1982 with Howard Marshall as director. The Center, originally housed in the Conley House, quickly became a major force in the study of folklore in the state, offering internships, public programming, publications, architectural surveys, and other research.[7]

When Roberts left the University of Missouri for the University of Pennsylvania in 1983, he was recognized for "leadership and devotion developing our folklore offerings" in *The Newsletter of the English Department*, which continued to publish notices of Missouri Folklore Society activities for several years (University of Missouri 1983). The three folklorists hired after Roberts inaugurated an era in the study of folklore at the University of Missouri marked by a concern with power, equity, and justice. Together, John Miles Foley, Elaine J. Lawless, and Anand Prahlad built a program that worked to make the study of folklore a responsible, ethical, participatory, and humanistic practice.

Theoretical Emphases and New Ways of Knowing

Foley was hired as a professor of classics and English in 1979. After completing his doctoral work at the University of Massachusetts Amherst, Foley was assistant professor at Emory University, a visiting fellow at Harvard, and a visiting assistant professor at the University of Belgrade. At the University of Missouri, Foley taught undergraduate and graduate courses that included Oral Tradition, Epic, Old English (including *Beowulf* and seminars on the Exeter and Vercelli books), Homeric Poetry, Latin, and Greek. As part of the *Beowulf* graduate seminar, Foley hosted the "Beowulfathon," a four-hour event at his rural home, wherein students and faculty took turns reading the poem aloud (in Old English), taking short breaks for food and drink.

Foley made the University of Missouri an international hub for the study of oral tradition. In the 1986 proposal to establish the Center for Studies in Oral Tradition, Foley wrote, "Since coming to UMC [the University of Missouri–Columbia] in 1979, I have made a concerted effort to put the university into a position to take on leadership in this new field. Until two years ago this position was occupied very prominently by Harvard, but with the retirement of Albert Lord and the absence of a successor to him, a (temporary) vacuum has been created. It is quite clear that some university will take over Harvard's role; if UMC does not do it, perhaps Berkeley, Indiana, or Pennsylvania will step in. None of these other schools is, however, as well prepared as we" (Foley 1986). Through a vigorous publishing and public relations agenda, regular academic events including the Missouri Oral Literature Symposium (1984) and the annual Lord and Parry Lecture Series (established in 1985), and the journal *Oral Tradition* (founded in 1986), the University of Missouri became a leader in the study of oral tradition and Foley the recognized successor to Harvard's Albert Lord. Foley's work in oral traditional theory built on Lord and Milman Parry's *The Singer of Tales*, and Foley's early fieldwork documented the continued oral traditions in Yugoslavia previously studied by Parry and Lord. His prolific and wide-ranging lifelong contributions redefined even the key terms of his field (Garner 2012). By making *Oral Tradition* an online open access source, Foley ensured that academic and community scholars of oral tradition worldwide could make use of current scholarship.

Like Foley, Elaine Lawless emphasized the importance of theoretical approaches in the analysis of collected material. When Lawless joined the faculty in 1985, she was already known for bringing together feminist theory and folk religion in her doctoral work at Indiana University and at Idaho. At the University of Missouri, Lawless began to build a folklore program that drew graduate students who wanted to study folklore and literature, women's folklore, feminist theory, and vernacular religion.

Lawless's work with Pentecostal communities and the role of women's unofficial preaching in those communities led her to develop the theory and practice of reciprocal ethnography. Reciprocal ethnography undermines the hierarchy of power that places the ethnographic researcher above the ethnographic subject by requiring the researcher to share the work with the group under study and to present the interpretations of the researcher and the group in dialogue.[8]

Recognizing the personal and the political in her own field interests, Lawless began researching and writing about narratives of domestic violence, which culminated in *Women Escaping Violence* (2001). Lawless's collaboration with Heather Carver in the Theater Department resulted in the Troubling Violence Performance Troupe, a group of graduate students in folklore and theater who performed personal experience narratives of domestic violence given to them by friends, family, and audience members. Lawless and David Todd Lawrence (PhD, University of Missouri, 2003), produced *Taking Pinhook* (2014), an ethnographic documentary about an all-Black Missouri town that was destroyed when the Army Corps of Engineers breached the Birds Point–New Madrid floodway in 2011. The displaced residents were denied not only compensation, but even Federal Emergency Management Agency assistance. Lawrence and Lawless won the 2019 Chicago Folklore Prize for their book, *When They Blew the Levee* (2018), which charts the political, racial, and cultural conflict as the battle for justice for Pinhook unfolded.

The programmatic focus on social justice, antiracism, and ethical ethnography was reinforced when Sw. Anand Prahlad joined the faculty in 1990 as a poet and professor of folklore (with graduate degrees from UC Berkeley and UCLA). Prahlad bridged the gap between creative writing and ethnography and revived the focus on African American folklore and folklore of the African diaspora that had begun in 1977 with Roberts. Prahlad's work with Jamaican proverbs, Black

Fig. 23.1. Elaine Lawless (*second from left*) with former University of Missouri graduate students Abel Gomez, Kate Kelley, and Danae Faulk (*left to right*) at the American Folklore Society meetings in Buffalo, NY, October 2018. Photograph by Thomas A. McKean, courtesy of Elaine J. Lawless.

cinema and speculative fiction, and later *The Greenwood Encyclopedia of African American Folklore* (2005) drew a pool of graduate students whose doctoral research sought to understand structures of power linked to race and economics within the framework of folkloristics. Prahlad's creative work, including poetry collections (1982, 2012), and his prize-winning memoir, *The Secret Life of a Black Aspie: A Memoir* (2017), support his teaching and research focus that refuses binaries and comfortable answers.

Prahlad's teaching reinforced the focus on theory emphasized by Lawless and Foley. He offered graduate seminars in Postcolonial Approaches to Folklore Study, The Theory of the Fetish, Humor Theory, and Disability Theory. In addition, Prahlad taught courses in African American Folklore, Folklore and Film, Poetry, and Songwriting. Prahlad was awarded the William T. Kemper Fellowship for Teaching Excellence in 2010, in part because of his fierce commitment to inclusion, whether of gender, sexuality, race, religion, or ability.

Together, Foley, Lawless, and Prahlad emphasized the importance of creative ethnography and the responsibility of the researcher to the humans who become

Fig. 23.2. Anand Prahlad taught courses in folklore, creative writing, Black studies, and disability studies at the University of Missouri. Photograph ca.2010 courtesy of Anand Prahlad.

the subject of published research. They encouraged their students to engage with questions that affect the lives of those who dwell in the margins, and their students have gone on to become leaders in the field.

From the official launch of the Folklore, Oral Tradition, and Culture Studies program in 1992, the University of Missouri admitted several folklore doctoral and master's students every year, graduating more than fifty MA and PhD students. Through a departmental policy of supporting MA and PhD students through tuition waivers, stipends, and health insurance, the program was able to attract a wide range of talented students. The Student Folklore Society was a vigorous community of students who raised funds to support student travel to the annual meetings of the American Folklore Society and the Western States Folklore Society, often through bake sales that attained legendary proportions. Each year, the Student Folklore Society selected and hosted a prominent folklorist to give a lecture on campus. Graduate students in folklore soon took over teaching introductory folklore courses, specifically Introduction to Folklore and Folklore

Fieldwork. When Lawless served as editor of the *Journal of American Folklore* in the early 2000s, the journal provided additional opportunities for graduate students as editorial assistants.

When the Missouri Cultural Heritage Center closed in 1993 due to budget cuts, the Missouri Folk Arts Program (MFAP) was created to fill the vacuum. Currently, MFAP is housed within the university's Museum of Art and Archaeology and funded through national grants and the Missouri Arts Council. The MFAP began offering graduate internships in 1993 to doctoral and master's students in folklore, providing mentoring and training in public folklore. MFAP directors have included Barry Bergey, Amy Skillman, Dana Everts-Boehm, and Lisa Higgins. In addition to the Traditional Arts Apprenticeship program, the MFAP offers workshops to support community scholars as they collect, archive, and promote folk arts in their home communities.

Looking Ahead

After serving as president of the American Folklore Society (2007–10) and receiving the AFS Lifetime Scholarly Achievement Award in 2015 as well as numerous teaching and research awards at the University of Missouri, Elaine Lawless retired in 2015. In 2017, Prahlad became Director of the Creative Writing Program, leaving less time for teaching and advising folklore graduate students. Foley's death in 2012 left a vacancy in teaching and research that, due to persistent budget freezes, remains unfilled. Budget cuts and austerity measures have meant that no folklorists have been hired to replace Foley or Lawless, and the English faculty voted in 2017 to stop admitting graduate students in folklore until there are faculty to support them. While other folklorists remain at Mizzou (including Sandy Rikoon, Dean of Human Environmental Sciences; Richard Callahan in Religious Studies, and Joanna Hearne in English and film), the future of the study of folklore at the University of Missouri is in transition. Despite this, the Missouri Folklore Society, the Missouri Folk Arts Program, and the many collaborative relationships across the academic, public, and amateur realms remain strong and creative, ensuring a statewide commitment to the study of folklore in the state of Missouri.

Acknowledgments

Many thanks to my indefatigable research assistant, Katanna Davis, for her hours spent tracking down information, sifting through materials, and arranging visits to archives. Additional thanks are due to Kristopher L. Anstine of the University of Missouri Archive and the staff at the Missouri State Historical Society. I would also like to thank David Para, Cathy Barton Para, Lyn Wolz, and Richard

Schroeder, who shared information about the Missouri Folklore Society, the folk music performances at Chez Chandelle, and local efforts to share Missouri folklore with a wide audience through the Missouri Heritage Readers series.

Notes

1. I do not use the term *amateur* disparagingly but as meaning "one who loves or is fond of," per the *Oxford English Dictionary*.

2. See Smith (2016), Wolz (1986–87), and Pentlin and Schroeder (1986–87) on contributions of individual undergraduate students. During Belden's tenure, several graduate students wrote master's theses on ballads and ballad traditions, including Sara Frances Bradham (1931); Edward Weatherly (1929), who went on to teach courses in the ballad; and John Robert Moore (1914), who became a prominent Defoe scholar at Indiana University. For the latter, see "Dr. John R. Moore, Defoe Scholar Who Taught at Indiana U., Dead," *New York Times*, July 20, 1973, https://www.nytimes.com/1973/07/20/archives/dr-john-r-moore-defoe-scholar-who-taught-at-indiana-u-dead-taught.html.

3. John W. Roberts Folklore Collection. 1975–76. Boxes 1–6. CA 4756. State Historical Society of Missouri State Archive.

4. See also "Missouri Folklore Society Membership Information." Schroeder, Adolf and Rebecca Collection, CA5648. State Historical Society of Missouri Archive.

5. The Missouri Folk Arts Program Traditional Arts Apprenticeship Program continues to support old-time fiddling in the state of Missouri.

6. Schroeder Collection, CA5648, Box 6.

7. The Conley House on the University of Missouri campus was reputed to be haunted. See the University of Missouri Archive for the Missouri Cultural Heritage Center's administrative records, and the Missouri State Historical Society Archives for correspondence, grants, working files, research materials, project materials, and publications.

8. See Holtgrave (2015) for Lawless's reflections about her career as an ethnographer.

References

Belden, H. M. 1905. "The Study of Folk-Song in America." *Modern Philology* 2: 573–79.

———. 1906. "Old-Country Ballads in Missouri." *Journal of American Folklore* 19, no. 1: 231–40; 19, no. 2: 281–99.

———. 1940. *Ballads and Songs of the Missouri Folk-Lore Society*. Columbia: University of Missouri Press.

Foley, John Miles. 1986. "Prospectus for Center for Studies in Oral Tradition: Phase I." Box 2, Folder 1, C:1/18/2. University of Missouri Archives.

Garner, Lori Ann. 2012. "In Memoriam: John Miles Foley." *Old English Newsletter*. http://www.oenewsletter.org/OEN/print.php/memorials/foley/Array.

Holtgrave, Darcy. 2015. "Coining 'Reciprocal Ethnography': A Visit with Elaine Lawless." *Syndicate Mizzou*. University of Missouri. https://www.youtube.com/watch?v=M4-U_Lrm2HM.

Howland, Jack. 2014. "Discovery Reignites Memories of the Chez at First Presbyterian." *Columbia Missourian*. October 27. https://www.columbiamissourian.com/news/discovery-reignites-memories-of-the-chez-at-first-presbyterian/article_57ab66fo-9156-54fb-bfcb-1481a692e5ef.html.

Lawless, Elaine J. 2001. *Women Escaping Violence: Empowerment through Narrative*. Columbia: University of Missouri Press.

Lawless, Elaine J., and David Todd Lawrence. 2014. *Taking Pinhook*. https://rebuildpinhook.org/documentary/.

Lawrence, David Todd, and Elaine J. Lawless. 2018. *When They Blew the Levee: Race, Politics, and Community in Pinhook, Missouri*. Jackson: University Press of Mississippi.

Pentlin, Susan L., and Rebecca B. Schroeder. 1986–87. "H. M. Belden, the English Club, and the Missouri Folk-Lore Society." *Missouri Folklore Society Journal* 8–9: 1–44.

Prahlad, Anand. 1982. *Hear My Story and Other Poems*. Berkeley, CA: Berkeley Poets Workshop and Press.

———, ed., 2005. *The Greenwood Encyclopedia of African American Folklore*. Westport, CT: Greenwood.

———. 2012. *As Good as Mango*. Nacogdoches, TX: Stephen F. Austin University Press.

———. 2017. *The Secret Life of a Black Aspie: A Memoir*. Fairbanks: University of Alaska Press.

Smith, Dale. 2016. "Ballad of Ada Belle." *Mizzou News*. March 30. https://news.missouri.edu/2016/ballad-of-ada-belle/.

University of Missouri. 1966–74. *University of Missouri Bulletin*. University Archives, University of Missouri.

University of Missouri Department of English. 1975. *Newsletter of the English Department* 1, no. 1. University Archives, University of Missouri.

———. 1977. *Newsletter of the English Department* 3, no. 1. University Archives, University of Missouri.

———. 1983. *Newsletter of the English Department* 8, no. 1. University Archives, University of Missouri.

Wolz, Lyn. 1986–87. "Folk Music in Missouri: An Annotated Bibliography." *Missouri Folklore Society Journal* 8–9: 193–214.

Zumwalt, Rosemary Lévy. 1988. *American Folklore Scholarship: A Dialogue of Dissent*. Bloomington: Indiana University Press.

CLAIRE SCHMIDT is Assistant Professor of English and Director of the Honors Program at Missouri Valley College. She is author of *If You Don't Laugh You'll Cry: The Occupational Folklore of White Wisconsin Prison Workers*.

24 This Is the Right Place for It

The Development of the Folklore Program at Cape Breton University

Jodi McDavid

The folklore program at Cape Breton University (CBU) in Sydney, Nova Scotia, is one of the younger programs in North America. Both the institution and its development are wrapped up in issues of Cape Breton identity, a subject familiar to folklorists. Cape Breton is an island, and from 1785 to 1820, it was a British colony. Some residents still consider its reabsorption into Nova Scotia a betrayal by Halifax- and London-centered interests and perennially advocate separation. The end of steel and coal as an economic base makes this proposition untenable, but the collapse of industry narrative (and the inability to foresee, forestall, or remedy it) lays responsibility on outside governance. Unemployment and a lack of capital have caused local populations to decline.

The university began as Xavier Junior College (an extension of St. Francis Xavier University) in 1951, became the College of Cape Breton in 1974, the University College of Cape Breton in 1982, and finally Cape Breton University in 2005. CBU has always been a small, reactive institution, quickly changing paths to chase funding. There are several reasons for the university culture developing this way. One is simply its being one of seven public, taxpayer-funded universities in Nova Scotia (compared to other Atlantic provinces, two of which have one university each) and its relatively modest size, with 3,500 students in 2017 but rapidly ballooning to 5,100 in 2019. Another reason may be the seeming willingness to accept and promote the have-not dialogue that positions the Island (invariably capitalized in local usage) against the capital, Halifax, where governmental power and four of the seven universities are located. CBU must thus strategize and jockey for opportunities in competition with larger key players.

The Island's main industry is arguably tourism, including an emphasis on cultural tourism. As with other folklore programs that have emerged in contexts where local culture is locally understood as rich, distinct, and under threat, advocates frequently state that having a folklore program at CBU is a no-brainer, its rationale self-evident because Cape Breton is immersed in vernacular traditions.

Further proving the depth of the local material, international folklorists such as Michael Taft (1991), Margaret Bennett (1989), Burt Feintuch (2010), and Mats Melin (2015) have done significant research here.

Despite the common perception and projection that Cape Breton is ethnically homogeneous, there is considerable diversity in the local population. Cape Breton Island's First Nations peoples are the Mi'kmaq, who live throughout Atlantic Canada but whose largest population and most sacred geography are in Cape Breton. Acadian settlers were followed by a more deliberate French colonial and military presence before being ousted by the British in the years prior to the American Revolution. As the British presence became entrenched (by, among other means, forcing the Acadians into exile), Irish immigrants and, significantly, Scots Highlanders settled and soon became the largest population, albeit divided by Catholic/Protestant tensions and removed from the Anglocentric corridors of political and economic power. Industrialization (and tensions in Europe) brought greater diversity as Eastern European Jews, Italians, Poles, Ukrainians, Syrians, Lebanese, and West Indians arrived to work in coal and steel, populating the increasingly metropolitan Sydney. In recent decades, the university and the hospital system have attracted further populations, although out-migration has decimated others.

That said, the dominant narrative in tourism in Cape Breton is Scottishness. Ian McKay cites "tartanism" and antimodernism as factors in the deliberate crafting of Nova Scotia as traditional (1992; McKay and Bates 2010). But when Cape Breton presents itself as an inherently Scots place, it erases other identities and experiences. The dominant narrative is that of the settler and colonizer and inherently one of a white Cape Breton. There is an ongoing effort to recast that narrative to represent the more complex and multicultural history of the Island, and good examples of cross-cultural partnerships in local tourism practice have arisen (MacPherson et al. 2016), but it is a work in progress. All of this has affected the development of a folklore program in a place that popularly considers itself to have one identity and cultivates that identity for the tourist gaze.

There were many precursors to the development of the program and the hiring of the first person into the discipline of folklore at CBU. Over time, an atmosphere that was conducive to folklore scholarship emerged due to a constellation of seemingly unrelated events. As early as 1955, Sister Margaret Beaton, a librarian, established a collection of archival materials and cultural anecdotes with an emphasis on Scots and Gaelic materials. That collection grew and eventually became the Beaton Institute, one of the largest archives in Nova Scotia. In the late 1970s, Elizabeth Beaton, a folklorist, became the senior researcher at the Beaton Institute.

Another seemingly unrelated event was the development of the bachelor of arts degree in community studies (BACS) at CBU, a unique program and the first full degree offered when it was granted university status in 1974, combining humanities and social science approaches with direct community action, co-op placements, and cultural interventions. Richard MacKinnon first taught a special topics course in folklore in 1982 in the time between completing his master's degree in folklore at Memorial University of Newfoundland (MUN) and returning there in the fall to begin his doctorate. In 1984, MacKinnon accepted a one-year contract to teach folklore and community studies and developed three courses: Introduction to Folklore, Oral Literature, and Folklife Studies. In 1984, folklorist David Buchan was invited to CBU to give a lecture, but he also spoke to upper administration, advocating for the development of a folklore program. A full-time position was created within the BACS program, and for the next twenty years, MacKinnon taught folklore courses along with his responsibilities to the BACS program.

From 1999 to 2000, Michael Robidoux, another graduate from MUN's folklore program and an ethnographer of sport, taught in the BACS program in the sport, heritage, and culture stream and was allowed to offer the Culture and Tradition course. Although Robidoux had some research-active peers in the institution, including MacKinnon (1990) and colleagues in the Department of History, the department's overall lack of a research focus made Robidoux's decision to leave for the University of Lethbridge easier, despite CBU's offering him a full-time position. Robidoux's time at CBU was marked by labor grievances and the first faculty strike, in which he was an active participant. Ironically, this strike and the resultant collective agreement impelled the university toward becoming more research-active.

Meanwhile, MacKinnon worked with Parks Canada to develop a certificate to be delivered at CBU. This postbaccalaureate heritage certificate (still much requested but no longer available) was meant to both provide specialization and allow further training for professionals working in the heritage field. A lot of CBU's early programs, especially ones related to folklore, had an emphasis on work skills and job preparedness, which posed significant problems as the program emerged and developed. Terry MacLean, a Parks Canada employee, was at the forefront of developing and teaching the program. In retrospect, it is evident that MacLean pushed for the acceptance of folklore at CBU, encouraging Robidoux to apply for the position. MacLean thus played a key role in the development of the program but was not a folklorist and was initially involved as a government, rather than university, employee.

The pivotal moment for the establishment of folklore at CBU was the appointment of MacKinnon as the Canada Research Chair (CRC) in Intangible Cultural Heritage in 2005. MacKinnon fondly recounts the university development office calling him and reading some terms from a list, at which point the caller said, "Intangible cultural heritage is on this list; that is what you do,

Fig. 24.1. Culture and Heritage Building, Cape Breton University, built in 1994. Photograph ca. 2015, courtesy of Cape Breton University.

right?" The proposition to apply for the federally funded CRC already marked a seismic shift for CBU, as the university began both to see itself and to be seen as a research institution. When a CRC is hired, the opportunity to backfill the person's position with new tenure-track hires often arises, because the program pays the chair's salary. CRCs also have significant course reductions, and so while it increases the research capacity of the program, it simultaneously reduces the teaching capacity of the CRC. It was in this context that a position in folklore was created, which was filled by Ian Brodie in 2005. Simultaneously, Heather Sparling was hired for a one-year contract in ethnomusicology, a position subsequently regularized to full-time in 2006.

One of Brodie's first tasks was to assist with the development of MacKinnon's newly established Centre for Cape Breton Studies. Although a recent transplant to the community, Brodie was also expected to develop regional courses and a local program of research. In time, Brodie learned that his digitization and website development work on the MacEdward Leach collection for Beverly Diamond, a CRC in ethnomusicology at Memorial University (Diamond and Brodie 2013) had cinched his job offer, although Brodie's involvement had stemmed more from a need for employment than from a facility with or affinity for Atlantic Canadian balladry. From 2005 to 2011, Brodie and Jodi McDavid (also a PhD in folklore from MUN and at the time Brodie's spouse) developed several courses in the folklore program, supplementing inherited courses with new offerings to fill in any gaps. They also worked to design the program as a system, determining where students would get theory, method, and vocabulary, sensitive both to breadth and depth requirements while being aware of the Cape Breton culture narrative that attracts students to the program to begin with. Brodie began to cultivate local—and fundable—research interests and began publishing on local topics (2015).

Another key factor in the development of this program was not to renew MacKinnon's CRC after seven years but instead to create two CRC positions—one in ethnomusicology and one in folklore. However, two ethnomusicologists, Sparling and Marcia Ostashewski, were appointed to these positions. These chairs created another backfill opportunity, and another ethnomusicologist, Chris McDonald, was hired. The narrative of the development of the ethnomusicology and music program fits better with the local understanding of what a cultural program should be than the way folklore has historically represented itself. MacKinnon is a well-known local musician, and folklore at CBU always had an awareness of, and focus on, music. Unfortunately, CBU does not have the resources to create more positions in folklore, and it has not been easy to justify additional folklore hires while other programs are similarly struggling for positions.

Several "clever hires" have been made or proposed over the years to get more folklorists into the institution under the mantle of other programs. Thus, there are or have been a number of folklorists affiliated with CBU, but they are not in the folklore program full-time or at all. Folklorist Ronald Labelle joined the French program in 2012 as one of only two full-time faculty members. His courses included language acquisition, French Canadian cultures, and literature, as well as folklore. He created two cross-listed courses, *Contes et légendes du Canada français* and *Chansons traditionnelles françaises*. Because these courses demanded French fluency, however, the cross-listing did not result in strong enrollments. Elizabeth Beaton held a tenured position in the BACS program after she left the archive. She was never enlisted to teach folklore courses, however, although her research at that time was cutting-edge public-sector folklore work, fieldwork heavy and engaging with notions of class and diversity.

In the relatively brief time from 2005 to 2018, the departments housing folklore have gone through five name changes as folklore is shunted from one interdisciplinary home to another. The name changes and departmental restructuring are part of a strategy: as a popular elective, folklore helps balance undersubscribed courses and thus serves to ameliorate budgetary tensions. At this stage, the folklore program has one full-time position. MacKinnon has taken full-time administrative leave to serve as CBU's vice president academic, and Labelle in the

French program retired in 2019. Neither was replaced with a folklore specialist. Ethnomusicology has one CRC (the second was not renewed) and two full-time faculty members alongside regular contingent faculty.

Another setback for a deeper commitment to a program at CBU is the ready availability of contingent labor. Per-course instruction, often performed by women or underemployed musicians, was and remains a dominant mode of employment in the folklore and ethnomusicology programs. McDavid was instrumental in creating the courses that she, Brodie, and MacKinnon later taught, but is not noted in many of the official documents of the university. During her position as archivist of Beaton Institute but under separate contract, McDavid also developed and taught an archives course for folklore and published local research based on her doctoral work (2008). In her subsequent position in the Office of Research and Graduate Studies, she supported the CRCs in culture studies and contributed to many strategic plans that included reference to CBU's cultural programs. Adding to the pool of per-course instructors, Janice Esther Tulk joined the university from 2008 to 2010 as MacKinnon's postdoctoral student and returned in 2011 as a full-time researcher with the Purdy Crawford Chair in Aboriginal Business at CBU. An ethnomusicologist with an expertise in Mi'kmaq music, Tulk had also graduated from MUN, where folklore courses are integrated into the ethnomusicology program. Tulk periodically teaches folklore and music courses and is fully employed in CBU administration. When Gerald Pocius retired in 2016 after almost four decades of teaching folklore at MUN, he moved to Sydney and became affiliated with the CBU folklore program, periodically offering courses as a per-course instructor.

Perhaps CBU has yet to realize its potential as a program, having been cut off at the knees several times. Some key reasons for this may be structural: Access to per-course instructors disincentivizes planning for long-term growth; a lack of basic administrative support places the burdens of paperwork and committee scheduling on the shoulders of faculty; and university-wide budgetary crises and labor conflict produce ongoing tensions. For example, in 2017, following the faculty union's near-strike, usual budget propositions, the public and controversial termination of the university president's contract, and dropping enrollments, McDavid concluded that it would be wise to diversify the household income and left her administrative position of seven years to establish her own consultancy.

What will the CBU folklore program look like in the next twenty years? CBU has had a few initiatives that it may return to, including a plan to develop a heritage management master's or certificate program that would involve the folklore and MBA programs. Ideally, the institution will dig deep and complement Brodie's academic strengths with a public-sector folklorist to create a balance in the program that is more suited to the public perception of folklore as involving practical as well as theoretical studies. The institution also has several resources on which to capitalize more fully, such as the recording and digitization lab at MacKinnon's Centre for Cape Breton Studies, and some currently untapped ones, like a large folk art collection.

Enrollment for folklore courses, at least as electives, continues to hold steady, and the faculty and those affiliated with the program are very research-active. Research interests fit the parameters of and have found success with Canadian funding agencies such as the CRC program and the Social Science and Humanities Research Council. For that reason, along with the public perception of folklore and the attractiveness of the courses to students, folklore at CBU is currently stable, although ideally it should be growing. What makes this program unique is the strength of its researchers and their commitment to being public intellectuals. Labelle was the storyteller in residence in the regional library and started a storytelling festival, while Tulk studied indigenous dancing at powwows. MacKinnon explored protest songs and changed local perception about what folklore could be when he examined counterhegemonic songs of working-class people and broke down local perceptions of ethnic-based folklore. Beaton examined the architecture of Whitney Pier, a working-class area, and built a huge repository of interviews in the Beaton Institute. Brodie studied localized popular culture and youth culture. Collectively, the folklorists at CBU have won national recognition, published extensively, and, above all, have done so in the face of many challenges. The strength of the program is its people and their ability to pull together and weather storms.

Those currently and recently involved find it disheartening to see a program so full of promise suffer under the chaotic nature of the institution, and it is likely that in the next decade they will be calling on colleagues to help argue for the maintenance of what we have managed to eke out against all odds.

Acknowledgments

I thank Ian Brodie, Elizabeth Beaton, Ronald Labelle, Richard MacKinnon, Janice Esther Tulk, and Michael Robidoux for providing details of their employment for this article.

References

Bennett, Margaret. 1989. *The Last Stronghold: Scottish Gaelic Traditions of Newfoundland*. Edinburgh: Canongate.

Brodie, Ian. 2015. *Old Trout Funnies: The Comic Origins of the Cape Breton Liberation Army*. With Paul MacKinnon. Sydney, Nova Scotia: Cape Breton University Press.

Diamond, Beverley, and Ian Brodie. 2013. "MacEdward Leach and the Songs of Atlantic Canada." *Oral Tradition* 28, no. 2: 335–40.

Feintuch, Burt. 2010. *In the Blood: Cape Breton Conversations on Culture*. Photographs by Garry Samson. Logan: Utah State University Press; Sydney, Nova Scotia: Cape Breton University Press.

MacKinnon, Richard. 1990. "Cape Breton Tradition: Public Image and Private Reality." *Forerunner*, Spring: 28–31.

MacPherson, Stephanie, Patrick T. Maher, Janice Esther Tulk, Mary Beth Doucette, and Tracy Menge. 2016. "Eskasoni Cultural Journeys: A Community-Led Approach to Sustainable Tourism Development." Paper presented at the Travel and Tourism Research Association 2016 Conference. https://scholarworks.umass.edu/ttracanada_2016_conference/21.

McDavid, Jodi. 2008. "The Fiddle Burning Priest of Mabou." *Ethnologies* 30, no. 2: 115–36.

McKay, Ian. 1992. "Tartanism Triumphant: The Construction of Scottishness in Nova Scotia, 1933–1954." *Acadiensis* 21, no. 2: 5–47.

McKay, Ian, and Robin Bates. 2010. *In the Province of History: The Making of the Public Past in Twentieth-Century Nova Scotia*. Montreal: McGill-Queen's University Press.

Melin, Mats. 2015. *One with the Music: Cape Breton Step Dance Tradition and Transmission*. Sydney, Nova Scotia: Cape Breton University Press.

Taft, Michael. 1991. "Tracking the Cheshire Cat: Ethnic Americans and American Ethnicity on Cape Breton Island." *Canadian Folklore Canadien* 13, no. 1: 35–44.

JODI McDAVID is the owner of McDavid Brodie Consulting, and an Instructor at Cape Breton University.

25 Practical Cultural Work

The MA in Cultural Sustainability at Goucher College

Amy E. Skillman and Rory Turner

THE IDEA FOR a graduate program that would immerse students in "practical cultural work" sprang into the mind of Rory Turner, assistant professor of sociology and anthropology, one day as he was walking down Goucher College's central walkway. A folklorist and cofounder of the Maryland State Art Council's Maryland Traditions program, Turner shared these thoughts with a colleague, who told him to contact the Welch Center for Graduate and Professional Studies, because the center was on the verge of launching new programs.

Following this recommendation, in a November 2007 email to Debbie Cebula, then assistant dean of the Welch Center, Turner outlined a prospective two-year program aimed at cultural community leaders to "provide the tools and perspectives for more effective, indeed, transformative work by these cultural catalysts in creating the conditions for local deeply held cultural forms to flourish in an era of globalization and change." He noted, "The capacity for communities to make meaningful choices about cultural heritage is eroding . . . we need to develop stronger and healthier local economies and cultures, stronger communities that provide cultural scaffolding for people's well-being." This program would be the first of its kind, evolving from and synthesizing applied anthropology, public folklore, arts administration, community arts, social identity theory, and cultural policy studies to create a platform for effective cultural stewardship and partnership. In short, the two-year program would be "grounded in the sensibilities and interests of the liberal arts, including humanities, but equip students with the professional and management skills that they need to be successful in the workplace."[1]

Why Goucher College?

Goucher College (originally the Woman's College of Baltimore City) was founded in 1885 by a group of influential Methodists led by the Reverend John Franklin Goucher, who, with his wife, Mary Fisher Goucher, deeded the land to begin its original campus in downtown Baltimore. The college was renamed in honor of the Gouchers in 1910 and relocated in 1954 to a 287-acre wooded campus in Towson, Maryland, eight miles north of the heart of the city. The college has been coeducational since 1986 (Goucher College 2018b).

Goucher has built a strong, innovative tradition of liberal arts education with a reputation for social justice and activism. Faculty members work with the Office of Community-Based Learning to create opportunities that connect students to nonprofit organizations working in Baltimore's neighborhoods. A highlight of Goucher's curriculum is the requirement that all undergraduates study abroad before graduation. In 2015, Goucher adopted an academic philosophy focused on relationships, resilience, and reflection. Coursework reflects the core values of a liberal arts education: proficiency in English composition and in a foreign language and solid foundations in history, abstract reasoning, scientific discovery and experimentation, problem solving, social structures, and environmental sustainability (Goucher College 2018b).

Graduate Programs at an Undergraduate College

In the 1990s, the college added its first graduate programs: Historic Preservation, Creative Nonfiction, Arts Administration, and Education and Teaching. Turner believed an MA in cultural sustainability would fit into this environment. His experiences with the Maryland Traditions program persuaded him that public folklore had an important tool kit and set of perspectives for meaningful cultural work that deserved wider attention and application. Inspired by the work of organizations such as the Philadelphia Folklore Project and City Lore, and by the depth of inquiry and critical reflection shared with colleagues and artists throughout the region, Turner envisioned a field of practice grounded in partnership with communities and fostered through ethnographic engagement that led to cultural empowerment.

The motivating idea behind the MA in cultural sustainability is that, by valuing and beginning with the gifts of culture, communities and scholars in collaboration can do work that strengthens the capacity of people to claim agency and live better lives. Participants in this mode of action must pay careful attention to the ethics of relationships in the context of complex and unequal social, economic, and political landscapes. This work demands practical strategies to develop projects that will strengthen valued cultural processes in their own terms rather than through the imposition of dominant models with their own epistemological and normative baggage. The humble work of public folklore, as practitioners have transformed it over the past several decades, offers crucial tools for doing this work with the nuanced ethical care and cultural sensibility it demands. Identifying and building from the gifts of communities that so often take form as folklore enables an important type of cultural work with wide application and far-reaching potential. This paradigm further recognizes that many people and organizations are already engaged in this kind of action and that a global network of activists inspired by a common care for valued cultures has enormous potential.

Why Cultural Sustainability?

In early 2008, the Welch Center decided to move forward in developing this program, emboldened by market research indicating strong demand for such an offering from potential students. Turner recruited faculty colleagues, and they developed and formulated a curriculum to realize this vision. Together with Cebula, this group developed a set of offerings in the program that included both culturally focused courses and professional courses centered on management competencies. In considering an appealing name for this new offering, they chose *Cultural Sustainability* to reflect the program's emphasis on community-centered approaches geared toward supporting the agency and capacity of communities to shape their own destinies. In selecting this name, the program connected with an existing body of policy development and inquiry that was exploring matters of culture and well-being in relationship to broader concerns regarding sustainability. This has proven to be a positive resonance that has invited the realization that the health of local cultures and community life has an important role to play in the systemic transformations of political, social, economic, and environmental practices needed to move toward a more sustainable world.

An advisory council was identified and convened in fall 2008. This group included leaders in practical cultural work: Christina Barr, Robert Baron, Peggy Bulger, Kurt Dewhurst, Elaine Eff, James Bau Graves, Debora Kodish, Jon Lohman, Michael Atwood Mason, Melissa McLoud, Betsy Peterson, Carole Rosenstein, Guha Shankar, Betsy Taylor, Jeff Todd Titon, and Bill Westerman. These scholars and professionals reviewed the proposed curriculum, educational objectives, and program learning outcomes and endorsed the endeavor. The first group of eleven students began the program in January 2010 in a nine-day residency. In 2011, Turner stepped down as academic director and Amy Skillman took on this role, which she still maintains.

Mission and Learning Objectives

The mission of the MA in Cultural Sustainability (MACS) Program is to teach students "to work closely with individuals and communities to identify, protect, enhance, and advocate for important traditions, ways of life, cherished spaces, and our vital relationships to each other and the world. As a result, you [a prospective student] will become a leader, writer, thinker, teacher, activist, and/or entrepreneur who will take action to counter the powerful forces that endanger communities and threaten cultural equity around the world" (Goucher College 2018a).

In the MACS Program, cultural sustainability is understood as both introducing culture into larger discussions of sustainability and applying the principles of sustainability into cultural practices and concerns. Borrowing from Robert Cantwell's notion of cultural inalienable rights, we understand sustainability to be about creating the conditions in which cultures can thrive (Cantwell 2001). In this way, the curriculum is action-oriented and the learning outcomes reflect the ideals of a theoretical grounding, ethical practice, community engagement, action, professional preparation, and creating a community of practice. The faculty adopted the following outcomes after a 2014 program review.

> Outcome 1: Research, demonstrate and apply knowledge of cultural practices and contemporary issues pertaining to cultural sustainability, which contribute to human and ecological well-being.
>
> Outcome 2: Exhibit professional and ethical responsibility in managing partnerships that foster community self-determination and empower community efforts in cultural documentation, preservation, revitalization, and social equity.
>
> Outcome 3: Design, undertake and critique cultural documentation field projects applying diverse research methods such as observation, writing, photography, video, and/or sound recording to identify and nurture traditions of knowledge and practice that are meaningful and valued by communities.
>
> Outcome 4: Devise, implement and evaluate actions that support cultural sustainability such as educational programs, exhibitions, performances, workshops, projects, media productions, websites, festivals and other initiatives that align with community practices.
>
> Outcome 5: Identify and demonstrate a range of professional management skills that contribute to organizational sustainability such as financial skills, communications, and leadership through collaboration, teamwork, and consensus building.
>
> Outcome 6: Identify strategies for cultivating a professional network of practitioners and organizations in support of a community of practice. (Goucher College 2019)

Faculty

The faculty members in the MACS Program are all practitioners who have transformed their respective fields through interdisciplinary thinking, action, and practice. MACS faculty are passionate about ensuring cultural equity as well as

Fig. 25.1. MACS student Jessica Guild (*left*) explores documents with Chesapeake Bay working waterman Jimmy Murphy while on a field visit with students and faculty as part of a July 2012 residency. Immediately following this introductory overview, the students boarded a traditional skipjack sailboat and learned about the cultural, economic, and environmental issues facing working waterman today. Photograph courtesy of Rory Turner.

supporting the continued success of their students. While many are folklorists, we have intentionally brought on board filmmakers, arts advocates, museum consultants, social entrepreneurs, environmental activists, economists, and social theorists to ensure a diverse perspective on issues of cultural sustainability. Several members of the original advisory council have joined the faculty—a testament to their belief in the goals and purpose of the program.

Format

Courses are offered during intensive weeklong residency sessions twice a year, in January and July, as well as through fully online sessions in the fall, spring, and summer. This blended learning approach provides flexibility and academic integrity for students. The residency fosters a solid foundation for personal relationships to develop with faculty and students and an opportunity to learn hands-on skills such as cultural documentation and dialogue design. The retreat-like residency invites the creation of a community of practice, which carries students through their online courses and into their professional lives. Visits to sites of cultural sustainability in the Baltimore area provide models and create a shared sense of purpose among the students. Thus, the residency delivers not only intensive courses but also experiential learning opportunities to explore cultural sustainability practices in situ.

The online courses provide flexibility for students to continue working and/or raising families while in graduate school. Courses often guide the students into academically grounded research to engage in projects where they live, encouraging civic engagement and professional networks in the very communities that matter to them.

Curriculum

Rather than focus on the genres of folklore (e.g., narrative, material culture, vernacular architecture), the MACS Program offers students tools and strategies that enable them to work with their communities in whatever ways those communities need. Thus, the core courses reinforce cultural equity, community partnership, self-reflexivity, and community action research. Students take required courses in Cultural Partnerships, Cultural Policy, Cultural Documentation, and Ethnographic Methodologies.

Electives, such as Arts and Social Change, Principles of Cultural Mediation, Museums and Communities, and Dynamics of Identity, allow students to focus on a sector or issue in their community, connecting them to potential local resources while they gain the skills and knowledge to make a difference in those communities. Students may also select electives from many of the other graduate programs at Goucher (Arts Administration, Digital Arts, and Environmental Studies are popular options). Although the MACS Program does not have tracks or concentrations, students often use their electives to create one. Common themes include: arts and community-based activism; environment, culture, and community; food justice and sustainability; museums and public education; and social justice policy and planning.

All students must take at least nine credits from the management core, ensuring that when they leave the program they have professional skills to bring to their chosen sector, which often leads them to positions of decision making and even policy making. Courses in leadership, financial skills, communications, grant writing, marketing, social entrepreneurship, ethics, and intellectual property help prepare students for professional careers.

All this coursework culminates in a capstone that builds on what students have learned and encourages them to imagine who they might become. Whether an academic thesis or a community-based project, the MACS capstone synthesizes practice and theory into real-world applications.

Fig. 25.2. Leadership is a popular management course, which ends with four days of sailing on the Chesapeake Bay. Students implement leadership strategies and styles as part of the crew. Here, two students plot the vessel's course, 2014. Photograph courtesy of Thomas Walker.

So, Who Chooses a Degree in Cultural Sustainability?

As of May 2019, eighty-one students had completed their coursework and received their MA degrees in cultural sustainability. The program attracts aspiring professionals working in public agencies, museums, cultural organizations, tribal councils, and other nonprofits as well as schools engaged either directly or indirectly with community-based forms of culture. Some of the students are traditional artists, others are community leaders; some have recently graduated from BA programs, while others are returning to graduate school after many years of work in another field. The program creates a framework for educating artists, writers, cultural leaders, and community activists eager to address well-being and equity in their communities and beyond. Many see what is happening across the globe and yearn for the tools to heal an ailing planet. Others seek strategies for using their traditional art forms to empower their neighborhood or tribe. What follows is a sampling of graduates and their capstone topics:

Michelle Banks spends half her year in Guatemala, where she created an intergenerational organization that partners with highland Mayan communities to reclaim traditional agricultural knowledge and ensure the survival of the landscape as well as the next generation's relationship to it and their culture. She is pursuing a PhD in sustainability education and has returned to Goucher to teach Ethnographic Research.

Mike Vlahovich, descended from a Croatian fishing family, is a working waterman and activist living on the Eastern Shore of Maryland. He came to the MACS Program to gain skills that would lend credibility and growth to his traditional boat restoration project, Coastal Heritage Alliance. He has created a training program with local skipjack captains to support heritage tourism opportunities using their own boats when they are not oystering. While in the program, Vlahovich expanded this work to his ancestral country of Croatia. In 2016, he was awarded a National Endowment for the Arts National Heritage Award honoring his leadership and artistry as a boat builder.

Amber Dodge has worked in the refugee resettlement sector for over ten years, first as an English teacher in refugee camps in Thailand and more recently as a caseworker and liaison in Jacksonville, Florida. Her time in the MACS Program gave her the skills and opportunity to develop a crafts initiative for refugee artists who continue to practice their traditional art forms as a source of income as well as healing from the personal, social, and spiritual disruptions that forced them to leave their countries. Dodge has created a website that serves as an international clearinghouse for information on how and why to develop such programs.

Heidi Thomas is a well-established landscape architect in Baltimore who came to the program thinking about changing careers. However, the more courses she took, the more she realized she was in a position to build knowledge around the intersection of landscape design, cultural equity, and food justice. Her work continues in Baltimore, where she works with African American neighborhoods to reclaim public spaces and ensure access to healthy food.

A native of Minnesota, Michele Anderson is the director of Springboard for the Arts in rural Fergus Falls. The town has been battling a development issue around the 100-year-old state hospital, a Kirkbride building designed like a rambling castle on the hill. The structure has been facing the wrecking ball, much to the angst of the town's residents, who know it as a powerful part of the local landscape embodying poignant and transformative memories. Anderson worked with local artists to gather narratives and to create artistic opportunities for residents to advocate for repurposing the building instead of destroying it.

Karen (Queen Nur) Abdul-Malik is a recent past president of the National Association of Black Storytellers. She is not only a storyteller but also an advocate for the use of storytelling as a strategy for solving community problems. Her work documents creative placemaking environments where relationships that extend past self and family are generated through the foundation of storytelling to strengthen communities. She is currently the Folklife Center Director at the Perkins Center for the Arts in New Jersey.

Deborah Spears Moorehead is an artist and member of the Seaconke Pokanoket Wampanoag Tribal Nation in Massachusetts. She used her time in the program to draw on scholarly discourse, oral traditions, research, documentation, and interviews to clarify the history of the Wampanoag homeland and establish continuity for her tribe—a requirement of federal recognition by the US government. Spears Moorehead is a direct descendant from Massasoit, the great leader who first met and befriended the Pilgrims in 1620. Her work and her continued artistic endeavors are serving to heal her tribe from the injustices of invisibility.

These are just some examples of what our remarkable graduates are doing. They are action-oriented, doing work in their own communities to address community well-being through cultural equity and voice.

The MACS Program retains a strong relationship with the field of folklore. It emerged from public folklore practice and critical dialogue among practitioners, and the majority of MACS faculty members are folklorists or ethnomusicologists. The primary commitment of the program to ethical practice is informed by the partnership models of ethnographic research developed in public folklore. The program's conceptualization of expressive culture begins from a folkloristic vantage point: contextualized, genre-based forms of communicative action—gifts, if you will, shaped by and shaping social life through performance and emergence, connecting people in significant relationships, past, present, and future. In identifying the key role of such practice and cultural material in the well-being of human and environmental communities, MACS hopes to expand and demonstrate the relevance and value of folklore for a sustainable and sustaining world.

Note

1. Rory Turner, email to Debbie Cebula, November 18, 2007.

References

Cantwell, Robert. 2001. "Folklore's Pathetic Fallacy." *Journal of American Folklore* 114, no. 451: 56–67.

Goucher College. 2018a. "Master of Arts in Cultural Sustainability." Accessed April 11, 2018. www.goucher.edu/macs.

———. 2018b. "Who We Are." Accessed April 11, 2018. https://www.goucher.edu/explore/who-we-are/history/.

———. 2019. "Master of Arts in Cultural Sustainability, Program Mission and Learning Outcomes." Accessed June 11, 2019. https://www.goucher.edu/learn/graduate-programs/ma-in-cultural-sustainability/mission-and-outcomes.

AMY E. SKILLMAN is Director of the Master of Arts in Cultural Sustainability Program at Goucher College.

RORY TURNER is Professor of Practice in the Center for People, Politics, and Markets at Goucher College.

26 The Future out of the Past

The View from the Conference on the Future of American Folkloristics

Jesse A. Fivecoate, Kristina Downs, and Meredith A. E. McGriff

EVERY SUCCESSIVE GENERATION of scholars must create a vision of the future for its scholarly community and traditions. In 2016 with this in mind, three junior scholars at Indiana University, graduate students and recent graduates, formed a conference planning committee and tasked themselves with curating productive discussions about the future of folkloristics. There were two key components to this charge: a beginning assumption that folkloristics will continue and a commitment to ensuring that the discussions at the conference would be constructive and practical.

The impetus for this conference was not simply the generational thirst for future-oriented action but also a response to graduate student colleagues who seriously questioned a future of any kind for the discipline. These outspoken colleagues, though their numbers were small, asserted that folkloristics was nearing its end as a distinct area of study and practice. They believed folklore studies would eventually be absorbed into larger disciplines that have more clout and a stronger foothold in the academy, such as anthropology. Along with this reconfiguration, they argued, our departments, academic programs, and jobs would cease to be autonomous and would no longer carry the name of folklore.

To be sure, this was not the first prediction of this kind. Most folklorists are familiar with the lengthy list of publications that seek to throw into the spotlight the crises of the folklorists' identity, knowledge base, and academic status; we do not have space here to enumerate those arguments again. One, however, stands as an example, both for the way it was framed and for the manner in which folklorists responded to it. John Dorfman, not a folklorist himself, put folkloristics on the endangered disciplines list in his piece "That's All, Folks" (1997), and placed the blame for its demise on folklorists themselves.

Alan Dundes addressed Dorfman's comments in his 2004 American Folklore Society Presidential-Invited Lecture in which he took the leadership of the society and folklore faculty around the country to task for not speaking back to Dorfman directly. It was the graduate students at Indiana University, Dundes noted, who had taken up that mantle. Liz Locke, along with eighty other graduate students at the Folklore Institute, signed a rebuttal to Dorfman claiming that students of folkloristics do not enter the field because they are misinformed about the maligned status of their discipline within the academy (Dundes 2005, 387). The signatories were determined to actualize a future for the discipline. In solidarity with that group of graduate students, the planning committee for the Conference on the Future of American Folkloristics sought to produce a conference that would not shy away from discussions about the difficulties of ensuring a future for folkloristics and would create solutions to the problems that the discipline might face.

The Conference on the Future of American Folkloristics was thus conceived as a space for junior scholars to convene to (re)imagine the future of our discipline. We, the initial committee and lead planners throughout the conference—Jesse A. Fivecoate, Kristina Downs, and Meredith A. E. McGriff—began to discuss the shape such a conference would take. After speaking with and receiving support from John H. McDowell, chair of the Department of Folklore and Ethnomusicology at Indiana University, and Timothy Lloyd, executive director of the American Folklore Society, we sent out a survey to the society membership to gauge interest in the conference. When survey responses indicated widespread enthusiasm for the proposed conference, we decided to open participation to a wider range of voices. We reframed the conference to one in which scholars from all career stages and a variety of affiliations could participate in the conversation.

After more than a year of planning, the Future of American Folkloristics conference took place May 18–20, 2017, on the campus of Indiana University in Bloomington, Indiana. More than one hundred folklorists attended from more than fifteen different academic programs and nearly as many public programs. They included graduate students, retired scholars, public folklorists, and faculty at all career stages. Attendees were geographically dispersed as well, coming from across the United States and from as far away as Korea and Ireland.

Although we had originally planned to limit the number of daily sessions to three and to maintain a unified conversation by having no concurrent sessions, the number of high-quality submissions we received prompted us to modify our plans. The final program consisted of four sessions per day with two concurrent sessions in each time slot. The sessions consisted primarily of workshops and roundtables designed to include the audience and to stimulate productive conversations, though a handful of traditional paper sessions were mixed in. Each

2017 FOAF

CONFERENCE ON THE FUTURE OF AMERICAN FOLKLORISTICS
BLOOMINGTON, INDIANA
MAY 18-20, 2017

Fig. 26.1. Logo from the Future of American Folkloristics conference program, May 2017. By Meredith McGriff.

day's programming concluded with a plenary address. Thursday evening, Diane E. Goldstein spoke about what today's folklorists can learn from the history of applied folkloristics; Friday, Debra Lattanzi Shutika spoke on leadership and leadership training as a way to guarantee a place for folkloristics amid changing academic and political realities; and Kay Turner brought the conference to a close on Saturday with a discussion of how folklore studies can benefit from engagement with contemporary artists and by developing a queer folkloristics.

Sessions at the conference confronted some of the most pressing issues facing the discipline. We used as our guiding principle a quote from Diane Goldstein's 2013 presidential address at the annual meeting of the American Folklore Society: "Do great work and call yourself a folklorist" (2015, 138). Participants discussed the important work that folklorists need to be doing and the importance of folkloristics maintaining a distinct disciplinary identity. Social justice was perhaps one of the most pervasive themes, including positioning folklorists as social justice activists, addressing social justice through folklore pedagogy, and ameliorating social injustices bequeathed to us from the discipline's history. Another common thread was an examination of ways folklorists can better communicate with diverse audiences, including the general public, government officials, academics in other disciplines, and university administrators. We know that the discipline has value to offer outside the academy. Many participants stressed the importance of learning to communicate that value effectively to those who do not know what a folklorist is, perhaps one of the most critical challenges to the future of folkloristics.

In planning this conference, we acknowledged that the future of American folkloristics will be shaped by folklorists from across the continent, and those folklorists will inevitably be influenced by the folklore programs where they study and earn their degrees. It seemed pertinent to provide a forum in which the stakeholders in those programs could come together and discuss their past challenges and future goals. To facilitate such conversations, we developed a poster session on the histories and futures of folklore programs in higher education. This was inspired in part by two paper sessions at the 2016 meeting of the Western States Folklore Society on the "History of Folklore Programs in the United States." A call was sent to institutions, and in the end, five were able to participate: the University of Missouri, represented by Elaine Lawless; the University of North Carolina at Chapel Hill, represented by Patricia Sawin; Western Kentucky University, represented by Ann K. Ferrell; the University of Wisconsin–Madison, represented by Christine J. Widmayer; and Indiana University, represented by Lydia Campbell-Maher. In addition to presenting basic chronologies and historical facts, we asked that participants consider including challenges their programs had faced, distinct contributions their department has made to folkloristics, and the ways that those leading the program currently envisioned the future of teaching folkloristics. Each thus had unique focal points depending on the program's or department's size, longevity, pedagogical focus, or position within the greater institution/university.

The audience was eager to participate in discussion, and topics were varied. Recruitment was a recurrent theme, ranging from the appeal to incoming students of departments that support research within their own particular regions to the lack of faculty of color as a challenge in attracting and supporting students of color. The question, "Why would students go somewhere where they won't find people who are like them?" was repeated throughout the conference. Andrea Kitta also brought up the recurrent problem of having more students interested in folkloristics than available spots in graduate programs. The inevitable ebb and flow of departments was a point of concern, though it was noted by many in the audience that while some departments may become smaller or cease to exist (such as at the University of Pennsylvania), other departments, such as at Western Kentucky University and George Mason University, are growing under the careful cultivation of their current faculty. In this regard, Debra Lattanzi Shutika, Lisa Higgins, and others noted the importance of finding resources for building infrastructure to ensure a program is not dependent on a few specific individuals.

Faculty in the audience also brought up the problem of being in split positions, since in many cases folklorists teach in departments that are positioned within other disciplines (such as anthropology, English, or area studies). In these cases, they must often negotiate between the different goals and priorities of those fields, and they feel as though they are doing more work and still not meeting the requirements for success in either. Faculty members, particularly those with experience in administrative roles within their departments, also discussed the differences and similarities in their relationships with university administrators as well as the variety of ways departmental success is evaluated in different locations. Furthermore, regarding evaluation, some noted we should develop metrics for considering the relative success of folklore departments in comparison to departments within other (particularly larger) disciplines. Reflecting on Lattanzi Shutika's keynote address, audience members discussed the importance of developing relationships with university administrators. It was noted that we should employ our own folkloristic training in this endeavor, pursuing an ethnography of universities in order to learn the cultures of deans, chairs, and other administrators and to move effectively within those power structures.

Remarkably, there were many points during the poster session when a presenter or audience member exclaimed a sentiment along the lines of, "I didn't know that," usually regarding an institution where they had little or no personal experience. Each university folklore program constitutes a dynamic reconfiguration of the discipline, and not every component of folkloristics is taught at each location. By facilitating ongoing discussions between department administrators, educators, students, and potential future employers of those students, we can help ensure that more folklorists have a better sense of the dynamic flow of folkloristic education through institutions in North America and beyond. All folklorists, whatever their career path or research focus, are likely to encounter potential students who are intrigued by the work. To be responsible stewards of the discipline, we should be prepared to guide these potential folklorists to the program best suited to their interests. Certainly this points to the benefits of such sessions (and, indeed, this book), which enable folklorists to be better educated about the teaching traditions in programs around the country.

The conversations at the poster session were not unique; many played on themes that echoed throughout the three-day conference. Three additional sessions focused on programs where folkloristics is taught, even though the name of the program does not include the word *folklore*: Gregory Hansen presented on heritage studies at the University of Arkansas; Esther Clinton and Jeremy Wallach led a session about teaching popular culture at Bowling Green University; and Leslie Soble, Susan Eleuterio, and Heather Gerhart discussed the cultural sustainability program at Goucher College. Multiple sessions addressed social justice as pedagogy. Rachel V. González-Martin from the University of Texas at Austin and Mintzi Martínez-Rivera from Indiana University presented an indictment of the challenges faced by instructors of color, discussing persistent racism in the academy and the discipline of folkloristics as well as the additional work that scholars of color are expected to do to educate their white colleagues on theoretical issues related to race. A complementary perspective on ways that white teachers can do the work of confronting whiteness and issues of race in the classroom through a folkloristic lens was presented by graduate students Caroline Miller and Jessie Riddle from Indiana University and Jared Schmidt and Christine J. Widmayer from the University of Wisconsin–Madison.

Another highly participatory roundtable session organized by Kay Turner focused specifically on reevaluating the folklore canon and the need to include more women, scholars of color, and generally more diverse perspectives. Discussions in other sessions also followed this thread, including Katherine Borland's presentation on Susan Stewart's work. Many presenters called for engagement with critical race theory, queer communities, queer theory, and intersectionality and demonstrated the important contributions that folklorists can be (and, indeed, already are) making in these realms. In addition to expanding the discipline's theoretical perspectives, some sessions discussed how folklorists could reevaluate their engagement with subject matter such as science, food, and play, and considered how American folklorists can better collaborate with international scholars who have different views on what folklore and folkloristics are.

Another thread of discussion throughout the conference addressed the myriad ways the skills of a folklorist can be of high value in realms of university life outside of teaching folkloristics, including administration, advising, first-year programs, and libraries, as well as more "traditional" folklorist roles in archives and museums. Overall, there was a sense in these conversations that in continuing to identify oneself as both a folklorist and administrator, folklorist and adviser, or folklorist and librarian, those who do such work can both promote the field and play important roles in academia. This conversation dovetailed with another discussion on the state of the job market for folklorists. Considering the decline in tenure-track positions and political trends that can result in cuts to public programs, a common question that arose was, "Can one be a folklorist when there are no jobs advertised for folklorists?" The answer that emerged during the conference was a clear yes. There are, in fact, numerous jobs advertised in the field (Rini Larson 2018), but since the competition is high for those jobs, the perception is that there is insufficient work specifically requesting credentialed folklorists. Rather than lamenting a lack of jobs labeled folklorist, most discussions focused on ways we can separate our identities as folklorists from our job titles and on owning those folklore identities no matter where we are working and what we are working on.

It became clear during the Future of American Folkloristics conference that the future of folkloristics is about the critical work that folklorists do in attending to power dynamics in relationships of all types; it is about our ability to acknowledge, listen to, and advocate for the subaltern; it is about taking seriously all that which is trivialized, especially when it is our own discipline. We must continue to attend to the everyday lives of all people, and this conference highlighted the fact that we must do better when it comes to the "all." Folklorists can and should work to decolonize the discipline and contribute to cutting-edge work on queer theory, critical race theory, and intersectionality.

It seems self-evident, but we need to be curators of a contemporary folkloristics that trains folklorists to be educators and administrators, scholars and advocates, and producers of knowledge as well as critical examiners of such products. We must be willing to be vulnerable and to discuss with one another our downfalls as well as our successes if we are to benefit from the lessons of the past. We need to engage with others in the academy as well as with those outside it. Folkloristics promises to democratize the academy, and to effectively realize this, we need to be critical of our vocabularies, assumptions, theoretical frameworks, and the positions from and voices with which we speak.

This promise is within our grasp. We build on the knowledge of our disciplinary past, but we do not rest. Criticism of the discipline is necessary for advancement, and if we turn a critical eye on our contemporary work, it is not to throw our projects into question but rather to strengthen them from within. Part of our work is to speak to ourselves, like any scholarly community does, but we must also speak beyond our borders. The history of the discipline has been one of trying to understand professionally the nonprofessional; formally the nonformal; officially the nonofficial. We have cultivated a multitude of toolboxes that help us approach these objects of inquiry, often pulling from other disciplines when it is apparent that we lack a vocabulary, method, or theory to aid us in understanding. For some, this has been our weakness; for others, our strength. The Conference on the Future of American Folkloristics underscored that the discipline cannot speak with one voice, but that when we speak together, and to each other, we clarify visions of our future and make progress toward realizing them.

References

Dorfman, John. 1997. "That's All, Folks." *Lingua Franca* 7, no. 8: 8–9.

Dundes, Alan. 2005. "Folkloristics in the Twenty-First Century (AFS Presidential-Invited Lecture, 2004)." *Journal of American Folklore* 118, no. 470: 385–408.

Goldstein, Diane. 2015. "Vernacular Turns: Narrative, Local Knowledge, and the Changed Context of Folklore." *Journal of American Folklore* 128, no. 508: 125–45.

Rini Larson, Rosalind V. 2018. "Report on Recent Job Prospects for Folklorists." American Folklore Society, AFS Review: Reports. https://www.afsnet.org/news/4C0198/Report-on-Recent-Job-Prospects-for-Folklorists.htm?fbclid=IwAR1aU_CsUBt_m6VMecn38GEUuPy-BBLCC3anCtvF4Pk7SWAfQAB6T-HG5zE.

JESSE A. FIVECOATE is a doctoral candidate in folklore at Indiana University.

KRISTINA DOWNS is Managing Editor of the *Journal of Folklore Research*.

MEREDITH A. E. McGRIFF is Membership Director of the American Folklore Society. She is author of *The Michiana Potters: Art, Community, and Collaboration in the Midwest*.

Conclusion

Patricia Sawin and Rosemary Lévy Zumwalt

We conclude by recognizing the reality of loss, the innovations accomplished even as some programs disappeared, and folklorists' ongoing creativity in devising and defending productive academic programs despite the unpredictability of academic futures.

From the 1940s through the 1970s, folklore programs developed while universities operated according to a Deweyan, democratic model (Hufford, this volume; Schultz 2015). Faculty promulgated novel disciplinary models and shared newly generated knowledge to foster a broadly educated populace, and administrators and the public acknowledged faculty members' expertise and right to determine curricula. Universities competing for status relative to national and European peers recognized innovative degree-granting programs as valuable additions. Growing interest in traditional culture and ethnic "roots" ushered in one of those historical moments when folklorists can readily make the case that we offer valuable perspectives on important social issues.

Since the 1980s, however, folklore programs have functioned amid economic austerity and the ongoing corporatization of the university. Higher education responded to increasing distrust of intellectual expertise and to expectations for training with direct practical application in lucrative employment. "The corporate university took control of the curriculum in order to generate revenue" (Schultz 2015), which resulted in an emphasis on professional programs, a battle between university administrations and faculty over faculty governance, and increasing recruitment of part-time faculty to produce teaching hours without investing in tenure-track faculty lines. As these struggles played out, folklorists witnessed the dissolution or outright assassination of three major PhD-granting programs in the United States, at the University of Pennsylvania, the University of Texas, and the University of California, Los Angeles. At the University of Texas, "the folklore component of the program waned" after 1986 and was supplanted by an "emphasis on cultural studies" (Bauman, this volume). At UCLA, the Graduate Council "suspended student admission to the program" in June 1997 (Jones, this volume). And the board of trustees at Penn suspended the Department of Folklore and Folklife in June 1999 and ceased admitting graduate students to the program in 2004–5 despite vigorous resistance (Hufford, this volume).

Other programs have repeatedly struggled to revamp or justify themselves to meet the challenges of changing demographics and administrative priorities. Haring and Bendix observe, "University programs [in the United States] were reduced or eliminated, evidently under the impression that a discipline dedicated to the obsolescence of trivia could afford to wither" (2012, 300). Canadian universities were by no means immune to the effects of budget cuts and shifting administrative priorities, but these have been mitigated by support from the Canadian federal and provincial governments, foundations, and individual donors. Major research grants from the Social Sciences and Humanities Research Council and Fonds québécois de recherche–société et culture, extensive private fundraising from supportive communities (notably Canadian Ukrainians) and the Canada Foundation for Innovation, and/or the multi-year endowment of Canada Research Chairs or chairs supported by private donors have enabled scholars at Laval, Alberta, MUN, and Cape Breton to embark upon long-term research projects that enhanced their careers, contributed to archival collections, brought new faculty to universities, and provided monetary support and research experience for students and postdoctoral fellows. Scale also mattered. Folklore programs like the ones at Indiana University and Memorial University of Newfoundland that were relatively large and had achieved departmental status with concomitant control of dedicated budget and faculty lines and graduate admissions proved more stable, while administrators directed their budgetary shears toward small programs seen as low-hanging fruit.

Nevertheless, over the past forty years—even with the loss of three PhD-granting programs—most of the established graduate folklore programs have maintained their standing while others have emerged or expanded. Both developments illustrate the strength of what Barre Toelken called the twins laws of folklore, conservatism and dynamism—the "conservative force of tradition itself" and the "dynamism of change" (1979, 34)—a dedication to hold on to the discipline's central theoretical insights, research methodologies, and ethical commitments coupled with a creative willingness to seek out new interdisciplinary partners, new career applications for folklore study, and new populations of students. Simon Bronner identifies a "decentering of folkloristic education," which he connects "to shifts in twenty-first-century scholarship." IU's Richard Dorson, Bronner notes, "worked from the assumption that a few doctorate-granting academic centers in the United States took the lead in guiding students." But starting in the 1980s, "American folklore and folklife studies branched out and became integrated into a broad range of academic programs and institutions aimed not only at emerging adults in college but also at older learners and K–12 schools" (2019, 14).

An increased number of MA programs now prepares students to apply folkloristic perspectives in a wide range of careers (from archives and historical preservation to creative writing and audio production) and feeds some students into the new and remaining PhD programs. The MA Program in Cultural Sustainability at Goucher College provides activists with an applied folklore tool kit to foster cultural equity sustainability. In her 2013 presidential address to the American Folklore Society, Diane Goldstein issued a rallying cry to all those who have studied folklore, whatever their official job title: "Do great work and call yourself a folklorist" (2015, 138).

At the same time, the discipline faces a not-insignificant challenge to maintain a large enough pool of doctoral scholars trained at different universities to be able to populate new and established programs and to raise new generations of folklorists. Proliferating fixed-term and adjunct positions offer folklore PhDs less secure employment than tenure-track lines. Recognizing the improbability of creating new PhD-granting departments, folklorists have approached the practical dimension creatively, devising new versions of older interdisciplinary models to offer doctoral minors (as at the University of California, Berkeley) or concentrations within departments (as at the University of Louisiana, Utah State University, and Brigham Young University) or crafting interdisciplinary programs (as at the University of Wisconsin–Madison and the Ohio State University) within which students research folklore topics and establish identities as folklorists regardless of whether they officially earn degrees labeled "folklore." To assure the viability of master's and especially doctoral programs, faculty must also persuade students and administrators alike that the discipline of folklore offers crucial insight into relevant intellectual issues. While each doctoral program in folklore has particular strengths, many now draw on multiple theoretical or methodological approaches to stake their intellectual claim, including ones for which that particular program might not have been noted in the past. These include offering comprehensive study of folklore genres; strengthening collaboration with local communities and/or expanding international coverage; emphasizing the study of contemporary online creativity; highlighting the relevance of folklore's grasp of narrative and vernacular artistry to economic and political issues; challenging limiting Eurocentric and colonialist "genealogies" of the discipline (Briggs, this volume); and encouraging engagement with crucial contemporary critiques of race, gender, and sexuality. This embrace of multiple approaches and the spirited debate about the priorities among them—such as at the Future of American Folkloristics conference (Fivecoate, Downs, and McGriff, this volume)—suggest the liveliness and promise of contemporary graduate education in folklore.

The discipline of folklore cannot return to the early period when administrators might be impressed by a unique discipline and when establishing a new program required a minimum of bureaucratic negotiation; nor can it return to the effervescent growth of folklore programs fostered by government investment in higher education and widespread fascination with traditional cultures of the 1960s and 1970s. There is no silver bullet to slay our antagonists or detractors, no magical elixir to transform folklore programs into invincible giants, no time-travel portal to return us to those legendary days. We can, however, take pride in the academic legacy bequeathed to us in the United States and Canada by intellectual leaders who developed distinctive emphases within the discipline and whose students dispersed to other programs, cross-pollinating the study of folklore and training subsequent generations of folklorists.

References

Bronner, Simon. 2019. "Introduction, Definitions, Concepts, and Questions of Folklore and Folklife in a Diverse, Mobile Nation." In *Oxford Handbook of American Folklore and Folklife Studies*, edited by Simon J. Bronner, 3–37. New York: Oxford University Press.

Goldstein, Diane. 2015. "Vernacular Turns: Narrative, Local Knowledge, and the Changed Context of Folklore." *Journal of American Folklore* 128, no. 508: 125–45.

Haring, Lee, and Regina F. Bendix. 2012. "Folklore Studies in the United States." In *A Companion to Folklore*, edited by Regina F. Bendix and Galit Hasan-Rokem, 286–304. Hoboken, NJ: Blackwell.

Schultz, David. 2015. "The Rise and Coming Demise of the Corporate University." *Academe*, September–October. https://www.aaup.org/article/rise-and-coming-demise-corporate-university.

Toelken, Barre. 1979. *The Dynamics of Folklore*. Boston: Houghton Mifflin.

PATRICIA SAWIN is Associate Professor and Coordinator of the Folklore Program in the Department of American Studies at the University of North Carolina at Chapel Hill. She is author of *Listening for a Life: A Dialogic Ethnography of Bessie Eldreth through Her Songs and Stories.*

ROSEMARY LÉVY ZUMWALT is Vice President Emerita and Professor Emerita of Anthropology at Agnes Scott College. She is author of *American Folklore Scholarship: A Dialogue of Dissent* and (with Isaac Jack Lévy) *Ritual Medical Lore of Sephardic Women: Sweetening the Spirits and Healing the Sick.*

Index

Page numbers in italics refer to illustrations

www.ingramcontent.com/pod-product-compliance
Lightning Source LLC
Chambersburg PA
CBHW021220270326
41929CB00010B/1203

* 9 7 8 0 2 5 3 0 5 2 8 9 6 *